Campus Recreation

Essentials for the Professional

NIRSA

National Intramural-Recreational Sports Association

HUMAN KINETICS

Library of Congress Cataloging-in-Publication Data

Campus recreation : essentials for the professional / NIRSA, National Intramural-Recreational Sports Association.
    p. cm.
  Includes bibliographical references and index.
  ISBN-13: 978-0-7360-5975-6 (hard cover)
  ISBN-10: 0-7360-5975-X (hard cover)
  1. College students--Recreation--United States. 2. Intramural sports--United States--Management. 3. College sports--United States--Management. 4. Recreation centers--United States--Management. 5. Sports facilities--United States--Management. I. National Intramural-Recreational Sports Association (U.S.)
  LB3608.C35 2008
  796.04'3--dc22
                                    2007025783

ISBN-10: 0-7360-5975-X
ISBN-13: 978-0-7360-5975-6

The Web addresses cited in this text were current as of October 9, 2007, unless otherwise noted.

NIRSA Managing Editor: Mary Callender, CRSS, NIRSA Director of Publications & Educational Resources; **Acquisitions Editor:** Gayle Kassing, PhD; **Developmental Editor:** Melissa Feld; **Assistant Editor:** Martha Gullo; **Copyeditor:** Patsy Fortney; **Proofreader:** Erin Cler; **Indexer:** Nancy Gerth; **Permission Manager:** Dalene Reeder; **Graphic Designer:** Nancy Rasmus; **Graphic Artist:** Kathleen Boudreau-Fuoss; **Cover Designer:** Keith Blomberg; **Photo Asset Manager:** Laura Fitch; **Photo Office Assistant:** Jason Allen; **Art Manager:** Kelly Hendren; **Associate Art Manager:** Alan L. Wilborn; **Illustrator:** Accurate Art, Inc.; **Printer:** Sheridan Books

Printed in the United States of America   10   9   8   7   6   5   4   3   2   1

Human Kinetics
Web site: www.HumanKinetics.com

United States: Human Kinetics
P.O. Box 5076, Champaign, IL 61825-5076
800-747-4457
e-mail: humank@hkusa.com

Canada: Human Kinetics
475 Devonshire Road Unit 100, Windsor, ON N8Y 2L5
800-465-7301 (in Canada only)
e-mail: info@hkcanada.com

Europe: Human Kinetics
107 Bradford Road, Stanningley, Leeds LS28 6AT, United Kingdom
+44 (0) 113 255 5665
e-mail: hk@hkeurope.com

Australia: Human Kinetics
57A Price Avenue, Lower Mitcham, South Australia 5062
08 8372 0999
e-mail: info@hkaustralia.com

New Zealand: Human Kinetics
Division of Sports Distributors NZ Ltd.
P.O. Box 300 226 Albany, North Shore City, Auckland
0064 9 448 1207
e-mail: info@humankinetics.co.nz

NIRSA
4185 S.W. Research Way, Corvallis, OR 97333
541-766-8211
www.nirsa.org

CONTENTS

CONTENTS

PART IV   Professional Aspects of Campus Recreation

PREFACE

PREFACE

Describing campus recreation to the unaccustomed often necessitates a variety of examples to elaborate its broad scope. Many use the term *campus recreation* to denote "a major sector of recreation programming designed to meet the needs of older teenagers and young adults" (Kraus, Barber, & Shapiro, 2001, p. 128). As a professional and program-defining term, it is used interchangeably with *recreational sports, intramural sports,* and *intramural-recreational sports.* The term *campus recreation* narrows the broader field of recreational sports to those facilities, services, and activities specifically offered on college and university campuses.

The key descriptive term for campus recreation that comes to mind for baby boomers might be *intramurals.* It is a term that conjures up memories of a student's extracurricular life in college playing flag football or participating in a racquetball ladder tournament. But those defined as the "Y generation" are much more sophisticated in their definition, as well as their expectations. Program participants have come to expect opportunities to raft a class IV or class V river, participate in a kickboxing class, compete in an indoor soccer league, travel with their Ultimate disc sport club team, or spend some downtime in the leisure pool before taking in a fruit smoothie and a veggie wrap at the rec center cafe. Campus recreation has grown to offer a smorgasbord of programs and activities that students, faculty, and staff can choose from.

Campus Recreation: Essentials for the Professional was written to explain the essentials to students preparing for a career in campus recreation as well as to new professionals wanting to strengthen and broaden their knowledge in the field. Part I introduces the philosophies and theories of student development and addresses how recreation contributes to that development. It also offers a history of campus recreation and the National Intramural-Recreational Sports Association (NIRSA) that provides students and professionals with lifelong learning opportunities. Rounding out part I is a discussion of the effect that Title IX has had beyond athletics and what it means for campus recreation.

Part II focuses on programming and facilities on campus. Chapters address how to plan, implement, evaluate, and assess a variety of programming areas, including aquatics, intramurals, sport clubs, instructional programs, outdoor recreation, fitness, and wellness, in addition to familiarizing readers with standard indoor and outdoor facility offerings and structures.

Part III delves into managerial areas, introducing readers to more advanced functions. The chapter on writing a business plan includes information on establishing department values, philosophies, priorities, and guiding principles and creating mission statements and financial forecasts. Marketing is vital for promoting the programs, services, and facilities of a campus recreation department. College students have high technological expectations for communication, and marketing must take advantage of those opportunities. An introduction to risk management is a must for every professional, no matter what field he or she is in. And finally, the art of assessment is vital to ensure that the program is accountable to and valued in the overall university environment.

Part IV provides information on the professional aspects of campus recreation. The question of whether ethics can be taught or whether it is innate is an intriguing one for the professional. Some believe that codes of ethics do not motivate people to behave well; they only assist people who already want to do so. Sustainability is a concept that is growing exponentially throughout higher education. How colleges and universities can reduce their impact on the environment through facility planning, landscaping, recycling, and the use of renewable resources is addressed in this part. The final chapter addresses careers and professional standards in campus recreation, exploring the type of career progression to expect, job titles, responsibilities and qualifications, and salary averages for various positions. In addition, this chapter addresses the types of standards that are expected both professionally and programmatically.

A CD-ROM is included at the back of the book. It includes full-size worksheets, forms, and checklists to help new professionals in their day-to-day responsibilities in recreation programming and administration. These forms are shown in the book at thumbnail size and indicated with a CD-ROM icon.

Campus Recreation: Essentials for the Professional helps readers understand the important role campus recreation has in developing the "whole student." Participation in recreational sport programs and activities is a key determinant of college satisfaction, success, recruitment, and retention. A well-run campus recreation program helps participants by improving their emotional well-being, reducing stress, and providing happiness. The programs build self-confidence and character, promote diversity, teach team building, and improve leadership skills (National Intramural-Recreational Sports Association, 2004, p. 5).

High school senior tour days and freshman orientation sessions often include tours of the recreational sport facilities and programs on campus. Prospective students are often swayed to attend a university based on its recreational facilities and programs. A significant amount of time is spent outside of the classroom, studying, working, or participating in a variety of campus offerings. This out-of-class experience contributes significantly to a student's overall development.

We hope this book serves as a valuable resource to the ever-developing campus recreation professional.

References

Kraus, R., Barber, E., & Shapiro, I. (2001). *Introduction to leisure services: Career perspectives.* Champaign, IL: Sagamore.

National Intramural-Recreational Sports Association. (2004). *The value of recreational sports in higher education.* Champaign, IL: Human Kinetics.

PART I

Foundations

Philosophical and Theoretical Foundations of Campus Recreation: Crossroads of Theory

Douglas S. Franklin, CRSS, PhD, Assistant Dean for Recreation and Wellness, Ohio University at Athens

Sarah E. Hardin, CRSS, PhD, Associate Director of Campus Recreation, DePaul University

It is often argued that one of the reasons for a campus recreation program at a college or university is the positive impact that the use of such programs, services, and facilities has on the quality of life of its users.

Lewis, Barcelona, and Jones, 2002

Practitioners in the professional field of **campus recreation** provide a variety of services to students, faculty, and staff on campuses. Most institutions require that these employees bring a certain level of knowledge and experience to their positions. A bachelor's degree and a minimum of several years of experience in the campus setting are usual requirements for someone to be a candidate for campus recreation positions. Many positions in this field, even those considered entry level, require a master's degree. However, most campus recreation job descriptions do not specify the academic program required of a candidate. As long as a candidate meets the experiential, certification, skill, and degree requirements for the position, the academic curriculum he or she followed seems unimportant. Campus recreation administrators gain theoretical preparation in a variety of areas. Their educational backgrounds influence the direction and purpose of the programs, services, and policies of their departments.

This chapter describes the philosophical foundations of the field as determined by one national professional organization and one accrediting body. These philosophies are expressed in the mission statements of various campus recreation and sport departments. The chapter then explores the "crossroads of theory" that is created by the multitude of academic backgrounds campus recreation professionals possess and the potential impact of those theoretical foundations.

Philosophical Foundations That Guide Mission

The complexity of higher education is manifested in the various functions and activities offered through curricular and cocurricular programs on a campus, including the recreation program. Although collegiate intramural or recreational sport programs have been on campuses since the early 19th century, it is only within the last 50 years that these programs have become "professionalized."

Through its standards and curriculum committees, the National Intramural-Recreational Sports Association (NIRSA) established standards for recreational sport or campus recreation programs and "provided direction in terms of competencies" for professionals (Young & Ross, 2004). The National Intramural-Recreational Sports Association's *General and Specialty Standards for Collegiate Recreational Sports* (1996) defined the purpose of campus recreation as follows:

1. **Service:** To satisfy varying degrees of interest in cooperative or competitive play activity in the game form by utilizing available resources in the most efficient and effective manner
2. **Development:** To provide learning opportunities for sport participants and leaders
3. **Relations:** To establish and maintain quality in programming that contributes to a positive image of the institution

The Council for the Advancement of Standards in Higher Education (CAS), in conjunction with NIRSA, devised specific standards for recreational sport or campus recreation programs (see chapter 17, pages 308-309, for specific information about CAS). According to CAS (Dean, 2006):

Recreational sports are viewed as an essential component of higher education, supplementing the educational process through enhancement of students' physical & mental development. (p. 283)

With regard to mission, the CAS standards and guidelines provide specific direction:

The recreational sports program (RSP) must incorporate student learning and student development in its mission. The program must enhance overall educational experiences. The RSP must develop, record, disseminate, implement and regularly review its mission and goals. Mission statements must be consistent with the mission and goals of the institution and with the standards in this document. The RSP must operate as an integral part of the institution's overall mission. (Dean, 2006, p. 285)

The missions and focuses of campus recreation departments across the country reveal that NIRSA's principles of purpose and adherence to the CAS standards are articulated in many ways. Campus recreation is a continually evolving field and is evolving differently at every institution. However, the development of these principles and standards has helped many institutions to better understand and determine the role that campus recreation programs may and should play within their educational missions. The following section looks at three areas that affect the philosophical foundation and orientation of the campus recreation department within an institution.

Commonalities and Differences Among Campus Recreation Programs

Campus recreation mission statements from institutions across the United States reveal a variety of focuses. Although service, opportunity, lifestyle enhancement, and personal development are key factors in most, other factors may be emphasized. For example, the Florida Gulf Coast University department of campus recreation emphasizes health and wellness as well as diversity.

> The Department of Campus Recreation at Florida Gulf Coast University provides diverse activities that enhance personal development, healthy lifestyles, education, and a positive campus experience. We accomplish this by promoting social interaction, competitiveness, personal wellness, and fun. (Florida Gulf Coast University, n.d.)

The University of South Carolina focuses on the first two purposes listed in the NIRSA standards—service and development:

> To provide appropriate recreation programs and services to the University's students, faculty, and staff for the purpose of promoting growth and development, positive interpersonal relationships, and healthy lifestyles. (University of South Carolina Campus Recreation, n.d.)

The University of Tennessee at Knoxville's Recreational Sports Department specifically follows the NIRSA standards in its mission statement:

> To satisfy varying degrees of interest in cooperative and competitive activities by utilizing all available resources in the most efficient and effective manner; to provide learning experiences for sport participants and leaders; and to establish and maintain quality programming that contributes to a positive image of the institution and academic experience at the University of Tennessee, Knoxville. (University of Tennessee at Knoxville Recreational Sports, n.d.)

To truly examine the mission, focus, and purpose of campus recreation organizations, one must look at three major issues:

1. The mission and scope of the institution in which it is housed
2. The campus recreation department's placement within the university structure
3. The disciplines from which campus recreation administrative professionals have received their foundation and training (see table 1.1); these include, but are not limited to, higher education, sport management, leisure studies, physical education, and exercise science

Table 1.1 Campus Recreation Professionals' Disciplines

Discipline	Sport and play	Student development	Organization and management	Historical mission focus
Sport or recreation management	High skills and knowledge in sport and activity	Low knowledge and understanding of developmental theory	High skills in management	Historical programs and sport activities
Exercise science and physiology	High skills in fitness-related functions	Low knowledge and understanding of developmental theory	Limited skills in management	Programs and activity
College student personnel or higher education	Low skills in sport, activity, and fitness	High skills and knowledge of developmental theory	Limited skills in management	Programs used for holistic personal development
Business	Low skills in sport, activity, and fitness	Low knowledge and understanding of developmental theory	High skills in management	Efficient use of funds to provide programs

Institutional Mission and Scope

The campus recreation department's mission may be affected by the institutional mission. Campus recreation and recreational sport administrators frequently view the mission of their departments as part of the university mission of lifelong learning and education. They describe their efforts as part of the curriculum and significant to the mission and purpose of the institution. Therefore, the institutional mission is a guiding factor when defining the role that these programs and services play in students' lives. SUNY at Geneseo's mission statement for intercollegiate athletics, intramurals, and recreation exemplifies adherence to the institution's principles:

Intercollegiate athletics, intramurals and recreation at Geneseo are considered an integral part of the educational process that aspires to combine a rich co-curricular life with an already established rigorous curriculum. . . . The promotion of leadership, responsibility and an appreciation of the similarities and differences we all embody, contribute to the advancement of the overall mission of the College. (SUNY at Geneseo Department of Intercollegiate Athletics and Recreation, 2002)

Eastern Illinois University indicates that its campus recreation services assist in the development of the university community:

The primary mission of Campus Recreation is to provide a broad range of co-curricular recreational activities allowing for the personal, intellectual, physical, civic and social growth of students, faculty, and staff with the ultimate objective being the development of constructive use of leisure time and healthful lifestyle throughout life. (Eastern Illinois University Campus Recreation, n.d.)

The University of Pennsylvania states its support of the institution's goals by saying that it provides "value-added experiences":

The mission of recreation is to create value-added experiences for the university and community's growth and development by encouraging involvement in the present, which will enrich and challenge the future. (University of Pennsylvania Department of Recreation, 2005)

The scope of the institution's mission affects the focus of the mission statement of the campus recreation department. For instance, a program housed at a regional university is more likely to include the external community within its mission, whereas one at a research institution may include a devotion to research in its mission. This is the case at the Division of Campus Recreation of the University of Illinois at Urbana-Champaign, where the mission is

to provide recreation and wellness opportunities which enhance the quality of life of the students and other members of the university community. The Division promotes this mission through diverse programming, service, teaching and research. (University of Illinois at Urbana-Champaign Division of Campus Recreation, n.d.)

Placement Within the University Structure

The placement of the campus recreation department within the university structure is a second factor that influences its mission and focus. A department within a student affairs department may provide more developmental programs and opportunities, whereas one under an athletics department may focus more on the competitive aspects of recreation programming. At the University of California at Irvine, the recreation program is housed within the athletics department, and its purpose is that of

complementing the university's mission by enhancing the campus community through recreational sports and fitness. (University of California at Irvine Campus Recreation, n.d.)

Following are other major factors mentioned frequently in mission statements:

- Holistic approach to life-enhancing opportunities in the physical, mental, and emotional domains
- Physical development of the individual
- Active lifestyle
- Creative development

Administrators' Educational Foundations

The educational foundations of administrative personnel affect the missions and programs and services offered by campus recreation departments. For example, a director with a sport management background may focus on the efficiency of the recreation operation. One with a degree in recreation and leisure, on the other hand, may focus more on leisure theory, student self-determination, and control. Table 1.1 offers more insights into this issue.

The focus is further complicated when the administrator has been influenced by several foundational disciplines. Consider a woman with a bachelor's degree in sport management who pursues a master's degree in exercise science. As a graduate student, she works in a recreation program for an administrator with a background in student affairs. After graduation, her first job is at an institution where campus recreation is administered through the athletics department, but her immediate supervisor has a leisure services background. When she eventually becomes the director of campus recreation at another university, her direct supervisor is the executive director of the student union. She has now been exposed to six areas of theory and application in program and service offerings. How this diversity of backgrounds influences her organizational focus is difficult to predict.

It is important to recognize that the varied philosophical foundations of those who administer campus recreation affect the missions of the departments they direct. Consequently, aspiring recreational sport professionals should understand the philosophies and theories that undergird and provide direction for the profession.

Theoretical Foundations

Philosophy is a theory underlying or regarding a sphere of activity or thought; it encompasses the most general beliefs, concepts, and attitudes of an individual or group. A philosophy helps to guide behavior through the establishment of systematically defined values, beliefs, and preferences (Edginton, Jordan, DeGraff, & Edginton, 2002). For organizations it is defined as the broad policies and ideological principles that guide group actions (Schein, 1992). A theory is a well-substantiated explanation of some aspect of the natural world or an organized system of accepted knowledge that applies in a variety of circumstances to explain a specific set of phenomena (Princeton, 2007). Theories attempt to explain and predict behavior in organizational structure, cultures, and circumstances (Shafritz & Ott, 2001).

Understanding the role theory plays in campus recreation is essential to program success and to the interaction with other campus entities. "Theory attempts to explain why facts are what they are" (Henderson, Presley, & Bialeschki, 2004, p. 412) and provides "insight into what can be or has been observed" (Henderson, 1994). Theory grows as it is tested in practice and refined through scholarly effort. As a basis for campus recreation practice, theory expands exponentially as programs grow, evolve, and become more encompassing. Consequently, it is essential for campus recreation professionals or students studying in the field to gain perspective from various disciplines. The following section provides a survey of theories affecting campus recreation and recreational sport professionals.

At the Crossroads of Theory

Picture a highway intersection in a crowded city. Intersections with strange names such as Mixing Bowl, Malfunction Junction, Mousetrap, Full House, Death Merge, and Spaghetti Bowl provide images of what happens when roads converge. In the days before modern loops, figure eights, and cloverleaves, travelers came to a stop to verify that the road was clear and they could proceed; it was a simple system for a simple time.

Unfortunately, those intersections were often the cause of deadly crashes when traffic became more complex. Multilane highways with interchanges were developed to handle the complex flow of traffic. The interstate highway system and progressive highway designs created a system to safely move traffic through the interchanges. The goal of traffic planners is similar to that of campus recreation professionals, who must integrate recreation, student development, and management.

As mentioned earlier, campus recreation professionals come from divergent backgrounds, resulting in a variety of perspectives and methods. Unlike the traditional disciplines of business, communications, and education, campus recreation programs have no singular source of theory from which to draw or develop new knowledge. Instead, campus recreation is a convergence of multiple theories, a "mixing bowl of theory," which makes the profession rich and open to new and innovative approaches. The purpose of this section is to explore how the confluence of these perspectives affects campus recreation professionals.

Sport, Recreation, and Leisure: The Traditional Route

Sport, recreation, and leisure theory form the foundation for the existence of collegiate recreation programs. As far back as 1826, when the Harvard faculty supported Carl Follen's ideas to develop a gymnasium to "work the devil out of the students" (Brubacher & Rudy, 2002, p. 49), physical activity programs have provided a form of stress reduction and served as a healthy form of leisure for college students. A familiarity with some applicable terms will help develop an understanding of leisure, recreation, and sport theories.

Leisure is a term with multiple definitions, including those related to time and state of mind. "Leisure consists of a number of occupations in which the individual may indulge of his own free will—either to rest, to amuse himself, to add to his knowledge or improve his skills" (Dumazedier, 1960, p. 522). However, for the majority of the population leisure is time free of structured activities. For most of us, leisure is the evening or weekend time that we look forward to after a day or week of work. For college students, leisure is the unencumbered time free of class, study, or other obligations, in which to participate in structured or unstructured activity or just to kick back, hang, or chill with friends.

Recreation is the time or activity that we use to renew and re-create ourselves by taking part in pleasurable activities or enjoying pleasurable surroundings. Like leisure, recreation is usually accomplished during our free, or nonwork, time. Some people like to recreate by participating in unstructured activities. An early morning jog on the bike path might provide an opportunity to prepare for the stress of the day, whereas an evening jog might provide an opportunity to unwind from a stressful day. Some enjoy recreating through more structured activities such as participating in organized softball or basketball leagues; others might recreate through more meditative activities such as tai chi or yoga. Any activity that helps college students re-create themselves through the healthy use of leisure time is considered recreation.

Play is a form of human or animal behavior that is self-motivated and carried on for intrinsic purposes. Generally pleasurable, it is often marked by elements of competition, exploration, problem solving, and role playing. Play may appear in both leisure and work and may be marked by freedom and lack of structure or by a set of rules and prescribed actions (Kraus, 1990). In campus recreation programs play usually involves engaging in a sport or recreational activity such as intramural or club sports.

Sport consists of "playing cooperative–competitive activity in the game form" (Mull, Bayless, & Jamieson, 2005, p. 7). Sport has its origins in the 15th century as a "pleasant pastime or diversion" (Gudden, 1979), a concept still in use today. College campuses usually have a variety of competitive levels of sports, including varsity, club, and intramural, each with its own special functions. Campus recreation programs provide a variety of competitive team and individual sport activities to create opportunities for student growth and development.

Intramural is defined as being or occurring within the walls of something. Intramural sports provide an opportunity for students to participate in competitive sports against other students within the walls of the same institution. Some professional staff believe that the logical progression of this type of activity is to take the best and most competitive intramural sport teams and have them compete extramurally—that is, against other institutions with similar skill levels.

Sport clubs provide students with opportunities to participate in sport-related activities with a greater level of commitment than intramural sports provide. Whether students are learning a new sport or participating in one they have always been involved in, clubs provide an opportunity to keep fit while competing against students in other colleges and universities. Some sport clubs are student run and allow club members to acquire skills in program planning, organizational management, and leadership.

Fitness programs, usually activities limited to physical development, are often confused with the more holistic concept of wellness: activities that address physical, intellectual, social, emotional, spiritual, occupational, and environmental needs. Fitness programs are structured and unstructured activities that enhance cardiorespiratory endurance, as well as muscular strength, power, and endurance. Activities range from individual equipment such as treadmills and elliptical trainers, to selectorized equipment and free weights, to group exercise programs including aerobic dance and spinning. Many fitness programs now offer personal training, nutrition counseling, body mass imaging, and massage therapy.

Outdoor adventure programs provide adventure trips, instructional clinics and classes, climb-

William A. Cotton, Colorado State University.

Group exercise programs like this ballet fitness class are among the many structured activities that may be offered by campus fitness programs.

ing operations, equipment rentals, and in some cases a challenge course for team building and leadership development. These programs often focus on experiential learning and environmental awareness.

So how do we bring these functions together? Because campus recreation evolved from sport, an understanding of the underlying theories of sport, play, and physical activity is useful. Following are descriptions of five sport theories that inform our understanding of campus recreation:

1. **Functionalism.** This theory suggests sports serve as an inspiration and a method to either maintain societal balance or assist in societal change. Functionalists view sport in society from a systems approach, suggesting the function of sport is to provide social balance (Anshel, 2003).

2. **Conflict theory.** This theory refutes functionalism and instead proposes that social order is based on the coercion, exploitation, and manipulation of individuals; the distribution of power; and the use of that power to facilitate change. Conflict theory suggests sport is used as a social mechanism for alienation, coercion, and social control to maintain the interests of the elite (Anshel, 2003).

3. **Critical theory.** This theory asserts that the forces of history, cultural ideology, and material conditions constrain people's view of the social order. Critical theory casts doubt on the established definition, purpose, and role of sport in societal change (Anshel, 2003).

4. **Feminist theory.** This theory assumes that the social order reflects the values, experiences, and interests of men to the exclusion of women. It claims that sports reproduce and serve to maintain existing gender relations and challenges and opposes current conceptions regarding masculinity and femininity (Anshel, 2003).

5. **Interactionist theory.** This theory states that the social order depends on shared meanings which are created and maintained through the interaction of people and the world around them. Sport-related interactionist theory focuses on the athlete's self-views and the culture and subculture of sport. Conclusions from the interactionist theory in sport suggest that the formation and maintenance of an athlete's identity depend on reaffirmation through social interaction and that behavior in sports is best understood within the context of sport subcultures and in connection with the identities formed in these subcultures (Anshel, 2003).

The practical application of each of these sport theories is evident in the modern campus recreation program. The interaction of participants and staff members creates opportunities for continual social interaction. Examples may help illustrate these theories. A *functionalist* might view participation on an intramural or sport club team as a source of inspiration that would ultimately benefit society, whereas a *conflict theorist* might view that same participation as a link between big-time athletics and big-time money. A *critical theorist* might suggest that a corecreational soccer game with international students provides an opportunity to liberate or empower participants to transform society through interactions with varied cultures, whereas a *feminist* might look at that same event as an opportunity to transform participants' views of masculinity and femininity. Finally, an *interactionist* might focus on each participant's view of himself or herself as an athlete but only within the context of that specific activity.

Play theory forms the basis for recreational activity. *Play* is defined as engaging in sport or recreation. Several play theories provide a rationale for participation in recreational sports:

• The *surplus energy theory* (Schiller, 1875; Spencer, 1873) offers that play is motivated by the need to release surplus energy, similar to the way a volcano releases steam and ash to make room for the lava to flow. Students running or playing basketball to reduce stress have surplus energy to burn off.

• In 1883 Lazarus proposed the *recreation theory of play;* he viewed play as performing a restorative or re-creative function. An example of a re-creative player is a student participating in an outdoor adventure trip that provides solitude for thought and reflection.

• The *relaxation theory* posits that play provides an avenue to relax from the stresses of daily life (Patrick, 1916). Recreation activities for relaxation might include yoga or use of a leisure pool.

• The *cathartic theory* states that people play because they need to express disorganized and painful emotions in a harmless way (Kraus, Barber, & Shapiro, 2001). Anyone who has been on the losing end of an intramural sport contest can attest to this theory.

• The *compensatory theory* proposes that play is a substitute for unachievable goals and desires and provides an outlet to make up for unpleasant or unavailable experiences (Kraus et al., 2001). Many students who suffer from academic failures compensate by participating in recreational sport programs. A careful balance between academic and recreational pursuits must be stressed to participants.

• The *achievement-motivation theory* suggests that play, like other endeavors, involves the desire to strive, excel, master, and succeed through risk taking (Levy, 1978). Recreation programs provide this outlet through controlled risk-taking activities such as using climbing walls and challenge courses.

• The *optimal arousal theory* supposes that play is a combination of complexity, novelty, and dissonance (conflict or difference) and that when people become bored, they seek stimulation (Ellis, 1973). The unstructured use of campus recreation facilities is often a way for students to overcome their boredom and internal conflict.

• *Csikszentmihalyi's flow theory* (1990) suggests that play provides the opportunity to become so involved with the activity that the person loses ego and self-consciousness. Through skill and mastery, participants achieve a state of flow in which they have feelings of personal power and control. Participants who are "in the zone" can control most, if not all, aspects of their performances.

• The *conflict-enculturation theory* suggests that play provides an opportunity for the participant to learn new behaviors and skills by experiencing them in a controlled environment with minimal emotional risk (Sutton-Smith, 1995). Recreation programs provide opportunities to learn the essential skill of conflict resolution during structured and unstructured play. Every conflict provides a "teachable moment."

Theories of recreation, sport, play, and leisure provided the rationale for many early campus recreation programs. However, because of the recent organizational shift to student affairs departments (Franklin, 2007), there is a growing need to understand the role campus recreation plays in the growth and development of the whole student. We must therefore look at a different road: the road from student development.

The Road From Student Development: Helping Students Grow, Develop, and Learn

In 1995 *Athletic Business* magazine indicated that housing campus recreation programs within student affairs offices was the prevalent organizational model of the 1990s. Forty-six percent of small institutions and 65 percent of large institutions ascribed to this model (Cohen, 1995). A 2007 study (Franklin, 2007) revealed that 72 percent of all campus recreation programs were located in student affairs offices. The relocation of campus recreation programs to student affairs organizations suggests that the focus is now on **student development** and learning—the primary emphases of student affairs (Evans, Forney, & Guido-DiBrito, 1998).

Institutions of higher education play a unique role in society by educating "traditional-aged students" (ages 18 to 24), transitioning them from children to adults and producing society's citizens and future leaders. This transition occurs through developing students' cognitive, social and emotional, environmental, physical, spiritual, and vocational skills. In the broadest context, this growth, called student development, is extensively used in college student affairs practice (Evans et al., 1998). The term *student development* describes the process of growth and maturation of students in a particular environment. Campus recreation assists in student development through its programs and operations. Because campus recreation professionals are involved in student development and student learning, they should be aware of theories related to this specialized field of higher education.

Astin's Theory of Involvement

Alexander Astin (1999) believes that the type of involvement campus recreation programs provide enhances student growth and development, which ultimately leads to their overall success. Astin's theory contends the following:

- The more students are involved in both the academic and social aspects of the collegiate experience, the more they learn.

- Student involvement consists of energetic participation in academics, being on campus, participating actively in student organizations and activities, and interacting with faculty.

- The student plays a fundamental role in determining his or her own extent of involvement in courses and cocurricular and social activities.

- The more quality resources available, the more likely students will be to grow or develop.

- Faculty interaction both in and out of class, high-quality programs, and institutional policies that reflect a commitment to student learning are necessary for student growth.

Involvement theory was recently supported in a NIRSA-sponsored study titled *The Value of Recreational Sports in Higher Education* (National Intramural-Recreational Sports Association, 2004), which linked involvement in recreational sport programs to factors of student satisfaction and success.

Erikson's Epigenetic Principle Theory

Erik Erikson, a Freudian psychiatrist, believed that development occurs through a series of eight age-linked stages across a lifetime (1959/1980). Erikson's first four stages occur during childhood and form the basis for identity (Evans et al., 1998). Stage 1, trust versus mistrust, happens during infancy. Stage 2 occurs with toddlers and consists of balancing autonomy and shame and doubt. Stage 3 happens during preschool and consists of initiative versus guilt while forming the basis for conscience and sexual identity. Industry versus inferiority arises during the school-age years and occurs during stage 4. Stages 5 and 6 transpire during adolescence and young adulthood, the stages of traditional college students. Identity and role confusion, stage 5, comprises the transition from childhood to adulthood and forms the basis for defining self, whereas stage 6 involves the struggle between intimacy and isolation. Stage 7, generativity versus stagnation, and stage 8, integrity versus despair, take place during adulthood.

Erikson provided the foundation for much of student development psychosocial theories and suggested that the convergence of social environment and biological maturation would result in a series of crises to be resolved. Each crisis resolution provided a foundation for dealing with each new crisis (Huitt, 1997). Traditional-aged college students and student employees of campus recreation programs fall into Erikson's adolescent and young adult categories. As such, campus recreation professionals must understand how to deal with students in crisis.

Sanford's Theory of Challenge and Support

Nevitt Sanford built on Erikson's idea that developmental crises are resolved by a moderate, growth-enhancing level of discomfort and suggested that a balance of challenge and support must be present for development to occur (Sanford, 1966). He postulated that too little challenge would create feelings of safety and comfort and preclude development, whereas too much challenge would produce anxiety and result in an inability to adapt.

Challenge and support form the basis for many campus recreation programs. Challenging activities provided in a supportive environment, whether intramural sports or challenge courses in an outdoor program, are keys to programmatic success. The balance of how much responsibility student employees are given within the operation of a campus recreation program is often weighed on the principle of challenge and support.

Perry's Theory of Intellectual and Moral Development

W.G. Perry's theory is a continuum of nine developmental positions from which a person views the world (1981). Rapaport (2006) offered an easy-to-understand outline of Perry's theory, which categorizes Perry's original nine positions into four:

1. *Dualism/received knowledge.* Dualistic people view the world in terms of black or white, good or bad, or right or wrong. The transition to multiplicity is achieved through cognitive dissonance (Festinger, 1957), the psychological phenomenon that refers to the discomfort felt when confronted with a discrepancy between what one knows or believes and new information or a new interpretation (Evans et al., 1998).

2. *Multiplicity/subjective knowledge.* Multiplicity is characterized by a valuing of diverse views and opinions; all views are equally valued. The transition from multiplicity to relativistic thinking occurs by the "recognition of the need to support opinions" (Evans et al., 1998).

3. *Relativism/procedural knowledge.* Relativism is the acceptance of multiple opinions, values, and judgments developed from credible sources, evidence, logic, systems, and patterns and clarified by analysis and comparison (Perry, 1981).

4. *Commitment/constructed knowledge.* Commitment is a confirmation, choice, or decision about such things as a career, values, politics, or personal relationship that was made from the vantage point of relativism (Evans et al., 1998).

Understanding that students develop from dualism through multiplicity to relativism and commitment is important for the campus recreation professional. Each program area can play a unique role in dealing with developmental positions.

Intramural sports, by their nature, focus on dualism supported by rule enforcement, order, and discipline. The student-run aspect of sport clubs provides for development beyond the dualism of rules and regulations and focuses on viewing the club from the multiple perspectives of team members and advisors. A sport club team grows and progresses when team leaders and members gain consensus from multiple viewpoints supported by well-thought-out and substantiated (relativistic) facts that ultimately lead team members to commitment.

Chickering's Seven Vectors

In 1969 Arthur Chickering developed the theory of education and identity and proposed the following vectors that lead to identity: developing competence, managing emotions, moving through autonomy toward interdependence, developing mature interpersonal relationships, establishing identity, developing purpose, and developing integrity. Chickering and L. Reisser revised the theory in 1993 to adjust for the social, emotional, and intellectual elements of well-being. This revision suggests that students move through vectors randomly and at dissimilar rates, often reprocessing and revisiting previous stages.

The practical application of Chickering's theory takes place daily in a campus recreation program through the development and implementation of a wide range of activities that account for the developing nature of students. While a rafting trip (or any activity) may not, in and of itself, create identity or provide purpose in students' lives, the culmination of this and other experiences creates a sense of possibility, through which students develop purpose and identity.

Kohlberg's Theory of Moral Development

Lawrence Kohlberg identified six stages of moral reasoning grouped into three major levels. Each level represents a fundamental shift in the social-moral perspective of the individual.

• Level 1, preconventional, includes stage 1, reward and punishment, and stage 2, "you scratch my back and I'll scratch yours."

• Level 2, conventional morality, includes stage 3, reflects the concept of good boy or good girl, and is followed by stage 4, authority and social-order maintenance, usually called "law and order."

• Level 3, postconventional, consists of stage 5, the social contract orientation and universal ethical principles, which suggest the greatest good for the greatest number, and stage 6, exemplified by selfless acts without regard to personal loss.

Stages 1 through 5 have some type of empirical basis and stage 6 is more theoretical.

The practical application of Kohlberg's theory relates to the stated and implied rules within recreation programs. Players participate in intramural or extramural sport contests based on rules and regulations and are held accountable for their actions within those parameters. Campus recreation professionals are placed in a unique position to influence the moral and ethical development of participants and student employees through various meetings, training seminars, and corrective action meetings.

A profound change is occurring within the field of student affairs, and by extension campus recreation. The focus on student development is being broadened to include the engagement of students in the process of learning and the assessment of their learning through established outcomes.

Learning Reconsidered (National Association of Student Personnel Administrators, 2004) refocused the efforts of collegiate student affairs professionals toward the importance of learning and suggested that "learning is a complex, holistic, multi-centric activity that occurs throughout and across the college experience" (p. 5). The subsequent publication, *Learning Reconsidered 2: A Practical Guide to Implementing a Campus-Wide Focus on the Student Experience* (*LR2*; Keeling, 2006), added a learning focus for the campus recreation program. NIRSA provided the content for the recreational sport sections of *LR2* and thus established the expectation for recreation professionals to implement a learning outcomes approach to the profession. To apply this approach to practice, campus recreation professionals should have a working knowledge of and be able to apply learning theory. Bloom's taxonomy (Bloom, Englehart, Furst, Hill, & Krathwohl, 1956) provides a foundation for implementing a learning-centered approach to practice.

In the *Taxonomy of Educational Objectives: The Classification of Education Goals: Handbook I: Cognitive Domain*, the focus on cognitive development by Bloom et al. is particularly relevant in approaching learning outcomes. Most helpful to the modern campus recreation professional is the identification of action verbs aligned with these stages.

1. Knowledge is the most basic level of cognitive development, and knowledge verbs include *define, describe, identify, label, list, match, name, recall, reproduce, select,* and *state.* An example of a learning outcome for knowledge for a campus recreation student would be "the student official will recall from memory the rules and regulations for softball."

2. Comprehension, the next stage of the taxonomy, is the ability to understand the importance of the material. The verbs associated with comprehension include *convert, defend, distinguish, estimate, explain, infer, paraphrase, predict, rewrite,* and *summarize.* A student learning outcome for comprehension might be "the student assistant will summarize the key elements of the program plan for the Choose Campus Rec special event."

3. Application is the ability to use the information learned, and related verbs include *change,* compute, demonstrate, discover, manipulate, prepare, produce, relate, show,* and *use.* A sample outcome is "the student manager will compute the cost related to personnel for the Learn to Swim program."

4. Analysis is the ability to deconstruct the information into its basic components in order to differentiate between its multiple uses. Verbs associated with analysis are *break down, diagram, differentiate, discriminate, distinguish, outline, point out, relate, select, separate,* and *subdivide.* A possible student learning outcome is "the student facility director will diagram the point-of-sale process and identify potential areas for improvement."

5. Synthesis brings divergent pieces together. Related verbs include *compile, compose, create, devise, design, generate, modify, organize, plan, rearrange, reconstruct, relate, revise, rewrite,* and *write.* A sample learning outcome for synthesis is "the student program manager will design a complete array of individual and dual sports for competition by students during the fall semester."

6. Finally, evaluation is the ability to determine the value of the knowledge by using or establishing criteria for assessment. Associated verbs include *appraise, compare, conclude, contrast, critique, justify, interpret, relate,* and *support.* A possible learning outcome for evaluation is "the student facility director will compare and contrast methods of addressing risk management issues related to the operation of the student recreation facility."

The Road From Organization and Management: The Glue That Holds Us Together

Campus recreation no longer toils in the shadow of athletics or academic programs. Old worn-out gyms with warped floors and narrow-lane pools have been replaced by multistoried recreation facilities with soaring climbing towers and pools with lazy rivers. The fact that many collegiate recreation programs have dedicated fees creating operational budgets in the millions of dollars underscores the importance of understanding how to efficiently manage and organize large and complex operations.

Classical Organizational Theories

Classical organizational theories (Shafritz & Ott, 2001) form the basis for understanding organizations. Selected theories include the following:

Courtesy of University of Alabama.

Today's campus recreational facilities are often spacious and architecturally significant, reflecting the importance of recreation initiatives within the campus community.

- In *Of the Division of Labor* (1776), a seminal work in organizational management, Adam Smith suggested looking at what an organization does and how best to deploy labor resources.

- In his book *General and Industrial Management*, Henri Fayol's general principles of management go beyond dividing labor and identify 14 areas essential to managing the endeavor. These include the division of work, authority and responsibility, discipline, unity of command, unity of direction, subordination of individual interest to the general interest, remuneration of personnel, centralization, scalar chain (line of authority), order, equity, stability of tenure of personnel, initiative, and esprit de corps (Fayol, 1916).

- In his essay "Bureaucracy" (1946), Max Weber explains that a bureaucracy has fixed and official jurisdictional areas that are generated by rules, hierarchy, and graded levels of authority; uses office documents to manage; provides the thorough and expert training of managers; demands the full working capacity for organizational officials; and has a stable and easily learned set of office rules.

These classical organization theories form the foundation for every campus recreation program. Departments are organized by functional services, institutional size, and program function. The use of documents to determine usage and activity patterns and organizational strengths and weaknesses is standard practice in many organizations, as is the practice of professional development (training) for student and professional staff.

Neoclassical Theories

Neoclassical organizational theorists refute the rigidity and adherence to principles found in classical theories but offer only slight modifications to these classic works (Shafritz & Ott, 2001).

One such theorist is Peter Drucker, who developed management by objectives (MBO) in 1954. MBO is a systematic approach in which management identifies and links achievable goals with available resources, resulting in optimizing performance. Campus recreation programs that use MBO operate with a clear sense of purpose and direction by using incentives as well as other goal-related practices.

Human Resources Management

The human resources management period follows the neoclassic period of organizational theory. In 1924 and 1927 George Elton Mayo's experiments on worker productivity provided insights into the management–worker relationship. The Hawthorne experiments were an effort to study the effect of light on worker output by subjecting employees to various amounts of light. The results revealed that regardless of the amount of light, worker productivity improved. Researchers surmised that the increased productivity was due to the added attention workers received and concluded that behavior could not be set apart from feelings and sentiments. They also concluded that manifestations of sentiment can only be understood within the context of the total situation of the employee as a person and that work is a social entity.

In "The Human Side of Enterprise" (1957), Douglas Murray McGregor provided a view of theory X and theory Y management. McGregor suggested that the conventional view, theory X, has three main tenets: Management is responsible for organizing the money, materials, equipment, and people in the interest of economic ends; workers need to have their efforts directed, be motivated, have their actions controlled, and have their behavior modified to fit organizational needs; and, without active intervention from management, workers would be passive, even resistant to organizational needs. The basic premise of theory X managers is that the average worker is lazy by nature, lacks ambition, prefers to be led, is inherently self-centered, is indifferent to organizational needs, is resistant to change, is gullible, and is not very bright. After questioning the validity of theory X based on workers' physiological, safety, social, ego, and self-fulfillment needs, McGregor postulated a new theory for management, theory Y. As in theory X, management is responsible for the organization of the elements of a productive enterprise; however, in theory Y workers are not assumed to be passive by nature or resistant to organizational needs. Workers are assumed to have the potential for motivation, development, and readiness, and management is responsible for recognizing and developing these characteristics.

Because campus recreation is a people business, recreation professionals must establish environments that foster human interaction and growth. Understanding why people work within

Creative team-building exercises provide the impetus and incentive to cooperate and can cultivate trust and mutual respect between recreation professionals.

Reprinted, by permission, from Project Adventure, 2007, *Adventure education: Theory and application* (Champaign, IL: Human Kinetics), 11.

organizations and what motivates or inhibits optimal performance is critical for the recreation professional. Overly intrusive and restrictive supervision based on the perception that people are lazy and need constant direction will likely create an environment that will foster this type of behavior. Conversely, an environment that supports the development of staff creativity through trust and mutual respect is likely to result in a more open and collaborative culture.

Modern Structural Organizational Theories

Modern structural organizational theorists view organizations from a post–World War II perspective and are influenced by neoclassical and human resources theories (Shafritz & Ott, 2001).

Organizations have evolved over time, and leaders are now faced with new problems. Peter Senge (1990) suggested that organizational leaders take a systems approach because of the complexity they are now facing. In Norbert Wiener's (1948) system model, the basic elements of a system include inputs leading to processes that result in outputs, which produce feedbacks that alter inputs. This simple design forms the basis for all planning models. Daft and Sharfman (1995) suggested that a system is a set of interrelated elements that takes input from the environment, subjects it to transformational processes, and produces output. Katz and Kahn (1978) described organizations as open systems that display degrees of internal interdependence or interrelatedness, have the capacity for feedback, and move toward a state of balance.

The modern campus recreation program is sufficiently complex to warrant a systems management approach. Many programs use a cyclical planning process that includes a set of inputs (i.e., funding, time, and effort) processed through a set of activities and internal services (i.e., budget and funds distribution) that result in measured outputs of program satisfaction and successful student development. These outputs are then used as input qualifiers for the new cycle.

W. Edwards Deming is considered the father of total quality management (TQM). In his book *Out of Crisis* (1986), he highlighted the following 14 points for managers to consider in developing a culture of quality within their organizations:

1. Create constancy of purpose toward improvement of service.
2. Adopt a new philosophy of quality.
3. Cease dependence on inspection to achieve quality. Eliminate the need for inspection on a mass basis by building quality into the product in the first place.
4. End the practice of awarding business on the basis of price tag. Instead minimize total cost. Move toward a single supplier for any one item, on a long-term relationship of loyalty and trust.
5. Improve constantly and forever the system of production and service to improve quality and productivity and thus constantly decrease costs.
6. Institute training on the job.
7. Institute leadership. The aim of supervision should be to help people and machines and gadgets to do a better job. Supervision of management is in need of overhaul, as well as supervision of production workers.
8. Drive out fear so that everyone may work effectively for the [organization].
9. Break down barriers between departments.
10. Eliminate slogans, exhortations, and targets for the workforce asking for zero defects and new levels of productivity. Such exhortations only create adversarial relationships, as the bulk of the causes of low quality and low productivity belong to the system and thus lie beyond the power of the workforce.
11. Eliminate work standards (quotas), eliminate management by objective, numbers, or goals, and substitute leadership.
12. Remove barriers that rob people of their right to pride in workmanship. Abolish annual merit systems and management by objective.
13. Institute a vigorous program of education and self-improvement.
14. Put everybody in the company to work to accomplish the transformation.

Deming's focus is applicable to service organizations such as campus recreation programs that strive to develop an atmosphere conducive to constant improvement of service. Participants, employees, and professional staff often adopt a philosophy of quality and place an emphasis on planning and service. Although it is often difficult in an institutional setting to avoid purchasing "low bid," costs are contained by developing mutually beneficial relationships with vendors. On-the-job training is often continuous, but does not replace annual training. Student leaders are developed by giving them responsibility and the tools necessary to lead. Fear created by budget shortfalls and dwindling resources is often replaced with an atmosphere of trust and an environment of collaboration among programs and facilities. Campus recreation programs, particularly those involved in NIRSA, are actively engaged in continuing professional development by hosting, attending, and presenting seminars. Finally, participants and employees often feel empowered to transform the program into one of quality.

There is no shortage of books on modern organizational management theories. Bookstores throughout the country have immense business sections dedicated to this topic. Therefore, to single out any one book or theory is an iffy proposition at best. However, Stephen Covey's *Seven Habits of Highly Effective People* (1989), on the *New York Times* bestseller list for over a decade, is worthy of attention. Covey provided a set of guiding principles to move individuals as well as organizations from dependence to independence and finally to interdependence. Covey suggested that an individual must be principle centered and that, although moral values guide behavior, habits derived from principles enhance the ability to be successful.

Covey's first three habits of independence— "pro-activity," "begin with the end in mind" (personal mission building and goal setting), and "first things first" (time management)—provide the basis for personal independence. Interdependence is created by communication and collaboration stemming from obtaining "win–win agreements," "seeking first to understand and then to be understood" (empathetic listening), and "synergizing." Finally, "sharpening the saw" (attaining balance in our lives) solidifies the individual's ability to achieve success.

Seven Habits provides an ideal model for campus recreation programs. Student participants and employees often lack the ability to clearly organize themselves or their experience. However, by using positive thinking, goal setting, and time management, students can move from asking, What should I do? to saying, I will do this. It is only after independence that the student can actually participate in the advanced stages of interdependent collaboration necessary to succeed in a campus recreation program. Recreation professionals understand that it is in the best interest of both the staff and participants to understand each other's perspectives and synergize to provide effective programs. Finally, an overworked and unbalanced staff cannot sustain the program over long periods of time. Personal and team balance is viewed as foundational by department leadership.

Covey's *The 8th Habit: From Effectiveness to Greatness* (2004) provided foundational principles to move people and organizations by suggesting that leaders "find their voice and help others find theirs." Fundamentally, this is a growth and development role, previously discussed in the section on student development.

The road from organization and management is both old and new. Like a highway with several layers of concrete and asphalt, organizational theorists continue to add new ideas about how organizations operate. Campus recreation professionals are urged to stay abreast of new trends to manage their complex organizations effectively.

Traffic Flow at the Crossroads

Now that we have looked at the roads that lead to campus recreation as a profession, how do these relate to the CAS standards discussed earlier in this chapter and in chapter 17? Table 1.2 outlines some strengths and weaknesses of the most

Table 1.2 Strengths and Weaknesses of Background Areas

Standard	Recreation, sport, and leisure	Student development	Organization and management
Essential component of higher education, supplementing the educational process through enhancement of students' physical and mental development	Emphasis is on physical activity and development	High emphasis is on involvement and moral and mental development	Emphasis is on organizing to achieve both efficiently
Incorporate student learning and student development in its mission	Historically limited emphasis on activity rather than development	High emphasis on student learning and development	Historically, no emphasis

(continued)

Table 1.2 *(continued)*

Standard	Recreation, sport, and leisure	Student development	Organization and management
Satisfy varying degrees of interest in cooperative/competitive play activity in the game form by using available resources in the most efficient and effective manner	Key historical strength and emphasis of most programs	Historically this has not been the focus of student affairs	Emphasis on providing appropriate resources to accomplish function
Learning opportunities for sport participants and leaders	Historical strength and emphasis of some programs	Historical strength for nonsport programs; growing emphasis	Rising emphasis as a result of expanding operations
Programming that contributes to a positive image of the institution	Key historical strength and emphasis of most programs	Historical strength for nonsport programs; growing emphasis	Rising emphasis as a result of expanding operations

popular background areas from which campus recreation professionals gain their foundational education and theory.

Conclusion

At first glance, all of the theories discussed in this chapter may seem to be a confusing conglomeration of ideas that are difficult to understand and use. However, they actually provide the profession with very colorful and useful foundations. Administrators with varying backgrounds can assist each other in understanding how the purpose and direction of their programs and services may be influenced and enhanced by different viewpoints and perceptions. The education of the future campus recreation professional is best achieved by balancing a strong understanding of sport management, student development, learning, and organizational theories with practical and constructed learning gained through experience within the campus recreation program.

References

Anshel, M.H. (2003). *Sport psychology: From theory to practice* (4th ed., pp. 29-40). San Francisco: Benjamin Cummings.

Astin, A. (1999). Student involvement: A developmental theory for higher education. *Journal of College Student Personnel, 40*(5), 518-529.

Bloom, B., Englehart, M., Furst, E., Hill, W., & Krathwohl, D. (1956). *Taxonomy of educational objectives: The classification of educational goals. Handbook I: Cognitive domain.* New York, Toronto: Longmans, Green.

Brubacher, J.S., & Rudy, W. (2002). *Higher education in transition* (4th ed., p. 331). New Brunswick, NJ: Transaction Publishers..

Chickering, A.W. (1969). *Education and identity.* San Francisco: Jossey-Bass.

Chickering, A.W., & Reisser, L. (1993). *Education and identity* (2nd ed.). San Francisco: Jossey-Bass.

Cohen, A. (1995, April). College recreation: Separate but equal. *Athletic Business,* 29-38.

Covey, S.R. (1989). *Seven habits of highly effective people: Restoring the character ethic.* New York: Simon and Schuster.

Covey, S.R. (2004). *The 8th Habit: From effectiveness to greatness.* New York: Simon and Schuster.

Csikszentmihalyi, M. (1990). *Flow: The psychology of optimal experience.* San Francisco: Jossey-Bass.

Daft, R.L., & Sharfman, M.P. (1995). *Organization theory: Case & applications* (4th ed., p. xiii). St. Paul, MN: West.

Dean, L.A. (2006). *CAS professional standards for higher education* (6th ed.), pp. 285-291). Washington, DC: Council for the Advancement of Standards in Higher Education.

Deming, W.E. (1986). *Out of crisis.* Cambridge, MA: The Massachusetts Institute of Technology.

Dumazedier, J. (1960). Current problems of the sociology of leisure. *International Social Science Journal, 4*(4), 522-531.

Eastern Illinois University (n.d.). Mission statement. Retrieved from www.eiu.edu/~crecsrc/Mission.htm.

Edginton, C.R., Jordan, D.J., DeGraff, D.G., & Edginton, S.R. (2002). *Leisure and life satisfaction: Foundational perspectives* (3rd ed.). New York: McGraw-Hill.

Ellis, M. (1973). *Why people play.* Englewood Cliffs, NJ: Prentice Hall.

Erikson, E.H. (1980). *Identity and the life cycle.* New York: Norton. (Original work published 1959.)

Evans, N.J., Forney, D.S., & Guido-DiBrito, F. (1998). *Student development in college: Theory, research, and practice* (pp. 124, 125, 162). San Francisco: Jossey-Bass.

Fayol, H. (1916). *General and industrial management.* Constance Storrs (Trans.). London: Pitman Publishing. In Jay M. Shafritz & J. Steven Ott, *Classics of organization theory* (5th ed., p. 48). Belmont, CA: Wadsworth.

Festinger, Leon. (1957). *Theory of cognitive dissonance.* Stanford, CA: Stanford UP.

Florida Gulf Coast University Campus Recreation. (n.d). Retrieved from www.fgcu.edu/CampusRec/mission.html.

Franklin, D.S. (2007). Student development and learning in campus recreation: Assessing recreational sports directors' awareness, perceived importance, application and satisfaction with CAS standards. Dissertation Abstracts International (UMI no. 3269236).

Gudden, J.A. (1979). *The international dictionary of sports and games.* New York: Schocken Books.

Henderson, K.A. (1994). Theory, application and development in recreation, park, and leisure research. *Journal of Park and Recreation Administration 12*(1), 51-64.

Henderson, K.A., Presley, J., & Bialeschki, M.D. (2004). Theory in recreation leisure research: Reflections from the editors. *Leisure Sciences 26*, 411-425.

Huitt, W. (1997). *Socioemotional development. Educational psychology interactive.* Valdosta, GA: Valdosta State University. Retrieved from http://chiron.valdosta.edu/whuitt/col/affsys/erikson.html.

Katz, D., & Kahn, R. (1978). *The social psychology of organizations* (2nd ed.). New York: Wiley.

Keeling, R.P. (2006). *Learning reconsidered 2: Implementing a campus-wide focus on the student experience.* Washington DC: American College Personnel Association (ACPA), Association of College and University Housing Officers—International (ACUHO-I), Association of College Unions—International (ACUI), National Academic Advising Association (NACADA), National Association of Campus Activities (NACA), National Association of Student Personnel Administrators (NASPA), and National Intramural-Recreational Sports Association (NIRSA).

Kraus, R. (1990). *Recreation and leisure in modern society* (4th ed.). New York: Harper Collins.

Kraus, R., Barber, E., & Shapiro, I. (2001). *Introduction to leisure services: Career perspectives.* Champaign, IL: Sagamore Publishing.

Lazarus, M. (1883). *About the attractions of play.* Berlin: Dummler.

Lewis, J., Barcelona, B., & Jones, T. (2002). Leisure satisfaction and quality of life: Issues for the justification of campus recreation. *National Intramural-Recreational Sports Journal, 25*(2), 57-63

Levy, J. (1978). *Play behavior.* New York: Wiley.

McGregor, D.M. (1957). The human side of enterprise. In Jay M. Shafritz & J. Steven Ott, *Classics of organization theory* (5th ed., p. 179). Belmont, CA: Wadsworth.

Mull, R.F., Bayless, K.G., & Jamieson, L.M. (2005). *Recreational sport management* (4th ed.). Champaign, IL: Human Kinetics.

National Association of Student Personnel Administrators. (2004). *Learning reconsidered: A campus wide focus on the student experience.* Retrieved from www.naspa.org/membership/leader_ex_pdf/lr_long.pdf.

National Intramural-Recreational Sports Association. (1996). *General and specialty standards for collegiate recreational sports.* Corvallis, OR: Author.

National Intramural-Recreational Sports Association. (2004). *The value of recreational sports in higher education: Impact on student enrollment, success and buying power.* Champaign, IL: Human Kinetics.

Patrick, G.T.W. (1916). *The psychology of relaxation.* Boston: Houghton Mifflin.

Perry, W.G. (1981). Cognitive and ethical growth: The making of meaning. In Arthur Chickering et al. (Eds.), *The modern American college: Responding to the new realities of diverse students and a changing society.* San Francisco: Jossey-Bass.

Princeton University. (2007). Definition of theory. Retrieved from http://wordnet.princeton.edu/perl/webwn?s=theory&o2=&o0=1&o7=&o5=&o1=1&o6=&o4=&o3=&h=.

Rapaport, W.J. (2006). William Perry's scheme of intellectual and ethical development. Retrieved from www.cse.buffalo.edu/~rapaport/perry.positions.html.

Sanford, N. (1966). *Self and society.* New York: Atherton.

Schein, E. (1992). *Organizational culture and leadership* (2nd ed.). San Francisco: Jossey-Bass.

Schiller, F.V. (1875). *Essays esthetical and philosophical.* London: George Bell.

Senge, P. (1990). *The fifth discipline: The art and practice of the learning organization.* New York: Doubleday.

Shafritz, J.M., & Ott, J.S. (2001). *Classics of organization theory* (5th ed.). Belmont, CA: Wadsworth.

Smith, A. (1776). An inquiry into the nature and causes of the wealth of nations. In Jay M. Shafritz & J. Steven Ott, *Classics of organization theory* (5th ed., p. 37). Belmont, CA: Wadsworth.

Spencer, H. (1873). *Principles of psychology.* New York: Appleton.

State University of New York at Geneseo. Mission statement. Retrieved from http://knights.geneseo.edu/index.php?pg=mission.php.

Sutton-Smith, B. (1995). Conclusion: The persuasive rhetorics of play. In A.D. Pellegrini (Ed.), *The future of play theory: A multidisciplinary inquiry into the contributions of Brian Sutton-Smith* (pp. 275-295). Albany, NY: State University of New York Press.

University of California at Irvine Campus Recreation. (n.d.). Mission statement. Retrieved from www.campusrec.uci.edu.

University of Illinois at Champaign-Urbana Division of Campus Recreation. (n.d.). Mission statement. Retrieved from www.campusrec.uiuc.edu/staff/index.html

University of Pennsylvania. (n.d.). Mission statement. Retrieved from www.upenn.edu/recreation/mission.htm.

University of South Carolina Campus Recreation. (n.d.). Retrieved from http://campusrec.sc.edu.

University of Tennessee at Knoxville Recreational Sports. (n.d.). Retrieved from http://recsports.utk.edu.

Weber, M. (1946). Bureaucracy. From *Essays in sociology,* edited and translated by H.H. Gerth and C. Wright Mills. In Jay M. Shafritz & J. Steven Ott, *Classics of organization theory* (5th ed., p. 73). Belmont, CA: Wadsworth.

Wiener, N. (1948). *Cybernetics or control and communication in the animal and the machine.* Paris: Hermann et Cie. Cambridge, MA: MIT Press.

Young, S.J., & Ross, C.M. (2004). Professional preparation for the recreational sports specialist. *Journal of Recreation and Leisure.* Retrieved from www.byu.edu/cpe/swdaahperd/2004journal.html.

Glossary

campus recreation—A major sector of recreation programming designed to meet the needs of older teenagers and young adults in college settings; often used interchangeably with *recreational sports.*

fitness programs—Programs linked to the physical realm of wellness that offer structured and unstructured activities that enhance cardiorespiratory endurance, as well as muscular strength, power, and endurance.

intramural—Derived from the Latin words *intra,* meaning "within," and *muralis,* meaning "wall." The term is usually paired with other words such as *sports, athletics,* or *activities* and, when so combined, implies that these programs are conducted "within the walls" or imaginary boundaries of some organization or institution.

leisure—Unencumbered time, free from class, study, or other obligations, in which to participate in structured or unstructured activity.

outdoor adventure programs—Programs that provide adventure trips, instructional clinics and classes, climbing equipment rentals, and in some cases challenge courses for team building and leadership development and focus on experiential learning and environmental awareness.

play—A behavior that is self-motivated and carried on for intrinsic purposes; it usually involves sport or recreational activity.

recreation—Time or activity used to renew and re-create ourselves.

sport—A team or individual competitive activity.

sport club—A group of students (and if the institution allows, faculty, staff, and community members) who voluntarily organize to further their common interests in a sport through participation and competition.

student development—The process of growth and maturation of students in a particular environment.

CHAPTER 2

History and Evolution of Campus Recreation

NIRSA, in consultation with Paul E. Wilson, CRSS, BS, NIRSA Historian

Experience is not what happens to a man; it is what a man does with what happens to him.

Aldous Huxley

Before today's all-inclusive campus recreation programs, there was an amalgam of physical education and intercollegiate athletics that often ignored the athletic needs of the majority of students. The blur between the inception of collegiate intramural sports and varsity athletics began in the early years of America's higher education. Initially, all sports were informal, composed of student teams engaged in leisure-time play. As these informal games grew in popularity, college administrators eventually allowed organized athletic varsity teams. However, the demand for informal sports, later called intramurals, continued because the games attracted too many students who could not, would not, or simply did not participate in intercollegiate athletics (Lewis, Jones, Lamke, & Dunn, 1998).

Intramurals grew up as a "stepchild," ignored by the more prominent and competitive programs. The word *intramural* is derived from the Latin words *intra*, meaning "within," and *muralis*, meaning "wall." The term is usually paired with other words such as *sports, athletics,* or *activities* and, when so combined, implies that these programs are conducted "within the walls" or imaginary boundaries of some organization or institution. Intramural programs are found in educational institutions at all levels—elementary schools; junior high schools; high schools; colleges and universities; and in military, commercial, and community organizations (Mueller, 1971).

Using a historical time line of significant events, this chapter describes the evolution of intramural programs into well-integrated, ever-expanding campus recreation programs. In addition, the history of the National Intramural-Recreational Sports Association and its importance to the development of professionals and programming in the field of campus recreation are discussed.

Growth and Evolution of Sports on College Campuses: 1600 to 1860

When the first American colleges were established, the educational spirit and religious beliefs of the colonists were antagonistic to any form of physical education or play (Stewart, 1992). Young people were too busy clearing forests and building shelter to play games (Means, 1952). The first institutions of higher learning were Harvard College (1636, just 16 years after the arrival of the

Pilgrims at Plymouth Rock), the College of William and Mary (1693), and Yale (founded as Collegiate College in 1701 and renamed Yale College in 1718). Students attended only to gain a liberal education or entry into the elite professions (Rice, 1929). Play was discouraged. As early as 1761, the trustees of Princeton University invoked a severe penalty for "any students caught playing ball in certain areas of the campus," and even by 1787, its trustees continued to object to games with sticks and balls, stating that these were "low and unbecoming to gentlemen students" (Means, 1952, p. 10).

Greek organizations, generally credited with the popularity of football, initially played as a form of fraternity "rush." Although played by teams on campuses as far back as 1827, when Harvard introduced the sport, the style of play at these early football matches closely resembled modern day soccer and not the rugby-like game that eventually emerged (Turano, 2001). Fraternities, because of their organization and permanency on campus, were among the first groups to promote athletics on an interfraternity basis.

A boat race between Harvard and Yale in 1852 is the earliest recorded intercollegiate meet (Stewart, 1992). Yale also had a dozen intramural competitive boating (rowing) clubs by 1859, which eventually developed into interclass teams, or crews (Means, 1952).

Baseball, known in 16th-century England as "rounders," was growing in popularity in small American towns where it was called "townball," "base," or "baseball" (Monser, 1995). Informal baseball games on college campuses were becoming popular in many regions of the country (Dulles, 1965). The first recorded baseball game on a college campus was held between Williams and Amherst at Pittsfield, Massachusetts, in July 1859. Amherst won by a score of 66 to 32 (Stewart, 1992).

Significant Developments: 1860 to 1870

During the 1860s American colleges and universities began to borrow outright the English idea of sports. The majority of early American sport clubs were influenced by the sports of English and European origin. However the English conception of "games" soon lost its original intention in America as the various groups began to adapt or change the rules to fit their way of life and to seek competition with other city and school teams (Means, 1952).

When the American Civil War began in 1861, the need for recruits meant that sport activities were deferred. The organized physical activity program at the University of Minnesota in 1862 was compulsory military training for all men in the freshman class (Burton & Wade, 2003).

Even though many sports on campuses abated as men went off to battle, some expanded as a result of the Civil War. Baseball continued as Union soldiers played it in their army camps. Enlisting soldiers brought their bats and balls with them and taught their comrades to play. The Union military leaders encouraged this recreation (Kirsch, 1998).

When the war ended in 1865, baseball grew in popularity as soldiers returned home and introduced the game to their towns (Kirsch, 1998). It resumed—and grew in popularity—on college campuses as well as in the national leagues. By 1872 "the magazine *Sports and Games* categorically stated that it had become 'the national game of the United States'" (Dulles, 1965, p. 189).

During the period after the Civil War, intercollegiate games became more frequent in schools nationwide. The prevalent viewpoint at the higher administrative levels was that these sports had to be "either tolerated or restricted." According to Snyder and Spreitzer (1978), in their book *Social Aspects of Sport*, the students joined clubs to participate in activities that were generally dismissed by faculty as frivolous. Only a few schools thought of them as having any importance or educational value (Means, 1952).

More Than Baseball and Football: 1870 to 1900

Baseball wasn't the only sport to be revived on college campuses following the Civil War. The first intercollegiate football game after the war occurred between Princeton and Rutgers in 1869 (Turano, 2001).

Although football was obviously becoming one of the most popular collegiate sports (4,000 spectators watched the first Princeton–Yale game in 1878; 40,000 watched 10 years later) (Dulles, 1965), the game was extremely dangerous and inflicted many injuries and deaths. Many institutions wanted to abolish football while others urged that it be reformed. In 1894, when public outcry and school administrators' concerns for the safety of students had escalated, additional rules were put into place.

Around this time physical education teachers began to try to expand their role in school settings. In 1885 William Gilbert Anderson, a physical training instructor in Brooklyn, New York, founded the Association for the Advancement of Physical Education (AAPE, now known as AAHPERD) by inviting a group of people who were working in the gymnastics field to come together to discuss their profession. As physical education and varsity athletics became more solidified on college campuses, students across the country who were not involved with varsity sports still wanted extracurricular informal sport activities. They also wanted physical exercise that was more interesting and fun than the rigid calisthenics, marching and drilling, and exercise or gymnastics programs that were favored by campus faculties (Mueller & Mitchell, 1960).

Some of the earliest intramural programs began in the late 1800s, generally under the auspices of varsity coaches or physical education teachers. Intramural activities at the University of Wisconsin began in 1893 when its Armory Gymnasium was built. Interclass and intercollege participation in baseball, contact football, gymnastics, and track and field existed under the direction of various physical education department staff members (University of Wisconsin at Madison, n.d.). In 1895 the Women's Athletic Association began at the University of Minnesota with the formation of the Ladies Tennis Association (Burton & Wade, 2003). Princeton and Yale played the "Caledonian Games" brought to America by Scottish immigrants (Means, 1952). These events generally consisted of dancing, music, and athletic competitions such as foot races; hurdle races; wrestling; pole-vaulting; high and long jumping; hopping, skipping, and jumping; and putting heavy stones (Rural Hill Center of Scottish Heritage, n.d.).

Shift in Philosophy: 1900 to 1913

The first 10 years after the turn of the 20th century marked a dramatic increase in both athletics and intramural sports. When school administrators finally realized the numbers of students who were actually participating in these informal games, the shift in philosophy began. Students were now interested in playing sports for the sake of participation instead of competition.

Although schools all over the United States record earlier intramural events, recreational sport is generally recognized as being "born" at Cornell University in 1904 (Lewis et al., 1998). The collegiate coaching staff at Cornell provided specialized instruction to students who were not on intercollegiate teams (Meuller & Reznik, 1979). The president of Cornell thought it appropriate that students be allowed to pursue athletic interests without joining intercollegiate teams (Lewis et al., 1998). Thus, the concept of playing sports for the sake of participation began to take hold on college campuses.

In the early years, collegiate recreational sports were mostly organized by students. However, college and university administrators began to feel the need to supervise these activities. Not only were they concerned for the students' safety and felt the obligation to prevent injuries; there also was the need to enforce game rules, as well as supervise the daily issues of logistics of facility and equipment use. In addition, varsity coaches were very supportive of intramural programs, believing the structured competition would develop athletes that could be recruited to varsity sports (Means, 1952). College physical education teachers liked the informal intramural competitions because they introduced a competitive element that increased student interest in physical activity.

Departmental Control and Other Significant Beginnings: 1913 to 1930

In the second two decades of the 20th century, as the intramural movement expanded, more colleges and universities began to develop intramural programs. Some of the major events during this period were as follows:

1913 Both the University of Michigan and Ohio State University inaugurated the first departments of intramural athletics, each under the direction of one man who was expected to handle the demands for competition in the various leading sports (Means, 1952, p. 11). The sole purpose of those departments was the organizing and scheduling of sport for the recreational enjoyment of the students (Lewis et al., 1998).

1916 Oregon State University, the University of Texas at Austin, and the University of

Illinois followed the lead of Michigan and Ohio State and inaugurated extensive intramural programs (Means, 1952).

1917 The Athletics Research Society's Committee on Intramural Sports, a group of scientific educators, recommended a comprehensive classification of playing units in its annual report. In these early phases of intramural development, the athletics associations had the idea that the intramural program would provide a source of recruiting for future varsity athletics (Mueller, 1971).

1917 At the University of Wisconsin, the National Athletics Conference of American College Women was organized. This group maintained a firm stand against varsity athletics for women and promoted the intramural concepts of "sports for all" (Mueller, 1971).

1918 The growth of intramural sports in colleges and universities suffered a temporary setback during the World War I years of 1914-1918. Results of medical examinations for the draft of military service indicated that programs of physical education and athletics in high schools and colleges around the country were not satisfactory for preparing men for the military service. After the war the whole nation was made aware of the need for a program that would reach the youth of the nation. Because of the increased public interest in all forms of athletics and the importance ascribed to athletics in the military training camps during World War I, college intramurals boomed after the war with the return of the servicemen (Mueller, 1971).

1919 Dr. Elmer Mitchell became the director of intramurals at the University of Michigan, the first college to give the title to the head of this work.

1920 At the University of Texas at Austin, Anna Hiss was named director of the Intramural Sports for Women program. She created programs for women in tennis, golf, riding, archery, fencing, badminton, bowling, tumbling, and riflery (University of Texas at Austin, 2003).

1921 Kansas State College created a program for all intramural sports and intercollegiate activities (Means, 1952).

1922 The University of Minnesota created a new Department of Physical Education and Athletics that would be responsible for all intramural and intercollegiate activities.

1925 The University of Oklahoma started its intramural program under the direction of Bennie Owen (Means, 1952).

1925 The first book on intramurals, *Intramural Athletics,* was written by Dr. Elmer D. Mitchell, considered by many to be the "father of intramurals" in America. He became the recognized leader in the field (Mueller, 1971).

1928 Because of Dr. Mitchell's influence in the field, the University of Michigan built the first building dedicated primarily to intramural sport at a cost of $743,000 (Stevenson, Reznik, & Pitcher, 1978).

Americans Begin to Value Leisure Time: 1930 to 1950

The next two decades saw changes in the values of Americans as a result of a number of significant events. The Great Depression was a worldwide economic downturn starting in 1929 and lasting through most of the 1930s. The most industrialized countries were most affected, including the United States, and unemployment and homelessness soared.

People were desperate for help to end the unemployment and economic crisis that gripped the country during the Depression, and the 1932 presidential election produced a landslide victory for Franklin Delano Roosevelt. In what would later be known as "The Hundred Days," during his first three months in office Roosevelt revitalized the faith of the nation by introducing programs such as the Civilian Conservation Corps (CCC). By creating the CCC, he brought together two resources that were being underused: young men and the land. During the height of the CCC, the enrollees were working hard, eating heartily, and gaining weight while they improved millions of acres of federal and state lands and parks. In the years of its existence, the CCC built 3,470 fire towers and 97,000 miles of fire roads, devoted 4,235,000 man-days to fighting fires, and planted more than 3 billion trees.

Participation in the CCC began to decline in the early 1940s as men joined the armed forces and was decimated after the Pearl Harbor bombing in 1941. It soon became obvious that, in a nation dedicated to war, any federal project not directly associated with the war effort was in trouble (National Association of Civilian Conservation Corps Alumni, n.d.).

Following the Great Depression, the work of the CCC, and World War II, Americans began to view recreation as a wise use of leisure time. After World War II there was an interest in erecting living war memorials in the form of recreational and athletics buildings. Industrialization led to shorter working days and weeks, necessitating that future citizens be taught hobbies, sports, and recreational activities that they could take part in during their new leisure time (Means, 1952).

At the 1947 annual conference of the American Association for Health, Physical Education and Recreation, the question arose as to who was responsible for the development of the purely recreational programs in the colleges of the future. Forward-looking departments began to create this modern program. Many colleges and universities increased the scope and offerings of their programs as well as integrating the men's and women's programs to provide corecreational activities (Means, 1952).

William Wasson, a biology teacher, head track coach, and assistant football and basketball coach at Dillard University in New Orleans, developed an intramural program for the Dillard students. In 1948 he sought and received a grant from the Carnegie Foundation to tour black colleges throughout the country to study their student intramural programs. Once he had collected the data and written *A Comparative Study of Intramural Programs in Negro Colleges*, he sent the document to all of the participating colleges he had visited. During this time he had the idea of a national organization that would serve as a reference, resource, and meeting of the minds of men and women interested in developing intramural programs. This ultimately led to the meeting of 22 male and female intramural directors from 11 historically black colleges that was held at Dillard University on February 22, 1950. It was at this meeting that the National Intramural Association (NIA)—later known as NIRSA—was created.

Campus Recreation Programs Provide for All: 1950 to Present

During the 1950s the popularity of intramural sports, seen solely as competitive programming, began to wane. Noncompetitive activities began to

25

William Wasson

Born in Chattanooga, Tennessee, William Wasson grew up in Louisville, Kentucky, graduated from Central High School, and then attended Louisville Municipal College, where he received a bachelor of science degree in biology in 1937. While in college, he played football and basketball and ran track. After he graduated with a master's in biology from Atlanta University, he taught and served as a principal for two years in Homerville, Georgia.

It was at the University of Michigan (Ann Arbor) where Wasson developed his lifelong interest in intramural sports. In 1946, while pursuing a master's in physical education, he took a class from Dr. Elmer Mitchell. Mitchell's enthusiasm and passion for creating physical activities for all students was contagious.

After he finished his second master's, Wasson moved to Dillard University in New Orleans, Louisiana, to teach biology, but he continued his interest in sports. He was an assistant coach for both football and basketball, was the head track coach, and he developed an intramural program for Dillard students. His interest in this activity grew, and he sought and received a grant from the Carnegie Foundation in 1948 to tour black colleges throughout the country, to study their student intramural programs.

Once he had collected the data and written *A Comparative Study of Intramural Programs in Negro Colleges,* he sent the document to all of the participating colleges that he had visited. It was also during this time that he got the idea of having a national organization that would serve as a reference, resource, and meeting of the minds of men and women interested developing intramural programs. This ultimately led to the meeting of 22 male and female intramural directors from 11 historically black colleges that was held at Dillard University on February 22, 1950. It was at this meeting that the National Intramural Association (NIA)—later known as NIRSA—was created, and Dr. Wasson has since been known as the founder of the association.

That same year, Wasson returned to the University of Michigan to pursue a doctorate. While there, he received a teaching fellowship in the campus intramurals program. After he earned his doctorate in 1954, he moved to Grambling College (Louisiana) to teach biology. Three years later, he moved to Wayne State University, where he taught kinesiology, anatomy, physiology, and the physiology of exercise until he retired as Professor Emeritus in 1980.

Through the years, Wasson served on 100 doctoral committees. He was a visiting professor at McMaster University in Hamilton, Ontario, and at Windsor, Canada, from 1961 to 1963. In 1961 he authored *Physiology of Exercise,* and in 1962 he published a laboratory manual, *Anatomy and Kinesiology.*

When Dr. Wasson passed away in 1991 in Sun City West, Arizona, where he had gone to live after he retired, he left a rich legacy of service and involvement. He served as president of the NIA for the first five years, received the NIRSA Honor Award in 1969, and published numerous articles on intramural and recreational sports. He also served as a consultant for the establishment of a National Intramural Association of Canada.

He was director of the National Undergraduate Leadership Conference for Kappa Alpha Psi fraternity. He also served as cochair of the Motor City International Indoor Track Meet and was a member of Phi Epsilon Kappa, Phi Delta Kappa, and Beta Kappa Chi honor societies. He was also a member of the board of directors of the Camp Fire Girls, associate fellow of the American College of Sports Medicine, and the president of the Detroit Varsity Club.

Dr. Wasson was once asked how he would like NIRSA to remember him. He humbly responded, "As the person who accidentally happened to have been there because, certainly not in the back of my mind, did I think we would get organized and become a national, or rather an international, organization."

Source: *NIRSA Know* newsletter, February 2004.

emerge toward the end of the decade, including outing-type, social, and creative activities. Informal physical recreation, which emphasized the recreational aspect of intramurals rather than the competitive aspects, was expanded (Maurer, 1978).

After Title IX became law in 1972, women's intramural programs were hurt because the more athletic participants in them moved on to varsity sports. At the same time, many universities began to consolidate men's and women's physical education departments. In most cases, the women's department became a subordinate unit of the men's department (Dudenhoeffer, 1997). It was soon after this that many female students began to realize their potential in regard to sport participation. No longer was it a choice between being a woman or an athlete. The evolution of the modern-thinking woman came about as a direct result of the Women's Liberation Movement, which led to a growing acceptance of female participants in sport and recreational activities (Yager, 1978). The 1920s slogan "athletics for all" had morphed into "recreational sports opportunities for all" (Maurer, 1978).

Two professional associations that helped mold the future of campus recreation had many interactions over the years. In 1959 the NIA became an affiliate of the American Association for Health, Physical Education and Recreation (AAHPER), but in 1961 it rejected an offer to merge with them into one association. Since then, AAHPERD has been recognized as the largest organization of professionals supporting and assisting those involved in physical education, leisure, fitness, dance, health promotion, and education, while NIRSA is known as the leading resource for professional and student development, education, and research in collegiate recreational sports.

In 1975 the NIA voted to change its name to the National Intramural-Recreational Sports Association (NIRSA), because the field of campus recreation had broadened to encompass more than just intramurals. The name change professionalized recreational sports.

The 1980s and 1990s saw significant growth in campus recreation programs as more universities began to recognize the opportunities for student involvement that the programs provided, making campus recreation a significant contributor to the mission of higher education (Barcelona & Ross, 2002).

Campus recreation programs expanded into new areas to meet the needs of the diverse student population. Besides the traditional intramural offerings, programs developed and evolved to include sport clubs; instructional programs; informal recreation, aquatics, fitness, wellness, outdoor recreation, family, and youth programs; summer camps; and special events.

With more programs came more participation and the need for new and expanded facilities. According to NIRSA's *Collegiate Recreational Sports Facility Construction Report for 2006-2011,* 220 colleges and universities reported that during the five-year period from 2006 to 2011, schools would spend over $3.17 billion on new construction, additions, remodels, and expansions of campus recreation facilities.

Conclusion

Over the years, the expanding role of campus recreation has often led to the need to justify those programs, services, and facilities to the university community. The role of campus recreation in the recruitment and retention of students is becoming well documented, as is the value students place on their participation in these programs in correlation to their overall college satisfaction and success. Campus recreation programs, and the professionals who administer them, are truly a cornerstone to students' overall collegiate education and experience.

References

Barcelona, R.J., & Ross, C.M. (2002). Participation patterns in campus recreational sports: An examination of quality of student effort from 1983 to 1998. *Recreational Sports Journal 26*(1): 41-53.

Burton, A.W., & Wade, M.G. (2003). History of the University of Minnesota, School of Kinesiology. Retrieved from www.education.umn.edu/Kin/school/history.html.

Dudenhoeffer, F.T. (1997). Life before NIRSA: A brief history of women's intramurals in the 20th century. *NIRSA Journal 21*(2): 3-7.

Dulles, F.R. (1965). *A history of recreation: America learns to play* (2nd ed.). New York: Meredith.

Kirsch, G.B. (1998, May). Bats, balls, and bullets. *Civil War Times Illustrated 37*(2): 30-37.

Lewis, J., Jones, T., Lamke, G., & Dunn, J.M. (1998, December). Recreational sport: Making the grade on college campuses. *Parks and Recreation.* Retrieved from www.findarticles.com/p/articles/mi_m1145/is_12_33/ai_53479082.

Maurer, B. (1978). Intramural programming—The old and the new. *NIRSA Journal 2*(2): 20-21.

The Founding of the National Intramural-Recreational Sports Association (NIRSA)

The National Intramural-Recreational Sports Association was founded in 1950 at Dillard University in New Orleans. William Wasson invited men and women intramural directors from 11 historically black colleges and universities (HBCUs) to a meeting to discuss ways to improve intramural programs at colleges.

© NIRSA

Founding members of the NIA.

NIA Founding Members

Dillard University
William Wasson (founder)
Armstead Pierro
Annette Akins

Texas State University
Juanita Pierce
Dimples Lee
Viggo Wallace

Xavier University
James E. Hawkins
Victor Kerr
Alfred Priestly
Hiram Workman

Bethune-Cookman College
Rudolph Mathews
Roosevelt Grattic

Albany State College
George James

Tuskegee Institute
Cleve Abbott

Wiley College
Ross Townes

North Carolina College
Allen Weatherford

Arkansas A&M College
Alvin Brown

Southern University
Horace Moody

Tillotson College
Grant Gray

Other attendees:

Morris X.F. Jeff (New Orleans Recreation Department)
Jim Hall (Louisiana Weekly)
Reverend Norman A. Holmes

Today, NIRSA's 4,000 professional and student members are located across the nation and internationally on more than 675 institutional member campuses, at U.S. military installations, at city and public recreation programs, and at private and not-for-profit organizations. The mission of the National Intramural-Recreational Sports Association is to provide for the education and development of professional and student members and to foster quality recreation programs, facilities, and services for diverse populations. NIRSA demonstrates its commitment to excellence by using resources that promote ethical and healthy lifestyle choices.

When the administration of the NIRSA national office became a full-time operation in 1986, it was first headquartered on the campus at Oregon State University. In July 1998 the association built a 16,089-square-foot, $2.2 million facility, the NIRSA National Center, in Corvallis, Oregon (National Intramural-Recreational Sports Association [NIRSA], n.d.).

NIRSA headquarters in Corvallis, Oregon.

Significant Happenings in the History of NIRSA

Logos from past to present: *(a)* NIA logo from 1950 to 1975, *(b)* NIRSA logo from 1975 to 1997, and *(c)* NIRSA logo from 1997 to the present day.

1950 The inaugural meeting of the National Intramural Association (NIA) was held February 22-23 at Dillard University in New Orleans, Louisiana.

1952 The Third Annual Conference of the National Intramural Association was held at Howard University, with Herman Tyrance serving as host. With the presence of S. Bischoff and Al Lumley, the organization became an interracial association. The name of the association was changed to the National Intramural and Recreation Association, although historians state that no one referred to the association as anything but the NIA.

>> *continued*

>> continued

1959 The National Intramural Association became an affiliate of the American Association for Health, Physical Education and Recreation (AAHPER). The Executive Committee met in December and rewrote the constitution, dropping "Recreation" from the name and eliminating women's membership.

1960 At the annual business meeting, the revised constitution as proposed by the Executive Committee was unanimously accepted by the membership, thereby excluding women from membership and returning to the original name of the NIA.

1961 The National Intramural Association rejected an offer to merge with AAHPER.

1966 The first edition of the *NIA Directory* (later called the *Recreational Sports Directory*) was published.

1969 An executive secretary position was created, and Paul H. Gunsten was given responsibility for establishing a national headquarters, mailing institutional membership certificates, and publishing and mailing the newsletter, directory, and proceedings.

1971 Carol Harding and Carolyn Hewatt, two well-respected women's intramural directors, were invited to give professional presentations at the annual conference. Their attendance, along with President Lynn Reading's urging, encouraged the passage of a constitutional revision that accepted women as members in the NIA. Edsel Buchanan became the executive secretary.

1972 Job placement services were made available at the annual conference by committee chair Will Holsberry.

1973 Will Holsberry became the executive secretary and was responsible for managing the office.

1975 The National Intramural Association membership voted to change its name to the National Intramural-Recreational Sports Association (NIRSA). The NIRSA national office was moved to Oregon State University.

1977 The first issue of the *NIRSA Journal* was published in March under editor Jim Peterson.

1986 The national office became a full-time operation. The constitution was changed to change the title of the association's chief executive officer, Will Holsberry, from executive secretary to executive director.

1987 Mary Daniels was elected as the first female president of NIRSA.

1991 Dr. William Wasson, NIRSA founder, passed away.

1994 Land was purchased (2.3 acres) in the Sunset Research Park area on the southwest side of Corvallis, Oregon, for the building of a NIRSA National Center.

1997 July 11: Groundbreaking ceremony for the NIRSA National Center in Corvallis, Oregon.

1997 July: Will Holsberry, NIRSA's first executive director, retired. Dr. Kent Blumenthal, CRSS (certified recreational sports specialist), CAE (certified association executive), became NIRSA's second executive director.

1998 Dedication of the NIRSA National Center. The last surviving founder of the NIA, Horace Moody, passed away.

1999 The 50th NIRSA annual conference was held in Milwaukee, Wisconsin.

2002 NIRSA was accepted as a member of the Council of Higher Education Management Associations (CHEMA).

Means, L.E. (1952). *The organization and administration of intramural sports* (2nd ed.). St. Louis: C.V. Mosby. (Original work published 1949.)

Mitchell, E.D. (1939). *Intramural sports.* New York: A.S. Barnes and Company.

Monser, Chris. (1995). Townball—Description and rules. The baseball archives. Retrieved from www.baseball1.com.

Mueller, P. (1971). *Intramurals: Programming and administration* (4th ed.). New York: The Ronald Press.

Mueller, P., and Mitchell, E.D. (1960). *Intramural sports.* New York: The Ronald Press.

Mueller, P., and Reznik, J.W. (1979). *Intramural-recreational sports: Programming and administration* (5th ed.). New York: John Wiley and Sons.

National Association of Civilian Conservation Corps Alumni. (n.d.). Roosevelt's tree army: A brief history of the Civilian Conservation Corps. Retrieved from www.cccalumni.org/history1.html.

National Intramural-Recreational Sports Association. (n.d.). Retrieved from www.nirsa.org.

Rice, E.A. (1929). *A brief history of physical education.* New York: A.S. Barnes.

Rural Hill Center of Scottish Heritage. (n.d.). Origin of the Scottish games. Retrieved from www.ruralhill.net/origin.htm.

Snyder, E., & Spreitzer, E. (1978). *Social aspects of sport.* Englewood Cliffs, NJ: Prentice Hall.

Stevenson, M.J., Reznik, J.W., & Pitcher, R.W. (1978). First intramural-recreation facility celebrates 50th year. Retrieved from www.recsports.umich.edu/facilities/imsbhistory.html.

Stewart, R.E. (1992). A brief history of the intramural movement. *NIRSA Journal: 17*(1): 12.

Turano, C. (2001). The rise of intercollegiate football and its portrayal in American popular literature. Retrieved from www.uga.edu/honors/curo/juro/2001_10_13/Turano2.html.

University of Texas at Austin. (2003). History of recreational sports. UT Division of Recreational Sports. Retrieved from www.utrecsports.org/about/history/history.php.

University of Wisconsin at Madison. (n.d.). Intramural sports history. Retrieved from www.recsports.wisc.edu/intramurals/im_history.htm.

Yager, G.M. (1978). Women: Campus recreational sport (IM). *NIRSA Journal 3*(1): 44-48.

CHAPTER 3

Title IX Legacy and Beyond

Kathryn G. Bayless, CRSS, MSPE, Director, Campus Recreational Sports, Indiana University at Bloomington

As we empower girls in sport, we empower girls for life.

Sharon Shields, professor and vice provost, Vanderbilt University

This chapter presents the history of Title IX legislation and addresses its impact on girls and women in sport, both athletic and recreational. It includes a brief explanation of the evolution of the regulations and policy interpretations that have been developed to help guide implementation and discusses some of the challenges associated with implementation. This is followed by views on the impact of Title IX among recreational sport professionals. Because of a lack of research in this area, information is admittedly anecdotal.

Finally, implications for the future of Title IX in recreational sports are considered.

The Law, Regulations, and Interpretations

Take a moment to think back on your childhood, especially as a child at play. You may resonate with the following thoughts and feelings of Patsy Neal, three-time AAU All American basketball player:

I was born an athlete.

I cradled balls and ran barefoot through the fields.

I took tree limbs and batted rocks into the sky.

I chased balls and birds and butterflies in a never-ending stream of ecstasy.

I moved; therefore I existed.

I enjoyed; therefore I lived.

I was young then, and life to me was just another game.

I grew older, but not much wiser.

I still ran and jumped and played with pure joy.

I only thought of this moment, this day, this time.

My legs moved, my hands threw, my heart beat . . . Lord, I worked.

My being, my self, my body, my soul—

It beat as one unit.

I lived.

I was.

I did not care to know how or why, for I was a child, and children

Just are without knowing.

It was a period of bliss.

And then . . . ever so slowly . . . I grew up.

There were subtle changes.

I still felt the beauty of coordination between body and mind.

I still loved the flow of the body in the afternoon sun and in the morning mist.

But the rules changed.

I became more responsible for my actions—and more aware of the consequences

Involved in action.

Sometimes I even worked at my play.

I sought perfection where before there had only been joy.

I struggled toward goals where once I had found them freely as happenings.

The supreme pureness of movement slowly gave way to other things—

Practiced and rehearsed things.

And yet . . . yet . . . that joy, that song of gladness, that beauty of simply being alive,

That supreme ecstasy of movement endured and survived even the

Growth of maturity.

I lived in my body, and I loved my being.

And then one day I was an adult.

I no longer jumped over mud puddles and hurdled bushes.

I no longer bounced balls off the house or caught raindrops in my mouth.

Reprinted from P. Neal, 1974, *I was born an athlete* (Grand Rapids, MI: Zondervan Corporation). By permission of Patsy Neal.

What a vivid portrayal of the joy of play and movement often associated with childhood and the adolescent years. What a sobering picture of adulthood expressed by the author!

Perhaps this portrayal of adulthood is foreign to you, and you continue to enjoy play and recreational pursuits; but, for many people, especially women prior to the 1970s, maturing into adulthood typically meant being discouraged from, and even denied, participation in sport and recreational activities. Although the reasons are varied, prominent among them were the beliefs that girls and women were biologically weaker and had to be protected from physically demanding activities, and that involvement in sport violated conventional views about the meaning of being "feminine."

Changing Times: The Adoption of Title IX

In the late 1960s and during the 1970s, traditional views of women and sport were not only challenged, but also altered as a part of the social revolution rooted in the modern feminist movement and civil rights unrest that raised awareness about **discrimination** in this country. One of the most significant indicators of this social revolution was the passage of legislation in 1972 known as **Title IX of the Education Amendments (P.L. 92-318, 20 U.S.C.S. section 1681 et seq.)**. This landmark legislation bans sex discrimination (against either males or females) in schools, whether it is in academics or athletics. Title IX states:

> No person in the U.S. shall, on the basis of sex, be excluded from participation in, or denied the benefits of, or be subjected to discrimination under any educational program or activity receiving federal aid.

This **law,** in 37 words, reflected an intensifying effort to extend equal opportunities and fair treatment to girls and women at work and play within education settings. It signaled a significant social revolution and provided a legal mandate through which traditionally male-dominated strongholds could be challenged.

When Title IX was enacted in 1972, schools were provided a six-year period in which to move toward **compliance** and in which the **regulations** could be written to determine whether schools were in compliance. Delays in compliance with Title IX were not permitted in any programs except athletics. High school and college athlet-ics programs were given until July 21, 1978, to comply.

Title IX legislation was written to address many issues of sex discrimination and applies to all programs within schools, colleges, and universities that receive federal funding. Yet the greatest public controversy has surrounded implementation within recreation, physical education, and athletic settings in particular. Carpenter and Acosta (2005) reported:

> Over 10,000 comments were received during the review process. The comments came from lobbyists, athletics directors, parents, teachers, lawyers, coaches, and educational administrators; the comments came from a broad spectrum of interested individuals and groups. Over 90 percent of those comments related to the application of Title IX to athletics, yet less than 10 percent of the regulations deal directly with athletics, physical education, recreation, or sports. (p. 6)

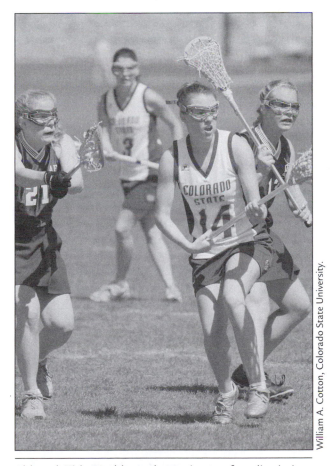

William A. Cotton, Colorado State University.

Although Title IX addressed many issues of sex discrimination, public controversy focused on the implementation of the legislation in athletic settings.

The controversy surrounding implementation is rooted in the broad language of the one-sentence law, which resulted in varied interpretations about implementation. Subsequently, the Office for Civil Rights (OCR), part of the Department of Education, was charged with the following:

- Developing regulations
- Providing greater details for implementation and measuring compliance
- Enforcing Title IX

Developing Regulations

As it turned out, the regulations provided minimal information about what was required for athletics, and even less information about requirements for recreational sports. Nevertheless, an overview of those regulations related to athletics provides a foundation to better understand the expectations of the law and the struggles with its ambiguity, as well as its application to recreational sports. The pertinent sections are as follows:

Section 106.8 Designation of Responsible Employee and Adoption of Grievance Procedures (34 Code of Federal Regulations, Part 106)

a. *Designation of responsible employee.* Each recipient shall designate at least one employee to coordinate its efforts to comply with and carry out its responsibilities under this part, including any investigation of any complaint communicated to such recipient alleging its noncompliance with this part or alleging any actions that would be prohibited by this part. The recipient shall notify all its students and employees of the name, office address, and telephone number of the employee or employees appointed pursuant to this paragraph.

b. *Complaint procedure of recipient.* A recipient shall adopt and publish grievance procedures providing for prompt and equitable resolution of student and employee complaints alleging any action, which would be prohibited by this part.

Section 106.33 Comparable Facilities

A recipient may provide separate toilet, locker room, and shower facilities on the basis of sex, but such facilities provided for students of one sex shall be comparable to such facilities provided for students of the other sex.

Section 106.37 Financial Assistance

1. To the extent that a recipient awards athletic scholarships or grants-in-aid, it must provide reasonable opportunities for such awards for members of each sex in proportion to the number of students of each sex participating in interscholastic or intercollegiate athletics.

2. Separate athletic scholarships or grants-in-aid for members of each sex may be provided as part of separate athletic teams for members of each sex to the extent consistent with this paragraph and section 106.41.

Section 106.41 Athletics

a. *General.* No person shall on the basis of sex, be excluded from participation in, be denied the benefits of, be treated differently from another person or otherwise be discriminated against in any interscholastic, intercollegiate, club or intramural athletics offered by a recipient, and no recipient shall provide any such athletics separately on such basis.

b. *Separate teams.* Notwithstanding the requirements of paragraph [a.] of this section, a recipient may operate or sponsor separate teams for members of each sex where selection for such teams is based upon competitive skill or the activity involved is a contact sport.

However, where a recipient operates or sponsors a team in a particular sport for members of one sex but operates or sponsors no such team for members of the other sex, and athletic opportunities for members of the excluded sex have previously been limited, members of the excluded sex must be allowed to try-out for the team offered unless the sport involved is a contact sport. For the purposes of this part, contact sports include boxing, wrestling, rugby, ice hockey, football, basketball and other sports the purpose or major activity of which involves bodily contact.

c. *Equal opportunity.* A recipient who operates or sponsors interscholastic, intercollegiate, club or intramural athletics shall provide equal athletic opportunity for members of both sexes. In determining whether equal opportunities are available, the Director will consider, among other factors:

- Whether the selection of sports and levels of competition effectively accommodate the interests and abilities of members of both sexes
- The provision of equipment and supplies
- Scheduling of games and practice time
- Travel and per diem allowance

- Opportunity to receive coaching and academic tutoring
- Assignment and compensation of coaches and tutors
- Provision of locker rooms, practice and competitive facilities
- Provision of medical and training facilities and services
- Provision of housing and dining facilities and services
- Publicity
- Recruitment
- Support services
- Financial assistance

Unequal aggregate expenditures for members of each sex or unequal expenditures for male and female teams, if a recipient operates or sponsors separate teams, will not constitute noncompliance with this section, but the Assistant Secretary, the Office for Civil Rights (OCR), part of the Department of Education, may consider the failure to provide necessary funds for teams for one sex in assessing equality of opportunity for members of each sex.

Although the regulations are not law, once accepted by Congress in 1975, they had the "force of the law," and courts were required to give the regulations the same weight as they did the actual law.

Policy Interpretations and Compliance

The regulations for Title IX did provide some guidance, but a challenging drawback of the initial regulations was the lack of specificity on how to measure compliance. In response, a set of **policy interpretations** (*Federal Register*, volume 44, number 239, at 71413) was published by the Department of Health, Education, and Welfare (now called the Department of Education) in 1979 to provide details on methods for measuring compliance (see Web site www.ed.gov/news/fedregister/index.html).

Although the law and regulations both have the "force of the law," the policy interpretations do not. Instead, they are given considerable deference. This means that in a dispute, the courts are required to give weight to the law and its corresponding regulations. When it comes to policy interpretations, the courts give them weight, but not as much as the words contained in the law and regulations.

Rather than bringing greater clarity to the issue, sometimes the policy interpretations of a method for measuring compliance actually generated controversy because the courts place lesser weight on policy interpretations than on regulations. For example, heated debate escalated surrounding the regulation requiring equal access to participation opportunities and a three-part test for measuring compliance found in the policy interpretations. The regulation says that equitable athletic opportunities must be provided to both sexes, but the regulations do not provide direction on how to measure compliance.

On the other hand, the policy interpretations provide some direction on the application of Title IX directly to athletics through the three-part test (also referred to as the three-prong test). This interpretation said that a school may demonstrate compliance by meeting any one of the following three parts:

1. Whether the institution provides opportunities in sports for male and female students in numbers that are substantially proportionate to their respective enrollments
2. Whether the institution can show a history and continuing practice of program expansion that is demonstrably responsive to the developing interests and abilities of the members of the sex that is underrepresented among athletes
3. Whether the institution can show that the present program has fully and effectively accommodated the interests and abilities of the members of that sex

Although only one option must be met to comply with the participation requirement, the debates continued because some opponents did not like the presence of the proportionality option and wanted it modified or removed. Opponents also claimed that compliance with the other two options was difficult to achieve (Carpenter & Acosta, 2005, pp. 14 and 15).

Although the policy interpretations of 1979 did address some areas of ambiguity, the Office for Civil Rights, the agency charged with enforcing Title IX, developed additional details about the requirements and how to comply. These materials include an *Investigator's Manual* to instruct investigators in how to investigate complaints and the three letters of clarification outlined here (for a copy of the actual letters, go to www.chronicle.com/indepth/titleix):

1. *1996 letter of clarification.* Responded to requests for specific guidance, including examples, regarding the three-prong test for measuring nondiscriminatory participation opportunities

2. *1998 letter of clarification.* Dealt with the requirement to provide equitable financial aid to both males and females

3. *2003 letter of clarification.* Reaffirmed the proportionality prong of the three-prong test

In addition to these documents, other findings resulting from complaints to the Office of Civil Rights and lawsuits provide sources of information that further constitute the body of information to guide enforcement and implementation of Title IX. Since its inception, Title IX has elicited strong sentiments both for and against its implementation and enforcement. An overview of major benchmarks in the tempestuous chronology of Title IX is provided in figure 3.1. This time line also appears on the Women's Sports Foundation Web site (www.womenssportsfoundation.org) and in *Title IX* by Carpenter and Acosta (2005).

Included in figure 3.1 are references to the most current sequence of challenges since the 1996 letter of clarification, culminating in events associated with the formation of a special federal commission. The impetus for the creation of the commission began in 1995 and was tied to congressional hearings (House Subcommittee on Postsecondary Education) and lawsuits attacking the proportionality prong of the three-prong test.

Chief among the Title IX opponents at this time was Representative Dennis J. Hastert (R-Illinois), who became speaker of the house in 1999. Hastert was a former wrestling coach, former president of the Wrestling Coaches Association, and an inductee to the Wrestling Hall of Fame. His testimony at the hearings centered on his belief that the proportionality prong was directly linked to colleges' decisions to terminate men's "minor" sport teams such as wrestling.

Although these hearings produced no changes, the proportionality debate heated up largely as a result of ongoing frustrations with decisions by college administrators to terminate men's "minor" sport teams rather than increase opportunities for women.

The year 1996 saw the promulgation of the clarification letter by the Office of Civil Rights; the 1996 clarification letter supported the three-prong test for participation found

in the policy interpretations. The judiciary similarly found no reason to reinterpret the issue. Eight of the 12 United States Courts of Appeal had ruled on Title IX cases involving proportionality, and all eight supported it as an appropriate legal measure for assessing equitable participation. The loudness of the proportionality debate was unabated even though Congress, the Office for Civil Rights, and the courts had all tried to close the discussion. (Carpenter & Acosta, 2005, p. 189)

Commission to Review Title IX

Undeterred, by 2002 Speaker of the House Hastert supported the creation of the commission to review Title IX in general and the proportionality prong in particular. On June 27, 2002, the federal Commission on Opportunities in Athletics was established under the direction of the secretary for the Department of Education, Rod Paige. The purpose of the commission was to collect information (see the questions that follow), analyze issues, and obtain broad public input directed at improving the application of current federal standards for measuring equal opportunity for men and women and boys and girls to participate in athletics under Title IX. Further, the commission was charged to submit its report no later than January 31, 2003. The report was to include its recommendations and to address the following eight questions (for more information, see www.hhs.gov/ocr/hipaa):

1. Are Title IX standards for assessing equal opportunity in athletics working to promote opportunities for male and female athletes?

2. Is there adequate Title IX guidance that enables colleges and school districts to know what is expected of them and to plan for an athletics program that effectively meets the needs and interests of their students?

3. Is further guidance or other steps needed at the junior and senior high school levels, where the availability or absence of opportunities will critically affect the prospective interests and abilities of student athletes when they reach college age?

4. How should activities such as cheerleading or bowling factor into the analysis of equitable opportunities?

5. The department has heard from some parties that whereas some men athletes will "walk-on" to intercollegiate teams without

Title IX Chronology

June 23, 1972

Title IX of the Education Amendments is enacted by Congress and is signed into law by Richard Nixon. The sponsors of Title IX were Birch Bayh from the Senate and Edith Green from the House. Title IX prohibits sex discrimination in any educational program or activity within an institution receiving any type of federal financial aid.

May 20, 1974

Senator Tower proposes the "Tower Amendment," which would exempt revenue-producing sports from being tabulated when determining Title IX compliance. The amendment is rejected.

July 1974

In lieu of Senator Tower's failed amendment, Senator Javits proposes that the Department of Health, Education, and Welfare (HEW) must issue Title IX regulations including, "with respect to intercollegiate athletic activities, reasonable provisions considering the nature of particular sports" (e.g., event-management needs, etc.).

May 27, 1975

President Ford signs Title IX and submits it to Congress for review (persuant to Section 431(d)(1) of the General Education Provisions Act).

June 1975

Representative O'Hara introduces House Bill (H.R. 8394), proposing to use sports revenues first to offset the cost of that sport, then to support other sports. He wants to alter Title IX's coverage in athletics. This bill dies in committees before reaching the House floor.

July 21, 1975

Congress reviews and approves Title IX regulations and rejects resolutions disapproving them.

- June 4, 1975: The present Title IX regulation was transmitted to Congress.
- June 5, 1975: Senator Helms (S. Con. Res. 46), and June 17, 1975, Representative Martin (H. Con. Res. 310), disapproving entire Title IX legislation.
- June 17, 1975: Representative Martin (H. Con. Res. 311), disapproving Title IX legislation only as it relates to intercollegiate athletics.
- July 16, 1975: Senators Laxalt, Curtis, and Fannin (S. Con. Res. 52), disapproving application of Title IX to intercollegiate athletics.
- July 21, 1975: Senator Helms introduced S. 2146 in an attempt to prohibit the application of Title IX regulations to athletics where participation in those athletic activities is not a required part of the educational institution's curriculum. (He reintroduced S. 2146 as S. 535 in 1977.)

Title IX federal regulation is issued in the area of athletics. High schools and colleges are given three years, and elementary schools one year, to come into compliance.

February 17, 1976

NCAA legally challenges Title IX.

July 15, 1977

Senators Tower, Bartlett, and Hruska introduce Senate Bill (S. 2106), proposing to exclude revenue-producing sports from Title IX coverage. The bill dies in committees before reaching the Senate floor.

(continued)

Figure 3.1 The chronology of Title IX legislation.

Reprinted, by permission, from Women's Sports Foundation, 2006.

1978

HEW issues proposed policy "Title IX and Intercollegiate Athletics" for notice and comment.

July 21, 1978

Deadline for high schools and colleges to comply with Title IX in athletics.

December 11, 1979

HEW issues final policy interpretation on "Title IX and Intercollegiate Athletics." Rather than relying exclusively on presumption-of-compliance standard, the final policy focuses on each institution's obligation to provide equal opportunity and details the factors to be considered in assessing actual compliance (currently referred to as the three-prong test).

1980

Department of Education is established and given oversight of Title IX through the Office for Civil Rights (OCR).

February 28, 1984

Grove City v. Bell limits the scope of Title IX, effectively taking away coverage of athletics except for athletic scholarships. The Supreme Court concludes that only the specific program (i.e., office of student financial aid) that receives federal funds needs to comply with Title IX.

March 22, 1988

Civil Rights Restoration Act of 1987 passes, overriding a presidential veto by President Ronald Reagan. This act reversed *Grove City,* restoring Title IX to institution-wide coverage. If any program or activity in the school or college receives federal funds, all programs and activities must comply with Title IX.

September 6, 1988

Haffer v. Temple settles, giving new direction to athletics departments regarding their budgets, with respect to participation rates of male and female athletes.

April 2, 1990

Valerie M. Bonnette and Lamar Daniel authored *A Title IX Athletics Investigator's Manual,* issued by the Office for Civil Rights.

February 26, 1992

In *Franklin v. Gwinnett County Public Schools,* the Supreme Court rules that monetary damages are available under Title IX. Previously, only injunctive relief was available (i.e., the institution would be forced to stop discriminating).

1992

Shortly after the *Franklin* decision, the NCAA completes and publishes a landmark gender equity study of its member institutions.

1994

Senator Mosley-Braun (S. 1468) and Representative Collins (H.R. 921) sponsor the Equity in Athletics Disclosure Act (EADA), stating that any coeducational institution of higher education that participates in any federal student financial aid program and has an intercollegiate athletics program must disclose certain information concerning its intercollegiate athletics program. Now, annual reports are required.

January 16, 1996

OCR issues clarifications of the three-part "Effective Accommodation Test."

(continued)

Figure 3.1 *(continued)*

Reprinted, by permission, from Women's Sports Foundation, 2006.

October 1, 1996

All institutions of higher education must have available, to all who inquire, specific information on their intercollegiate athletics departments, as required by the Equity in Athletics Disclosure Act.

November 21, 1996

Federal appeals court upholds a lower court's ruling in *Cohen v. Brown University* that Brown University illegally discriminated against female athletes. Brown argues that it is not in violation of Title IX because women are less interested in sports than men. Both the district court and the court of appeals reject Brown's argument. Many of the arguments Brown made unsuccessfully are similar to those relied upon by colleges and universities all over the country.

June 23, 1997

Twenty-fifth anniversary of the passage of Title IX.

February 20, 2001

The Supreme Court issues a decision in *Brentwood v. Tennessee Secondary School Athletic Association* holding that the high school athletic association is a "state actor" and thus subject to the Constitution. This means, for example, that in gender equity suits under the Equal Protection Clause of the 14th Amendment, athletic associations cannot argue that they are not covered.

December 17, 2001

The court issues a decision in *Communities for Equity v. Michigan High School Athletic Association* holding a state athletic association liable under Title IX, the Equal Protection Clause, and Michigan state law for discriminating against girls by scheduling six girls' sports in nontraditional and/or disadvantageous seasons.

February 2002

The National Wrestling Coaches Association, College Gymnastics Association, and the U.S. Track Coaches Association, along with several other groups representing male athletes and alumni of wrestling programs at Bucknell, Marquette, and Yale, filed suit alleging that Title IX regulations and policies were unconstitutional.

May 29, 2002

The U.S. Department of Justice filed a motion to dismiss on narrow procedural grounds the complaint by the National Wrestling Coaches Association, College Gymnastics Association, and the U.S. Track Coaches Association filed in federal court against the U.S. Department of Education attacking the three-prong test developed for schools to determine their compliance with Title IX in women's athletics programs.

June 2002

The National Wrestling Coaches Association filed a cross-motion asking that the Department of Education be ordered to withdraw the 1979 policy interpretations and the 1996 clarification letter.

June 23, 2002

Thirtieth anniversary of the passage of Title IX.

June 27, 2002

U.S. Secretary of Education Rod Paige announces the establishment of a Commission on Opportunities in Athletics. The stated purpose of the commission is to collect information, analyze issues, and obtain broad public input directed at improving the application of current federal standards for measuring equal opportunity for men and women and boys and girls to participate in athletics under Title IX. The commission will recommend to the secretary, in a written report, whether those standards should be revised, and if so, how the standards should be revised. The commission will also recommend other steps

(continued)

Figure 3.1 *(continued)*

Reprinted, by permission, from Women's Sports Foundation, 2006.

to improve the effectiveness of Title IX and to maintain and build upon the extraordinary progress that has resulted from its passage 30 years ago.

February 2003

The commission issues its report. U.S. Secretary of Education Rod Paige says that he will only move forward with the 15 unanimous recommendations (out of 23 recommendations) by the commission.

June 11, 2003

The National Wrestling Coaches Association lawsuit against the Department of Education is dismissed.

July 11, 2003

The Office for Civil Rights of the U.S. Department of Education issued its "Further Clarification of Intercollegiate Athletics Policy Guidance Regarding Title IX Compliance." The clarification reaffirms the validity and effectiveness of long-standing administrative regulations and policies governing this application.

August 15, 2003

The College Sports Council, a group including the National Wrestling Coaches Association, announces that they will file an appeal of the June 11, 2003, dismissal of the "wrestlers" case.

May 2004

The appeal by the College Sports Council is denied.

March 17, 2005

The Department of Education issues a policy guidance (the "Additional Clarification") that significantly weakens Title IX. Schools can now simply send out an e-mail survey to their female students, asking them what additional sports they might have the interest in and ability to play. If the survey responses do not show enough interest or ability, schools do not have to add any sports—and are presumed to be in compliance with Title IX.

June 23, 2007

Thirty-fifth anniversary of the passage of Title IX.

Figure 3.1   *(continued)*

Reprinted, by permission, from Women's Sports Foundation, 2006.

athletic financial aid and without having been recruited, women rarely do this. Is this accurate, and, if so, what are its implications for Title IX analysis?

6. How do revenue-producing and large-roster teams affect the provision of equal athletic opportunities?

7. In what ways do opportunities in other sports venues such as the Olympics, professional leagues, and community recreation programs interact with the obligations of colleges and school districts to provide equal athletic opportunity?

8. Apart from Title IX enforcement, are there other efforts to promote athletic opportunities for male and female students that the department might support, such as public–private partnerships to support

the efforts of schools and colleges in this area?

Speculation about the outcome of the commission's work revealed that both foes and supporters recognized the potential for either sweeping changes away from significant enforcement or the reaffirmation of Title IX. Subsequently, an outpouring of opinions was directed at commission members to sway them to particular points of view.

Along with this onslaught of public opinion came strong criticisms of the composition of the commission, as well as the background, perceived biases, and experiences of commission members. The criticisms continued throughout the 12-month life span of the commission, including allegations of ineptitude and ignorance on the parts of commissioners, the commission staff, and

Department of Education administrators. Clearly, these concerns added to the growing trepidation over the way the results would be used:

> By itself, the report had no power, but how it would be used created great anxiety. Its potential contents took on an importance beyond their actual power. The report could either be ignored *in toto* or used as support to accomplish whatever predetermined decisions the Department of Education might have had in mind through enforcement emphases or, through executive order, whatever the president of the United States might have wanted all along. Nonetheless, the commission occupied a central place in the field of attention from June 2002 to February 2003, when the final report was issued. (Carpenter & Acosta, 2005, p. 191)

Of the 23 final recommendations contained in the report (titled "Open to All: Title IX at 30"), 15 received a unanimous vote by commission members and became the focal point of an announcement from Secretary of Education Rod Paige that the Department of Education would only "move forward" on the 15 unanimous proposals. Unfortunately, significant unrest and divergent views remained. A prominent example of the levels of dissatisfaction with the report was the preparation of a minority report submitted by two commission members who felt that the process and final report were flawed. Then, on July 11, 2003, Assistant Secretary for Civil Rights Gerald Reynolds issued the *2003 Further Clarification of Intercollegiate Athletics Policy Guidelines Regarding Title IX Compliance*. Following are the highlights from the 2003 letter of clarification:

- Reaffirmation of the three-prong test for participation with no one prong given preference

- Reminder that nothing in Title IX materials requires or recommends cutting or limiting male participation

- Notice to schools that the OCR will aggressively enforce Title IX standards, including implementing sanctions for institutions that do not comply

- Reaffirmation allowing private sponsorship of athletic teams, with the reminder that such sponsorship does not change or diminish obligations under Title IX

- Pledge by the OCR to ensure that its enforcement practices do not vary from region to region

For a complete copy of these guidelines, go to www.chronicle.com/indepth/titleix.

Application to Recreational Sports

Admittedly, as noted by Carpenter and Acosta (2005, p. 65), the application of Title IX to athletics has commanded more intense attention from the judicial, legislative, and executive branches than any other endeavor under its jurisdiction. They offer two reasons for this:

1. Because athletics involves a mainly sex-segregated construct, discrimination is readily apparent.

2. Athletics involves a domain that is historically male-centered, so that opening the door to new participants means having to share resources previously thought to be for males alone.

Regardless of the reasons, it is clear from a review of any coverage of Title IX—whether it is in the literature, in the media, on the Internet, or in case law—that athletics has been the focal point. Yet, Title IX also applies to opportunities for girls and women in collegiate recreational sport participation and employment if the institution receives federal financial assistance. Once Title IX jurisdiction has been established, the provisions of Title IX and its regulations apply equally. Although the regulations and policy interpretations do not specifically address recreational sports, the program providers are expected to comply with those regulations and interpretations that have applicability. For example, the portion of the regulations related to athletic scholarships does not apply, whereas those related to equitable facility access may.

Carpenter and Acosta (2005) note that few lawsuits have been lodged against operators of intramural, club, or recreation sports. They speculate that the reasons for the lack of complaints may be that they have not yet been filed or that discrimination in such programs is still taken for granted in its somewhat informal participation climate. Although either or both may be true, perhaps the best explanation is rooted in the "sport for all" philosophy of recreational sport. By definition, recreational sport means "playing cooperative, competitive activity in the game form" and is

William A. Cotton, Colorado State University.

Title IX applies to opportunities for girls and women to participate in collegiate recreational sport programs if the institution is federally funded.

intended to serve all people regardless of gender, race, ethnicity, age, ability, or interest (Mull, Bayless, & Jamieson, 2005, p. 7).

The inclusive nature of recreational sport mitigates against discrimination, but it does not guarantee nondiscriminatory practices. For this reason it is important that recreational sport professionals have systems in place to monitor compliance.

At present, no research or publications specifically address Title IX within recreational sport. Further, the resources, Web sites, and organizations cited at the conclusion of this chapter have athletics as their primary focus. Although these resources provide invaluable information on Title IX, there is a significant need for recreational sport professionals to provide leadership in addressing this gap in information about the history and impact of Title IX on the involvement of girls and women in recreational sport. Possible questions to consider include the following:

- How has participation by girls and women in recreational sport changed?

- How have opportunities for women in employment changed in entry-level positions, middle management positions, and administrative positions?

- How have salaries changed for women compared to men?

- What are the participation trends for girls and women? How do they compare with trends for boys and men?

- How have opportunities changed for girls and women in part-time employment as officials, lifeguards, sport supervisors, and the like?

- Has there been any change in involvement by women in leadership positions within professional organizations and associations?

Conclusion

Today, many historical barriers for girls and women in academic and sport settings have been reduced or eliminated thanks to the dedication and perseverance of countless individuals, agencies, and organizations. However, much remains to be done to achieve the desired outcome of the legislation: equality of opportunity and benefits of participation to all, regardless of gender. What will the women of tomorrow be like? Will they be like the adults who no longer play, or will they be able to say this (Neal, 1974):

I no longer jump. I soar!
I no longer jog. I run!
I am free to live, thank God, with dignity.
O . . . what a joy it all is!

Resources

American Alliance for Health, Physical Education, Recreation & Dance (AAHPERD)
1900 Association Dr.
Reston, VA 20191-1598
703-476-3400
800-213-7193 (list of departments)
www.aahperd.org

This is an excellent site to find many articles on Title IX and women in sports. It also has a list of related Title IX Web sites.

American Association of University Women (AAUW)
AAUW Educational Foundation

AAUW Legal Advocacy Fund
1111 Sixteenth St. N.W.
Washington, DC 20036
Phone: 800-326-AAUW
Fax: 202-872-1425
TDD: 202-785-7777
Web site: www.aauw.org
E-mail: info@aauw.org

This site contains online museum, grants, and research information. It also lists a site to access the 2002 *Title IX at 30, a Report Card on Gender Equity—A Report of the National Coalition for Women and Girls in Education* and 60 Title IX-related articles.

Good Sports, Inc.

Title IX and gender equity specialists
11451 Spruce Run Dr.
San Diego, CA 92131
858-695-9995

U.S. Department of Education Commission on Opportunity in Athletics, *Title IX Briefing Book,* November 2002.

National Association of Collegiate Women Athletic Administrators

Web site: www.nacwaa.org

National Coalition for Women and Girls in Education (NCWGE)

Director of Communications: 202-785-7745
Web site: www.ncwge.org

This site provides information on the coalition, current activities, updates on relevant federal education legislation, useful resources, and NCWGE publications. One report of note is "Title IX Athletic Policies: Issues and Data for Education Decision Makers," August 27, 2002.

National Collegiate Athletic Association (NCAA)

700 W. Washington St.
P.O. Box 6222
Indianapolis, IN 46206-6222
Phone: 317-917-6222
Fax: 317-917-6888
Web site: www.ncaa.org

Achieving gender equity manual: A basic guide to Title IX and gender equity in athletics for colleges and universities. Retrieved from www.ncaa. org/library/general/achieving_gender_equity. Review the following sections:

Introduction, written by NCAA Education Outreach Office.

Title IX Basics by Valerie M. Bonnette, from Good Sports, Inc., Title IX and gender equity specialists.

Current case law: Litigation, pages 1-21. Retrieved from www.ncaa.org/library/general/achieving_gender_equity/current_case_law.pdf.

Division I Athletics Certification, pages 1-4. Retrieved from www.ncaa.org/library/general/achieving_gender_equity/certification.pdf.

Promotion ideas, pages 1-5. Retrieved from www.ncaa.org/library/general/achieving_gender_equity/promotion_ideas.pdf.

Emerging Sports, pages 1-9. Retrieved from www.ncaa.org/library/general/achieving_gender_equity/emerging_sports.pdf.

National Federation of State High School Associations

Web site: www.nfhs.org

National Association for Girls and Women in Sports (NAGWS)

Web site: www. aahperd.org/nagws

Title IX Tool Box, Volumes I and II

Gender equity in sports is a challenge for participants, coaches, and administrators. This double-volume publication, an essential reference for school administrators, athletics directors, and anyone working with girls' and women's sports, contains the definition of the law, Title IX, evaluation guidelines for compliance, suggestions on creating change and finding support, and a list of contacts for professional assistance.

Equity in the Gymnasium: Coed Physical Education: Finding Solutions and Meeting the Challenges

This booklet takes a fresh look at the challenges and potential solutions involved in coeducational physical education. It provides techniques for evaluating programs for both compliance and efficacy.

National Women's Law Center

Web site: www.nwlc.org

Office for Civil Rights

Web site: www.hhs.gov/ocr/hipaa

Office for Civil Rights Equity Assistance Centers

Title IV of the Civil Rights Act: Equity Assistance Centers Program. (2001). Retrieved from www. ed.gov/pubs/AnnualPlan2001/025b-red.doc.

University of Iowa

Gender equity in sports. Retrieved from http://bailiwick.lib.uiowa.edu/ge/.

U.S. Department of Education

Web site: www.ed.gov/news/fedregister/index. html

Utilize the search feature to locate information on Title IX.

Women's Sports Foundation

Web site: www.womenssportsfoundation.org.

This site contains information on research, grant opportunities, career opportunities, and so on, including:

School Report Card. (2000). Retrieved from www.womenssportsfoundation.org/cgi-bin/iowa/issues/geena/school/repcard.html.

Newspaper Report Card. (2000). Retrieved from www.womenssportsfoundation.org/cgi-bin/iowa/issues/geena/media/repcard.html

Playing Fair: A Guide to Title IX. (2001). Retrieved from www.womenssportsfoundation.org/cgi-bin/iowa/issues/rights/article.html?record=195

References

Carpenter, L.J., & Acosta, R.V. (2005). *Title IX*. Champaign, IL: Human Kinetics.

Department of Health, Education, and Welfare. (1979). *Federal Register*, volume 44, number 239, at 71413. Retrieved from www.ed.gov/news/fedregister/index.html.

Mull, R.F., Bayless, K.G., & Jamieson, L.Y. (2005). *Recreational sport management.* Champaign, IL: Human Kinetics.

Neal, P. (1974). *So run your race: An athlete's view of God.* Grand Rapids, MI: Zondervan Corporation.

Glossary

compliance—The state or act of conforming with or agreeing to do something.

discrimination—The unfair treatment of one person or group, usually due to prejudice about race, religion, ethnic group, age, or gender.

law—A rule of conduct or procedure recognized by a community as binding or enforceable by authority; an act passed by a legislature or similar body.

policy interpretation—An explanation or establishment of the meaning or significance of something; further explanation on how to comply with a law or regulation.

regulations—Official rules or orders stating what may or may not be done or how something must be done.

Title IX of the Education Amendments (P.L. 92-318, 20 U.S.C.S. section 1681 et seq.)—Landmark legislation that bans sex discrimination (against either males or females) in schools in both academics and athletics.

PART II

Programming and Facilities

CHAPTER 4

Instructional Programs

Diane K. Belz, CRSS, MA, Building/Equipment Services Manager, University of Colorado at Boulder

Vicki D. Highstreet, CRSS, MPE, Senior Assistant Director, Campus Recreation, University of Nebraska at Lincoln

Nancy L. Rapp, BA, Director, Parks and Recreation, City of Santa Barbara, California

There is no one I cannot teach something to, and no one I cannot learn something from.

Source unknown

This chapter was adapted and revised from NIRSA's *Instructional Programs: A Resource Manual*.

Recreation instructional programs provide learning experiences through lessons, clinics, workshops, and instructor-led group activities. With the goal of promoting healthy, active lifestyles, programs offer a broad variety of opportunities for people to experience and develop lifelong recreation interests and skills. Programs often feature sport and recreational activities such as swimming, tennis, martial arts, fitness, dance, arts and leisure interests, and much more.

Instructional programs are often found in several traditional campus venues, including student unions, residence halls, continuing education, and most commonly, campus recreation departments. Within campus recreation, instructional programs can be housed under one umbrella or structured by specific program areas such as sports, outdoor recreation, or fitness and wellness.

This chapter outlines the basic principles for developing and operating a successful, comprehensive instructional program. The foundational framework provides the building blocks for developing a program for a particular institution. This includes identifying the populations that can be served (students, faculty, staff, alumni, community), surveying potential facility resources to support the program, identifying specific campus programming opportunities and limitations, determining funding and cost recovery expectations, and considering how campus recreation will or will not integrate with academic programs. Basic tenets of program administration are covered, including determining program and interest areas, scheduling activities, developing a qualified instructional staff, establishing fees, advertising and promoting, organizing activity registration, and evaluating the program.

Foundational Framework

During the initial planning stages for implementation of a campus recreation instructional program, the following factors should be carefully weighed as they relate to the specific institution:

- Clients or populations served
- Facility availability
- Programming opportunities and limitations
- Funding and cost recovery expectations
- Integration with academics
- Program administration

From campus to campus the structure of instructional programs will vary based on the impact of each of the preceding factors on the development and operation of the program. The beauty is that there is no one right way to structure a program. Beyond a few basic planning principles, the instructional programmer has unlimited possibilities for types of classes and extensive room for creativity in designing the program. As a program develops and expands, the program administrator must continually analyze local market competition, participation trends, and ways to streamline and improve business operations for greater efficiency and cost effectiveness.

Clients or Populations Served

On any campus a variety of populations can be targeted for participation. These include traditional and nontraditional students, faculty, staff, alumni, spouses, family members, and in some cases, the local community. Decisions about whom to serve are based on the institution's mission and priorities. For instance, an institution with limited facilities for programming may elect to limit its services to only students, whereas an institution with greater resources and looking for additional revenue streams to offset or reduce costs for students may choose to offer programs to alumni or the community. It is not uncommon for programs to charge a lower fee to priority populations (i.e., students versus faculty or staff).

Facility Availability

Planning should begin with an inventory of the available recreation and activity facility spaces. Campus recreation centers and facilities, athletic facilities, residence halls, student unions, Greek houses, academic classrooms, as well as off-site locations should be considered. For each facility, planners should look at what time blocks can be scheduled, what priorities, if any, exist for programmatic use of the facility, and whether those limitations can be negotiated to facilitate other programs.

For each facility, planners should also look at the space in terms of size, flooring, lighting, equipment storage options, compatibility with surrounding activities (i.e., whether the location will support placement of a dance or aerobics activity next to a quieter activity such as a lecture or yoga class), attractiveness of time availability to potential clients, and any facility use fees that may be applied. The facility should be clean, accessible, safe, and convenient. Con-

William A. Cotton, Colorado State University.

Facility planners must consider the compatibility of different activities in a proximate area, such as whether an aerobics class should be held near a quieter activity like a yoga class.

sideration should be give to whether shower, locker, and changing facilities are needed in close proximity to where the activity will take place.

Programming Opportunities and Limitations

Because various campus entities may be offering recreation instructional programs, it is important to survey who is offering what on your campus, and why. Competition among physical education, student unions, residential life, continuing education, and campus recreation instructional programs occurs on most campuses at one time or another. Ideally, departments should approach this issue in a collaborative fashion based on a shared mission to provide effective services to clients. The discussions should take into account whether certain departments might be better suited to offer particular programs, staff, and facilities. The institution is far better served by departments working together in a collaborative manner than by competing.

What can, or should, the campus recreation department offer in instructional programming? What unique activities can the department offer that are different from programs offered elsewhere on campus? Examples of instructional activities found in the campus recreational setting include fitness and wellness, sports, dance, art, music, martial arts or self-defense, aquatics, outdoor recreation, certification courses, and other leisure activities. For a more detailed list of course options, see figure 4.1.

Successful programs anticipate and meet participant demand and interest and show solid, steady participation over time. One of the best ways to stay up-to-date on current participant trends is by networking with other schools, local park and recreation agencies, and professional associations. Remember that programs that work in one institution may not work in another, based on regional interests, local market competition, and so forth. When developing a program, planners should avoid duplication of services, maximize use of the campus recreation facilities, and think creatively when planning for equipment needs and storage options.

Sample of Course Suggestions by Category

Aerobics/Exercise

Abdominal workout: L, W	High-impact aerobics: L	Stretch and tone: L, W
Aerobic funk: L, S	High/low combo: L	Swim conditioning: W
Aqua aerobics: W	Low-impact aerobics: L	Total mat work: L, S, W
Aqua step aerobics: S, W	Power step aerobics: S	Water combo: S, W
Circuit training: L, S, W	Running/jogging: L, W	Weight training: L
Deep water: W	Ski conditioning combo: L, S	Yoga: L
Fitness walking: L, W	Step aerobics: L, S	

Key: L = land, S = step, W = water

Certification Classes

Advanced First Aid	Lifeguard Training
Cardiopulmonary Resuscitation (CPR)	Water Safety Instruction
Community Health and First Aid	

Dance/Art/Music

Ballet	Guitar	Modern	West African drumming
Ballroom/social dance	Jazz	Square	West Coast swing
Country swing/line dance	Jitterbug	Swing	
Ethnic dance	Latin ballroom	Tap	

Martial Arts/Self-Defense

Aikido	Kendo	Self-defense	Taekwondo
Japanese shotokan	Ki aikido	Shotokan karate	Tai chi chuan
Judo	Kung fu		

Sports

Archery	Golf	Lacrosse	Sailing	Softball	Tennis
Badminton	Gymnastics	Marksmanship	Scuba diving	Squash	Volleyball
Bowling	Handball	Pickleball	Snorkeling	Swimming	Wallyball
Cricket	Horseshoes	Racquetball	Soccer	Table tennis	Windsurfing
Fencing	Ice hockey	Rugby			

Massage

Couples	Reflexology
Foot	Swedish
Introductory	

Miscellaneous

Beaded earrings	Chess	Handwriting analysis	Painting	Quilting
Bridge	Cooking	Knitting/crocheting	Photography	Theater excursions
Calligraphy	Drawing	Nutrition seminars	Pottery	Theater performance

Figure 4.1   Sample of course suggestions by category.

Funding and Cost Recovery Expectations

Most, but not all, instructional programs have **activity fees** that generate revenue to offset program costs. Economic challenges and revenue expectations differ by institution.

The level of institutional funding support, or **subsidy,** for the program will determine the level of cost recovery the program will operate under. Some programs are partially or fully subsidized through department or institutional funding; others must generate sufficient revenue to cover all costs associated with the program.

Planning should include the development of a comprehensive business plan (see chapter 11), which is an in-depth assessment of the program's financial potential. The business plan considers interest and demand for proposed activities; program expenses such as instructor salaries, equipment, facility costs, staff support, marketing and publicity costs, supplies, utilities, and department overhead; recommended fee levels; marketability; and participation expectations (minimums and maximums).

Cost recovery considerations can include **direct** and **indirect expenses,** as determined by the institution. Determining appropriate fees for activities is part art and part science, with expertise derived from trial and error over time. Fees are discussed later in this chapter in the section called The Art of Determining Activity Fees.

Programs often have different cost recovery levels for different populations; for example, faculty and staff may pay more than students, and alumni and community members may pay more than campus participants. Higher fees may be charged for activities scheduled during prime times, smaller group or private instruction, or very popular, trendy classes with strong participant demand.

Popular classes that generate substantial revenues beyond what is necessary to cover program expenses can be used to offset the costs of less popular or more expensive classes. This can allow the program to maintain a broader variety of activities at affordable fees.

Integration With Academics

With the elimination of physical education departments in colleges and universities as a result of challenging fiscal situations, more campus recreation departments are becoming administrators of both **credit and noncredit courses.** The opportunity to include physical education courses for academic credit through the recreation instructional program provides the campus recreation department yet another tie to the institution's academic mission.

Campus recreation departments may elect to get involved in offering academic credit courses for a variety of reasons, including support of the institution's academic mission, financial benefit, access to facilities, or expansion of program offerings. Such relationships are framed differently based on the needs and structure of the particular institution. This is discussed further in the section Academic Credit Courses as Part of the Curriculum.

Program Administration

The **program administrator** determines the curricula, schedules, hires instructors, purchases equipment, sets policies, develops marketing and publicity materials, oversees activity registration, and conducts program evaluation. Depending on the breadth of the campus recreation department, there may be one or more program administrators in specific program areas such as fitness and wellness, outdoor recreation, aquatics, or general instruction programs. Instructional programs require a significant level of general office support for those working in front line reception, activity registration, data entry, publicity, preparation of course materials, and so on.

Program Design and Development

A recreation instructional program can be small or large, feature one or more core areas of instruction, and offer courses in a variety of formats. Simply put, the program should be designed to meet the needs and interests of the identified clientele using all of the resources available, such as facilities and funding, and within any constraints placed on the scope of programming as defined by the department or the institution (to avoid conflicts with other service providers within the department or institution).

A comprehensive recreation instructional program would most likely include any number of courses in core areas such as dance, art, sports, fitness, outdoor recreation, martial arts, tennis, aquatics, cooking and leisure interests, and certification courses (such as CPR and first aid). The program should feature a good balance of physical

William A. Cotton, Colorado State University.

Campus recreation programs should balance physical training courses with skill acquisition and development courses.

training courses with skill acquisition and development courses (beginning through advanced). A well-designed program offers a variety of formats and courses to meet the scheduling needs and interests of the clientele in order to attract the largest number of participants.

The size of the program should be based on the size of the eligible or targeted population. In smaller settings, the program administrator would be wise to avoid offering too many activity choices, which would run the risk of not achieving minimum enrollment.

Course Descriptions

The **course description** is used to explain to potential participants exactly what the activity is, what skills or knowledge will be taught, and the potential benefits that will be gained from taking the course. See figure 4.2 for an example.

Because most instructional programs publish a catalog or brochure to promote classes, and because space in the brochure is often limited, writing effective and inviting course descriptions with as few words as possible is very important. In one or two brief, well-crafted sentences, the description should pique interest while providing sufficient information so clients can determine whether the course is right for them. Program administrators are well known for collecting activity brochures from other schools and agencies to get ideas for classes and catchy course descriptions.

The following elements are generally included in promotional materials as part of the course description:

- Activity or program title (describes the activity and generates interest)
- Brief narrative course description that explains the course content and what will be achieved by taking the course
- Course schedule, including beginning and ending dates
- Meeting dates and times, including holidays when class will not be held
- Location of the course
- Fee, if any
- Prerequisites, if any

Some programs include the following information as part of their course descriptions, depending on the space available in the course catalog or the needs of the program:

Hip-Hop Dance

This fun, nonintimidating class encourages self-expression through sensual and earthy urban choreography. Perfect for both the beginner and more experienced dancer, this class is an exciting nonstop workout followed by yoga stretches and meditative breathing.

| #8142 | Wed | 6:00-7:00 p.m. | 9/20-11/15 | $24 | Rm. 115, Knowles Ctr. |

Figure 4.2 Sample course description.

- Instructor name
- Instructor bio
- Special registration information
- Required minimum class enrollment for class to be held

Course Formats

Course formats vary based on the subject matter, skill level, target audience, facility scheduling options, affordability of course fee, or attendance.

The length, frequency, and duration of the activity refer to the length of time of an individual class meeting, the number of times per week the class meets, the number of weeks the class meets, and how often the class is held per semester or quarter. This scheduling is influenced by the type of activity and whether the emphasis is on skill acquisition, maintaining fitness, or industry standards. The following should be considered:

- Age, skill level, and physical condition of the participants
- Whether the focus will be on skill building or conducting a fitness workout
- Time needed to learn, practice, and master a particular set of skills
- Designated industry standards, if any, for particular activities (i.e., warm-up, cool-down, recommended aerobic conditioning phase)

Individual **class meetings** can be anywhere from 15 minutes to an hour or more. Most common are the 60- to 90-minute class meetings. The duration of a course also varies. A course may be offered once an academic term or there may be two or more multiweek **sessions** per term. Also popular for some courses are clinic or workshop formats, which generally extend for a short period of time—one or two days, or even a half day. Examples of frequency scheduling are daily or two or more meetings per week.

Class formats can be modified to meet facility scheduling needs and program demands. As an example, with a three-hour block, it may be preferable to offer three 60-minute **sections** of a popular class; this schedule will serve more participants than two 90-minute classes will. Alternately, with a 90-minute block, two 45-minute classes may be preferable to one 90-minute class.

Drop-In Participation in Classes

An option that not only accommodates clientele but also presents an opportunity for additional revenue is to allow drop-in participation. Although there are many advantages to this form of class participation, there are also drawbacks. The course format will help decide the appropriateness of this type of participation. Drop-in participation is not an appropriate option for skill-acquisition courses, for example, because each lesson builds on skills developed in earlier lessons. For safety reasons, you would not want a less skilled person participating in a class that is beyond her skill level.

Drop-in participation is most effective in fitness and physical conditioning classes, especially if a number of sections of similar classes are available. Drop-in formats are very popular in the fitness realm, in which well-attended classes are scheduled multiple times throughout the day. The drop-in format also takes into consideration the desire of clients to mix and match various fitness classes to meet their personal fitness regimens.

Another reason to consider including drop-in participation is because certain types of fitness courses inherently have high registration numbers initially, but experience lower attendance numbers over the scheduled cycle due to **attrition.** Structuring the program to facilitate drop-in participation allows interested clients to take the place of those who choose not to participate on a regular basis or who stop attending altogether.

Courses can be structured as either enrolled courses that allow drop-in participation on a space available basis or as drop-in courses. Creating a drop-in card at a premium price increases revenues for the program while ensuring more stability in class attendance. Such cards are popular with clients because they offer the flexibility to attend classes that fit best into their daily schedules and personal fitness regimens.

Number of Class Offerings

Successful program administrators build their programs in response to participant demand. One of the most challenging aspects is determining how many classes of a specific activity or interest should be offered to meet demand. If too many sections of a popular class are offered, enrollment may be low in several of the classes, necessitating their cancellation.

From a business perspective, programs should average a high **fill rate** (the number of people enrolled compared to the number of spaces available) to ensure the greatest return on the costs to offer the program. The fill rate percentage target will change from program to program, but generally you want to achieve an average in the 75 to 100 percent range.

For example, if a course costs $350 to offer and the course fee is $35, the cost is the same whether there are 10 people enrolled (class minimum) or 15 people enrolled (class maximum). Any registrations beyond the first 10 become net profit to the program. Using the example, operating with a full, 15-person class, the program generates $175 in net profit.

Popular activities that fill quickly during the registration period can generate good "buzz" among prospective clientele. However, this must be balanced with the need to meet the demands for additional offerings and grow the program over time. It is a delicate balance.

Activity Skill Levels

Activities can be offered at the introductory, beginning, intermediate, and advanced skill levels. A well-constructed and well-designed program that offers progressive instruction requires lesson planning that considers careful building of skills over time. Course descriptions for the different skill levels must be clearly explained in terms of the basic skills required and the skills that will be taught in the class.

Because of their mission, philosophy, funding, or availability of facilities, some institutions restrict recreation programs to the introductory and beginning levels. As an example, priority may be given to introducing lifetime recreational skills, with the expectation that participants will acquire more advanced skills elsewhere.

Determining Instructor Qualifications

The instructional program administrator can do everything possible to facilitate a successful program, but can lose ground quickly if the program does not feature competent instructors. The instructional staff is the backbone of the program. They represent the program to the public and interact with clients on a regular basis. To obtain the right people for their programs, administrators must have proper recruitment and selection procedures in place. The following factors should be considered: education, certification, experience, leadership qualities, ability to communicate and establish rapport with patrons, and attention to administrative details.

Education and Certification

Program administrators should be familiar with the education, credentials, and certification options or requirements within particular subject areas. Many program areas have independent training courses that instructors may or should have completed. Completed course work and certification from nationally recognized associations or programs are good indicators that instructors are qualified, as are college course credits or related college degrees. Before hiring, administrators should verify any required certification or credentials, and they should keep records throughout the course of employment that such requirements are maintained.

Experience

One of the greatest indicators of a good instructor is previous teaching experience. This demonstrates a genuine interest in teaching in a particular specialty and allows the administrator to interview past employers and, in some cases, past course participants.

Leadership Qualities

Having a degree or certification in a specialty area should not be relied on as the sole determining factor for a good instructor. Some people have the credentials and knowledge required to teach a class but lack the leadership qualities that are necessary to successfully guide patrons through the learning process. This characteristic, along with the ability to establish a rapport with patrons, is difficult to identify up front. Employment and personal reference checks provide essential feedback for determining these characteristics in potential instructors.

Effective Communication and Rapport With Patrons

Instructors are only as good as their students perceive them to be. An instructor who communicates effectively and is personable, a good listener, and able to develop rapport with people will be able to teach the information and provide an environment that encourages learning and participation. Instructors should be able to adapt to the desires of patrons while staying within the guidelines of good instruction.

Attention to Administrative Details

Sometimes good instructors have difficulty with the administrative details of the class. This can become problematic for program administration and can affect the operation of the program. For example, an instructor may repeatedly fail to follow established registration or substitution procedures or have trouble with some other administrative aspect of the program. In dealing with instructor performance, program administrators must weigh the pros and cons of retaining instructors who are struggling with administrative issues. If the instructor is particularly popular, teaches a class that is unique to the program, or has a specialty that makes locating alternative instructors a challenge, the program administrator may choose to compensate for the instructor's deficiencies in order to retain his or her services.

Determining Class Size

Determining the class size is dependent on the following factors:

- Standard used for student–instructor ratios (institution or governing body)
- Facility availability (appropriately sized space for the type of activity and the number of people)
- Equipment availability (provided, rented, or purchased)
- Minimum or maximum numbers to meet the financial requirement (i.e., amount of revenue generated to recover the cost of providing the activity)
- Instructor recommendations (limited number of students, equipment needed for each person, limited or extended contact hours)

The decision to alter the established minimum or maximum number of participants for an activity should be restricted to the program administrator, who has the responsibility to weigh each of the preceding factors. This becomes important during registration periods, when program staff may be inclined to exceed a course maximum to accommodate disappointed clients.

Equipment Considerations

Once an administrator has identified the courses to be offered, a full program review is necessary to determine the equipment needed for each course. The following questions can assist with these considerations:

- Are there items that can be shared within a class, or will each participant need his or her own items?

- Can participants provide their own equipment, thereby eliminating the need for the program to purchase and store the items?
- What are the repair and replacement considerations, and how should that cost be recovered through the class fee? (Some courses have equipment fees in addition to the course fee for just this purpose.)
- Is the initial outlay of equipment cost justified when considering the goals of the overall program? Can cost be recouped over a period of one or more years?
- Does another department or another area in the campus recreation department have equipment it might be willing to share?
- What are the storage and access issues of the facility where the activity will be held?

Program administrators should be creative when considering equipment needs and storage options for their programs. Sharing equipment between programs and departments is not uncommon. After a thorough review of equipment needs and options, an administrator may determine that a class is not feasible because the cost of equipment is prohibitive or because storage options are insufficient.

Risk Management

Risk management is identifying and taking actions to minimize areas of risk that have the potential for causing injury. Risk management is an ongoing program, often the focus of a larger program within the institution. Campus recreation departments generally have a comprehensive risk management plan that is applied to all department programs and activities, with the expectation that it will be consistently and conscientiously implemented by all associated employees or agents (e.g., independent contractors, volunteers). (Chapter 13 in this book addresses risk management.)

The program administrator must take all appropriate actions to ensure the safety of those who will participate in the program. Instructors should be appropriately qualified, conditions in the teaching space should be safe, and activities in the classroom should be managed to ensure that each person can participate without causing injury to him- or herself or others. Employees or agents should be knowledgeable on all related policies, procedures, and practices. Risk management concerns should be thoroughly incorporated into policy manuals and ongoing training programs.

The risk management plans of all recreation instructional programs should include the following:

- Evacuation procedures
- Medical emergency procedures, defined for specific facility locations as needed
- Severe weather procedures, defined for specific facility locations as needed
- Incident report forms
- Accident and injury report forms
- Facility safety checklist, work order and notification procedures, emergency maintenance procedures
- Harassment and workplace violence policies
- Drug and alcohol policy
- Vehicle and driving policies
- Misconduct and ejection policy
- Workers' compensation policies, procedures, and reporting forms
- Media authorization procedures
- Age, physical condition, or ability considerations
- Risk avoidance procedures, including guidelines for identifying and responding to the following:
  - Loud, aggressive, inappropriate, or risky behavior in the classroom or activity, including fighting
  - Participants being overly stressed or tired or participant skill level above or below the median skill level for the class
  - Improper body mechanics, insufficient warm-up or cool-down
  - Cults and cultlike behavior

Recognition

No one works alone in a service program. Recognizing the efforts of employees, instructors, sponsors, and volunteers is an investment in a program's continued success. This can be done with a simple thank-you or through more formal recognition events in which individuals or teams are singled out for their contributions. These mechanisms enhance the program's public relations efforts. Moreover, recognizing programmatic improvements or specific contributions by individuals or teams of people is good for morale and provides positive reinforcement for everyone who works so hard for the success of the program. Recognition may take the form of certificates, trophies, T-shirts, photographs, and so on.

Scheduling

The success of an instructional program depends largely on effective scheduling. When determining session times, administrators should consider participants' lifestyles and interests, the popularity of the activity, and the time of year. Additional considerations are as follows:

- Off-site programs can be more difficult to supervise.
- Offering activities during a nontraditional season, such as basketball during the fall, may mean a greater opportunity for facility access.
- Sharing facilities with other programs during prime times provides the opportunity for both activities to take place. For example, aikido and fencing classes could each use half a court in the gym, or an aquatic exercise class and lap swimmers could share pool space.
- With back-to-back classes, time may be needed for equipment setup and breakdown, transitions between classes, and any custodial needs.
- As a program grows and changes, flexibility in scheduling is vital to ensure the accommodation of all programs.

The availability of instructors can also determine when classes can be scheduled. A large pool of qualified available instructors allows greater scheduling flexibility. However, if extensive experience or education is required to teach a course, adjusting the schedule may be necessary to accommodate a particular instructor's availability.

Facility reservation processes may vary by institution, department, and even facility. Typically, requests are made on a designated form and are submitted up to a year in advance. Requests can sometimes be made in blocks of time for a specific program, with actual activities added to the request form further into the year.

Facility Requirements for Activities

Some activities have facility requirements in addition to size that must be considered during the scheduling process—for safety and accommodation. For instance, certain fitness or dance activities require specific types of flooring, sound equipment, equipment storage, and ventilation. A gymnastics class is generally held in a specially designed facility exclusive to that activity with permanent or semipermanent equipment in place. Certain types of art classes require good lighting, access to sinks and water, or privacy (e.g., figure drawing with live models).

Time of Day

Although some activities are successful regardless of when they are scheduled, others depend on the attractiveness of the hour. A time suitable for one activity is not necessarily suitable for another. For instance, early morning swim times in an outdoor facility may be attractive to fitness swimmers, but will not typically attract beginning swimmers.

Administrators should carefully consider the best time to reach a target audience, whether it is early morning, midmorning, noontime or lunch hour, midafternoon, evening, or weekends. The needs of the commuter student or employee may be different from the needs of those who live on campus or in the immediate community. Weekend classes can also be popular, particularly Saturday mornings and Sunday afternoons.

Prime time is the term applied to those hours in which facilities have the heaviest use and demand. For most campuses, prime time is 7:00 to 8:00 a.m., the lunch hour, and 4:00 to 8:00 p.m. Slotting courses during prime time hours should take into consideration popularity, demand, and being able to meet the needs of a variety of skill and fitness levels—as well as one can.

Academic Credit Courses as Part of the Curriculum

As discussed earlier in this chapter in the section Integration With Academics, many instructional programs find themselves administering academic credit courses as part of a larger noncredit recreation instructional program. The foundational framework for noncredit courses is the same as that for credit courses.

Program Administration

The overall administration of a program that includes academic credit courses and noncredit courses is not substantially different from that of strictly noncredit programs. A strong collaborative relationship with the respective coordinating academic unit is a must. The program administrator will often negotiate the financial terms for administering the course with the academic unit responsible for the credit. In addition, the program administrator will often interact with the campus bookstore, registration and records offices, the classroom facility reservation process, and campus academic advisors.

Negotiating reimbursement to campus recreation for administering and conducting the credit courses generally involves upper levels of department and campus administration. Financial terms will vary by institution, but should include the following:

- Determination of the allowable fee range, if any
- Whether cost recovery will include direct and indirect costs incurred by campus recreation, and any predetermined overhead percentage
- Accounting procedure and financial reporting requirements
- Refund and other fee-related policies
- Attendance policies and reporting requirements

Course Design and Requirements

The academic unit responsible for the credit hours generally provides guidelines regarding contact hours per student, evaluation procedures, course curriculum, and learning objectives. Recreation instructional program administrators are held to the standard of the academic unit for course content and instructor performance.

The following should be considered when developing a course syllabus for an academic credit course:

- Number of contact hours needed to meet the college or university requirement
- Student–instructor ratio based on the standards provided by the institution
- Percentage of grade required to demonstrate cognitive learning
- Learning objectives and sources used to accomplish objectives
- Grading procedures
- Attendance requirements to meet minimum grade levels
- Letter grade or pass-or-fail grade option
- Number of credit hours per course

Credit Versus Noncredit Recreation Courses

Students choose to register for credit recreation courses for a variety of reasons. Sometimes it is because the course of interest is only available as an academic credit course, or because it is available at a time and day the student prefers. Other times it is because the student needs the academic units to supplement his or her academic record.

The variety of formats found in the campus recreation instructional program schedule often offers students many options for including additional academic units in their quarter or semester. For instance, a shorter-format class added midterm can provide additional credit or replace credit from a course that was dropped earlier in the term. Program administrators should take this into consideration when scheduling credit as well as noncredit courses.

The administration of an academic course schedule includes determining the type of class, the day or time the class will meet, the facility availability, qualified instructors, instructor and class evaluation, and a salary schedule relevant to the needs of the program and the instructor. This process is not much different from the administration of a noncredit class. Occasionally there can be administrative challenges when determining which courses will be offered, how attendance and grades will be reported, and how to ensure that courses are conducted in compliance with specified criteria to meet course requirements and learning objectives. Each institution will have policies and procedures that may dictate the recreation program administrator's level of authority when developing or changing one or all of the preceding responsibilities as they relate to the academic course criteria.

Managing for an Effective Instructional Staff

Smart program administrators invest the time and effort to attract and retain a high-caliber, dynamic instructional staff, which is the program's greatest asset. Instructors are the primary service providers—when they shine, so does the overall program. Likewise, when they do poorly, their reputation spreads to the entire program.

Good instructors are prepared and have clear goals for the class and well-developed lesson plans. They engage participants in the excitement and joy of the learning or participatory experience;

most of all, they represent the program in a professional manner. The following list highlights some of the characteristics to look for when building an instructional staff:

- Is people-oriented and relates well to participants

- Is enthusiastic about sharing knowledge and skills with others

- Displays a friendly, helpful, sharing attitude

- Demonstrates an ability for managing and conducting classes

- Understands the importance of being well prepared and punctual

- Accepts responsibility for complying with policies and procedures

- Has a good understanding of conditioning, etiquette, and equipment as each relates to the subject area

- Knows the standards pertaining to risk management and practices good class design and management skills that reduce the potential for injury and negligence

- Possesses appropriate certification issued by an accredited agency or professional association

- Presents and conducts him- or herself in a professional manner

Recruitment and retention of highly qualified instructors are continual challenges. Programs that build a solid reputation for quality and professionalism attract potential instructors—either to teach courses currently offered or to bring new courses to the program. Administrators often spend a great deal of time searching for the right person to teach that unique or special course.

Three Kinds of Instructors

Three kinds of instructors serve campus recreation programs: institutional employees, volunteer instructors, and **independent contractors.** Any given program may use instructors from one or more of these categories

It is important to understand the impact and legal implications of these three employment options, especially the differences between the institutional employee and the independent contractor. Although it happens rarely, some agencies and institutions have had the status of their instructors as independent contractors challenged by the IRS. An IRS determination that an independent contractor has been acting within the definition of an employee can result in the institution compensating the instructor with employee benefits retroactive to the start of employment.

Institutional Employees

In this instance, instructors are hired as employees of the institution. The employee has a job description, a supervisor, and a defined reporting structure. The employee is evaluated and can be dismissed for appropriate cause. The institution maintains control over all aspects of the program and is held accountable for workers' compensation and unemployment benefits for the employee. Primary liability remains with the institution while the employee is performing within the scope of job responsibilities. (See chapter 13.)

Volunteer Instructors

Programs occasionally use volunteers to teach some of their courses. Less common is an all-volunteer instructional staff. From time to time an instructor will approach a program and offer to teach a particular course on a volunteer basis either out of a spirit of goodwill, a desire to affiliate with the institution, or to get a foot in the door and build a following. Also common is a program that provides instructor training and development in exchange for volunteers teaching or assisting with classes.

Coordination with the institution's personnel and risk management departments is important before using the services of volunteers. Some institutions require volunteers to complete applications to formalize their relationship with the institution, and others provide workers' compensation or some level of liability insurance coverage. Using volunteers in the instructional setting has greater risk for programs, and it is important for the program administrator to understand exactly what those risks are and the institution's preferences for modifying that risk. Whether paid or volunteer, the instructor must be qualified to teach the course.

Table 4.1 outlines some of the pros and cons to consider when employing professional staff, students, or volunteers in recreation programs.

Independent Contractors

In a contractual relationship, the institution legally contracts with an outside agency or individual for a specific service. Care must be taken to select a reputable contractor, define the terms and conditions of the contract, and establish a strong working relationship.

The contracted instructor or agency does the following:

- Provides the services specified in the terms of the contract
- Follows the policies and procedures set forth by the contract
- Has the necessary skills to do the job
- Does not receive direct supervision by the institution
- Carries the responsibility and liability for the program or service

Institutions often choose to outsource services to independent contractors to reduce overhead costs related to the salaries and benefits associated with institutional employees, to shift liability from the institution to the service provider, and when services can more efficiently be provided by the contractor. Independent contractors are commonly used when the instructional setting for the course is high risk or features expensive equipment or when off-campus facilities are required for activities, such as horseback riding, photography, or white-water rafting. Every institution has a level of risk it is willing to take. The wise administrator works closely with risk management personnel when weighing decisions about whether or how to offer such activities.

The argument for independent contractor status is stronger if the service is provided off campus in a contractor-owned, -rented, or -managed site, and if the contractor is engaged in an independently established trade, occupation, profession, or business (Strong, 1992).

Before entering into a contract with an independent contractor, the administrator should investigate several service providers to select the best for the program. This practice, combined with a well-worded contract, should alleviate many problems (Meyers, 1991).

Instructor Salaries

Salary considerations depend heavily on budget conditions and revenue sources. Instructors expect to be compensated at a rate comparable to the industry standard. However, if institutional restrictions limit an administrator's ability to pay on this scale, there are many benefits to consider beyond salary. These include additional training opportunities, having access to materials that

Table 4.1 Instructor Hiring Pool

Category	Pros	Cons
Professional staff: fully qualified and experienced instructors	· Have a higher level of experience and qualifications · More likely to provide consistent, high-quality instruction · Are generally more mature · Require little or no training · Have a higher level of employment commitment (attendance, etc.) · View teaching as their profession, and thus have greater involvement in and commitment to the field · Retention tends to be greater	· Higher salary demands · Often are more difficult to recruit · Can be less receptive to performance evaluation · Occasionally exhibit "prima donna" behavior
Students: reasonably qualified, less experienced instructors	· Salaries are generally lower, commensurate with education and experience · Tend to have greater availability and flexibility for scheduling · Are easier to recruit · Generally exhibit a high desire to work and learn from their supervisors · Desire on-campus employment · Are familiar with recreational sport department · Have loyalty to university or department program · Supports a university commitment to provide student development opportunities · Meets department mission to provide employment opportunities to students	· Usually are less skilled, educated, and experienced · Tend to be younger, less mature · Have less-developed professional judgment · Frequently have uneven employment attendance due to academic conflicts · Require training and instructional resources · May have difficulty teaching peers
Qualified volunteers: fully qualified and experienced instructors in unpaid positions	· No salary requirement · For programs with limited resources, provides opportunity for program development	· Require substantially increased level of supervision · Formal volunteer appreciation or recognition program recommended for retention · Formal volunteer agreement recommended to provide workers' compensation coverage for work-related injuries as needed (requires consultation with attorneys and risk management personnel)

enhance the teaching experience, taking advantage of the educational setting (many people enjoy teaching in a university setting because the participants are natural students), and the opportunity to attend classes at the institution.

When determining the instructor salary structure, administrators should do the following:

- Decide whether instructors for different activities will be paid at different levels.

- Determine what criteria constitute instructor base pay, opportunities for raises, and additional compensation for education and certification.

- Establish rehiring and seniority stipulations or procedures.

- Develop a pay classification system that distinguishes among the levels of instructors, such as activity leaders, student instructors, and professional instructors. Keep the plan flexible so it can be modified as new parameters arise.

- Research pay systems, including other recreation services within the department such as intramurals and sport clubs, other departments offering instructional programs, and other institutions.

Table 4.2 Instructor Compensation Comparison

Payment process	Pros	Cons
Percentage Payment is determined by a percentage of generated revenues, i.e., a predetermined percentage of each class registration fee goes to the instructor and the program. Depending on the institution, this method can be used for employees (less common) or contract instructors (more common).	· Great for beginning a program, as instructors are motivated to promote activities to generate increased registrations. · More registrations mean more income; great incentive for hardworking instructors.	· Over time, as activity becomes more successful and class size grows, instructor salaries can become exorbitant. · Setting a ceiling for compensation is recommended in these instances. · For employees, this payment method may conflict with institutional payroll policies.
Per Course An agreed-upon flat fee is paid for an entire class session. Depending on the institution, this method can be used for employees (less common) or contract instructors (more common).	· Easy payment process, no time sheets, and only one check is issued, at conclusion of session.	· Determining adjusted compensation for substitutions and cancellations can be problematic. · Some instructors request payment for class preparation time as well as classroom time. · For employees, this payment method may conflict with institutional payroll policies.
Hourly Payment is made on an hourly basis (employee only).	· Enhances employee–employer understanding. · Consistent with other department employment.	· Predetermine whether compensation will include both time in the classroom and time for class preparation. In some programs, instructors are paid preparation time as a ratio of teaching time (i.e., 1 hour of preparation for 4 hours of instruction). Others set the hourly rate to include any preparation. · Difficult to determine fair wages among various teaching theories; recommend periodic salary surveys with local providers.
Contractual: Independent Contract Payment is set by contract, i.e., per participant, per hour, per class, or a flat fee as negotiated with contractor providing the service.	· Easy payment process. · Program focus is on administration of the contract, insuring services are provided according to agreed-upon terms.	· Requires negotiating contract terms with independent contractor. · Contract terms must be carefully written in clear, concise terms with a complete description of services. · Requires greater administrative follow-up—confirming proof of insurance, securing appropriate contract approvals, for example.

- Review the historical trends within the program.
- Research similar jobs in the public and private sector.

Because instructor salary is the single largest program cost affecting fees and the program budget, administrators should consider the pros and cons of various compensation structures (see table 4.2).

Recruitment

To attract a variety of qualified instructors, administrators must create effective recruitment materials and place them in high-visibility loca-tions. The following is not an inclusive list, but provides some ideas.

- Flyers, posters, bulletin board listings, and video monitors in recreation facilities and other campus locations
- Campus employment e-mail listings, work-study, and placement service
- News releases: print, radio, university TV
- Word of mouth
- Other instructors, campus recreation staff, program participants, intramural and sport club meetings, student organizations, and continuing education and academic depart-ments

- American Red Cross, American Heart Association
- Commercial fitness centers, health clubs, dance studios, golf and tennis clubs
- Municipal recreation agencies, the YMCA, and so on

Hiring Process

Interviewing all candidates is a way of getting to know the applicants and gaining additional information on their education, experience, philosophies, and professional development. With the exception of nationally recognized standards that must be met, the instructional program administrator has some flexibility in determining job requirements. However, when hiring an instructor (or any staff), the program administrator must always do the following:

- Review the application
- Conduct the audition
- Verify credentials and certifications
- Check references

Auditions

It is a very good idea for all candidates passing the initial interview to audition in an actual or simulated class setting. This allows the program administrator to observe the following:

- Instructor skills and personality
- Effectiveness of teaching methods and techniques
- Ability to organize and manage a class
- Rapport with clientele

Instructor Agreement

Most program administrators choose to use an instructor agreement to define teaching commitments for each term. This agreement should not be confused with the legal contract associated with an independent contractor.

Generally, the instructor agreement (see figure 4.3) includes information on the classes that have been assigned to the instructor for the session, quarter, or semester, including class title and skill level, days, times, beginning and ending dates, salary, and holiday considerations, if any. The following are generally found in instructor agreements:

- Acknowledgment that policies and procedures have been read, discussed, understood, and signed by the instructor or administrator
- Acknowledgment of the program administrator's authority to terminate those who do not adhere to policies
- Acknowledgment of reading, understanding, and agreeing to abide by policies related to duties and responsibilities in the instructor manual
- A statement that all instructors are required to meet specified class dates
- A statement that no signs related to the class are to be posted without approval by the program administrator (promotional flyers, class canceled, class moved, etc.)
- Cancellation and substitution policies and procedures
- Provisions for equipment and supplies

Independent Contractor Contract

As discussed previously in the section Independent Contractors, many program administrators use independent contractors to teach for their programs.

Instructor Agreement

Indicate employment area:

☐ Sport clubs ☐ Outdoor recreation Other ____________

An employment contract between the Department of Recreation and the employee as named below to perform the job herein described pertaining to duties, time involvement, and salary.

PLEASE PRINT:

____
Name

____
Phone

____
Address

Social Security Number ____________

Job title ____________ Account Number ____________

Duties and responsibilities ____________

Special conditions (if any) ____________

Salary total $ ________ to be paid as follows: (monthly, weekly, etc.)

Beginning date ____________ Ending date ____________

Recreation Program Instructor's Guidelines:

1. All instructors must be CPR certified.
2. Each class has a set minimum of people needed to sign up. If the class does not meet this minimum, it will be cancelled.
3. All instructors must submit a class outline by ____________ (Date).
4. It is very important that each instructor make classes at the scheduled times. An instructor who is going to miss a class must call the administration office 24 hours prior to the scheduled class time. All students must be notified in advance of all planned cancellations. Each missed class must be rescheduled.
5. There will be no deviation from scheduled class time unless approved by the recreation program director.
6. All instructors are required to meet specified class dates. If extenuating circumstances arise, and the employment obligation cannot be fulfilled, two weeks' notice is mandatory.
7. The program area must be returned to the condition it was in upon arrival.
8. All signs dealing with class information must be approved by the recreation program director.
9. Other things to consider:
   - Acknowledgment that procedures have been read, discussed, understood, and signed by the instructor/administrator

Figure 4.3 Instructor agreement.

Developing the Contract   Basic contract language for independent contractors should be developed and reviewed by appropriate institutional representatives, including those in the legal, purchasing, and risk management divisions. The contract should describe what specific services will be provided by the institution and the contractor and how and when they will be provided. These are the terms of the contract, and they need to be clearly defined in unambiguous language.

To ensure a clean contractual relationship, program administrators should avoid situations in which they might be accused of exerting too much control over the activity. The role of the program administrator is to hold the contractor fully responsible for meeting the terms of the contract. If the contractor fails to do so, the program can terminate the contract as specified in the terms.

Contract terms generally define the scope of responsibilities, including the following:

- Scope of curriculum with lesson plans
- Policies for cancellations and makeup lessons
- Facility use and access
- Condition and quantity of provided equipment
- Fee collection and contractor payment, including minimum and maximum enrollments per class
- Specific qualification of instructors (with copies of certifications provided by the contractor as required)
- Standard contract terms for termination of the contract, insurance, workers' compensation, and so on

Contractor Compensation   Independent contractors are paid either a percentage of the fees paid by participants or a flat rate (e.g., per hour or per class). In each case the fee charged to participants is part of the negotiation.

Most common is paying the contractor a percentage of each fee paid by a participant. Percentage splits can be 50 percent to the instructor and 50 percent to the program, 60 percent to the instructor and 40 percent to the program, 70 percent to the instructor and 30 percent to the program, or any variation that is agreed to by both parties.

One advantage to using percentage splits is that contractors are motivated to improve the participation in their classes so that they make more money. They will do their own marketing and promotion and work to draw people to their class.

When introducing a new class or activity, program administrators can structure the compensation percentage to motivate the instructor. For instance, to fully invest the instructor in growing the class, the administrator can structure the agreement so that the contractor makes a higher percentage up to a designated number of registrations and then reduce that percentage when the number is exceeded.

Instructor Manual

A comprehensive instructor manual is an effective tool for communicating information about the department, program, policies, procedures, risk management practices, and general employee guidelines. This is usually a "living" document that is updated once a year (or from time to time), distributed to new instructors, and redistributed as needed to current instructors. Instructors may be asked to sign a document stating that they have read and understood the material in the manual and that they agree to uphold the policies and practices described within. As with all employee operations and training manuals, it is good to have the draft manual reviewed by department administration, as well as the institution's legal, personnel, and risk management departments.

Elements of Instruction

The primary role of the instructor is to teach. The most important quality found in a good instructor is a love of teaching. Effective instructors focus not only on what they are teaching, but also on how they are teaching it. They ensure that each person experiences a feeling of success and of being a valued member of the class. When students leave class with a positive feeling about themselves, the learning experience, and the activity, they are more likely to continue their participation in the activity and the program.

Importance of Lesson Plans

Instructors are expected to conduct competently prepared and executed lessons. A lack of preparation gives the impression that the instructor knows or cares very little about the subject—and demonstrates a lack of respect for the participants. The content of the class should be organized in a logical progression to achieve the objectives and the goal. This should be done in two parts: a general course outline and individual lesson plans for each class meeting.

A general course outline provides an overview of the objectives to be achieved for the duration of the course. For example, in week one, the objective could be to introduce basic fencing equipment, terminology, and footwork. Lesson plans are detailed plans for each class meeting. For example, for the first class, the lesson plan might include introductions, a brief history of fencing as sport and art, demonstrating and issuing equipment, modeling proper stance, and group practice. Lesson plans should be designed for progressive skill acquisition but be flexible enough to adapt to different situations, the unique dynamics of the class, and differing skill levels and physical abilities.

Objectives for each class session should serve as building blocks that move participants toward reaching the general class goal. For instance, the following objectives might be set to achieve the general goal of playing a singles racquetball match for a beginning racquetball class:

- Hit a solid backhand.
- Hit a solid forehand.
- Keep the score of a game.
- Know the basics of court positioning.
- Know the rules of singles racquetball.
- Serve three types of serves.

In developing the course outline, consider the following:

- Provide handouts on vocabulary, equipment, and off-campus locations for practice.
- Make the first week of class as stimulating and unique as possible. (Many participants attend the first week; then, lacking satisfaction, they don't return.)
- Propose field trips and outings (tournaments, concerts, films).
- Schedule guest speakers, exhibitions, and so forth.
- Vary the format or content as the class progresses.

See figure 4.4 for an overall course outline and an individual lesson plan for an eight-week (16-meeting) beginning-level volleyball class.

Instructional Delivery Methods

After setting the objectives of the course, the instructor determines the best method(s) by which to achieve them. For example, teaching students the basics of dance might include a short lecture at the beginning of each class, followed by a demonstration or a video of a professional dance performance, and then ending with the students practicing as the instructor moves about the class providing individual review and feedback. Following is a list of delivery methods instructors can use to ensure satisfactory student learning:

- Demonstration of skills and techniques
- Well-planned lectures
- Repetition of information, movements, or both, to reinforce learning
- Student participation, which could include drills, games, or play
- Opportunity for questions and discussions

Following are instructional aids that can enhance learning:

- Displays on classroom bulletin boards, handouts
- PowerPoint® presentations, DVDs, CDs
- Video recorders and specialized equipment

Videotaping can be an effective instructional aid when used appropriately. Often, when participants see their physical movements, style, and technique from the viewpoint of an observer, they are more apt to achieve the desired improvement.

Individual Instructor Techniques   No two people teach a class in the same way, and some people are more effective teachers than others. Following are some general teaching techniques. When used, they often reveal the difference between a good and great teacher.

- Having a sense of fun and play. Classes should involve elements of fun and pleasure. A sense of play, as well as discipline, is a quality of an effective instructor. Having fun with the class encourages the establishment of relationships between the instructor and students, and among students.
- Encouraging class interaction. Group interaction can broaden a participant's campus community experience and provides the opportunity for faculty, staff, and students to interact on a more informal basis outside of traditional classroom

Beginning Volleyball Course Outline

Framework for each class (length 60 minutes)

10 minutes: Warm-up and stretching

10-20 minutes: Presentation of skill or strategy

Remainder of class: Practice of skill and lead-up games

Meeting	Skill or objective(s)	Drills
1	Introduction to game: Basic positions; rules; concepts of bump, set, spike. Teach double forearm pass.	Demonstrate basic six-person formation. Use "partners," line, circle, and moving line drills for practice of "bump" pass.
2	Review forearm pass; teach underhand serve. Combination drill: Serve and bump to setter position.	Warm-up: Circle bump Group practice: Serving
3	Review underhand serve; teach overhand pass. Pass as in meeting 1.	Warm-up: Bump with partners Use same drills for overhand.
4	Review overhand pass; teach overhand serve and overhand pass.	Group practice: Serving Combination: Serve, bump
5	Review overhand serve, passing; introduce setting techniques.	Practice serve, bump, set; work on height and placement of set.
6	Teach spike.	Toss, set, and spike (setting done by instructor and intermediate players)
7	Review spike; teach dink.	Toss, set, and spike or dink
8	Review spike, dink; teach block.	Toss, set, spike, dink, and block: Rotation drill
9	Teach 4-2 offense, including switching after serve.	Demonstrate 4-2; practice 3-hit attack.
10	Review 4-2; teach covering of spiker and blocker.	Practice covering hitter and blocker.
11	Select teams.	King of the court
12	Tournament	Round robin
13	Tournament continues.	Videotape of one game
14	Review videotape, continue tournament.	
15	Tournament continues.	
16	Finals of tournament	

Figure 4.4 Sample course outline.

settings. The instructor should encourage this, carefully acknowledging differing ages, physical abilities, disabilities, and interests.

• Dressing appropriately. An instructor's attire should reflect an appropriate image. Teaching effectiveness is hindered if students are unable to clearly see the demonstrated movements because of figure-concealing clothes. Dress should not be overly distracting or revealing and should be appropriate for the subject matter, allowing for both movement and visibility.

• Using an appropriate tone of voice. The tone of voice an instructor uses can lead to different inter-

pretations of directions. Demanding, patronizing, unsure, or stressed tones do not encourage learning.

• Giving proper directions. When giving directions, an instructor should use appropriate vernacular for body parts or movements so that students learn more than just the movements themselves. Doing so enhances the instructor's professional image as well.

Effective Teaching Characteristics

Successful instructors keep students motivated to continue with the class, thereby reducing attrition. Such instructors share the following characteristics:

- Are conscious of body position and location in the classroom when demonstrating movements or techniques
- Provide encouragement and use students' names to enhance the learning experience
- Maintain a warm and friendly environment in the classroom
- Provide a class in which the participants feel safe and secure
- Give participants options and choices
- Set and work toward specific objectives
- Speak directly to the student
- Understand that a relaxed environment provides the most comfortable way to enjoy a recreation class
- Are open to receiving participant input
- Use cue words that allow the participant enough time to prepare for the next action
- Use positive language when making suggestions and corrections
- Provide positive reinforcement to students as often and as individually as possible (even simple comments of praise or correction are useful)
- Encourage students to come back to class even after several absences by offering reviews, peer teaching, and home practice sessions
- Solicit input from the class as to their expectations and background as soon as possible and adapt lesson plans and teaching style accordingly

Instructor Style Can Affect Retention

How an instructor teaches or conducts the class can result in attendance fluctuations or decline. Students who experience one or more of the following may be increasingly absent or withdraw from the course:

- Anxiety, embarrassment, or loss of skill when returning to class after one or more absences
- Lack of opportunity to express opinions or expectations to the instructor
- Lack of personal or individualized instruction

- Lack of socialization in the classes. This can be characterized as the lack of a social relationship between participants and the instructor, as well as between peers.
- Lack of understanding of the goals and direction of the course early in the session, resulting in misunderstood expectations and skill levels
- Pressure to learn too much material in too short a period of time
- Pressure to perform or excel beyond their ability and skill level
- Too much variation in skill levels within the class

Instructor Training

Instructor training programs will vary based on the needs of the program and the qualifications and experience of the instructional staff. In some institutions, training consists of an orientation to the institution, department, or program, covering policies, procedures, and general information. In other institutions, instructor training may occur in a highly structured teaching and development program.

The following topics should be included in a general orientation or training program:

- Department structure and organizational chart
- Employment policies and procedures
- Procedures for emergencies, accidents, and injuries
- Inappropriate behavior in the classroom (see figure 4.5)
- Safety, risk management, and liability (see chapter 13)
- Legal implications pertaining to equipment and the environment (see figure 4.6)

Instructor Performance Evaluation

To fully evaluate instructor performance, administrators will need to assess feedback from participants in the class, as well as their own observations of the instructor's teaching skills and abilities.

Instructor evaluation by the class provides immediate feedback to the instructor and the program administrator. Evaluation forms should be provided to each class taught by the instructor on a regular basis. Frequently, the evaluation of the instructor is combined with an evaluation of the class (see figure 4.7)

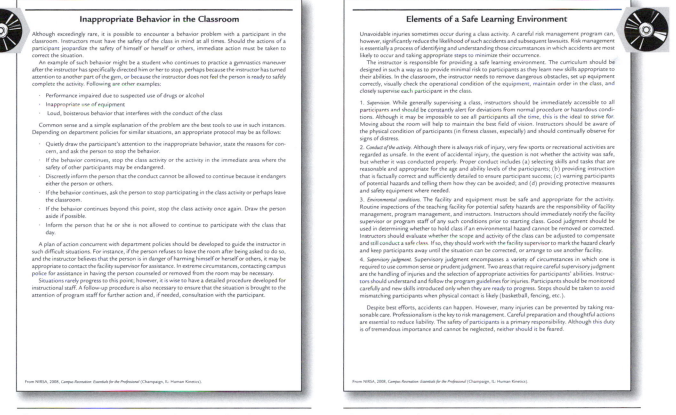

Figure 4.5 Inappropriate behavior in the classroom.

Figure 4.6 Elements of a safe learning environment.

Administrators should perform periodic instructor reviews themselves, encompassing the instructor's attitude, teaching proficiency, teaching methodology and curriculum adaptations, and teaching effectiveness. In addition to teaching skills and techniques, the evaluation should take into consideration compliance with established class protocols, appearance, punctuality, attendance, and safety (see figure 4.8).

The Art of Determining Activity Fees

Fees that are too high may result in fewer people participating, which could mean that the program fails. Alternatively, offering programs without fees or fees that are too low can send a message that the program has no value and is not worth participating in, which can also result in failure. Ideally, fees should be set within a range deemed tolerable by the population being served; this ensures strong participation and financial success.

Most instructional programs have revenue commitments that must be met for the program to continue. Fee levels will depend on the funding

Figure 4.7 Class evaluation form.

Instructor Evaluation Form

Please help us evaluate your instructor's job performance by checking the most appropriate responses below. Your input will remain anonymous and is greatly appreciated.

Instructor: _____

	Strongly disagree	Disagree	No opinion	Agree	Strongly agree
1. The instructor clearly explained course objectives (what was going to be learned).					
2. The instructor's course objectives were realistic.					
3. The instructor clearly explained the subject matter in a way I could understand.					
4. The instructor displayed adequate knowledge of the activity.					
5. The instructor recognized varied levels of ability and tried to help at each level.					
6. The instructor kept me interested in the activity.					
7. The instructor was organized.					
8. The instructor displayed a concern for my safety.					
9. The instructor was prompt.					
10. The instructor encouraged questions.					
11. The instructor was enthusiastic.					
12. The instructor was well groomed.					
13. The instructor spoke clearly.					
14. The instructor accepted suggestions and welcomed constructive criticism.					
15. I would take another course from this instructor.					

What were the instructor's weaknesses?

_____
_____
_____

What were the instructor's strengths?

_____
_____
_____

How can this instructor improve his or her teaching?

_____
_____
_____

From NIRSA, 2008, *Campus Recreation: Essentials for the Professional* (Champaign, IL: Human Kinetics).

Figure 4.8   Instructor evaluation form.

and cost recovery expectations of the particular institution. The fee formula or policy is generally established when the program develops its initial business plan.

An additional consideration in determining fees is whether the program will have a multilevel fee structure for different classifications of patrons. In the campus recreation setting, fee levels are often differentiated among students, faculty, staff, alumni, and community members.

Standard Fee Formula

The standard formula for determining fees is as follows:

$$\text{Program cost} \div \text{minimum number of participants} = \text{cost per person}$$

Determining fees is truly a learned art, as the administrator takes into consideration the need to recover costs, generate revenue, attract and retain participants, and compete with other markets offering similar products.

The program administrator can manipulate the standard fee formula in response to the situation. For instance, the standard formula may determine a fee that is higher than that of similar products offered by the competition. The standard formula can also determine a fee that is below market, or too low, which creates other problems. This happens especially in activities with low direct costs and large numbers of participants. In either case, the program administrator will want to modify the formula to achieve successful pricing. A change in the standard fee formula, such as changing the denominator (the minimum number of participants), can result in alternative pricing outcomes. Time and experience will give the program administrator greater confidence in predicting how patrons will respond to various fee levels and how to grow and protect key "profit centers" within the program.

Direct and Indirect Costs

Fees generally reflect appropriate considerations of the cost to offer the program. These can include direct costs, such as instructor salary, equipment, supplies, and facility rental, and indirect costs, such as administrative overhead, publicity, utilities, and facility maintenance. Because direct costs are easy to identify, they are usually easy to calculate. The breakdown of the indirect costs is more difficult, requiring complex formulas that are often specific to the institution.

Direct Costs

Most simply, direct costs are those costs specific to the particular course. As mentioned, these can include instructor salary, supplies, and any equipment costs being passed on to the participant. For some activities, there might also be facility rental charges, special promotional costs, and additional staffing costs.

Indirect Costs

Campus recreation programs whose business plans require full cost recovery will need to adjust the program cost part of the fee formula accordingly. This number can be difficult to determine because the equation disperses the total cost of a program, division, or department over a number of activities.

An instructional program hoping to recover 100 percent of costs related to the program will need to consider all direct costs as described earlier, plus salaries and benefits for other staff involved in the operation of the program, any supplies and equipment that are not already included as direct costs but are used to support the program, insurance, utilities, maintenance, janitorial services, and so on. If the program is to recover costs associated with higher levels of administration, such as a division or department, then those costs can become part of the equation as well.

Generally, indirect costs are determined through a complex formula that is then applied as a percentage of overhead expenses assigned to each activity. For instance, if the overhead costs are determined to be 10 percent, then a 10 percent charge is added to the fee formula. As an example, direct cost analysis sets the course fee at $30; however, the addition of the 10 percent overhead cost adds another $3 for a total course fee of $33. Overhead percentages are frequently derived through discussions and negotiations with department administration.

At the program level, the administrator may want to consider that some courses have a greater administrative demand than others, which can be taken into consideration when determining the overhead percentage charged to the course.

Fee Priorities for Groups of Clientele

For philosophical and also marketing reasons, some programs have two or more fee levels for specific groups of clientele. For instance, as mentioned earlier, many campus recreation programs feature tiered fee structures with lower prices for their student clientele, higher prices for faculty and staff, and even higher prices for alumni or community members. Some programs with a membership system offer a tiered fee system with a lower price for members and a higher price for nonmembers. This is similar to local park and recreation programs that have resident and nonresident fees. Fee levels are usually determined through discussions with the department administration and are set by policy. They can be either a set dollar amount or a percentage increase between categories.

Other Considerations When Setting Fees

Program cost, the most relevant element of the fee formula, is the most difficult component to identify. Administrators should follow their business plans and add or delete elements of cost deemed appropriate or inappropriate for each program. For a more detailed review of cost considerations, see figure 4.9.

Once they have completed their calculations, administrators can use the following questions and suggestions to reevaluate their fees:

- Involve the instructor when determining the number of participants that is appropriate for managing the class properly.
- Because beginning-level classes may need more instructor attention, they should have fewer participants.
- Check with the local parks and recreation programs or other schools to find the number of participants per class that has worked best for them.
- Consider the expenses necessary to plan, organize, and conduct the program.
- Evaluate what the market can handle.
- Determine when the activity becomes a private or semiprivate lesson versus a group lesson.
- Does the class need to realize a profit or merely break even?
- Evaluate the skill level the activity requires of participants (e.g., tennis requires high skill acquisition; aerobics is participatory).
- What additional equipment and supplies are needed?
- What costs are involved for administration and marketing?
- What additional staffing is needed and at what expense?
- Will there be a discount fee system (e.g., 12 classes for $15 versus $2 per class)?
- Will there be a multiple-class discount (e.g., 10 percent off the second class)?

Advertising and Promotion

An instructional program is an important service to the campus community. Creative, professional promotional techniques will increase consumer knowledge of the program's existence and what it offers. Promotions should be designed to inform, persuade, or remind the potential consumer about the benefits of participating in the program.

The personality, philosophy, and resources of each institution will influence the extensiveness of promotional efforts. Many campus recreation programs have a centralized publicity or marketing unit that is charged with publicizing and promoting department programs and services. This is a

Review of Course Expenditures for Fee Determination

What staffing is required to support the course?

- Instructors
  - Head instructor
  - Assistant instructor(s)
  - Class monitors
- Administrative staff
  - Clerical
  - Student support

What additional equipment and supplies are needed?

Each class or program area will have its own list of supplies and equipment. Use the following examples to assist you in creating a list for your specific class:

- Aerobics/exercise
  - Audio systems, portable or fixed
  - Steps, weights, mats
  - Music
- Certification courses
  - First aid equipment
  - Books/shipping
  - CPR mannequins
  - Certification fees

- Sports
  - Racquets, balls, and ball hoppers
  - Volleyballs, nets
  - Fencing jackets and foils
- Martial arts
  - Mats
  - Belts

What administrative and marketing expenses should be considered?

- Course materials
  - Handouts, syllabi
  - Laboratory and class manuals
  - Office supplies
- Registration supplies
- Promotion
  - Flyers
  - Brochures
  - Posters
  - Ads
- Telephone, office expenses
- Participant insurance
- Facility utilities and rental expenses

Figure 4.9 Determine fees by reviewing course expenditures.

tremendous benefit to the program administrator, who can tap that expertise and gain widespread exposure through inclusion in broader department promotion efforts. Generally, the program supplements departmental efforts with specially designed promotions to gain further exposure or to reach target audiences.

Two of the most effective tools for promoting the instructional program are inclusion in the department brochure, catalog, or activity guide and the department Web site. If a department brochure or Web site is not provided, the wise program administrator will develop both to specifically promote the program. Each of these tools is discussed in more detail in the next sections.

Other promotional efforts may include flyers, ads, or other marketing pieces designed for distribution through outlets such as campus newspapers, radio and television stations, bulletin boards (traditional and electronic), and campus networks.

Brochure, Catalog, or Activity Guide

For most recreation programs the most effective method of promotion is inclusion in a larger department brochure, catalog, or activity guide that is typically published several times per year, usually to coincide with the start of the academic quarter or semester. The brochure is typically a professionally produced, extensive document that features detailed information on department programs, services, and facilities. This marketing tool is a necessity, so if the department does not have one, the recreation program administrator should create one specifically for the instructional program.

The brochure should include information on the instructional program, course descriptions, registration information, and policies. Because production costs often restrict brochures to a limited number of pages, there is often a struggle to balance text-heavy course descriptions with photos and graphic images that create visually interesting pages to draw the reader in. Administrators and marketing staff get ideas and compare techniques by reviewing brochures and advertisements from other programs.

Department or Program Web Site

Another effective method of promotion is the department or program Web site. Most people today expect to find information and make purchases via the Internet; the same is true of campus audiences. A well-designed and easily navigated Web site that provides pertinent information in a reader-friendly manner is one of the most effective tools for drawing people to the program. Registration software can allow the Web site visitor to enroll and pay for courses online. (Online registration is discussed later in this chapter in the section Internet Registration.)

Making a Program Visible on Campus

Getting the message out to clientele across campus may seem easy, but remember that this group is receiving numerous "hits" of information each day. They will select what to read based on the "wow" factor of the message.

Whether distributing brochures, posters, or flyers, administrators will need to develop a distribution plan that takes into consideration the most traveled routes around campus, heavily visited buildings that offer display spaces for promotional materials, and any policies or restrictions on what can be displayed or for how long.

Here are some additional ideas for promoting programs and activities on campus:

- E-mail messages to campus e-mail groups
- Electronic message and data display boards in campus recreation facilities or other campus buildings
- Flyers and posters
- Program information placed in the academic registration materials
- Newsletters geared to specific groups such as campus recreation department staff, residence halls, faculty and staff, graduate students, or the personnel office

- Program information provided to campus representatives from groups such as residence halls, student government, faculty and staff groups, and Greek councils

Direct Mail

Although less common in the campus recreation setting because of cost, direct mail marketing ensures that the promotional piece reaches the target market. Costs often include production of the marketing piece itself and mail processing charges in addition to any per piece mail delivery costs. Analyzing the cost and benefits before implementing a direct mail campaign is important.

Mailing lists can be secured from various campus groups or departments or created from a database of previous or current activity registrations. Most effective is a targeted direct mail campaign to specific clientele. For instance, sending a tennis workshop brochure to previous participants in tennis instructional classes is likely to get a good response.

Careful timing throughout the production and distribution process is critical to ensure that the direct mail piece reaches the clientele in a timely manner. The schedule should consider time for creative development, print production, mail distribution services, including labeling and mailing the material, and the date materials should be "in hand" for registration. Generally, clientele should have information two to three weeks before the start of the registration period, although promotions for specific programs can be shorter than that.

Local Media and Advertising

Depending on the potential audiences that the program serves (campus, off campus), advertising beyond campus media may be cost beneficial. Most campuses have their own radio station(s) and newspaper(s). Programs can partner with them as well as local community outlets to get the word out about their programs. Following are some examples of media and what they offer:

- *Television and radio stations.* Feature stories, news stories, quick blurbs, and public service announcements.
- *Newspapers.* Advertisements and feature articles, high-readership publication days, display ads in sections popular with readers, teasers, and classified ads.

- *Calendars of events.* A listing of program, department, or institution events and activities often found in department promotional materials and publicized by campus media outlets.

Marketing Promotions

To attract new clients and build participation, administrators can consider the use of occasional promotional specials. Promotional specials give something away or discount the service with the goal of introducing new people to the program. Administrators can use their imaginations when it comes to designing promotional specials, but should consider the cost and benefits to the program before implementation. Promotional specials often involve some risk and an initial loss of revenue. If designed and implemented correctly, however, they should increase revenue and participation in the long run.

The following are examples of promotional specials:

- *Bring a Friend.* Set aside one day or week for class participants to bring an interested friend along—for free!

- *Open House Week.* Offer free classes for a week to encourage people to try new things.

- *Sign Up Two, Get One Free.* When someone brings two other people to sign up, he or she gets to register for free.

- *This One's on Us.* Offer participants a free coupon to try a class of their choice.

- *Birthday Benefit.* Offer a discount (such as 10 percent) to participants who sign up during their birthday week or month.

- *Buy Two, Get One at Half Price.* Participants who sign up for two consecutive sessions get the next one at half price.

ABCs of Program Registration

An effective **registration** process must function for the participants' ease and convenience while meeting administrative needs and the financial requirements of the program.

From the participant perspective, the process must be easily understood, convenient, time efficient, and customer friendly. For the program, the process must effectively enroll participants, facilitate payment and accounting needs, have the ability to generate class rosters and financial reports, and not overly tax staff operations in support of the program.

A well-planned, customer-friendly registration procedure that offers convenient options and is supported by reliable and flexible registration software and a well-designed registration form can go a long way to providing operational efficiency and customer satisfaction.

Registration Software

Many versions of activity registration software are available on the market today. Administrators buying registration software should conduct a thorough review and evaluation of various products before making their decision to ensure that they buy the best software for their programs. Most software products facilitate a staff person or clients themselves inputting the registration data into the system and offer phone and Internet applications.

Consulting with administrators of other instructional programs about their registration software, especially the following, can be helpful:

- Available software features and which are used most

- Ease of use by patrons and staff

- Frequency of service calls and satisfaction with customer service

- Responsiveness of provider to requests to modify the software or reports to better serve the program

- Overall cost and benefits

Administrators should also consult with department administration, technological personnel, and the finance department before selecting registration software to ensure that all related software systems and financial reports are compatible.

Programs that use staff to input registrations into the software should look to the future and anticipate the need to use other software-supported registration processes. Customers have come to expect the convenience of purchases via the Internet or phone, and programs will want to offer that same level of service.

Methods of Registration

Instructional programs should offer as many of the following methods of registration as practical, for the ease of potential clients:

- In person, at one or more locations, at one large registration event, or during regular office hours or special hours
- Internet
- Mail
- Fax
- Phone, either through an automated software program or live person

Decisions about which registration method(s) to use will most likely be based on the technological and staffing support available and whether credit card payments can be facilitated. The following sections provide brief descriptions of each method and some considerations.

In-Person Registration

In-person registration is conducted by staff on a face-to-face basis. The patron hands the completed registration form to the staff person, who processes the registration, accepts payment, and prints a receipt. In-person registration can be organized into a large "registration event" that initiates the registration period, conducted during special hours during a peak registration period, or offered during normal office hours.

The location of registration is an important consideration. Administrators should consider the hours of operation, the hours that registration will be accepted (i.e., business hours or all hours the facility is open), and whether to accept registration in more than one location. If registration software and the department technology system will support it, the registration software can be installed in several department locations so that patrons can register at their convenience. In some locations it may be helpful to offer a drop box or deposit slot to accept forms after hours.

Although it can be inconvenient for the patron to come to a facility to register during the available in-person hours, there are advantages:

- Payment and other errors are minimized by face-to-face interaction.
- Staff can provide additional information on the activities and answer questions.
- Patrons can be informed when a desired class is full, and staff can assist by suggesting alternative courses.
- Staff have opportunities to promote the program and additional classes during the course of conversation.

The registration process should be well organized and efficient in order to serve the greatest number of people in the shortest amount of time. This is particularly true for programs that have a large volume of registrations at the start of the registration period. Whenever possible, long lines of people waiting to be helped should be avoided.

Here are some ideas to help with handling high volumes of in-person registration during peak periods:

- Consider expanded registration hours, including early morning, evening, and weekend hours.
- Schedule registration for recreation programs to take place after academic class registration, which can reduce frequent requests for refunds or transfers as a result of changes in student academic schedules.
- Schedule and provide registration training for staff. They should be knowledgeable about the courses, policies, and operation of the program. Minimizing output of misinformation about such things is very important for good customer relations and the reputation of the program. If someone doesn't know the answer to a patron's question, be sure he or she can direct the patron to someone who does.
- Expand staff resources by using program volunteers to work registration in exchange for a priority enrollment or free class.
- If the registration process will include the Internet, in-person, mail, fax, and phone methods, determine which method, if any, will have priority over the others when registration begins.

Internet Registration

Online registration directly from the program's Web site is easily the most convenient and efficient method of registration for both the patron and program administration. Increasingly, the ability to register online is expected by technologically savvy consumers; failure to provide it can be perceived as poor customer service. Although a number of issues must be addressed before implementing online registration, the value to both the patron and the program is substantial.

Online registration can take place 24 hours a day, at the patron's convenience. The patron, rather than a staff member, completes the actual data entry. Registration is conducted in "real time"; the software provides immediate information on what spaces are available in various courses. If a person's first-choice course is full, he can immediately act to enroll in his second-choice course. This also means that a staff person processing a course registration for someone at the counter may be in the system at the same time as someone registering from another location. This is a seamless process to both parties; however, the registration is first come, first served. The staff person may have indicated to the patron at the counter that there is one space remaining in the course, only to see it disappear when processing the transaction. This is not normally a problem; it is mentioned merely to demonstrate the "real time" aspect of how the software application works. Because it is never a good policy to accept registration without payment, credit card payment should be required for online registration, and the patron should be able to print out a receipt at the close of the transaction.

In addition to offering registration, Web sites can provide links to additional sources of information that can help patrons decide whether the course is for them or what they will need once they are enrolled (special equipment and so forth). Also, most registration software programs have marketing applications that allow the database to include e-mail addresses. These can be sorted to facilitate targeted marketing of specific programs. For example, a promotion for a new tennis workshop can be sent to the e-mail addresses of people who registered for tennis classes in the past year.

When considering online registration, administrators should involve the finance, technology, and legal counsel departments of the institution, as discussed earlier. In addition, other program staff in the department should be consulted so that their registration needs can also be considered in the implementation process. All financial records and access to accounts must comply with the institution's financial framework, and hardware and server systems must be sufficient to handle the volume of transactions. Administrators should also discuss with campus legal counsel and risk management personnel the legalities of any waivers, consent forms, or release of liability forms associated with the online process.

To facilitate a smooth rollout of the program, all parties should come together for a series of meetings to brainstorm and problem solve all aspects of the operation in advance. Programs offering online registration have seen the percentage of registrations transacted online increase with each year. It is not unusual for online registrations to account for 50 percent or more of all registrations.

Mail-In Registration

With mail-in registration the patron completes a registration form that has been provided in advance, most likely in the activity catalog. Payment is made by check or credit card. Many patrons find mailing in their registration easy and quick. However, there are disadvantages to this form of registration. Occasionally registration forms are delayed or lost in the mail. Also, the patron will not have a receipt immediately following the transaction; one is generally sent out by return mail after processing. Errors in completing the form and including incorrect payment information are common and necessitate follow-up calls and actions to complete the transactions. Scheduling additional staff to process registration forms during high-volume periods can be helpful.

Faxed Registration

Similar to mail-in registration, patrons can fax completed registration forms to the program office. Faxing the forms is easy and convenient for patrons. Accepting faxed registration forms is particularly appreciated by patrons who have called the office with an inquiry and want to follow up with a registration. Staff can either fax a blank form to the patron, refer the patron to the registration form located in the activity catalog, or direct the patron to a downloadable version on the program Web site. The patron will generally follow up by faxing the registration form in to complete the transaction within a short period of time. Credit card payment should be required, because it is never a good policy to accept registration without payment.

It is important to check with the institution's legal counsel on the appropriateness of accepting a faxed signature on the informed consent and release agreement form (waiver), as well as the credit card authorization. Legal opinions vary on this issue. One disadvantage is that faxed forms can be difficult to read because of the poor quality of printing. Programs that accept faxed forms should have staff trained to carefully review each form received to ensure that the informed consent and release agreement language is completely shown on the faxed copy and is legible to the reader. Unreadable or partially obscured forms may be contested in court as invalid.

Phone-In Registration

With phone-in registration patrons call in and register over the phone using a credit card. The patron provides all of the information needed to the staff person during the call. Assuming that the program requires patrons to sign an informed consent and release agreement, a procedure will need to be in place for collecting the signed agreement at a later time.

Software applications that allow automated phone-in registration have also become popular. Similar to the online process, patrons call in to an automated program that accepts their verbal or touch-tone commands and processes the transaction.

Efficient and Customer-Friendly Operations

Regardless of the registration method used, the most important consideration should always be efficient and customer-friendly operations.

With online registration, the server should be configured to allow high volumes of concurrent registrations if a lot of people will be registering at one time. In-person registration processes should be designed so sufficient staff resources are available during peak registration periods.

Patrons can become very competitive for spaces in popular classes or extremely disappointed and unhappy if they do not get into the classes they want. Registration policies and practices should be clearly defined, well publicized, fair and equitable, and enforced consistently with a smile and without special preferences. All staff answering questions about the program and assisting patrons with registration should be trained so they are knowledgeable and prepared to provide the highest level of customer service.

Registration Forms

Registration forms should be designed to collect all of the information necessary to fully register the patron in the activity, while also meeting the administrative needs required for processing the form.

The following data fields are commonly found on registration forms:

Participant Information

Name

Address (campus, local, permanent)

Phone

M/F

Affiliation (student, faculty, staff, and so on)

Student or employee number

Age (when appropriate)

Emergency contact information

Course Information (one or more courses per form)

Title

Course number (accounting code, distinguishing class "call number")

Days

Times

Location

Fee

Payment Information

Total fees due

Payment method and related information (check made payable to XXX, cash amount, credit card number, expiration date, and authorized signature)

Informed Consent and Release Agreement

Refund and Transfer Policies

Photo Release

Office Use Only Section (to record processing date, staff initials, and receipt number)

Other forms that might be included with the registration process include the following:

- Interest surveys
- Statement of participant skill or ability forms
- Maps to class meeting site, if needed
- Equipment or supplies for specific courses

For a sample registration form, see figure 4.10.

Eligibility Requirements

Eligibility requirements should be consistent with the institution's policies and procedures for participation. This pertains to groups of eligible clientele, such as students, faculty, staff, alumni, and community. Appropriate identification must be presented and documented on the registration form. Participant eligibility may also pertain to age, skill level, health, and experience. Where required, it is a good idea to include course prerequisites in brochures, catalogs, and other promotional materials where the course is being advertised.

Late Registration

Late registration can refer to registration that occurs following the primary registration event or registration after the first class meeting. Most programs allow late registration to take place for

Figure 4.10 Registration form sample.

certain activities and for a specific period of time. For instance, it may not be appropriate to add students to a class using a progressive skill–based curriculum, or to a course in which equipment distribution and skills testing have already taken place.

Many programs determine the period for late registration, ending all late registration after the first, second, or third week of instruction. Some implement an "add" process that includes authorization by the instructor for someone to join a class that is already in session. Course fees may or may not be prorated for late registrations, depending on the program.

Wait Lists

Most programs have wait lists for some or all courses. Once a class has reached maximum enrollment, people can put their names on a first come, first served list to be added to the course whenever a space opens up. Registration software can facilitate this process, but it takes staff follow-up to complete the registration.

It is important that people who are on a wait list are added based on their position on the list. When someone withdraws from a class, the next person on the wait list should be contacted to determine whether he or she is still interested in registering. Registration is not complete until the patron fills out a registration form and pays for the course.

Transfers, Refunds, and Credits

Accommodating requests for transfers and refunds is good customer service. Policies should be determined at the start of a program. See figures 4.11 and 4.12 for sample transfer and refund request forms. Most programs try to monitor or control the number of transfers and refunds because these can directly affect class size and program consistency. For instance, allowing two people to transfer or withdraw may put the course at risk of being canceled because of low enrollment.

Administrators will want to consider the time period during which requests to transfer from one course to another are appropriate and will be accommodated. They should also consider whether an **administrative fee** will be charged to process the transfer request. Although allowing people to transfer to other classes keeps them in the instructional program, having an administrative fee can deter them from moving from class to class on a frequent basis.

When determining a program's refund policy, administrators should consider the following: customer satisfaction with the product (the course), loss of revenue (particularly if many refunds are given), and buying the goodwill of patrons over the long term (customer service).

To ensure that patrons are satisfied with the services provided, many programs offer unconditional satisfaction refunds. In other words, if the customer is unhappy with the class for any reason, the program will offer a full refund, no questions asked. Other programs offer a more conditional refund such as a percentage of the fee returned if the withdrawal occurs in the first week of instruction, a lesser percentage in the second week, and so on, or a prorated refund amount for each class meeting being refunded.

Determining the refund policy that is right for a given program may take trial and error and analysis of refunds over a period of time. A stiff refund policy can discourage withdrawals and refunds, whereas the unconditional satisfaction guarantee ensures a greater opportunity for return business and customer retention.

Some programs offer credit toward future purchases instead of cash or credit card refunds.

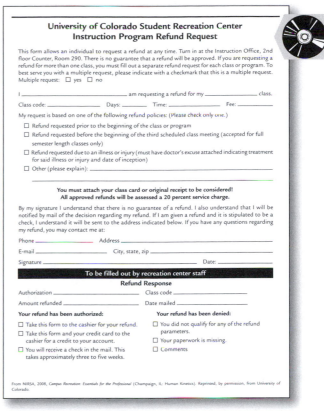

Figure 4.11 Sample transfer of funds request form.

Figure 4.12 Sample refund request form.

Evaluation

A credit system is not recommended unless it is supported through the registration software and appropriate staff resources are dedicated to ensuring that account records are properly maintained. Most programs issue immediate cash or credit card refunds to avoid the record-keeping requirements of a credit system.

Evaluation

To ensure quality, all instructional programs should have effective and continual evaluation processes in place. Several components of review must be considered: individual class evaluation, equipment and facility evaluation, instructor evaluation (discussed earlier), and overall program evaluation. The evaluation and review process itself presents additional opportunities for garnering patron perspective, generates improvement, promotes customer retention, and creates a positive program image.

Class Evaluation

The class evaluation is an important tool in a well-run instructional program. Feedback provided by participants allows program staff to learn whether the program is effective, meets the needs of those it is intended to serve, and fulfills program objectives. The class evaluation solicits critical feedback from the primary audience—program participants.

To maximize patrons' input regarding class evaluation, timing is as critical as implementation. Because participation sometimes drops off near the end of a course, evaluations should be distributed in the middle of the session to gather the greatest response.

Evaluation forms should be simple—either a self-mailing postcard or a one-sided sheet of paper (refer back to figure 4.7 for an example). Ranking statements allow people to score the course content, instructor ability, facility, and so on, using a scale of 1 to 5 or check marks to indicate whether the course was very good, good, poor, or completely unsatisfactory (or the rater has no opinion). Evaluations can also include multiple-choice questions, short-answer questions, and the opportunity to make additional comments.

Participants should evaluate the total class experience, including, but not limited to, the following:

- Overall quality of the instructor's teaching
- Course content
- Length and duration of the course
- Cleanliness and safety of the facility
- Availability and condition of equipment (if appropriate)

For new classes, and from time to time with ongoing classes, it is valuable to have instructors evaluate their courses. They can comment on participation levels, attendance over the course duration, continuing or declining participant interest, course format (including days, time, and duration), skill progression, facility and equipment condition, and whether content is what participants expect.

The program administrator will want to review all of the preceding as well, and make determinations about changes that could improve the course, instruction, or program. Moreover, the administrator will need to determine whether instructor performance meets the specific course needs, analyze whether the desired cost recovery target is being met, and decide whether the course can or should be modified to increase success.

Equipment and Facilities Safety and Adequacy Evaluation

The instructor and the administrator must conduct routine equipment and facility evaluations for the safety of the class participants. In particular, the instructor should be checking the safety of both the facility and equipment before the start of each class and reporting any concerns to the appropriate people in a timely manner. The program administrator is responsible for offering a safe program in a safe environment. Continual routine evaluations of both equipment and facilities will help maintain the safety of the participants and the integrity of the program.

Comprehensive Program Evaluation

Throughout each program cycle the administrator must be tuned in to the program in order to spot trends and indicators that call out for action to improve the program. Changes in the design and coordination of each subsequent class session can be implemented to keep programs from growing stale or suffering from declining enrollments.

However, a more comprehensive review of the instructional program should be conducted annually, or at least every two or three years, for a stable, ongoing program. The review should include evaluating the diversity of program offerings and program scheduling, the consistency and quality of instruction, the condition of facilities and equipment, the effectiveness and efficiency of registration procedures, customer satisfaction, and participation and fiscal analysis.

Conclusion

Designing, administering, and evaluating recreation instructional programs is a complex task. Because programs vary from one institution to another, administrators can benefit from networking and sharing ideas on current course trends, efficient and customer-friendly registration processes, and good administrative practices with those in other institutions. In the end, the value of a well-run, comprehensive program is seen in the numbers of clients who participate on a daily basis.

References

Meyers, P. (1991). Instructor employment: Independent contractor or employee? *NIRSA Journal 15*(3): 24-27.

Strong, R. (1992). Part-time teachers: Contractor vs. employee status. Learning Resources Network (LERN) Research Report 280, Manhattan, KS.

Glossary

activity or class fee—The price charged to the participant for an activity, class, or course.

administrative fee—A fee assessed by some programs in addition to the class fee, generally to cover the administrative costs of registration.

attrition—A decline in participation following the formal registration period.

class meeting—The specific time when members of the class meet for instruction. If the class meets twice a week for six weeks, it has 12 class meetings. A class meeting is not referred to as a session.

cost recovery—The level to which a program generates revenue to offset its cost. Cost recovery information should always specify whether the calculation includes indirect as well as direct expenses.

course description—Information that explains what activity will be taught, what skills or knowledge will be gained, and the potential benefits that will result from taking the course.

credit and noncredit courses—Participants who complete a course may receive academic credit, or there may be no academic credit offered to participants who complete a course.

direct costs (expenses)—Direct costs are those specific costs associated with a particular program or activity, such as instructor salary, equipment, supplies, and so on.

enrollment—See registration.

fill rate—The number of people enrolled compared to the number of spaces available.

independent contractor—A legal term referring to a provider of services purchased by contractual agreement. Some programs use independent contract instructors to teach all or some courses; others hire instructors as employees of the institution.

indirect costs (expenses)—Costs that are determined through extensive analysis or a complex formula to account for overhead expenses incurred as part of an activity or course. Such expenses can include facility maintenance, administrative salaries and benefits, utility and custodial costs, insurance, and so forth. Often this analysis results in an overhead percentage that is then applied to the total of direct costs incurred as part of an activity or course.

instructional program—A program that offers classes, activities, or courses designed to provide a participatory or learning experience that promotes physical health or develops lifelong recreational skills, or both. An instructional program can be an entire organization unto itself or part of a larger division or department.

prime time—The term applied to those hours in which facilities have the heaviest use and demand.

program administrator—The person with immediate administrative responsibility for the overall operation of the instructional program. Within institutions, titles may be program coordinator, program director, or assistant director.

registration—The act of signing up for, or enrolling, in a class or activity. One person taking one class or activity is considered one enrollment or registration. One person who takes two classes is considered two enrollments or registrations. Any fees due are collected at the time of registration.

section—A class or course may offer one or more sections. The sections may vary by day, time, instructor, or skill level. Each section is considered a separate class, independent of the others. If one course title has three sections, that would be considered three different classes with three different enrollments. A section is not the same as a single class meeting.

session—A period of time, usually 4 to 12 weeks, during which classes take place. Because recreation programs typically follow the academic schedule, a session can be equal to the length of the quarter or semester. In addition, the quarter or semester may be divided into two or more several-week sessions. A session is not the number of times a class meets during a given quarter or semester, and it is not the number of classes offered.

subsidy—Any monies not coming from direct fees for services. Subsidies include tuition reimbursement from state agencies, monies from a central institutional office, or staff salaries paid by means other than class registration income. To determine the percentage to which the program is subsidized, divide the subsidy income by the total income for a full recovery of all program expenses.

CHAPTER 5

Fitness and Wellness

Cher T. Harris, MS, Outreach Educational Programs Coordinator, College of Health and Human Performance, University of Florida

Jonathan Hart, CRSS, MS, Assistant Director of Campus Recreation—Facilities, Georgia Institute of Technology

Mila L. Padgett, MS, Assistant Director of Programs, Department of Campus Recreation, Oakland University

Lisa Stuppy, MS, Assistant Director of Fitness Programs, Boise State University

> Having access to group exercise classes, strength and conditioning rooms and other fitness opportunities is vital to the health and wellness of our nation. Fitness programs help college students formulate healthy lifestyle patterns at an early age and create a wellness culture on campus with our faculty/staff. Embrace this opportunity and be the best program you can be!
>
> *Carol Kennedy-Armbruster, School of Health, Physical Education, and Recreation, Indiana University at Bloomington*

This chapter discusses the key components of a comprehensive fitness and wellness program. This area of campus recreation focuses on the health and wellness of individuals. By providing educational programs that encourage healthy lifestyle choices, institutions offer opportunities for all users of the facility to enhance their quality of life through college, as well as throughout their lives. This chapter covers many aspects of fitness and wellness programs, including fitness center design and layout, group exercise, personal training, fitness assessments, and fitness and wellness personnel.

The Fitness Center

Whether you're working with a 2,000- or 200,000-square-foot fitness facility, the facility's success, as well as the success of the overall program, lies with the management of the employees and the facility space. Whether the facility consists of only a few pieces of **cardiorespiratory** equipment or is a multilevel fitness area, some basic principles apply.

Designing a Fitness Center

Throughout the past 20 years, colleges and universities nationwide have designed, developed, implemented, and incorporated state-of-the-art recreation facilities on their campuses. Recreational sports, fitness and wellness programs, and recreational facilities are a tremendous growth industry nationwide and provide a great marketable asset to colleges and universities. The booming facilities construction trend has not faltered even in a slow economy. In recent years, the cost of building a multimillion-dollar recreation complex has gone from $2 million to $140 million. Experts estimated that between 2005 and 2010 over $3.7 billion would be spent to build or renovate facilities on just 333 college and university campuses.

Recreation facilities are paid for with students' fees, state monies, bonds, or private funding. Because recreational sport and fitness services help recruit and retain students, regents and chancellors approve these new or renovated facilities and make sure they are built.

The students expect it. One of the driving forces behind updating, renovating, and erecting more modern recreation facilities is to keep up with the growing demand for good recreation opportunities (i.e., facilities, programs, and services)—especially when it comes to fitness. State-of-the-art recreational sport facilities and their programs attract and retain students and faculty.

Long gone are the days of fitness areas that are a hodgepodge of cardiorespiratory and strength machines and a sparse selection of free weights. Today's fitness enthusiasts have come to expect the very best in terms of fitness equipment and space accommodations. Thus, the bar has been raised for those in the fitness profession to deliver a good product (i.e., properly trained staff and state-of-the-art accommodations and equipment) that meets the needs of members.

By December 2004 more than half of the member institutions of the National Intramural-Recreational Sports Association (NIRSA) had either just opened a new facility, were in the process of building one, or were renovating existing facilities. The following pages offer a perspective on how to plan, design, and select the right equipment to get the job done.

Where to Start?

In designing the ideal fitness center, do not limit yourself to just being able to dream . . . dream big! The facility should encompass a wide variety of equipment with ample space for current and potential members. Begin by taking into consideration the facility's current state or condition. Ask yourself, How can we make things more functional, dynamic, and meaningful for our members? You may find that a fresh coat of paint, new mirrors, or rearranging the equipment to better serve your members can easily rectify some of the issues you are facing. However, your fitness center still needs to be functional to keep members satisfied.

Knowing Your Clients

To plan for a fitness center, you need to know your clients. Keep the following in mind:

- Know your members' motivations and what keeps them coming back day after day. Be sure to pay close attention to those with special needs and make accommodations to better serve their needs.

- Conduct a needs assessment to acquire better insight into and information about members' needs and wants, likes and dislikes. Do not limit yourself by deciding not to offer a wide variety of amenities such as towel service, support staff, ADA-compatible equipment and accommodations, and entertainment equipment (i.e., ambient acoustics for music or television).

- Orchestrate several fact-finding visits to other facilities to gain perspective on how they operate.

• Consult with reputable and experienced architects to assist in the development and design of a new fitness center.

• Attend trade shows and conventions to see what's the latest and greatest in the fitness industry.

• Think futuristic: Expand your knowledge and understanding of future fitness trends as well as membership growth and potential and how these might affect your facility in years to come.

• Fitness centers should be inviting to all. Focus on aesthetics and space use by paying attention to details. As you progress through the design phase, you should be able to visualize mirror placement effectively, the access and egress points, the effects of natural and artificial lighting, ceiling height, flooring, HVAC capacity, and most important, the placement of the exercise equipment.

Equipment Layout

In the planning and conceptual stage of designing the layout of the equipment, be mindful that there is no proven standard or scientific method for choosing the right exercise equipment and properly arranging it in your facility. The one consistent thing is to ensure balance by providing ample equipment and space for cardiorespiratory and strength equipment. Your members should dictate what to incorporate into the mix of equipment; it is up to you to ensure adequate space (see figure 5.1).

Use a blank schematic drawing or architectural blueprint to assist you in developing the layout of the fitness center. This will allow you to determine where to place the various pieces of equipment as well as allow you to visualize the layout on paper. Also, arranging the equipment on paper will enable you to make any adjustments, modifications, or changes prior to the installation of the equipment.

To assist with space allocation, anticipate providing a minimum of 1.5 square feet of space per member. For example, if you project your membership base to be around 10,000, you should plan to have at least 15,000 square feet of dedicated space for equipment. Be sure to project toward

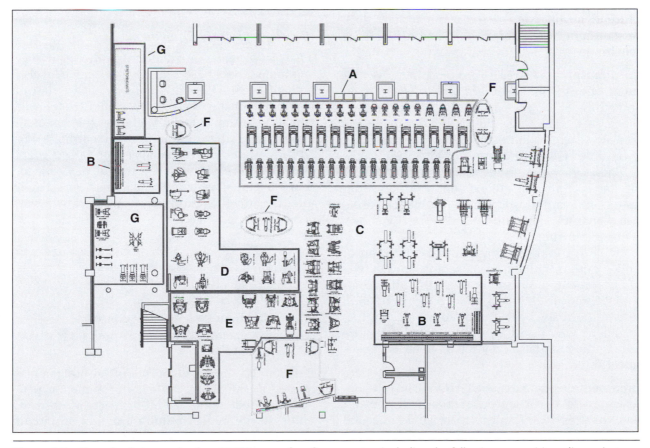

Figure 5.1 Example of a layout plan for a 15,000-square-foot fitness center, including the following areas: *(a)* cardiorespiratory, *(b)* free-weight, *(c)* plate-loaded, *(d)* beginner, *(e)* intermediate, *(f)* functional, and *(g)* stretching and body-weight.

the future; do not consider just your current membership.

Keep things simple. Design the layout so that the equipment is grouped into four areas:

1. Auxiliary areas (stretching, abdominal, and low back)
2. Introductory
3. Cardiorespiratory
4. Intermediate and advanced (i.e., plate-loaded and free weight areas)

Auxiliary Area Because the auxiliary area combines stretching mats, abdominal and back stations, and pull-up and dip towers, to avoid congestion, it should be on the outskirts of the fitness center. The introductory and auxiliary areas are great for those who want to use lighter free weights and do not want to have to venture into the advanced free weight area.

Introductory Area The introductory area should encompass a full line of selectorized machines that are geared specifically for beginners; however, this area should attract users of all fitness levels. In the design phase, make an effort to place these machines close to your support desk or station in case members need help using these machines.

Cardiorespiratory Area Cardiorespiratory equipment should not face bare walls. Users need something to keep them attentive while training. Staring at a blank wall is boring and not conducive to exercising. Do not be afraid to jazz things up by adding background music or television banks to entertain users. With today's technological advances, flat panel televisions are now integrated into cardiorespiratory equipment so users can watch and listen to their favorite TV shows while exercising.

Be sure to take into account the location of power outlets with the correct amps for each type of equipment and communication (audiovisual) line. If you are starting from scratch, be sure to communicate with the architect or contractor about where to locate power outlets before having the foundation poured or electrical boxes installed.

Intermediate and Advanced Area The intermediate and advanced area is for those with a higher level of expertise. Proper supervision is needed to ensure safety and rule enforcement because of the higher degree of risk associated with this equipment. If applicable, consider installing

mirrors to help users execute proper form while exercising.

Selecting the Right Equipment

The equipment that you choose for your fitness center has a significant impact on the success of your program. It is very important to do your homework before purchasing equipment. Definitely consider not only knowing your members' demographics, but also understanding their rationale for needing a variety of equipment. Base your decisions on their needs rather than yours. By knowing and understanding the interests of your participants, you will make the right purchasing decisions and improve membership retention.

Industry standards recommend an equipment mix of approximately 40 percent cardiorespiratory equipment, 30 percent selectorized machines, and 30 percent free weights. For programs with many older members, consider a 50:50 ratio of cardiorespiratory and strength equipment. Even facilities with a large number of strength-minded participants need to incorporate cardiorespiratory pieces into the mix.

Cardiorespiratory Equipment

One of the greatest attributes of cardiorespiratory equipment is that users do not need a high level of expertise to use the equipment. Select a variety of equipment that will give users of all fitness levels a wide selection of training choices (i.e., manual, quick start, hill, random, interval, cardio, 5K or 10K workouts, and distance or time calorie goal). Most cardiorespiratory equipment has easy-to-learn display consoles on which users can set their predetermined workout regimens. Following are a few essential pieces:

- Treadmills
- Ellipticals
- Cycles
- Steppers
- Stair climbers
- Ergometers (rowers and upper-body ergs—UBEs)

Treadmills Treadmills are one of the most popular pieces of equipment, are one of the most expensive, and require quite a bit of space. Most treadmills on the market require a dedicated circuit (20 amps) for power, so be sure that there is sufficient power to operate them where you want to place them.

William A. Cotton, Colorado State University.

Select cardiorespiratory equipment so that users of all fitness levels have a wide selection of training choices.

Things to Consider Before Purchasing a Treadmill

- What is the engine's horsepower (output)? Typically, commercial-grade motors range from 4 to 6 horsepower.

- What type of power source is needed to power the machine? Some treadmills run on 220 volts to keep their engines cooler. Machines that use 110 volts can easily be rotated with other powered machines and are more energy efficient. Interchanging equipment pieces in low-traffic and low-usage areas with those in high-traffic areas prolongs the life of the pieces. Treadmills should have dedicated power lines.

- What are the dimensions of the running and walking surface? Look for a deck with a minimum of 20 × 60 inches. Try to suit a variety of users, such as those with longer strides.

- What are the speed ranges? Speed should begin at 0.5 mph and go to 12 mph.

- Does the machine have decline and incline capability? Standard grade ranges from 0 to 15 percent grade for the incline and 0 to −3 percent gradation for the decline.

Ellipticals Introduced to the fitness industry almost a decade ago, ellipticals are still gaining in popularity. Like treadmills, these provide motions similar to those of running without the impact. Depending on the model of elliptical, users can oscillate in a forward or backward direction and have the option of moving their arms to train their upper bodies.

Things to Consider Before Purchasing an Elliptical Machine

- What is the preference of members? Do they want arm levers or the incline and decline of the ramp?

- What is the stride length of the machine? Shorter people may struggle with machines that have a long stride length, and tall people may struggle if the stride length is too short.

- Is power needed? Most ellipticals are self-powered; if you are considering one that requires power, just like the treadmills, be sure that you have sufficient electrical outlets.

Cycles   Cycles continue to be a staple in any fitness center because they can accommodate a wide range of users. Consider incorporating both types (recumbent and upright) into your cardiorespiratory selection.

Things to Consider Before Purchasing Cycles

- Can the seat adjust for proper leg flexion and extension to accommodate a variety of users?
- For upright cycles, do the handlebars accommodate good posture?
- For recumbent cycles, does the backrest have lumbar support?
- Do the cycles have wide seats for user comfort?

Other Machines to Think About Adding Into the Cardio Mix

- Stair steppers and climbers have declined in popularity since the inception of the elliptical machines; however, there are a few faithful followers who should be considered and included in the purchasing decision.
- **Ergometers** (rowers and upper-body ergs—UBEs) add great versatility to the cardiorespiratory and strength training mix. Look for UBEs that are compliant with the Americans with Disabilities Act (ADA). This would include the option to remove the seat so a wheelchair can be pulled up to the machine for upper-body use.

General Considerations Before Purchasing Any Cardiorespiratory Equipment

- How much space is needed to accommodate the equipment? Most manufacturers have space requirements in their informational brochures. If not, ask.
- Are there any added features that separate one machine from another? Examples include the number of programs or training modes, heart rate monitoring capability, portable radio or MP3 player, water bottle holders, and plastic shrouds for corrosion prevention.
- How durable are the machines? Machines graded for commercial use are more durable and can withstand greater usage than residential machines can. How many hours per day will the piece be used?
- What types of training or workout modules are incorporated into the machine? How

easy is it for users to navigate? Cardiorespiratory machines should have at least manual, interval, and cardio settings and should be easy to use. Look for machines that show how they work and offer advice on which training mode best suits the needs of the user.

- Do the machines make a lot of noise when in use? Most machines will make some noise; however, you do not want the noise to have an overpowering effect on the acoustics of the entire area.
- Take the time to try out products. Equipment representatives should be willing to deliver machines to your facility for you and your members to try. Be sure to be receptive to user feedback to determine preferences.
- Look for models that have heart rate (HR) monitoring capability: polar telemetry or HR contacts. This is a great feature, especially for special populations who may need to track their HR.
- Check the machines' warranties, service agreements, and buyback plans before purchasing. As the buyer, you have the upper hand in negotiating the terms and conditions with the manufacturer. It is imperative to have a three- or five-year replacement plan to ensure the proper rotation of equipment.

Strength Equipment

Choosing strength equipment is a two-part process. Begin by determining which type of equipment best suits your participants and then make certain that the equipment fits into the scheme of the fitness center's footprint; proper placement of the equipment is critical. Be careful not to squeeze too many machines into a small space. Allow enough room for egress while maintaining variety.

There are basically four types of strength equipment on the market: selectorized, plate-loaded, functional, and free-weight. All are unique in their functional and stabilizing capabilities, ability to accommodate dependent and independent movement, and defined paths of motion to target certain muscles or muscle groups.

- *Selectorized* pieces are generally considered introductory or basic equipment. These pieces follow a fixed plane of motion and allow a general user to feel safe and secure when

William A. Cotton, Colorado State University.

Offer a variety of equipment but maintain enough room between each piece to allow easy access.

using the equipment. Consider a full line of selectorized equipment that will complement your selection of more advanced machines. Be sure to include an assortment of machines that enable members to progress through a complete circuit (upper and lower body) for their workout. Typically, a line of 15 to 20 pieces will complete a full circuit line. Table 5.1 shows what machines could be included in the selectorized series.

Do not worry if there are some redundancies in your selectorized, functional, and plate-loaded equipment. The different types of equipment will attract various levels of users. You may also find that members want to be able to cross-train between the various types of strength lines.

• *Free-weight and plate-loaded* pieces are considered intermediate to advanced lines of strength equipment. If members are ready to advance to a wider array of strength training and

conditioning, these pieces will enable users to perform more advanced movements with or without a defined path of motion. Most of the intermediate pieces allow for independent or unilateral movement (or both) that enhances or promotes variety and muscle growth.

• *Functional* strength equipment is considered an advanced line. The advanced line of strength equipment encompasses more of the functional aspects of training by allowing the user to execute an unlimited range of motion, while performing an exercise. **Functional training,** however, is only recommended for more advanced users and should be carefully supervised by trained staff members.

Following are some considerations to make before purchasing strength equipment:

1. Does the equipment have a defined path of motion? You will want to ensure that you have equipment that is appropriate for all levels of users.

2. Are users able to easily identify the weight stack and make proper seat adjustments before using the machine? The beginner line should be user friendly and not overwhelming or intimidating.

3. Do the machines have a recognizable diagram and user instructions? The typical user is not going to ask how to use a machine. Therefore, instructional placards with easy-to-understand diagrams indicating proper form and targeted muscle(s) are essential.

4. How much space does the equipment require?

Table 5.1   Selectorized Series Machines

Area of exertion	Machines
Chest	Incline press, chest press, fly
Back	Pull-down, seated row
Shoulders	Shoulder press, lateral raise
Arms	Biceps curl, triceps extension
Core	Back extension, abdominal crunch, torso rotation
Quadriceps	Leg extension
Hamstrings	Leg curl
Calves	Seated calf raise, standing calf raise
Other	Glute trainer, hip rotator, abduction and adduction

Employees

The core of any great organization is its employees and the skills and strengths they bring with them. Therefore, hiring, training, and evaluating employees are processes critical to the success of any program. A standard interviewing procedure, basic in-house training programs, and a standard evaluation tool should be developed for consistent and adequate fitness center management.

Finding Applicants

A great place to look for employees is in the health, exercise, and wellness departments on campus. These people have the ability to put their academic learning to practical use. Chapter 4 lists other areas to look for qualified applicants.

Interviewing

The interviewing procedure may be linked to the other areas within the department or may be unique to your program. The depth of supervision required for each employee within the fitness area should determine the type of employee to seek.

The level of interaction with patrons, the hands-on knowledge needed, and the required education level should determine the nature of your interview questions. Supervision of the fitness area is often an entry-level position, and key qualities to look for are the same as for other such positions:

- Good work ethic
- Dependability
- Honesty
- Integrity
- Willingness to learn about the area of fitness and wellness

Hiring a Fitness Center Attendant

The level of training for a fitness center attendant depends on the expectations of the job. The position could require basic supervision and implementation of the emergency action plan, or it could involve offering assistance to participants such as spotting or equipment orientations. To ensure that this portion of the program is welcoming, staff should be friendly, be trained in emergency procedures, and have a customer service focus. If the role of the position is to provide assistance with exercises and implement fitness center programs, the training must be more in-depth and include exercise principles, basic anatomy and the biomechanics of exercise, emergency procedures, strength training principles, and proper form and technique in exercises and with equipment.

Most fitness centers will want attendants who are well versed in the area of exercise. This will encourage participants to ask questions related to exercise and feel confident about the people supervising their activity.

Hiring a Group Exercise Instructor

One key to developing a respected and well-attended group exercise program is the hiring, training, and evaluation of the instructional staff. Instructors have a different skill set than employees who work at the front desk or equipment counter.

A fitness director with a strong background in group exercise (having taught classes for many years) will know what makes a good instructor. If the director does not have an adequate background in group exercise, she may look to other area professionals, national fitness organizations such as the American Council on Exercise (ACE) or the Aerobic Fitness Association of America (AFAA) (see sidebar), or current instructors to assist with the hiring process. These resources can provide credentials and skill sets to look for in potential hires.

Although personality traits such as a positive attitude, a sense of responsibility, independence, and good communication skills are sought in people in all positions, instructors need to have basic educational and practical knowledge before they can jump in and teach. If at all possible, a national certification should be required as well as CPR and first aid certification. If a national certification is not easily accessible, substitute an in-house training program. The hiring should include a standard interview, as well as a practical audition. The practical audition would typically include a 10- to 15-minute version of the class type that is going to be taught. Key areas that should be demonstrated are proper warm-up and cool-down, modifications for all exercises, 32-count phrase teaching, and proper cueing techniques. A written examination should also be a component. Include basic exercise principles, the standard format of various classes, basic anatomy, and the biomechanics of exercise.

Depending on the structure of the department, fitness instructors who do not have a lot of practical knowledge or who have unrefined skills may need further training before teaching classes.

Certifying Agencies for Fitness-Related Certifications

Updated June 2007

**Aerobics & Fitness Association
of America (AFAA)**

15250 Ventura Blvd., Suite 200
Sherman Oaks, CA 91403
877-968-7263
www.afaa.com

**American College of Sports Medicine
(ACSM)**

401 W. Michigan St.
Indianapolis, IN 46202-3233
317-637-9200
www.acsm.org

American Council on Exercise (ACE)

4851 Paramount Dr.
Sand Diego, CA 92123
800-825-3636
www.acefitness.org

**Can-Fit-Pro
(Canadian Fitness Professionals Inc.)**

2851 John St.
P.O. Box 42011
Markham, ON l3R 5R7
800-667-5622
www.canfitpro.com

The Cooper Institute

12330 Preston Rd.
Dallas, Texas 75230
800-635-7050
www.cooperint.org

**International Sports Science Association
(ISSA)**

1015 Mark Ave.
Carpenteria, CA 93013
800-892-4772
www.issaonline.com

**National Academy of Sports Medicine
(NASM)**

26632 Agoura Rd.
Calabasas, CA 91302
800-460-6276
www.nasm.org

**National Exercise Trainers Association
(NETA) (formerly NDEITA)**

5955 Golden Valley Rd., Suite 240
Minneapolis, MN 55422
800-237-6242
www.ndeita.com

**National Strength and Conditioning
Association (NSCA)**

1885 Bob Johnson Dr.
Colorado Springs, CO 80906
800-815-6826
www.nsca-lift.org

Powder Blue Productions

23181 Verdugo Dr., Suite 105B
Laguna Hills, CA 92653
800-315-2505
www.turbokick.com

**World Instructor Training Schools
(WITS)**

206 76th St.
Virginia Beach, VA 23451-1915
888-330-9487
www.witseducation.com

YogaFit Training Systems Worldwide

2321 Torrance Blvd.
Torrance, CA 90501
888-786-3111
www.yogafit.com

Keep in mind that group exercise instructors can come from a variety of backgrounds. Unlike with personal trainers, formal education in the area of exercise science is not a necessity. A willingness to learn about the principles of exercise and how to implement these principles is a must, but group exercise instructors must also have the ability to communicate to small and large groups in sometimes intimidating situations.

Hiring a Personal Trainer

The purpose of personal training is to provide one-on-one exercise training that can help individuals reach their personal goals. The overall philosophy of a personal training program is determined by the recreational sport department and by the university. This program can be financially driven to create revenue for the department, or it can be an educational service provided at minimal or no cost to participants. In either case the level of training required of a personal trainer remains constant.

The personal trainer for a campus recreation program should be nationally certified as well as formally educated in the area of exercise science. This will give credibility to the training program and ensure that the personal trainer has knowledge and understanding of exercise principles. If a national certification is not required, then a solid in-house training program should be provided. A standard length of time for a training program is 10 to 15 weeks. This gives ample time to cover all the needed materials and provides the practical training experiences needed to become a well-educated personal trainer who can conduct a basic fitness assessment, develop an exercise program for various fitness levels, and demonstrate proper form and technique.

Even if your program requires personal trainers to have certification and base training, all interviews should include a basic screening process. This keeps the quality of your personal trainers at or above a minimum standard, as well as providing a standard interviewing tool that can be used to offer a fair and equitable interview session. The screening process should include the following:

- Proof of CPR and first aid certification
- Proof of national certification
- Proof of knowledge through written and practical examinations

The written test should address the following subjects:

- Anatomy
- Behavior change
- Biomechanics of exercise
- Exercise physiology
- Exercise program development
- Legal issues, such as risk management
- Fitness assessment procedures and protocol

The practical test should minimally address the development of an exercise program for a healthy person and for a person with risk factors. A fitness assessment component (to be discussed later in this chapter) should also be a part of the interview screening process.

Personal trainers are held to a higher standard than other employees within the fitness and wellness program because of their one-on-one interactions with patrons and the regulation of their educational skill levels. To ensure this skill level, a national certification in personal training should be required.

Personal trainers should be evaluated annually for the sake of their own growth. They should be expected to stay abreast of the research surrounding exercise and health, as well as to maintain appropriate relationships with clients.

An evaluation should consist of an observation of behavior, a practical evaluation similar to the one used in the screening process, and anonymous evaluations from clients. Such an evaluation keeps the program credible and the personal trainers challenged and up-to-date.

Hiring a Presenter for a Wellness Program

Hiring a presenter for a wellness program (see details later in this chapter) is often the trickiest piece of the fitness puzzle. The presenter will typically educate the audience on a health or wellness topic. Unless you have heard the person present at an event, you may not know exactly what her style is and whether she is an effective presenter. Referrals play a role in hiring presenters, but sometimes you just have to take a chance and see whether the person's style fits your audience.

Another tip is to check the content of a presenter's material before the presentation. As the director, you can ask for a wellness presentation outline a few weeks before the event. This gives you time to review the material and make sure that the information the person is going to present is in line with your expectations.

Hiring Other Department Employees

In addition to group exercise instructors, personal trainers, and fitness assessment staff working inside the fitness center, other employees may report to the fitness director, such as dieticians, massage therapists, and specialized instructors. Hiring and training within these areas should be very job and task specific. The credentials of candidates should be collected, and specific interview questions geared toward their specialty should be created. Referrals can also help you determine whether the person is right for the job. In some cases, hands-on interviews can be conducted; a candidate for a massage therapist position can perform a 15-minute massage, or a dietician can create a plan of action for a hypothetical client.

Certification of Employees

The accurate training and certification of employees help provide a safe and effective environment for all users of the facility. The amount of training and the requirement of certifications is a decision to be made within your specific department with the aid of the campus legal professionals. National certifications are always recommended; however, they should not replace a basic in-house training program and screening process.

If at all possible, group exercise instructors and personal trainers should possess a national certification. Before selecting a national certification, you should evaluate the content and testing procedures. Discussing the available certifications with colleagues within the industry, using your past experiences, and researching the certifying agency will help you to decide which certifications to accept.

Following are some questions to ask during this certification evaluation process:

- Does the test include all of the areas of group exercise and personal training that you believe are needed?
- Is only written testing used, or is there a practical component?
- What is the availability of the exam and the cost?

In addition to having a national certification, all fitness and wellness staff should obtain CPR and first aid certifications. Physical activity has inherent risks. Knowing that employees are mindful of these risks and have the basic knowledge required to help a person with an injury or illness will provide a sense of comfort to users of the facility.

Training New Employees

Training employees is a crucial component to managing a fitness and wellness program. These are often the first people patrons come in contact with on a daily basis. To ensure good customer service, a detailed in-house training program should be a priority.

Policies and Procedures of Department Employees

Continual training of employees is necessary to develop a well-respected staff. Training should be provided to employees in all departments, with specialized training available to employees in specific areas of fitness and wellness. Continuing education throughout the year will also help to build the staff as a team, which in turn will make the program stronger. All department policies and expectations should be discussed with new employees as well as during all staff trainings.

Policies and procedures are important for consistency within the fitness department, and a checklist is helpful during staff training to be sure everything is addressed (see figure 5.2). Staff members and participants should be able to easily ascertain why the policies and procedures are in place. Consistency provides the stability and reliability that participants need from the fitness program.

Developing department policies is really up to the fitness director. Procedures are used as a guide or road map for the group exercise staff to follow from the moment they enter the building to the time they leave. Following is an example of a fitness center policy:

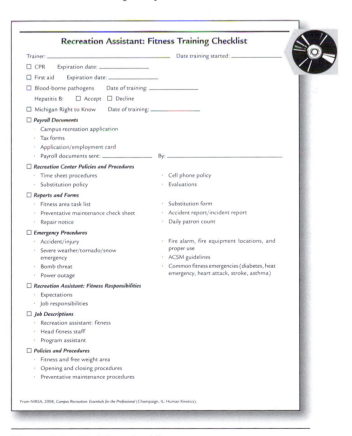

Figure 5.2 Training checklist.

Shift substitutions: If an employee is unable to work, it is his or her responsibility to find a substitute from the current list of employees. Employees must notify the fitness director when a substitution is made—at least one day before the shift. A no-show for the shift is unacceptable and would be subject to the disciplinary policy.

Following are other procedural items that might be included in a policy for fitness area employees:

- Being available 10 minutes before or after the class or shift to answer questions
- Checking out keys
- Clocking in
- Filling in attendance sheets

Give careful thought to how the department should operate with respect to the following:

- Attendance
- Certifications
- Communication
- In-service training
- Music selection for group exercise
- Pay raises
- Required apparel
- Scheduling
- Substitutions

In-House Fitness Training Programs

An in-house training program should be ongoing and given to all staff on a semester basis. This will ensure that everyone refreshes his or her skill set at least twice a year.

In-house training programs are developed based on the need within the department. Training programs will vary slightly for fitness attendants, group exercise instructors, and personal trainers, but at a minimum, all should cover departmental policies and procedures, as well as the educational knowledge and practical skills that every employee needs. Depending on the demographics of the college or university, national certifications or training workshops may or may not be available.

Group exercise instructors will benefit from conducting a mock class with the other trainees playing the role of students. This a valuable way to help new instructors with the nervousness, or "jitters," they may experience in front of a class.

The main goal of in-house training is to help employees feel comfortable and well trained in their working environments. Feeling confident within the area of fitness takes time, and the staff needs to be given the tools to succeed. A good training program gives employees the confidence to answer questions and create a safe and effective fitness program.

The length of a training program depends on how much time is available to dedicate to new employees as well as the level of training expected for the job. Although the job description of the fitness employee determines the type of in-house training, all in-house training should minimally include the following:

- Anatomy
- Biomechanics of exercise
- Emergency procedures
- Practical and written examinations for learning the muscles of the body
- Exercise physiology
- Exercise program development
- Expectations
- Fitness assessment testing
- Health appraisal
- Human behavior
- Legal responsibilities
- Department procedures
- Proper use of equipment
- Safety and injury management (i.e., risk management)
- Spotting techniques, if applicable
- University and department policies

Resources from the American College of Sports Medicine (ACSM), the American Council on Exercise (ACE), and the National Strength and Conditioning Association (NSCA) can help in the development of an outline for an in-house training program.

Team Teaching

Team teaching is a great component of the in-house training program. In team teaching, a new instructor works with a solid veteran instructor during scheduled classes. Each week they gradually begin to teach various parts of the class. This process allows the new instructor to implement small components of the class, meanwhile gaining confidence leading the group. The team teaching approach is a way to coach a new instructor who has a good educational background or a recent national certification on how to implement a class from start to finish.

Team teaching is good for both the trainee and the trainer. The added responsibility of training is a way to reward staff members who have demonstrated exceptional teaching ability and a high level of commitment to the department. Additionally, a contract including expectations and a specific training calendar should be followed.

This format can also be used for fitness attendants. Seasoned employees can have the responsibility of gradually introducing new hires to the fitness center and their responsibilities.

Employee Evaluations

An evaluation is a necessary and valuable tool to help all employees adapt and grow. It is a time to reiterate the expectations of the department, provide positive feedback, and offer constructive criticism to help improve the quality of their performance. **Employee evaluations** should occur at least once a year. This can also be a time to give rewards in the form of pay raises and other job perks.

An evaluation should be a one-on-one interaction between the supervisor and the employee. It can include a practical format, such as an audit of the person's work, or a written quiz and a review of basic work principles such as the following:

- Customer service
- Initiative
- Job knowledge
- Leadership
- Teamwork
- Timeliness

If changes need to be made in the employee's performance, this is the time to convey that information in a constructive way. Employees need to know how they are doing on the job. If they are not told they are doing well or where they need to do better, they will not have the tools to improve their overall job performance.

The goal of an evaluation is to identify areas that need refinement or additional training and improve the effectiveness of the employee. The evaluation tool that is used for fitness employees depends on their job description. A fitness attendant would not be evaluated on the same items as a personal trainer or a group exercise instructor.

An evaluation of a group exercise instructor would include the following practical items:

- Class content
- Cueing ability
- Department policies
- Interaction with participants
- Motivation

Because group exercise instruction varies from cardiorespiratory to strength and mind–body classes, instructors should not all be evaluated in a similar manner. Each type of class has a unique goal. For example, helping participants progress toward working in their target heart rate range might be a goal in a group cycling class, but not in a traditional yoga class. Therefore, different evaluation tools should be available to evaluate each class type effectively. See figures 5.3 through 5.5.

All instructors should be evaluated throughout their tenure in the department. New instructors should be evaluated the first semester or quarter of instructing, and all should be evaluated a minimum of once a year. Additionally, instructors who teach several class formats should be evaluated for each format.

Fitness Instructor Evaluation

Name ________________ Date ________

Class type ________ Evaluator ________________

CPR expiration ________ Years experience ________

Education/certifications and dates ________________

____

____

Instructor preparation	Score	Comments
Arrived >10 minutes before class		
Prepared music, tested mic, turned on lights, opened door 10 minutes before class		
Dressed appropriately		
Visited with and/or greeted participants		
Had a friendly and approachable attitude		
Helped new participants become oriented to the class		
The introduction was informative and complete (name, class type, if injured . . .)		
Read announcements		
Started class on time ___ : ___ ___ a.m./p.m.		

Class instruction	Score	Comments
Warm-up was adequate (increased HR, breathing, ROM)		
Followed correct class format as listed in class description		
Gradually increased intensity		
Emphasized form, injury prevention, alignment, and safety		
Demonstrated modifications for a variety of skill levels		
Broke down complex movements or combinations		
Monitored the intensity of the class with HR, RPE, talk test, or other appropriate method		
Reminded participants to work at their own levels		
Used proper variations of exercise selection and intensity		
Cues were precise, to the point, and given in advance (verbal and hand signals)		

From NIRSA, 2008, *Campus Recreation: Essentials for the Professional* (Champaign, IL: Human Kinetics).

Figure 5.3 Fitness instructor evaluation.

Pilates and Yoga Instructor Evaluation

Name ________________ Date ________

Class type ________ Evaluator ________________

CPR expiration ________ Years experience ________

Education/certifications and dates ________________

Instructor preparation	Score	Comments
Arrived >10 minutes before class		
Prepared music, tested mic, turned on lights, opened door 10 minutes before class		
Dressed appropriately		
Visited with and/or greeted participants		
Had a friendly and approachable attitude		
Helped new participants become oriented to the class		
The introduction was informative and complete (name, class type, if injured . . .)		
Read announcements		
Started class on time ___ : ___ ___ a.m./p.m.		

Class instruction	Score	Comments
Followed correct class format as listed in class description		
Gradually increased intensity, difficulty, and range of motion		
Placed continuous emphasis on form, injury prevention, alignment, and safety		
Demonstrated modifications		
Proper breathing was cued with movements and described at the beginning of class		
Promoted inward awareness		
Cues were easy to understand		

From NIRSA, 2008, *Campus Recreation: Essentials for the Professional* (Champaign, IL: Human Kinetics).

Figure 5.4 Pilates and yoga instructor evaluation.

Precision Cycling Instructor Evaluation

Name ________________ Date ________

Class type ________ Evaluator ________________

CPR expiration ________ Years experience ________

Education/certifications and dates ________________

Instructor preparation	Score	Comments
Prepared music, tested mic, turned on lights, opened door 10 minutes before class		
Dressed appropriately		
Visited with and/or greeted participants		
Had a friendly and approachable attitude		
Helped new participants become oriented to the class contents and bike setup		
The introduction was informative and complete (name, class type, if injured . . .)		
Read announcements		
Made sure all participants had water		
Started class on time ___ : ___ ___ a.m./p.m.		

Class instruction	Score	Comments
Warm-up was adequate (increased HR and breathing)		
Followed correct class format as listed in class description		
Gradually increased intensity		
Repeatedly emphasized form, injury prevention, alignment, and safety		
All cycling actions performed in class were logical and safe		
Monitored the intensity of the class with HR, RPE, talk test, or other appropriate method		
Reminded participants to work at their own levels		
Used proper variations of cycling action selection and intensity		
Cues were precise, to the point, and given in advance		
Transitions were smooth and logical		

From NIRSA, 2008, *Campus Recreation: Essentials for the Professional* (Champaign, IL: Human Kinetics).

Figure 5.5 Precision cycling instructor evaluation.

Participants

After focusing on the fitness center and your employees, you need to focus on the most essential part of your program: participants. In this section, we'll discuss fitness assessments and personal training.

Fitness Assessments

Health screening is the vital process of identifying people at high risk for exercise-induced heart problems and then referring them to appropriate medical care (American College of Sports Medicine and American Heart Association, 1998). According to the American Heart Association, more than one-fourth of all Americans have some form of cardiovascular disease (including high blood pressure), and the prevalence rises with age (American Heart Association, 1998).

The purpose of fitness assessments is to provide participants with information about their current fitness levels. This information is used to encourage participants to set realistic fitness goals and to enhance the ability of personal trainers to prescribe appropriate aerobic, flexibility, and resistance training programs. A fitness assessment **protocol** should include the following:

- Measurements of cardiorespiratory fitness
- Flexibility
- **Body composition**
- Muscular fitness

It is imperative that these protocols be administered in accordance with professionally derived standards to ensure the reliability and validity of results. Standard protocols for exercise testing can be found in the American College of Sports Medicine's (ACSM's) *Guidelines for Exercise Testing and Prescription,* seventh edition (2006). Following are the basic services provided in a fitness assessment:

- Body composition
- Flexibility assessment
- Height and weight
- Individual consultation
- Muscular endurance assessment

- Muscular strength assessment
- Resting blood pressure
- Resting heart rate
- Submaximal cardiorespiratory endurance test
- Waist-to-hip ratio

According to *ACSM's Health/Fitness Facility Standards and Guidelines* (1997), all of these assessments must be conducted by people who have the following credentials:

- College degree in health and fitness or a related exercise science field
- Current cardiopulmonary resuscitation certification
- Current professional certification from a nationally recognized organization in the health and fitness industry

A fitness assessment program in a collegiate setting can provide senior interns, graduate students, and practicum students with a valuable learning experience in a practical setting, provided they have the previously mentioned credentials. Such programs provide people with baseline values of their current physical health, including, but not limited to, cardiorespiratory endurance, muscular strength and endurance, body composition, flexibility, and blood pressure. To ensure you are getting the best student help available, create a collaborative effort on campus between your department and the various departments that provide exercise-related courses.

Pretest Procedures

Regardless of the amount of training staff members have had in the past, the information in this section is crucial to running a safe and efficient fitness assessment program.

According to ACSM's *Health/Fitness Facility Standards and Guidelines* (1997), a facility must offer each adult member a preactivity screening that is appropriate for the physical activities that the member will eventually perform.

Following are the steps to follow before beginning the testing of a participant:

1. Give all of the pretest instructions to the participant before making an appointment for the actual test.

2. The following information should be gathered prior to the actual fitness assessment. The assessment should not be conducted until all of this information is gathered and placed in the participant's file.

- Clearance form
- Health history questionnaire
- **Informed consent agreement**
- Membership category
- Personal training referral
- Physician's statement
- Emergency contact person

3. Let the participants know that all results obtained from the fitness assessment are strictly confidential.

4. Inform the participants that they may request to stop the test at any time.

5. Ask the participants if they have been tested previously. If so, comparing test results during the consultation can be valuable because those results will show where there has been improvement or where more focus is needed.

6. Anyone can experience a heart attack or stroke at any time; therefore, it is imperative that every staff member knows how to recognize and manage a heart attack or stroke victim. Early

Physician's Release for Activity

_____ has recently enrolled for membership at East Side/West Side Athletic Clubs. The club membership includes two complimentary orientation sessions with our qualified fitness professionals (degreed and/or certified in the field), as well as the opportunity to participate in numerous group fitness classes and individual programs.

On completion of the PAR-Q (Physical Activity Readiness Questionnaire), it has been determined that this new member is best served by additional or supplemental recommendations by his or her primary care provider.

Please take the time to review your client's medical history and the PAR-Q accompanying this request. If he/she can be released for physical activity, please complete the information below and let us know if there are any modifications or special needs.

Member's signature for release of information _____

Date _____

Club staff faxing this information (print name) _____

As a physician, it is my understanding that the person listed above wishes to participate in physical activity at the Club and has been referred to myself (his/her physician) before beginning a regular program. Here are my specific recommendations and/or comments regarding this new member and his/her involvement in an exercise program:

_____
_____
_____
_____
_____

Physician's printed name _____ Date _____

Physician's signature _____

From NIRSA, 2008, *Campus Recreation: Essentials for the Professional* (Champaign, IL: Human Kinetics). Reprinted, by permission, from East Side Athletic Club.

Figure 5.6 Physician's release for activity.

intervention is essential to survival. Many fatalities occur before the victim reaches the hospital; these deaths might have been prevented if someone had recognized the signs and responded quickly.

7. Confirm the age of the participant to see whether a physician's clearance is necessary. Any male participant older than 45 and any female participant older than 55 falls in the moderate risk category of ACSM's **risk stratification** for disease prevalence (American College of Sports Medicine, 2007) and should be required to submit a **physician's statement** and clearance form (see figure 5.6).

8. Review the physician's statement with the participant to determine whether the doctor should be consulted before the participant's fitness assessment.

9. Have the participant fill out the Physical Activity Readiness Questionnaire, or **PAR-Q**—a commonly used prescreening assessment for low to moderate physical activity that was created by Canadian researchers in the 1970s and then adopted by the Canadian Society of Exercise Physiology in 1996 (see figure 5.7).

10. You may also use a **medical information** sheet (see figure 5.8) to gather specific information about the participant's health and exercise habits.

11. Inform all participants of the risk of having a fitness test, the discomfort they may experience during the fitness assessment, and the soreness they may have the following day. It is recommended that participants under the age of 18 obtain parental consent by filling out an informed consent for voluntary fitness evaluation form (see figure 5.9) before participating in a fitness assessment. The participant's legal guardian must sign this form. If the participant is over 18, the form should be explained clearly, and the participant given ample opportunity to read it on her own. The participant should sign the consent form, and the staff member should witness her signature.

Fitness Assessment Area

It is important to have a fitness assessment area that is private and comfortable for participants in order to maintain testing reliability and validity. To reduce feelings of anxiety and uncertainty, those conducting the assessment should explain all of the testing procedures to participants before

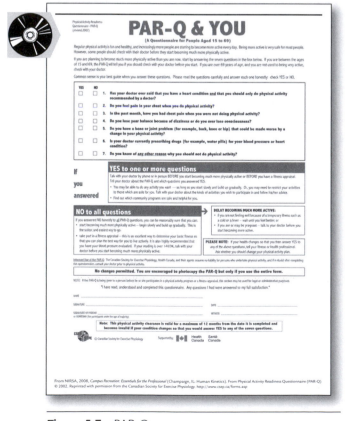

Figure 5.7 PAR-Q.

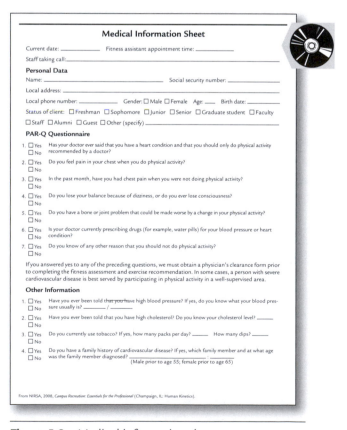

Figure 5.8 Medical information sheet.

Name of University or Department

Informed Consent Agreement

Name ____________________

The purpose of the fitness testing program is to evaluate cardiorespiratory fitness, body composition, flexibility, and muscular strength and endurance. The cardiorespiratory fitness test involves a submaximal cycle ergometry test using the YMCA protocol. Body composition is analyzed using skinfold calipers for predicting percent body fat. Flexibility is determined by the sit-and-reach test. Muscular endurance and strength is determined by an isometric biceps curl.

I understand and have been informed that there exists the remote possibility of adverse changes occurring during exercise including, but not limited to, abnormal blood pressure; fainting; dizziness; heart rhythm disorder; and very rare instances of heart attack, stroke, or even death. I further understand and I have been informed that there exists the risk of bodily injury including, but not limited to, injuries to the muscles, ligaments, tendons, and joints of the body. I have been told that every effort will be made to minimize these occurrences by proper staff assessments of my condition before each exercise session, by staff supervision during the exercise, and by my own careful control of exercise efforts. I fully understand the risks associated with the following procedures and it is my desire to participate as herein indicated.

I have been given the opportunity to ask questions regarding the procedures of this program. These questions have been answered to my satisfaction.

____________________ (Signature of participant) ____________________ (Date)

____________________ (Signature of person administering tests) ____________________ (Date)

Figure 5.9 Informed consent agreement.

Emergency procedures	
Dial 911	Explain exact location of the injured party, circumstances, and the number of injured people. Inform the dispatcher that a staff member will be outside to meet the ambulance. Our location is: (Insert location here)
Notify the supervisor on duty of the emergency	Have the supervisor call your campus police department at (____________) to inform them of the situation and that an ambulance has been called. Have the supervisor go outside to meet the ambulance.
Stay with the injured party at all times	Be prepared to perform CPR if necessary.
Complete an accident report form	Immediately after the emergency is over, complete and sign an accident report form.

Figure 5.10 Emergency procedures.

the assessment begins. They should also make sure that all equipment is maintained properly and cleaned after every assessment.

Cardiorespiratory Testing

The cardiorespiratory test measures a participant's aerobic capacity. The test can be either maximal or submaximal—which to use depends on the reason for the test and the availability of appropriate equipment and personnel. Maximal tests require a participant to exercise to the point of voluntary fatigue and are typically conducted under medical supervision. In recreation facilities, a **submaximal cardiorespiratory test** is preferred. A variety of equipment can be used for a submaximal test, including cycle ergometers, treadmills, walking tracks, and steps. Furthermore, within each of these tests there are different protocols that can be used to suit the needs of the participant. Which specific test to use will depend on the equipment needed and the employee's expertise and training. A complete description of the protocols and exercise testing procedures can be found in chapter 4 of the American College of Sports Medicine's *ASCM's Guidelines for Exercise Testing and Prescription.* It is highly recommended that these guidelines be followed in order to ensure that the testing is done correctly and completely. If the participant is injured or experiences any other **contraindication** during the assessment, follow the **emergency procedures** listed in figure 5.10.

Individual Consultation

On completion of a fitness assessment, a one-on-one consultation should be performed, with the participant's fitness level, goals, and knowledge of exercise taken into consideration. The consultation is an important component of the fitness assessment. During this session, all the results are covered and strategies for reaching individual goals are developed. The staff member should always be thoroughly aware of what the participant wants and why she is having a fitness assessment. It is imperative that staff be trained to tactfully explain the results of the assessments and how the participant can improve her results in a safe and efficient manner (see figure 5.11). If the participant chooses not to attend a consultation, she should be given the completed fitness assessment results packet (figure 5.12) to read at home. If your fitness assessment program uses software such as MicroFit or Polar, the participant

Figure 5.11 Health and fitness goals.

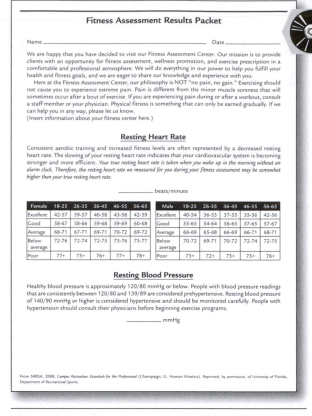

Figure 5.12 Fitness assessment results packet.

can receive a printout of the results immediately after the appointment.

Participant Results and Fitness Assessment Norms

The staff member should fill out the information gathered from the testing and measuring of the participant and use the fitness assessment norms tables to rank the participant's scores for each assessment. The staff member should then place each score on a continuum within the following three categories: *low* for below average, *healthy* for average, and *high* for above average. He should write the norms for each of the three categories under the continuum.

The staff member may want to go over with the participant any of the following during the consultation:

- Cardiorespiratory training (figure 5.13)
- Resistance training (figure 5.14)
- Basic nutrition recommendations (figure 5.15)
- **Exercise prescription** examples
- Goal setting (figure 5.11)

Figure 5.13 Cardiorespiratory training.

Resistance Training

Before beginning any resistance training program, remember to warm up for at least five minutes with light activity and to stretch your major muscle groups to reduce your risk of injury. At the completion of your program, you should again stretch all of your major muscle groups to maintain flexibility. Resistance training is an important part of any fitness program. The improvements made in endurance, strength, and overall health are an incentive to those who are just starting to work out. If your goal is to decrease body fat, resistance training will increase your muscle mass and therefore increase your resting metabolism. Resistance training can be done with free weights, selectorized equipment such as Nautilus or MedX, or through total body group exercise sessions. The following definitions and tips will help you to develop your own resistance training program.

Overload principle. For improvements to occur in strength or endurance, the muscles must be taxed beyond their accustomed loads.

Progressive resistance principle. The amount of weight that the muscle lifts must periodically be increased to make continued improvements in strength and endurance.

Specificity of training. For a muscle to increase in strength or endurance, resistance training exercises must use that specific muscle.

Principle of order. To achieve the most from a resistance training workout, larger muscle groups should be exercised before progressing to the smaller muscle groups. Exercising large muscle groups first is suggested to avoid premature fatigue of the smaller muscle groups. If you work your smaller muscles first, you limit the amount of work accomplished by larger muscle groups. Abdominal and low back exercises should be performed at the end of your training session. This will allow your abdominal and low back muscles to give your body sufficient support throughout your workout.

Repetitions and sets. A repetition is defined as one complete movement through a full range of motion during a weight training exercise. A set is the number of repetitions performed consecutively for a given weight training exercise without resting. The amount of repetitions and sets you should perform for a specific exercise will depend on your goals.

Types of Resistance Training Programs

	Endurance		Fitness	Hypertrophy	General Strength	Maximal Strength	Power	
Load/intensity	50%	60%	70%	75% 80%	85%	90%	95% 100%
Reps	20	15	12	10 8	6	4	2 1
Sets	1-3		1-3	3-6	3-5	3-5	3-8
Rest between sets	15-60 sec		1-2 min	1-3 min	2-3 min	3-5 min	3-8 min
Exercise/ body part	1-3		1-3	3-4	2-3	1-2	
Days/week	2-3		2-3	3-6	2-4	2-4	1-5
Muscular failure	Low to moderate		Moderate	High	Moderate to high	Moderate to high	Low to moderate

Important Guidelines

1. For improvements to occur, you must perform a resistance training routine at least twice a week.
2. More is not better. Without sufficient rest between workouts, you increase your risk of injury, because your muscles will be unable to repair themselves. A minimum of 48 hours between workouts for the same muscle groups is suggested.

From NIRSA, 2008, *Campus Recreation: Essentials for the Professional* (Champaign, IL: Human Kinetics). Reprinted, by permission, of University of Florida, Department of Recreational Sports.

Figure 5.14 Resistance training.

Basic Nutrition Recommendations

Nutrition is an important component of health and wellness and serves as a foundation for improving fitness and optimizing athletic performance. Although there is no one perfect diet, key building blocks to any healthy eating plan include adequacy, balance, variety, moderation, and enjoyment. Use the Food Guide Pyramid below to steer your eating habits (www.mypyramid.gov).

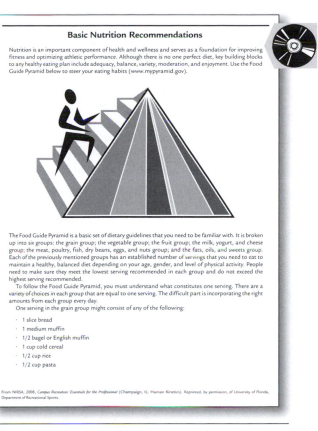

The Food Guide Pyramid is a basic set of dietary guidelines that you need to be familiar with. It is broken up into six groups: the grain group; the vegetable group; the fruit group; the milk, yogurt, and cheese group; the meat, poultry, fish, dry beans, eggs, and nuts group; and the fats, oils, and sweets group. Each of the previously mentioned groups has an established number of servings that you need to eat to maintain a healthy, balanced diet depending on your age, gender, and level of physical activity. People need to make sure they meet the lowest serving recommended in each group and do not exceed the highest serving recommended.

To follow the Food Guide Pyramid, you must understand what constitutes one serving. There are a variety of choices in each group that are equal to one serving. The difficult part is incorporating the right amounts from each group every day.

One serving in the grain group might consist of any of the following:

- 1 slice bread
- 1 medium muffin
- 1/2 bagel or English muffin
- 1 cup cold cereal
- 1/2 cup rice
- 1/2 cup pasta

From NIRSA, 2008, *Campus Recreation: Essentials for the Professional* (Champaign, IL: Human Kinetics). Reprinted, by permission, of University of Florida, Department of Recreational Sports.

Figure 5.15 Basic nutrition recommendations.

Personal Training

If your program offers personal training, you may want to refer participants from the fitness assessment program to personal training. If so, the staff member should provide information on the personal training program and have the participant complete a personal training referral form (see figure 5.16) after the fitness assessment or during the consultation. All information on the PAR-Q and health history questionnaires should be transferred directly to the personal training referral form, including all written comments and who wrote the comments.

Personal training is a great component to have in your campus recreation program. The overall philosophy of a personal training program is determined by the recreation department and by the university. The program can be used to create revenue for the department, or it can be provided for a small fee or at no cost as an educational service. The level of training required of a personal trainer remains constant, regardless of the philosophy used to support the program.

Personal Training Referral Form

Appt. date: _____ Appt. time: _____ Trainer: _____

Name: _____ Today's date: _____

Member ID#: _____ Member type (circle): Student Staff Faculty

Phone #: (H) _____ (W) _____ Academic year (circle): FR SO JR SR GRAD

E-mail: _____ Emergency contact (name, relationship, phone):

Date of birth: _____ Gender: _____

Place of residence (please circle one): Residence hall / off-campus / university apartments / Greek house

Ethnicity (*optional*) (please circle one): African American / Asian American / Hispanic American / Native American / White American / Non-American / Other: _____

1. Please place an X next to any of the following conditions that you have experienced.

Heart disease	Cholesterol over 260	Hernia
Rheumatic disease	Diagnosed hypoglycemia	Cancer
Chest pain	High blood pressure	Arthritis
Heart attack	Heart murmurs	Lung disease (asthma, emphysema)
Stroke	Frequent lightheadedness or fainting	Frequent or severe back pain
Epilepsy/seizure disorder	Joint, tendon, or muscle pain	Severe shortness of breath
Diabetes	Irregular heartbeats	Bulimia/anorexia

Other conditions not listed: _____

Please explain any conditions you marked with an X: _____

2. Please list and explain any medical conditions, including surgery, for which a physician has ever recommended restrictions on activity: _____

3. Please list any medications you take regularly and the reason for taking them: _____

To provide you with a safe and effective exercise program, the information on this form should be true to the best of your knowledge. If this questionnaire accurately reflects your health history and all medical limitations that may affect your personal training appointment, please sign below:

_____ _____ _____ _____
Client's signature   Date   Staff signature   Date

Personal Trainer Comments:

From NIRSA, 2008, *Campus Recreation: Essentials for the Professional* (Champaign, IL: Human Kinetics). Reprinted, by permission, of University of Florida, Department of Recreational Sports.

Figure 5.16 Personal training referral form.

Recruitment and Retention of Clients

Recreation programs should use the number of clients and the ability to retain those clients as gauges of the success of personal training programs. The marketing of the program will happen through the department resources as well as through the personal trainers themselves. (See additional information on advertising and marketing in chapters 4 and 12.) However, word of mouth plays a much larger role in obtaining clients than any flyer posted.

The retention of clients is just as important as recruitment. Personal trainers should strive to have returning clientele, because the more clients that are retained, the more the overall personal training program will grow.

Personal trainers can be rewarded based on their retention of clients, or client retention can be an expectation of their overall job. Client quotas can be another component of recruitment and retention. During the hiring of a personal trainer, a director can establish a quota of clients per week with the input of the new hire. This would then become part of the job requirement and the yearly evaluation.

Visibility

The more visible personal trainers are within the fitness area, the more curious patrons become about their abilities. A personal trainer who sits behind a desk will not gain the respect of the patrons as quickly as the trainer who is obviously providing exercise assistance on a regular basis. Personal trainers should wear attire that identifies them as personal trainers while using the fitness areas themselves; this helps promote their education and knowledge.

Forms and Paperwork for Personal Training Clients

The initial screening of personal training clients begins with the fitness assessment procedures discussed previously. All of the forms and testing protocols discussed in that section should be followed.

Clients referred to the personal training program complete a personal training referral form (see figure 5.16). This form, along with the fitness assessment results (see figure 5.12), is routed to the person responsible for pairing clients and personal trainers. A personal training referral form may also include the following items:

- Likes and dislikes of equipment
- Likes and dislikes of types of exercise

- Number of times a week and which days of the week training will occur
- Preference for male or female trainer
- Times for the training

The client should also complete a goal-setting form (see figure 5.11). This goes into more detail about the client's specific goals and his purpose for hiring a personal trainer. For example, if a client's main purpose is to train for a marathon, pairing him with a trainer who has a strength in marathon training will likely result in a positive experience for both the client and the trainer.

A client–personal trainer **contract** form should also be distributed (see figure 5.17). This contract may include the following items:

- Canceling and no-show policies
- Expectations in behavior from the client and the personal trainer
- Facility policies and procedures
- Steps to take if dissatisfied with the training program

The result of any personal training should be a positive experience on the part of the client. In

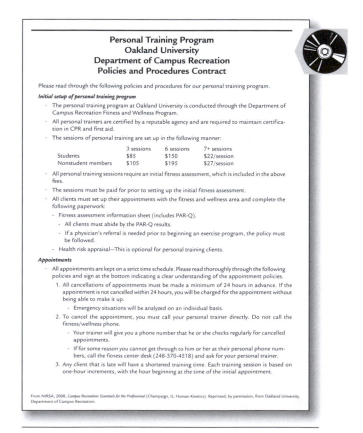

Figure 5.17 Client–personal trainer contract form.

some cases, however, the pairing of a client and trainer may not be ideal. Keep in mind that clients, as well as trainers, should be held to expectations. Depending on the severity of a situation, a client can be transferred to a new trainer or dismissed altogether. In any situation, the trainer should be held accountable for acting as a professional, and the client should be held accountable for acting in a civil and appropriate manner.

Wellness Programs

Wellness is a dynamic process of becoming aware of and making conscious choices about a balanced and healthy lifestyle. It includes learning new coping skills that address both the positive and negative aspects of life and balancing all six dimensions of wellness (National Wellness Institute, n.d.).

1. **Physical wellness.** Physical wellness focuses on taking care of the body through education, disease prevention, and the management of illness and injury. It encourages participation in regular activities and a lifestyle that promotes optimal health.

2. **Spiritual wellness.** Spiritual wellness focuses on having a guided sense of meaning or value in life as well as an understanding of and ability to express one's purpose in life. It addresses values and ethics and the degree to which one's actions are consistent with one's values.

3. **Intellectual wellness.** Intellectual wellness focuses on stimulating the mind through activities that are mentally challenging and nurtures a sense of being internally energized. It encourages continued learning and the ability to grow from experiences, especially through problem solving and decision making.

4. **Social wellness.** Social wellness involves contributing to the human and physical environment for the betterment of the community. It includes participation in activities that help to develop healthy relationships while enhancing the ability to enjoy social situations.

5. **Emotional wellness.** Emotional wellness refers to the ability to express feelings in an appropriate manner. It encourages participating in activities that focus on emotional self-care, including relaxation, managing stress, building self-confidence, and developing inner resources. It includes an awareness and acceptance of one's own feelings and the feelings of others.

6. **Occupational wellness.** Occupational wellness focuses on taking pride in one's work as well as maintaining a healthy balance between work and leisure. It encourages participation in activities that build skills for excelling in the workplace, including people skills and planning for the future.

Key Components of a Wellness Program

Educating and enhancing the experience of participants in all aspects of health and wellness are essential for campus recreation professionals. Offering diverse programs that fall into the wellness dimensions helps meet the needs of all people who enter the facility. However, creating a wellness program can be overwhelming. Its success will not happen without collaborating with other departments, planning for a diverse audience, and offering current topics that reflect the latest research.

Wellness Committee

A wellness committee is typically made up of people on campus who fall into one or more of the dimensions of wellness as well as student affairs and human resources professionals. Such a diversity of people on the committee is helpful in providing programs that cover all dimensions of wellness. Collaboration is a key component in the development of successful wellness programs. Taking the initiative to create relationships with professionals throughout the campus, as well as with wellness ambassadors in the community, enhances the development of the overall program.

Collaboration also means that not all wellness programs have to be sponsored or developed by the campus recreation program. Organizations on campus specifically oriented toward the areas of spirituality and emotional well-being might better serve as the sponsors of programs within these components of wellness. Collaboration can also include marketing through a variety of media and developing relationships that foster positive relationships throughout campus.

Planning for a Diverse Audience

Campus recreation programs serve diverse populations with a variety of wellness needs. To meet those needs, administrators must keep the audience in mind. An incoming freshman will not look at wellness in the same way as an employee of the university will, nor will she have the same needs.

Scheduling must also take into account diverse populations. A noon event may attract a completely different crowd than an evening event will. Although the two events may deliver the same message, the way the message is sent will differ. For example, if you were providing a nutrition-based program, noon attendees may include working people who want information on how to cook healthy foods while the evening presentation may be targeted at students, focusing on healthy eating in the campus dining halls. In the initial stages of program development, determining the market you are trying to reach and designing the program accordingly will create the most effective presentations.

Current Topics

The final component to developing creative wellness programs is to keep up with current topics and the latest research. Campus recreation is often a safe and inviting place for people to learn new life skills. Using professionals who are well educated in the following subjects will help the program become reputable and well attended:

- Cancer research
- Emotional well-being
- Holistic health
- Spirituality
- Stress

Wellness Programming

Even though campus recreation programs are initially built for the students of the college or university, other people are often allowed to purchase memberships. Faculty, staff, alumni, donors, and their respective families are some of the "other" user groups. Some facilities are even open to the general community. The scope of program offerings should be broad enough to meet the needs of the various clientele.

A bonus of offering programs to the following populations is bringing people into the facility at traditionally low-use times. Youth tend to use the facility on the weekends and during the summer months, for example, and seniors traditionally prefer early morning programs.

Youth Programs

Youth programming can be a way to entice non-traditional members to join the facility. Day camps, sport-specific camps, teen fitness pro-grams, and youth swimming lessons are great additions to campus recreation programs. Any offering that allows families to recreate together is a membership perk. Depending on the structure of the department, the program coordination may fall to the fitness department.

Senior Programs

Seniors represent another population to take a closer look at as a nontraditional user group. There is power in numbers. As a group, seniors have tremendous economic and political clout.

The older population (people 65 years or older) numbered 35.9 million in 2003 (the latest year for which data are available). It represented 12.4 percent of the U.S. population, or about one in every eight Americans. By 2030 there will be about 71.5 million older people (more than twice the number in 2000). This number of older adults is expected to be 20 percent of the population by 2030. The U.S. population is also living longer. In 2002 the life expectancy in the United States was the highest ever—77.4 years—for both men and women of all races, and it is continuing in an upward trend (U.S. Department of Health and Human Services Administration on Aging, n.d.).

Seniors with good health and lifestyle habits should fare significantly better than those with a more sedentary lifestyle. Promoting good nutrition and exercise can make the extra years more enjoyable (About, Inc., a part of the New York Times Company, n.d.).

With senior, or "mature adult," programming, the overall facility operation must be reviewed. The following should be discussed before implementing a senior fitness program:

- Do instructors have the desire to learn appropriate modifications for this population? (See www.asaging.org/students for information on the growth in future careers for an aging population.)
- Are the emergency action plan and staff training adequate to handle this population?
- Is the facility accessible to people with physical limitations?

Following are programs that can be developed for the senior population:

- Balance classes
- Blood pressure screenings
- Chair aerobics

- Low-impact aerobics
- Nutrition (See www.aarp.org/health/ Articles/a2003-03-10-diet.html for diet and exercise tips.)
- Stretching
- Tai chi
- Walking programs
- Yoga for seniors

Although many recreation facilities may not provide programming specific to seniors with advanced physical limitations, every facility has the opportunity to offer programs geared toward a healthy senior population.

Employee Wellness Programs

Employees represent another population that would benefit from wellness programs. Depending on the structure of the department, this program can be created in collaboration with the human resources department. The program may be an incentive-based program tied to the benefit system or just classes limited to faculty and staff. Programs that are offered often include those specific to the demographics of faculty and staff, such as ergonomics of a workstation, nutrition, caring for aging parents, communication within the workplace, and exercise for health.

Specialty Programs

Specialty programs, sometimes called mind–body programs, are another type of program that could be offered through the fitness department. These programs include Pilates, yoga, stress management, martial arts, massage, acupressure, reflexology, physical therapy, and nutrition. The list is endless depending on the focus of the program. The key is to offer programs that are relevant to the target population and that are on the cutting edge of the fitness and wellness industry. What this means is that a fitness director must keep up with the latest trends and research to maintain an effective fitness and wellness program.

Trends and Research

The opportunities available in fitness and wellness programs are astounding. There has been an explosion of variety in the last decade. Where once only hi/lo, step, and water aerobics were available on the aerobics schedule, now there is cycling, Pilates, yoga, core, kickboxing, and more. Fitness center programming has increased as well. Whereas a drop-in fitness center used to be the

norm, now classes are offered in the weight room to ensure that users are educated and comfortable in the environment. Such expansion is necessary for programs to survive, but it can come with its share of difficulties.

Fitness directors need to continually be versed in many class formats and have the ability to hire good instructors. Classes taught within a fitness center could include women on weights, free weight clinics, equipment orientations, exercise 101, interval training, circuit training, or trekking. Before adding classes to the schedule, be sure the instructors have the tools to deliver good instruction. Information should include the following:

- Breakdown of class in terms of timing
- Appropriate music tempo if music is used
- Class type and length
- Description of the class
- What the class should cover

The trend in the area of fitness is to offer something for everyone. In today's campus recreation market, facilities must be able to compete with the local clubs to attract users above and beyond the traditional student. Because most facilities offer membership to nontraditional users, programs must be provided to meet the needs of these groups. This is an excellent opportunity for the employees of the department to become well versed in customer service for a variety of age groups.

Conclusion

Fitness and wellness programs are on the increase, not the decline. In addition, as people live longer, the need for these will only get greater. Carol Kennedy-Armbruster, of the School of Health, Physical Education, and Recreation at Indiana University at Bloomington, said it this way:

The fitness component of a recreational sports program will continue to play a large role in the overall health and wellness of students, faculty, and staff. College is a time where students make lifestyle choices that often stick with them for years to come. With obesity at an all-time high within all age groups in the United States, we have an obligation now to offer a comprehensive fitness or wellness program. It is in these programs that participants experience the wonderful health benefits of exercise. If we make this experience fun, welcoming, safe, effective, and positive, we just might make a difference in the health and wellness of the nation as a whole.

References

About, Inc., a part of the New York Times Company. (n.d.). Retrieved from http://seniorhealth.about.com/library/weekly/aa081300a.htm.

American College of Sports Medicine. (1997). *ACSM's health/fitness facility standards and guidelines* (pp. 8, 37-41). Champaign, IL: Human Kinetics.

American College of Sports Medicine. (2006). *ACSM's guidelines for exercise testing and prescription* (7th ed.). Philadelphia: Lea & Febiger.

American College of Sports Medicine and American Heart Association. (1998). Recommendations for cardiovascular screening, staffing, and emergency policies at health/fitness facilities. *Medicine & Science in Sports & Exercise, 30,* 1009-1018.

American Heart Association. (1998). 1999 heart and stroke statistical update. In *Heart and stroke facts.* Dallas: American Heart Association.

Canadian Society of Exercise Physiology. (2002). Physical Activity Readiness Questionnaire. Retrieved from www.csep.ca/forms/asp.

National Wellness Institute. (n.d.). The 6 dimensions of wellness. Retrieved from www.nationalwellness.org.

U.S. Department of Health and Human Services Administration on Aging. (n.d.). Statistics on the aging population. Retrieved from www.aoa.dhhs.gov/prof/Statistics/statistics.asp.

Glossary

body composition assessment—A procedure used to determine body density in which fat mass and lean body mass are expressed as relative percentages of total body weight. Examples include skinfold assessment and hydrostatic weighing.

cardiorespiratory (CR)—The ability to perform large muscle, dynamic, moderate-to-high intensity exercise for prolonged periods. Related to the capacity of the heart-lung system to deliver oxygen for sustained energy production. Also called cardiorespiratory endurance or aerobic fitness.

contract—An agreement or promise between two or more parties that creates a legal obligation either to do or not to do something. Some examples are client–trainer contract, informed consent, assumption of risk, and employee contract.

contraindication—Any condition that renders a particular activity inappropriate.

emergency procedures—A set of guidelines and protocols for employees and others present in a facility to follow in an emergency situation such as an accident, fire, bomb threat, or tornado.

emotional wellness—The ability to express feelings in an appropriate manner. It encourages participating in activities that focus on emotional self-care, including relaxation, managing stress, building self-confidence, and developing inner resources. It includes an awareness and acceptance of one's own feelings and the feelings of others.

employee evaluations—A necessary and valuable tool to help all instructors adapt and grow in the department. In addition to recognizing past achievements, the goal of an evaluation is to improve the effectiveness of the employee. Evaluation helps identify areas that need refinement or additional training.

ergometer—An exercise machine equipped with an apparatus to measure the effects of exercise.

exercise prescription—The development of an exercise program to elicit a behavioral change that improves the participant's health.

functional training—A form of strength training that utilizes multiple muscle groups in a single exercise and trains the body for activities performed in daily life. This is an advanced form of training that includes balance, stability, and core function (abdominal and lower back) in each exercise.

informed consent agreement—A document that includes a written expression of what will occur during a specific activity as well as verbiage stating that a person has voluntarily accepted the known dangers by participating in that activity. This document should be orally explained and should include a statement confirming that the person was offered the opportunity to ask questions about the procedures to be followed during the activity.

intellectual wellness—Stimulating the mind through activities that are mentally challenging; a sense of being internally energized. It encourages continued learning and the ability to grow from experiences, especially through problem solving and decision making.

medical information sheet—A document that includes questions pertaining to the medical and health history of the participant. This document should be completed during the pretest portion of a fitness assessment.

occupational wellness—Taking pride in one's work as well as maintaining a healthy balance between work and leisure. It encourages participation in activities that build skills for excelling in the workplace, including people skills and planning for the future.

PAR-Q—A self-administered questionnaire that serves to alert those with elevated risk to consult their physician (or other appropriate health care provider) prior to participating in an exercise program.

physical wellness—Taking care of the body through education, disease prevention, and management of illness and injury. It encourages participation in regular activities and a lifestyle that promotes optimal health.

physician's statement—A document that is completed by the participant's physician clearing the participant to engage in an initial fitness assessment and a daily exercise program. Also called a physician's clearance.

protocol—A set of guidelines to follow when performing a fitness test to measure a specific component of cardiorespiratory health.

risk stratification—A set of categories that individuals are placed in following the identification in them of coronary artery disease risk factors or signs or symptoms of cardiovascular, pulmonary, metabolic, or other known disease. The categories include low risk, moderate risk, and high risk.

social wellness—Contributing to the human and physical environment for the betterment of the community. It includes participation in activities that help to develop healthy relationships while enhancing the ability to enjoy social situations.

spiritual wellness—A guided sense of meaning or value in life as well as an understanding of and an ability to express one's purpose in life. It addresses values and ethics and the degree to which one's actions are consistent with one's values.

submaximal cardiorespiratory test—Used to measure cardiovascular fitness, submaximal testing relies on the measurement of the participant's heart rate as increased workloads are performed. During this test, a participant is typically taken to 85 percent of his or her age-predicted maximal heart rate.

CHAPTER 6

Administration of Intramural and Extramural Sport

Robert J. Barcelona, PhD, Associate Professor, Recreation Management and Policy, University of New Hampshire

It is not enough just to introduce play and games. . . . Everything depends upon the way in which they are employed.

John Dewey, in Democracy in Education *(1916)*

The promotion of healthy, structured sport opportunities "within the walls" of various settings has been the historical focal point for recreational sport programs on college and university campuses and in community schools, municipal recreation departments, and nonprofit organizations such as YMCAs and Boys and Girls Clubs. The growing complexity of sport and recreation programming, driven by participants' needs and interests, fiscal realities, shifts in administrative priorities, and changing public policy, has expanded the nature and scope of the traditional intramural sport program. Participants' interest in both competitive and noncompetitive sport opportunities, participant-driven sport experiences, new avenues for competition, and nontraditional sport pursuits have created unique programming and management challenges for intramural and recreational sport administrators.

Defining Terms

The term **intramural** literally means "within the walls" and has been traditionally associated with school-based recreational sport pursuits involving some form of competition between two or more participants. The scope of intramural and extramural sport has grown beyond the traditional educational setting. Although the terminology may differ, the programmatic competencies can apply to any direct or indirect competitive recreational sport experience that occurs within the defined boundaries (geographical or social) of an organizational entity. In the case of campus recreation programs, the boundary is usually defined as members of the university community—often operationalized as students and perhaps faculty and staff as well. In community-based sport programs, such as community recreation departments; elementary, middle, and high schools; armed forces recreation programs; and nonprofit organizations, the boundary might be defined as town residents, students in a particular grade level, or members of a particular club. The important concept is that a defined jurisdiction regulates participant eligibility.

Intramural activities are sports. *Sport* has been defined in many ways, encompassing a range of activities and outcomes. At one end of the continuum, *sport* activities can be defined as competitive experiences performed by organized groups that demand physical exertion with the goal of defeating an opponent. This definition takes a narrow view of sport, focusing primarily on its form (competitive experiences that demand physical exertion).

Such a definition excludes many types of activities from consideration as sports, such as ballroom dancing competitions, bass fishing tournaments, competitive card playing, and weightlifting events. However, many of these activities are included in intramural sport calendars throughout the United States and Canada.

On the other end of the continuum, sport can be seen as a range of competitive or cooperative activities played in the game form (Mull, Bayless, Ross, & Jamieson, 1997). This definition provides a more wide-ranging view of sport, provided that the activities themselves are conducted as **games;** that is, they are organized, are structured, have rules and regulations, have specific strategies, occur within a defined time frame, and use specific facilities and equipment.

One differentiator between intramural sport and other types of sport experiences is the fact that intramural sport takes place during leisure time. *Leisure* literally means "to be free." In the context of intramural sport activities, participants freely choose to participate. They are free to choose the types of activities they play, the style in which they play them (i.e., more competitive, less competitive), and perhaps most important, the outcomes that they derive from the experience. For some participants, intramural sports are primarily an outlet for friendly competition or a chance to socialize with friends. For others, intramural sports are an opportunity to receive exercise and enjoy the benefits of physical activity. Many enjoy intramural sports for a combination of benefits and outcomes.

Intramural sport programs can be defined as sport activities offered in the game form that are freely chosen by a wide array of participants within a defined boundary for the benefits that they provide. The key to intramural sport programming is the freedom of choice that is inherent in the intramural concept. Although intramural sport represents structured sport participation and requires design, delivery, and leadership for its provision, the philosophical focus of intramural sport programs is on maximizing participant choice in terms of program types, formats, and outcomes. This view leads to an expanded view of sport opportunities in order to maximize the choices available for participants.

Program Philosophy

From an organizational standpoint, **philosophies** are consistent reference points from which to make decisions. Consistent with the idea of maximizing participant choice in activities and outcomes, the principal philosophical orientation for intramural sport programming should be as follows:

> Intramural sport programs should be accessible to a diverse group of participants, regardless of age, ability, gender, skill level, and other sociodemographic variables.

This simple statement of philosophy should drive decisions about the accessibility of sport opportunity for participants within an intramural sport program. Implicit in this statement is the idea that intramural sport administrators should provide sport opportunities that allow for a wide range of sport activities and participation styles and outcomes.

Intramural sport programming is participant centered. That is, intramural sport programs should be designed to meet the needs and preferences of participants. People participate in intramural sport activities for a number of reasons, including the following:

- Competition
- Fitness
- Fun
- Furthering a sport interest
- Goal attainment
- Skill development
- Socialization with friends

It is important to keep in mind the multiple outcomes associated with intramural sport participation, because often the competitive aspect of the sport experience—and the focus on goal attainment (such as winning)—takes precedence over other participation outcomes. Although winning is an important outcome of the intramural sport experience, it is just one outcome of participation.

Philosophically, success in intramural sport participation should be defined in terms of maximizing multiple outcomes. Successful intramural sport administrators provide opportunities for participants to achieve goals in a number of areas and emphasize the importance of these additional benefits of sport participation.

Similarly, competition is an important component of the sport experience. Numerous intramural programs have attempted to eliminate the competitive experience by not keeping game scores, not keeping track of league standings, eliminating trophies or other awards, and disallowing fans from cheering or making any noise while attending games. Although the intent of these programmatic interventions might have stemmed from worthwhile causes, the reality is that competition is a significant component of the sport experience and is one of the defining characteristics of sport.

Intramural sport administrators should create strategies that focus on the positive aspects of competition while minimizing the negative consequences that all too often are associated with the competitive sport experience. In addition to recognizing contest winners, administrators may also consider the following to minimize some of the negative aspects associated with the competitive experience:

- Promoting the concept of indirect competition, in which success is defined relative to an individual or team's past performance
- Recognizing the most improved team

Courtesy of Lynchburg College.

Meeting the needs and preferences of participants is the main goal of intramural sport programming.

- Acknowledging the team with the best sporting behavior
- Recognizing individual competitors who achieve personal bests

Finally, cooperation is a critical component of the sport experience and one that is often overlooked when examining intramural sport. Without some level of cooperation among participants, there can be no contest. At its most basic level, without some agreement as to when and where to play, there can be no game. Competitors must agree on the rules, the facility, the authority of the game officials, and other structural elements that make the contest possible.

In intramural sport, opponents should be viewed as facilitators of the sport experience, recognizing that competition is an activity with, rather than against, an opponent (Fraleigh, 1984). The relationship between competitors should focus on challenging rather than dominating. Intramural sport administrators can facilitate this relationship by promoting cooperation at every level of the sport experience. This can be accomplished through preseason meetings in which team captains mutually decide on game rules and formats, pre- and postgame rituals such as team introductions and handshakes, or postseason events such as recognition banquets or social gatherings.

Intramural Sport Basics

Although philosophy provides the overarching framework for program design, a number of other important steps must be taken to provide intramural sport opportunities that maximize participant choice. Specifically, successful intramural sport programs must be designed in a systematic manner that aligns participants' needs and program philosophy with sport offerings, policies, procedures, rules, and program structures that facilitate choice. This makes intramural sport programs intentional in their design and helps to ensure that participants can achieve the desired benefits of participation.

Understanding and Meeting Constituent Needs

Understanding why participants choose to participate or not to participate in intramural sport programs is of vital interest to administrators. To live up to the established philosophy, "sport for everyone, regardless of . . ." it is important to understand the needs and interests of the program's **constituent group**—those people in the institution's service area who currently participate in intramural sport programs and those who are interested but not currently participating.

To meet the philosophical goals of intramural sport programming on college campuses, administrators must understand how their programs can do a better job of meeting the needs of underserved populations (Barcelona & Ross, 2002; Young, Ross, & Barcelona, 2003). Examples of these groups include the following:

- Faculty and staff
- Families of students, faculty, and staff
- Nontraditional-aged students
- International students
- Off-campus residents

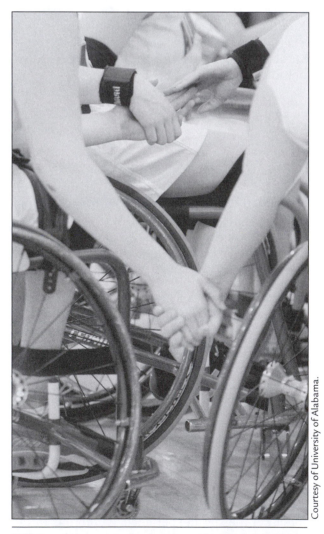

Courtesy of University of Alabama.

Offering options to underserved populations is among the philosophical goals of intramural sport programming.

- Students with disabilities
- Women

To understand the needs and interests of program participants, intramural sport administrators should conduct **needs assessments,** or systematic inquiries about the needs, attitudes, behaviors, and patterns of all constituents. Following are some methods for understanding and addressing constituent needs:

- Adopting programs that have demonstrated success at peer organizations
- Conducting formal assessment surveys (by mail, Web, telephone, and in person)
- Continuing to offer popular programs that serve constituents well
- Holding focus groups allowing for direct, face-to-face input
- Hosting "town meetings" or other forums to gather information
- Providing frequent opportunities for participant comments and feedback

- Using the input from participant advisory boards

Although it is important to understand the needs of constituents, it is equally important to consider the program's ability to meet these needs effectively. The capacity to meet the needs of constituents is an essential driver in program planning. For example, an intramural sport administrator might know that there is a need to accommodate additional flag football teams, but might not have access to enough outdoor field space to make it happen. It might be possible to meet this untapped need by offering different versions of flag football (such as an indoor program), offering an additional season, or adding weekend or nontraditional programming times to accommodate participant demand.

Facilitating Participant Choice

One of the most important programmatic concerns of intramural sport administrators is maximizing the choices available to participants. The diversity

Needs Assessment Example

Surveys are not the only method for assessing participant needs. The use of focus groups and other qualitative methods can give intramural sport administrators a good sense of what participants want. A description of an innovative needs assessment method follows.

How Much Is That Activity Worth?

This activity is a fun way of determining the popularity of existing offerings and can provide a forum for generating new programming ideas. Invite a representative group of intramural sport participants. Ideally, the group should represent key user groups in the intramural sport program: those who live in residence halls and Greek houses, off-campus residents, faculty and staff, women, and so on. This activity works best with approximately 20 participants. More than 20 drags the discussion down, and fewer than 20 risks not having a representative sample. Write down each of your intramural sport offerings on a separate manila folder and place these around the room. Give each of your participants $1,000 in play money. Have participants wander around the room and "spend" their money on the activities that are most important to them. How they divide their $1,000 is up to them: They may spend all of the $1,000 on one activity, divide it equally among multiple activities, or spend proportionally based on their interests. At the end of the session, have staff members count the money allocated to each activity and rank the activities based on their "value" to participants.

As a separate activity, you can encourage participants to generate ideas for new intramural activities. Create new folders and give each participant an additional $1,000 to spend on these new programming ideas, encouraging them to repeat the preceding game.

It is important to keep in mind the needs of nonparticipants as well. Many people have a desire to participate, but existing offerings do not meet their needs. Quantitative surveys are often the best technique for gauging the needs of nonparticipants. Making an effort to obtain enough responses to ensure that the results are representative and generalizable is important! See chapter 14 for more information on issues related to assessment.

that exists within the constituent base should be reflected in the types of programs offered, the way they are designed, and how they are delivered. To maximize participant choice, intramural sport programmers should provide a diverse array of options by focusing on four major areas:

- Sport offerings (sport classifications)
- Sport formats (methods of sport delivery)
- Participation categories (sport design elements)
- Game days, times, and locations

Intramural sport offerings can be grouped and classified as individual or dual sports, team sports, or meets.

Based on the needs of constituents, intramural sport calendars should have a diversity of offerings in each of these categories. For example, an intramural sport program might offer flag football,

William A. Cotton, Colorado State University.

Intramural sport calendars should have diverse offerings that are based on the needs of participants and include individual or dual sports, team sports, and meets.

soccer, basketball, volleyball, tennis, racquetball, a 5K or 10K road race, and track and field in the fall, and basketball, softball, Ultimate, bowling, badminton, table tennis, wrestling, and a swim meet in the spring. This calendar offers diverse choices of activities (sport offerings) and various classifications of sports (team, individual or dual, meets).

The format in which sport activities are offered can also expand participant choice. The **sport format** refers to the way an intramural program is designed. For example, there are numerous ways to offer basketball as an intramural activity. It might be offered as a 3-on-3 program or a traditional 5-on-5 program or as a special event consisting of free throws, three-point shooting, and dunk contests (DeGraaf, Jordan, & DeGraaf, 1999).

Offering a variety of formats provides even more choice within specific categories of sports. A participant might have enough friends interested in participating in a 3-on-3 flag football program or a 5-on-5 indoor soccer program, but not enough friends to field a team for a traditional flag football (7-on-7) or outdoor soccer (11-on-11) program. Similarly, special events such as a Basketball Bonanza or Softball Derby can meet the needs of participants who desire short-term, one-day sport experiences without the commitment to a team or league-oriented sport.

Another method for facilitating choice is to provide multiple **participation categories** that participants choose from based on their own sport needs. Participation categories differ depending on the organizational setting in which the sport program takes place and should be based on the needs and interests of program participants. Following are some examples of participation categories to consider in a collegiate intramural sport program:

- Age or school class (freshman, sophomore, junior, senior)
- Competitive level (noncompetitive, intermediate, competitive)
- Gender (male, female, or corecreational)
- Place of residence (residence halls, off-campus, Greek houses)
- Skill level (beginner, intermediate, advanced)
- University classification (undergraduate, graduate, faculty, staff)

Finally, when possible, participants should have a reasonable choice of game days, times, and locations. Although offering such options might be difficult given facility constraints, offering a range of choices in these areas encourages initial program participation and minimizes individual no-shows and team forfeits.

Sport Program Design

Sport program design is the systematic process of planning and providing structure for sport and recreation programs. Program design is the life-blood of the intramural sport program. Successful programs that yield the types of beneficial outcomes that constituents expect do not just happen. They are carefully planned and systematically designed with very specific goals in mind.

To use an analogy, the sport program is the car, the desired outcome (physical activity, fun, skill development, social interaction, friendly competition) is the destination, and the program planning process is the road map. A car can go many places, but a clearly defined destination and a good road map can get it there efficiently and effectively. Similarly, the outcomes of sport participation can be both positive and negative. A poorly designed sport program can end up doing more harm than good.

Focusing on the desired outcomes or benefits of intramural sport participation is the first step for intramural sport administrators. This benefits-based approach to program design (DeGraaf et al., 1999) has four major components:

1. Design programs to achieve desired benefits (physical activity, fun, skill development, social interaction).
2. Develop clear goals and objectives in terms of outcomes and benefits based on the organization's philosophy.
3. Evaluate and monitor programs to see whether these benefits have been achieved.
4. Inform the public of the positive benefits derived from intramural sport participation.

Knowing that successful intramural sport programs take into account the needs and interests of their constituents and offer the widest possible scope of sport activities, formats, and participation categories to facilitate and maximize participant choice, the successful intramural sport programmer takes care of the following:

- Equipment and supplies
- Participant governance systems
- Physical environment and facilities
- Policies, procedures, and rules
- Program budget
- Program evaluation
- Recognition or award systems
- Safety concerns and risk management
- Scheduling and tournament design
- Staff–customer interaction
- Staffing needs

Organizational Philosophy

Program design considerations should ideally flow from the overall organizational philosophy of the administrative unit housing the intramural sport program. The organization's philosophy—including its values, vision, mission, goals, and objectives—provides a framework for deciding the types of sport programs offered, to whom they are offered, and the way they are offered.

The organizational philosophy sets the stage for sport policy development. For example, if an intramural sport program at a college or university derives its budget solely from student activity fees, the organizational philosophy might dictate that students are the primary beneficiaries. An intramural sport program that has the motto "sport for everyone" should, in fact, live up to that philosophy by offering the widest variety of programs and program formats to its constituents.

Sport Policy Development

Policies are broad, general statements that flow from an organization's philosophy, goals, and objectives. Policies help provide a framework for decision making within an intramural sport program and help give the program direction. They are guides for participant and organizational behavior.

Policies should be written in a clear and unambiguous manner. Intramural sport programs that do not adequately address critical policy areas regarding eligibility, sporting behavior, safety, or weather will undoubtedly encounter problems related to fairness and equity, consistency, and overall organizational effectiveness.

Although policies reflect an organization's philosophy, goals, and objectives, the definition of *organization* can be broadly interpreted. For example, the organization might refer to the university, college, or school that is sponsoring the intramural sport program.

Policy might also be driven by the guidelines of a national association. Laws or specific pieces of legislation can also be sources for policy development. Because policies establish frameworks for decision making and behavior, they have consequences. In all cases, policies should be dynamic and should be revisited and reformulated if the current organizational environment demands such action.

Critical policy areas to consider within the intramural sport program are as follows:

- Activity governance (rules)
- Alcohol and other drugs
- Awards and recognition
- Coaching and team leadership
- Eligibility
- Facility use
- Forfeits and defaults
- Participant feedback
- Participation
- Preparticipation medical screening
- Protests
- Registration
- Sporting behavior and program control
- Staffing (officials and event staff)
- Uniforms and equipment

Sport Policies Versus Sport Procedures

Sport policies are different from **sport procedures.** Policies are broad statements reflecting the overall organizational philosophy. Policies do not dictate how programs will be carried out or enforced; they merely state the organization's position on a particular area. For example, a policy stating that only enrolled university students who have paid a student activity fee are eligible to participate in a collegiate intramural sport program does not indicate how this will be implemented within the program.

Sport procedures, on the other hand, are specific actions or steps designed to carry out a sport policy. In the preceding example regarding student fees, one or more specific procedures might be designed to address the eligibility issue within the intramural program. One procedure might be that only students showing current, valid university identification cards are eligible to play in a given intramural contest. Sport procedures

are specific and should serve to further define the actions associated with each policy.

Program-Related Rules

Even more specific than sport procedures, **program-related rules** guide the behavior of participants and staff. They stem directly from policies and procedures and provide a clear set of expectations.

For example, a policy stating that intramural teams must exhibit good sporting behavior can be enforced through a procedure of having the game officials assign a sporting behavior rating to teams after each game. A program-related rule might state that teams that do not average at least a "good" sporting behavior rating for each game will be ineligible for postseason play-offs. In this case, the policy (positive sporting behavior) is carried out by the procedure (official's ratings), and the rule (no play-offs for poor behavior) guides the behavior of participants (by maintaining a "good" sporting behavior average). It is important to remember that rules must be able to be enforced.

Policies, procedures, and program-related rules should be discussed with constituents before participation. In many cases, intramural sport programs can design a guide to participation to clearly communicate the program's policies. Where possible, policies should be developed in conjunction with constituent needs and interests and should be open for discussion and feedback.

Sport Rules

Sport rules govern the play of participants during the sport contest. They are specific to each sport activity. In many cases, standardized rule sets are provided by professional, collegiate, high school, or other national sport organizations. When standardized rule sets are not available, an entire set of rules governing a particular sport activity may be developed by the intramural sport program. This is generally the case with nontraditional sports such as kickball, Wiffleball, and similar activities. Today, a quick search of the Internet makes it easy to find standardized rule sets for even the most obscure sport activities.

Standardized rule sets for specific sports are popular because they are readily available and do not require intramural sport administrators to "reinvent the wheel." When choosing a particular standardized rule set for an intramural sport activity, administrators must once again keep the

William A. Cotton, Colorado State University.

Standardized rules for nontraditional sports such as 3-team handball can often be found on the Internet.

organization's philosophy and participants' best interests in mind.

For example, in an intramural basketball program, is it best to use the rules of the National Basketball Association or the rules of the National Federation of State High School Associations? Because many intramural basketball players have probably played high school basketball and are familiar with these rules, it might be more appropriate to choose the high school rule set.

Regardless of which set of standardized rule sets are chosen, many rules will not be applicable as a result of organizational philosophy, programmatic resources, or participant interest. Consider the following examples:

- An intramural sport program might choose to play with NCAA basketball rules, but might not have access to shot clocks.
- An intramural softball program might use Amateur Softball Association (ASA) rules,

but might choose to eliminate the strict uniform requirements to make the sport more accessible to college students on strict budgets.

- An intramural soccer program might use FIFA soccer rules, but allow for open substitution or dictate a minimum participation rule to ensure that everyone gets a chance to play.

Rule modifications based on specific programmatic needs or organizational philosophy should be considered in the following areas:

- Corecreational rules (no men in the lane, no back-to-back male plays)
- Facility considerations
- Game format (four quarters, two halves, three periods)
- Required equipment
- Safety considerations (no slide tackling, no contact)
- Sporting behavior
- Timing (running clock, 18-minute halves, 15-minute periods, time-outs)
- Uniforms

Tournament Design

Tournament design is an essential component of intramural sport programming. Simply put, tournament design refers to the style and format used to organize and schedule competitions. Although organizational philosophy, sport policy, procedures, and rules are all critical components of intramural sport programs, tournament design has perhaps the largest impact on participant perceptions of the program.

Choosing an appropriate tournament format goes beyond the individual preferences of the intramural sport administrator. It is not enough to use a tournament format just because it is familiar. Just like every other aspect of intramural sport programming, tournament design should flow from the goals, objectives, and intended outcomes of the program.

In general, the major tournament design formats are round-robin tournaments, elimination tournaments, and challenge tournaments, each of which has variations (Byl, 1999).

Round-Robin Tournaments

The **round-robin tournament design** is popular because it is familiar to most participants and guarantees the opportunity to continue playing regardless of wins and losses, as long as there are still games on the schedule. See figure 6.1 for examples of round-robins with different numbers of participating teams. Figure 6.2 shows an example of a round-robin tournament schedule. A classic round-robin format has each entry play every other entry once. When this has happened, the round-robin is complete. Although there are other variations of the round-robin (including double round-robins, in which each entry plays every other entry twice), the basic components of round-robin scheduling remain the same. Round-robin tournaments have the following advantages:

- They are easy to understand.
- They maximize participation over an extended period of time.
- They can be combined easily with other types of tournament formats (e.g., single elimination).
- They allow teams to be ranked at the end of league play for play-off seeding or other recognition purposes (Mull et al., 1997).

Although round-robin tournaments tend to be very popular with participants, they do require a significant investment of resources, especially in terms of facility availability.

Round-robin tournaments are popular because they allow teams to play multiple games, regardless of their win–loss records. However, the larger the numbers of entries in a round-robin league, the more games are required to ensure that every entry plays every other entry at least once. Although many participants want to play a large number of games, others can be overwhelmed by such long seasons and may lose interest. Shorter seasons requiring fewer games can be achieved by keeping round-robin league sizes small.

Elimination Tournaments

Elimination tournaments—commonly known as either single-elimination or double-elimination tournaments—are also popular with both participants and administrators, for several reasons.

Single-Elimination Tournaments The features of single-elimination tournaments are as follows:

- Single-elimination tournaments are efficient. They provide a true champion using fewer resources than round-robin or double-elimination tournaments of similar size.

- Single-elimination tournaments are useful formats when combined with multiple, preliminary round-robin play because they allow teams from different leagues to play against each other to determine a champion. For this reason, single-elimination tournaments are popular formats for postseason play-offs or tournament championships.

- Single-elimination tournaments do not maximize participation because of their "one loss and you're out" approach. They can lead to highly competitive matches, because participants must win to continue playing.

- In some cases, single-elimination tournaments are useful as stand-alone tournament formats (without the pairing with round-robin formats) when facilities or time to complete the tournament is limited.

See figure 6.3 for a sample single-elimination tournament.

Double-Elimination Tournaments Double-elimination tournaments can solve some of the problems of single-elimination tournaments, because they allow a team to lose a game yet still continue to play. Realistically, double-elimination tournaments guarantee entries at least two games. Double-elimination formats have their drawbacks as well. The following list outlines some of the concerns surrounding double-elimination tournaments:

- Because of the physical layout of the tournament bracket, double-elimination tournaments can be confusing for participants and spectators to understand.

- Double-elimination formats that do not use a "crossover" scheduling method run the risk of having participants eliminated by the same opponent that defeated them in their first contest (Byl, 1999).

- Double-elimination tournaments are more facility and time intensive than single-elimination tournaments.

Many intramural sport administrators are moving away from double-elimination tournaments in favor of three-team round-robin "pool play," followed by a single-elimination tournament to determine a true champion. The same objective of guaranteeing participants at least two games can be achieved with this method, and round-robin formats are generally more efficient to run and easier to understand than double-

Three-Team Round-Robin

Rounds	1	2	3
Bye	B – 3	B – 2	B – 1
Game 1	1v2	3v1	2v3

Four-Team Round-Robin

Rounds	1	2	3
Game 1	1v4	1v3	1v2
Game 2	2v3	4v2	3v4

Five-Team Round-Robin

Rounds	1	2	3	4	5
Bye	B – 5	B – 4	B – 3	B – 2	B – 1
Game 1	1v4	5v3	4v2	3v1	2v5
Game 2	2v3	1v2	5v1	4v5	3v4

Six-Team Round-Robin

Rounds	1	2	3	4	5
Game 1	1v6	1v5	1v4	1v3	1v2
Game 2	2v5	6v4	5v3	4v2	3v6
Game 3	3v4	2v3	6v2	5v6	4v5

Seven-Team Round-Robin

Rounds	1	2	3	4	5	6	7
Bye	B – 7	B – 6	B – 5	B – 4	B – 3	B – 2	B – 1
Game 1	1v6	7v5	6v4	5v3	4v2	3v1	2v7
Game 2	2v5	1v4	7v3	6v2	5v1	4v7	3v6
Game 3	3v4	2v3	1v2	7v1	6v7	5v6	4v5

Eight-Team Round-Robin

Rounds	1	2	3	4	5	6	7
Game 1	1v8	1v7	1v6	1v5	1v4	1v3	1v2
Game 2	2v7	8v6	7v5	6v4	5v3	4v2	3v8
Game 3	3v6	2v5	8v4	7v3	6v2	5v8	4v7
Game 4	4v5	3v4	2v3	8v2	7v8	6v7	5v6

Figure 6.1   Round-robin scheduling matchups.

Intramural Flag Football

Division: Men's Competitive

League: Comp-1

Teams

1. GATA

2. Sigma Chi

3. University Sporting Goods (USG)

4. Mad Elephants

5. Kinard Hall

Day	Date	Time	Location	Home		Visitor
Wed	9/13	6:00 p.m.	Turf 1	GATA	vs.	Mad Elephants
			Turf 2	Sigma Chi	vs.	USG
Wed	9/20	6:00 p.m.	Turf 1	USG	vs.	Kinard Hall
			Turf 2	Sigma Chi	vs.	GATA
Wed	9/27	6:00 p.m.	Turf 1	Mad Elephants	vs.	Sigma Chi
			Turf 2	Kinard Hall	vs.	GATA
Wed	10/4	6:00 p.m.	Turf 1	GATA	vs.	USG
			Turf 2	Mad Elephants	vs.	Kinard Hall
Wed	10/11	6:00 p.m.	Turf 1	Kinard Hall	vs.	Sigma Chi
			Turf 2	USG	vs.	Mad Elephants

All players must check in with the event supervisor prior to game time by showing a valid university identification card.

There is a 10-minute grace period for check-in. Teams not checked in by 6:10 will receive a forfeit.

Teams must control their spectators! Poor sporting behavior by spectators could result in team penalties.

Check the intramural Web site (www.intramurals.edu) or call Rec Check (555-5555) for weather-related game status.

Figure 6.2   A sample round-robin tournament schedule.

elimination tournaments. See figure 6.4 for a sample double-elimination tournament.

Challenge Tournaments

Challenge tournaments are creative tournament formats with the ultimate goal of ongoing participation over a period of time. Features include the following:

• Challenge tournaments allow participants to challenge each other to play matches, usually at a time and location agreeable to both participants.

• Challenge tournaments tend to be participant focused; the intramural administrator sets up the tournament structure and the time frame for completion, provides a basic set of rules, and provides contact information for all participants. The rest of the details involving scheduling matches, reporting results, and conducting play are generally the domain of the participants. Winners of challenges usually move up the tournament structure (or defend their position based on the relative position of the challenger). The participant or team that ends up at the top of the ladder, pyramid, or other challenge structure within a given time frame is deemed the winner of the tournament. See figure 6.5 for an example of a ladder tournament.

• Challenge tournaments work best with events that require minimal supervision and in

First Annual Campus Kickball Weekend
Women's Playoff Tournament

American League

(1) Delta Delta Delta

Th, 3:00 p.m. Field 1
(8) Stewart Hall

(4) Martin Hall

Th, 3:00 p.m. Field 2
(5) Lady Bugs

(3) Phi Mu

Th, 4:00 p.m. Field 1
(6) Crimson Tide

(2) Fun Bunch

Th, 4:00 p.m. Field 2
(7) Holmes Hall

Fri, 3:00 p.m. Field 1

Fri, 3:00 p.m. Field 2

Sat, 3:00 p.m. Field 1

Sun, 3:00 p.m. Field 1

National League Winner

Sat, 4:00 p.m. Field 1

American League Winner

National League

(1) Abner's

Th, 5:00 p.m. Field 1
(8) Chi Omega

(4) Lucky Eights

Th, 5:00 p.m. Field 2
(5) Alpha Phi

(3) Women's Soccer

Th, 6:00 p.m. Field 1
(6) Theta

(2) Crosby Crew

Th, 6:00 p.m. Field 2
(7) Lady Rebels

Fri, 4:00 p.m. Field 1

Fri, 4:00 p.m. Field 2

Women's Kickball Tournament Champions!

Figure 6.3 Sample single-elimination tournament.

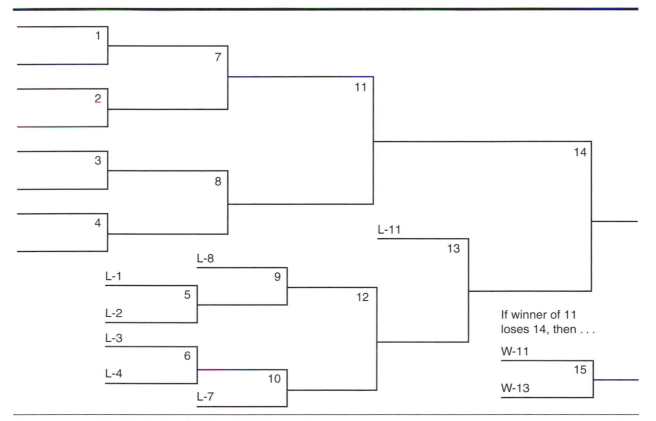

Figure 6.4 Double-elimination bracket with eight entries.

Intramural Raquetball Ladder Tournament

Division: Women's Intermediate

League: Intermediate Ladder 1

Place	Players	Place
1	Alicia Atwater	1
2	Betsy Brookover	2
3	Celeste Clem	3
4	Denise Donaldson	4
5	Emma Echenmeier	5
6	Fiona Ferdinand	6
7	Georgia Greenleaf	7
8	Harriet Hoffman	8
9	Ingrid Inhoff	9
10	Jacqueline Joyce	10
11	Kim Kilpatrick	11
12	Loraine Lamont	12
Place		Place

Rules:

1. Players have been assigned randomly to positions on the ladder.
2. To move up the ladder, you must challenge another player above you.
3. You may only challenge players who are up to two levels ahead (player 4 may challenge player 3 or 2).
4. Challenges are made by contacting opponents via their preferred contact method.
5. Go to www.intramurals.edu/racquetball to obtain contact information for opponents.
6. Challenges should be made early in the week for scheduling convenience.
7. Opponents have one week to accept a challenge and play a game.
8. Challenges not accepted within a one-week time frame (or no-shows) will be declared forfeits.
9. Challenges must be played in order!
10. It is the winner's responsibility to notify the intramural sport staff within 24 hours of contest results.
11. If the lower seed wins, positions are switched on the ladder.
12. If the higher seed wins, ladder positions stay the same.
13. You must play at least one game per week.
14. If you are not challenged in a week, you must challenge one of your opponents.
15. Official rules can be found at the IM Web site: www.intramurals.edu/racquetball/rules.
16. All questions or disputes will be settled by the intramural sport staff. Contact us at imstaff@im.edu.
17. The player at the top of the ladder on Friday, October 27, will be declared the winner.

Figure 6.5   A ladder tournament is an example of a challenge tournament format.

which participants are fairly familiar with the rules, norms, and standards of the sport. Individual, dual, and some team activities in which participants are highly motivated, have an interest in ongoing play, and need little supervision do well with a challenge tournament format. Following are some examples:

- Handball
- Racquetball
- Squash
- Tennis
- Wallyball
- Table tennis

Choosing Tournament Formats

The choice of tournament design format depends on a number of factors, including the following:

- Availability of facility space and number of available facility spots
- Level of competition
- Number of entries registered or expected to register
- Characteristics, needs, and interests of participants
- Program budget
- Program objectives
- Program personnel, including availability of officials and game staff

Availability of Facilities The availability of facilities plays a major role in tournament design decisions. In general, round-robin tournaments require more facility availability than single-elimination tournaments. Scheduling round-robin tournaments with large league sizes (more than six teams) will necessitate more facility space, both by the day and across the season. Intramural sport administrators often start with an available facility reservation and determine how many teams can be accommodated in the tournament based on various tournament formats.

Level of Competition The appropriate level of competition expected in a tournament also plays a role in tournament design format. The "one and done" nature of single-elimination tournaments, in which one loss eliminates a team or individual from further competition, yields a level of competitiveness to each game that may or may not be desired. Round-robin or challenge tournaments maintain the importance of competition, while at the same time guaranteeing future opportunities to play, regardless of wins and losses.

Number of Entries The number of expected entries is a major factor that drives the tournament design format. A flag football program that has 10 teams requires only nine games to be be complete a single-elimination tournament, whereas a 10-team round-robin league requires 45 games to be complete. In this case, the number of team entries and the availability of facility space to play the games are the most important tournament design factors.

Participant Characteristics, Needs, and Interests Different tournament formats meet the characteristics, needs, and interests of different participants in intramural sport programs. Consider the following:

- Participant characteristics such as age and skill level may be addressed through the use of specific types of tournament formats.
- Those with a primary interest in casual play and an emphasis on social interaction might be best served by round-robins or challenge tournaments.
- Highly skilled participants who are interested in playing a significant number of games and who want a competitive format with a true winner are best served by a round-robin tournament followed by a single-elimination play-off.

As in all cases with intramural sport programming, the participants' needs should play the prominent role in driving programmatic decisions.

Program Budget The budget is a pragmatic concern that intramural sport programmers face when deciding on tournament format. An intramural tennis tournament played on multiple tennis courts over the span of several months is generally more expensive to run than a weekend tournament played on one or two courts.

Program Objectives Answering the following questions will ensure that the tournament design format reflects the tournament's objectives. The answers will help the program administrator choose the type of tournament format and the style of tournament design.

- Is there an interest in determining an overall champion? If so, then elimination or challenge tournaments should be incorporated into the overall tournament design.
- Is there an interest in maximizing the number of entries? Scheduling three-team round-

robin leagues (the smallest league size) may yield the highest number of overall participant entries given a fixed facility reservation.

• Is there an interest in sustained involvement in a sport over time? Larger round-robin league sizes (leagues of eight entries or more) or double round-robin formats can provide a significant number of games per entry. Challenge tournaments, as well, can provide a longer playing season depending on the deadlines set by the tournament administrator.

• Does the tournament need to conclude within a short time span (such as in one day or over a weekend)? Single-elimination tournaments as stand-alone tournament formats, or a combination of small round-robin league sizes (three-team leagues) paired with a single-elimination championship tournament can accommodate short time frames.

• Is the tournament primarily led and run by participants? Challenge tournaments generally require little supervision and staffing, because participants are responsible for setting matches, determining game times, and reporting contest results.

Program Personnel Availability of program personnel is yet another component that determines tournament design. The games must have adequate staff coverage, including officials, program supervisors, and medical personnel to ensure program safety, integrity, and fair play. Tournament design formats that require multiple playing locations and play extended over long periods of time require significant staff coverage.

Officials are perhaps the most recognized intramural sport personnel and are critical to the success of an intramural contest. Different sports require different numbers of officials per contest. Flag football, for example, is usually called with three officials, but sometimes four can be used. Basketball should be called with a minimum of two officials, but in certain situations (postseason play-offs), three officials might be recommended. Soccer normally requires three officials, and volleyball is usually called with two. Programs might modify and limit the number of officials working each game based on a number of factors (the nature of the sport, cost, or the availability of staff). For example, softball can be called with one official, as can volleyball. In sports such as Ultimate and softball, games may be nonofficiated. Instead, players are responsible for calling the game and settling disputes. These decisions should not

be made lightly. The number of officials should not be limited if doing so will negatively affect the safety, integrity, or fair play of an intramural contest.

Large intramural programs that run on multiple fields or courts for several hours per night require a fairly large number of qualified officials to run games. Because intramural sport contests are usually modified for shorter play (18-minute running clock halves in basketball, for instance), officials are usually asked to work multiple games per shift. For example, an intramural basketball program that runs on three courts for six hours per night will require at least 12 officials per night if they are working in two-person crews and 18 per night if they are working in three-person crews. Under this arrangement, each official would work three games per shift.

Recruiting qualified officials is often a difficult task. A recent study found that word of mouth and encouragement from friends are often the best means for recruiting new officials (Scott, 2006). However, targeted recruiting tactics—including developing flyers; advertising in the student newspaper; encouraging intramural participants to officiate; and reaching out to academic classes in recreation, sport management, or physical education—can also help expand the pool of potential officials.

Because most intramural officials are inexperienced, training and development are necessary. Officials' training generally consists of an orientation, rules session, on-field or on-court clinic, and a test or exam. It is important for officials to receive continual feedback and evaluation even after training is completed. Encouragement and support from professional staff are critical in retaining intramural officials. The National Intramural-Recreational Sports Association (NIRSA) provides materials and resources to assist in officials' training and development.

Scott's (2006) study found that most intramural officials who begin officiating intend to continue to officiate in the future. Most expressed a desire to become student leaders within the intramural sport program. Officiating is often the gateway to further leadership opportunities in intramural sports as lead or head officials or event supervisors.

Intramural sport programs may also require scorekeepers, timekeepers, supervisors, and medical personnel to ensure that contests run smoothly. Not every program will need each of these positions, and in some cases tasks can be shared within one job category. For example, event supervisors are often trained in emergency first aid and CPR. Many times, an extra official might be scheduled per contest to handle scorekeeping and timekeeping duties. In some cases, teams are asked to supply their own scorekeepers. These decisions are program specific and are made with a variety of factors in mind (budget, staff availability, safety concerns).

Extramural Sport Basics

The growth of competitive sport opportunities for both men and women has increased the interest in sport competition beyond the boundaries of the intramural sport enterprise. Whereas intramural sport programs are designed to foster participation between individuals and teams within a designated sport space, **extramural sport programs** allow for competitive sport experiences between individuals and teams from different organizational settings.

Extramural sport has been described as an extension of the intramural sport program. Although the terms *intramural* and *extramural* have typically been associated with school and collegiate programs, the principles behind extramural sport programming can be applied to any number of recreational sport settings. National, regional, and state events—in fact, any type of sport contests composed of individuals and teams representing various organizational entities—can be considered extramural sport programs.

The same basic principles behind intramural sport program design apply to extramural sport. The benefits-based approach to program design is still the basis for extramural sport programs. For example, it is still important to understand participants' needs and interests, develop program goals and objectives based on the overall philosophy of the organization, and design the program accordingly. Also, the development of sound sport policy, procedures, and rules is just as important for extramural events as it is for intramural events

However, while intramural sport programs require a significant amount of planning and organization, extramural events, because they transcend the everyday sport experience, require additional levels of administration. The National Intramural-Recreational Sports Association also provides host organizations and administrators with information and criteria for administering extramural sport events (National Intramural-Recreational

Sports Association, n.d.). The following are some considerations for extramural sports:

- They require appropriate playing facilities and equipment. Just as the facility is one of the keys to effective intramural sport programs, an adequate facility is also a critical component to ensure a successful extramural sport event.

- The availability of playing space and equipment is a major factor that determines when and whether an extramural event will occur. A host institution must have access to a suitable number of playing spaces to accommodate the number of participants and teams that are expected to compete.

- Adequate lighting to play outdoor night games is critical in enabling all games to be completed in the time frame allotted for the event.

- All facilities should be reserved in advance, and contingency plans should be made in case of inclement weather or other unforeseen circumstances.

- Extramural sport events may require changing rooms, hospitality and concession areas, separate changing areas for game officials, and designated media space.

- Spectator seating, especially for games that might typically draw large crowds, is another consideration for the host institution.

- Providing access to a high-quality playing area for the semifinal and championship games where possible and appropriate provides an additional level of service and adds to the special nature of the event.

Event Structure and Scheduling

Along with reserving an appropriate playing facility, administrators of extramural sport events must strategically consider the timing of the events to avoid obvious (and not-so-obvious) conflicts that can prevent participation or detract from the overall experience. When possible, extramural sport contests should not conflict with other high-profile scheduled activities, such as intercollegiate athletics or other large-scale local events. It is also prudent to avoid other potential conflicts, such as holidays, exam periods, and the times of the year when inclement weather is likely to be a problem.

Because extramural events require most participants to travel some distance to compete, it is best to schedule formats that guarantee at least two and, where possible, three games at a given location. Although any number of scheduling formats can guarantee such participation levels, typically round-robin play followed by a single-elimination play-off is the recommended tournament design format.

Although double-elimination events guarantee teams at least two games, they are often unwieldy, confusing, difficult to reschedule, and time (and facility) intensive. A variety of participation categories, consisting of at least a men's and women's division and, when appropriate, corecreational play, should be offered. Depending on the event setting and participants involved, programs should offer additional divisions, including age divisions, skill-level divisions, geographical divisions, or others when appropriate.

Player and Team Eligibility

To ensure the integrity of the extramural sport event, policies governing the eligibility of players and teams must be stated clearly in advance of the event. These policies should be determined by the host institution in consultation with participating institutions and, where appropriate, the national governing bodies and principal event sponsors.

Because extramural sport is typically considered an extension of the intramural sport program, it follows that participating teams should be champions or designated representatives of participating institutions. Consider the following eligibility policies:

- Team eligibility might be restricted just to the champions of more localized intramural events.
- Team eligibility could be designated by representing institutions.
- Extramural events might consist of "open" play opportunities that allow for any team representing certain eligibility requirements to register and participate.
- Specific eligibility requirements might consist of enrollment or employment status at a participating college or university, active military status, age, amateur status, or nonvarsity status.

Program Control and Governance

Extramural administrators should establish standards of conduct to ensure safety and fair play for sport events. Although similar standards of conduct should also exist for intramural sport play, in an extramural game the host institution generally has less influence over the participants and spectators, thus necessitating clear guidelines and expectations for participant behavior. Generally, standards of conduct should address the following:

- Abuse of facilities or equipment
- Abuse of game rules or host institution policies
- Alcohol and other drug use
- Physical and verbal abuse of officials, game staff, opponents, and spectators
- Use of profanity or obscene gestures

In addition to clearly stating standards of conduct, policies should also clearly state the consequences related to a violation of such standards. The host institution should set up a governance structure that can provide due process in the case of disagreements related to the game, eligibility, or violations of the standards of conduct.

Risk Management

Administrators of extramural programs should consult an appropriate risk management officer to determine whether the level of risk that is being assumed by the host or representing institutions can be managed safely and effectively. The risk management officer should also be consulted about the following:

- Appropriate levels of staff coverage
- Developing informed consent or release of liability statements
- Personal injury procedures
- Property insurance
- Travel procedures

Host institutions should provide appropriate medical coverage for extramural sport contests, including certified athletic trainers, emergency medical technicians, and event staff trained in first aid, CPR, and automated external defibrillators (AEDs). In all cases, extramural sport programs should be included in the host or representing institution's comprehensive risk management plan.

Hotel Accommodations and Hospitality

Although extramural participants' principal focus is competing in their scheduled events, a significant portion of their time will be spent away from the playing facility. When participants travel out of town and require overnight stays, host institutions can be valuable resources to help visitors navigate their way through potentially unfamiliar towns or cities.

At a minimum, host institutions should provide information about local hotel accommodations, places to eat, local entertainment and shopping options, and other details that will help the visiting participants enjoy their experience.

Extramural sport events also provide an opportunity to forge partnerships between the host institution and local businesses. For example, securing discounted hotel rooms by designating a "host hotel" chosen through a competitive bid process can ensure the best value for participants. Administrators can negotiate with host hotels to provide free or discounted meeting rooms, catering, and complementary rooms for event staff and, where appropriate, game officials.

Sponsorship and Value-Added Promotions

Just as hotel accommodations can be a natural area for partnership creation, involvement by other types of local businesses can enhance both the quality of the event and the spending activity of event participants (Steinbach, 2000).

A **sponsorship** should be considered an exchange relationship; that is, it should ideally provide mutual benefits to the event host, participants, and the event sponsor. For the sport organization, business sponsorship of extramural events can provide the following:

- Cash
- Additional media attention
- In-kind support in the form of products
- In-kind expert personnel

Sponsorships offer participants giveaways, prizes, and promotional items that might not be available outside the event itself. This may give them the feeling of being at a "big-time" event.

Sponsoring businesses are able to raise the awareness of their products in the eyes of target consumers. Sponsorship also provides the opportunity for hands-on product trials through promotional giveaways, coupons, or other vehicles, enabling a direct and intimate relationship between the product and the consumer.

Offering sponsorship packages at different levels allows businesses to support the extramural event in different ways. One method for accomplishing this is to offer a sponsor a tiered benefit package based on its level of involvement with the extramural event. Consider the following:

1. *Title sponsorship.* The business's name is integrated with the event title.
2. *Official sponsorship.* The business aligns with the event in exchange for a lower level of sponsorship commitment.
3. *Presenting sponsorship.* The business receives the rights to associate with an event based on a product category.
4. *Official supplier.* The business provides goods or equipment to help stage the event.

Media Coverage

Depending on the event, the local, regional, or national print or broadcast media might be interested in providing coverage either in whole or in part. The media should be viewed from a publicity as well as promotion perspective. That is, it is important to use the media not only as a tool for promoting the event, but also as a source of publicity for sponsors and other event participants. In many cases, event sponsors want media coverage as a component of their sponsorship, so obtaining media support is a critical area of extramural sport programming.

At a minimum, it is advisable to send written press releases, as well as an e-mail, to the higher education reporters and the sports editors of local papers, as well as to television and radio stations. Daily results of extramural contests can be provided to the appropriate media outlets. To achieve optimal media coverage, event planners should provide the following:

- Designated media space or area
- Access to tournament staff, teams, and participants
- Hospitality opportunities (e.g., food, drinks, and socializing and networking opportunities)

A designated media relations director for the event can streamline this process and provide one consistent point of contact for media personnel interested in providing event coverage.

Event Staff

In many cases, extramural sport events require staffing levels above and beyond those needed for the normal intramural sport program. Although position titles and staff numbers will vary based on the type and scope of the event, critical staff positions are as follows:

- Tournament director
- Event supervisors
- Game officials
- Media relations director
- Medical personnel
- Officiating coordinator
- Officiating evaluators
- Photographer or videographer
- Registration staff
- Timekeepers, scorekeepers, statisticians
- Web master

In addition, extramural events should have a governance structure designed to handle issues concerning rule or eligibility protests. An "all-tournament committee" or other such committee that is charged with selecting "all-tournament teams" can also be included in the event staffing structure. Obtaining diverse representation on these committees, with volunteers representing a variety of participating institutions, helps to prevent charges of bias or other conflicts of interest.

Another critical task in planning for extramural sport events is ensuring an adequate quantity and quality of game officials. The number of officials needed differs depending on the event. Where possible, using the maximum number of officials promotes more opportunities for involvement and increases the quality of officiating in extramural events. Minimum qualifications for officials differ depending on the extramural event, but in all cases, administrators should demand the highest level possible on officials' qualifications and preparation (Popke, 2000).

Recognition

Because extramural sports are forms of recreational sports, recognizing participation is at the core of recognition and award protocols. However, it is important to remember that extramural sport events lend themselves to a formalized recognition protocol that transcends that of the typical intramural program.

Awards ceremonies, banquets, or other recognition rituals are appropriate for extramural sport events. In addition to recognizing participation, recognizing achievement in various divisions—men's, women's, corecreational, age group, and so forth—is entirely appropriate.

Recognizing achievement goes beyond just focusing on winners. Rewarding champions, runners-up, semifinalists, most valuable players, best sports, most improved teams, all-tournament players and officials, and others de-emphasizes winning and provides multiple avenues for team and individual recognition.

Event Evaluation and Impact

Consistent with the benefits-based model of program design, evaluation of the extramural sport program is a valuable component to determine whether the program goals and objectives were met. The content of the evaluation should encompass both the process and the product.

Process evaluation focuses on how the event was conducted, how it was delivered, and how it was implemented. Process evaluations are primarily concerned with the efficiency and effectiveness of program delivery.

Product evaluation focuses on the outcomes of the program: the number of teams and participants, demographic breakdowns, the number of officials and event staff, participant and staff satisfaction, and so on. Product evaluations may do the following:

- Address the relative public impact of the extramural event on key elements of the community
- Evaluate the economic impact of the event by investigating spending levels of event participants in the local community
- Measure the return on sponsorship investment by evaluating media coverage or participants' ability to recall or recognize program sponsors

Although evaluations are used to improve future events, the scope and impact of extramural sport programs can also yield public relations benefits for the host institution. Communicating these results to the appropriate audience—the institutional administration, corporate sponsors, and local businesses—builds community support for future hosting opportunities.

Conclusion

Intramural and extramural sports continue to be the signature programs in many recreational sport settings. Although the two differ in day-to-day programming issues, the same level of systematic and purposeful thinking is required to administer each.

Approaching intramural and extramural sport administration in a systematic manner, by focusing on and integrating program philosophy, goals, objectives, design elements, and evaluation maximizes the positive, beneficial outcomes associated with intramural and extramural sport participation.

References

Barcelona, R.J., & Ross, C.M. (2002). Participation patterns in campus recreational sports: An examination of quality of student effort from 1983 to 1998. *Recreational Sports Journal, 26*(1), 41-53.

Byl, J. (1999). *Organizing successful tournaments.* Champaign, IL: Human Kinetics.

DeGraaf, D.G., Jordan, D.J., & DeGraaf, K.H. (1999). *Programming for parks, recreation, and leisure services: A servant leadership approach.* State College, PA: Venture.

Fraleigh, W.P. (1984). *Right actions in sport: Ethics for contestants.* Champaign, IL: Human Kinetics.

Mull, R.F., Bayless, K.G., Ross, C.M., & Jamieson, L.M. (1997). *Recreational sport management.* Champaign, IL: Human Kinetics.

National Intramural-Recreational Sports Association. (n.d.). NIRSA extramural event criteria. Retrieved from www.nirsa.org/secure/staff/e_policies.htm.

Popke, M. (2000, May). Tournament time. *Athletic Business,* 69-73.

Scott, B. (2006). Recruitment, motivation, and retention of collegiate intramural sports officials. Unpublished master's project, University of New Hampshire.

Steinbach, P. (2000, January). Intramarketing: Corporate sponsorship trickles deeper into campus activities. *Athletic Business,* 27-28.

Young, S.J., Ross, C.M., & Barcelona, R.J. (2003). Perceived constraints by college students to participation in campus recreational sports programs. *Recreational Sports Journal, 27*(1), 47-62.

Glossary

constituent group—Those people residing within an institution's service area who currently participate in intramural sport programs and those who are interested but not currently participating.

extramural sport programs—Programs that allow for competitive sport experiences between individuals and teams from different organizational settings.

games—Activities that are organized, are structured, have rules and regulations, have specific strategies, occur within a defined time frame, and use specific facilities and equipment.

intramural—Derived from the Latin words *intra,* meaning "within," and *muralis,* meaning "wall." The term is usually paired with other words such as *sports, athletics,* or *activities* and, when so combined, implies that these programs are conducted "within the walls" or imaginary boundaries of some organization or institution.

needs assessments—Systematic inquiries about the needs, attitudes, behaviors, and patterns of all constituents.

participation categories—Different programming options or divisions that participants can choose from, based on their needs. Some examples are competitive level, sex/gender, and place of residence.

philosophies—Consistent reference points that organizations use to make decisions.

policies—Broad statements that flow from an organization's philosophy, goals, and objectives.

program-related rules—Rules that guide the behavior of participants and staff. More specific than sport procedures, they stem directly from policies and procedures and provide a clear set of expectations.

round-robin tournament design—A popular tournament format familiar to most participants. It guarantees the opportunity to continue playing regardless of wins and losses, as long as there are still games on the schedule.

sponsorship—A relationship between organizations for the purpose of enhancing a sport event through cash donations, in-kind support, media attention, or staff expertise.

sport format—The way an intramural program is designed and delivered. Sport can be offered as competitive leagues, informal opportunities, special events, or instructional opportunities.

sport procedures—Specific actions or steps designed to carry out sport policy. Procedures provide more specific information than policies and further define actions associated with them.

sport program design—The systematic process of planning and providing structure for sport and recreation programs.

sport rules—Rules that govern the play of participants during sport contests. They are specific to each sport activity.

tournament design—Essential component of intramural sport programming; refers to the style and format used to organize and schedule competitions. Tournament design may have the largest impact on participants' perceptions of the program.

CHAPTER 7

Aquatics Management

Carrie Tupper, MS, Director of Aquatics, University of Maryland
Gary Pogharian, CRSS, MSSEd, Aquatics Director, University of South Carolina
Jennifer Gudaz, MS, Director, Noyes Community Recreation Center, Cornell University

If you would thoroughly know anything, teach it to others.

Tryon Edwards (1809-1894)

From the days when hot springs supplied water to the Roman baths, the aquatic facility has been a place for social gathering. Today's computer-monitored and chemically treated **natatoriums** are the focal point for recreation, leisure, and competition as well as general socialization. Water activities such as swimming, water exercise, physical rehabilitation and therapeutics, and play attract people of all ages.

According to a 2004 National Sporting Goods Association survey, swimming ranks number three on the list of most popular U.S. sporting and recreational pastimes. A trend in the aquatics field over the past 15 years has been to emphasize the fun and social aspects of water. Fun features such as slides, fountains, lazy rivers, spas, and so on, have grown in popularity as people look to be entertained as well as to exercise. What were once special attractions have become requirements for the successful new facility. The collegiate setting is virtually the only venue that can limit itself to a purely competitive facility, although it still must be augmented to overcome the limitation of just such a design.

The sound management of an aquatic facility depends on the efficient coordination of several integrated functions. This is the result of a combination of the enduring popularity of swimming, increasing litigation, and the need for recreation and aquatic facilities to generate revenue. Many speak of the aquatics dilemma: An increased number of patrons causes increased potential litigation, thus increasing insurance costs, which decreases revenue. As a result, the facility must attract more people or increase the revenue per person, which could have an adverse effect on both patrons and revenue. It is a vicious cycle. This chapter covers the following aspects of aquatics management:

- Managerial responsibilities
- Staff hiring and training
- Budgets and revenue generation
- Programs
- Pool and spa facility maintenance, including water chemistry and quality
- Safety and risk management

Managerial Responsibilities

Aquatics managers and directors must have a working knowledge and a thorough understanding of related governmental health and safety codes (as well as any code that is specific to the facility) for the successful operation and maintenance

Courtesy of University of Alabama.

The desire for entertainment as well as exercise in campus aquatic environments has led to the popularity of slides, fountains, lazy rivers, and spas.

of the aquatic facility. They must also have a knowledge of the Americans with Disabilities Act (ADA) pertaining to aquatic facilities. This base of information is essential to minimizing litigation and creating a safe and healthy environment. There currently is no national aquatics standard; for example, managers of aquatic facilities in the state of Pennsylvania must be licensed, but the state of Kansas leaves that requirement up to the local municipalities. Thus, in Kansas you can be an operator in one city, but not be eligible to hold the same position in a different city in the same state! This requires that the aquatics professional continue to work with others.

For successful day-to-day operations, a major responsibility of an aquatics professional is to ensure that staff members are aware of their shifts well in advance. Staff should be on a rotation to ensure that they get proper breaks (this can be determined by using guidelines suggested by the American Red Cross, Ellis and Associates, and some state codes). At the beginning of the first shift of each day, a staff member must do the following:

• Complete a facility safety checklist to make sure all equipment is in proper working order, deploy the equipment to the proper location, and ensure that the facility is safe for staff and patrons. If these conditions are not met, the facility should not be opened. Remember that safety is the number one goal for the successful aquatics professional.

• Have a cleaning and maintenance list to complete throughout the day if there is no custodial staff. This list should consist of tasks that promote the safety of the facility, but are within the capabilities of the staff. It is also essential that the staff be given the necessary tools to accomplish these tasks (the staff should not be set up for failure).

• Perform the necessary chemical tests (at least twice a day or as required by local, state, or municipal codes) for pH and chlorine and record these in a log (this is necessary for the minimization of liability in the future if the need arises). Some states require facilities to post water temperature, so staff should make sure to maintain their checks in compliance with codes. Some states require that these readings be posted along with the time of their last check. (Posting your readings can be a great public relations move that protects staff from chemical or temperature complaints. If your readings are not good, however, it can be a nightmare.)

Staff Hiring and Training

An aquatic facility, like any other facility, is only as good as the staff it employs. The aquatics staff is responsible for the health and safety of aquatics program participants at all times and should be carefully trained, screened, and selected. All staff members must be properly trained for their specific facility in order to handle any situation that could occur. Because each facility has unique attributes (fountains, lazy rivers, diving boards) or designs (deck-level guttering, sunken pool, stainless steel guttering, brick copestones), facility-specific training is essential to a successful staff. Even those hired with current certifications should still be required to go through a specific training at your facility to be able to handle emergencies there. The aquatics professional is responsible for conducting safe and effective training programs for the staff to ensure the safety of participants. The staff must possess a maturity of judgment and a demonstrated ability in program and facility management for this to happen.

Aquatics Standards

Four major certifying agencies offer lifeguard training curricula:

• American Red Cross (ARC)

• Ellis and Associates

• YMCA of the USA

• United States Lifesaving Association (USLA)

Each of these agencies provides lifeguard, CPR, **automated external defibrillator (AED)**, and first aid training. Each aquatic facility should determine which agency best suits its facility.

There are three nationally recognized certifications for pool operators:

• **Certified pool operator (CPO)**, offered by the National Swimming Pool Foundation

• Aquatic facility operator (AFO), offered by the National Recreation and Park Association (NRPA)

• Pool operator on location (POOL), offered by the YMCA of the USA

Some states offer state-approved pool operator courses. These may be required in addition to the preceding certifications.

Lifeguards

Managers with the responsibilities of hiring, training, and evaluating the lifeguard staff must have lifeguard instructor certification. This will ensure that the staff has the proper training as dictated by codes. The aquatics professional should possess current lifeguard, CPR, AED, and first aid certifications, or the equivalents offered by the agencies listed previously, the same as the aquatics staff. They could also be familiar with, and certified as, if possible, a water safety instructor (WSI) or water fitness instructor (WFI) or the equivalent; scuba certification would also be beneficial. Having certification at a trainer level would help the professional enhance staff knowledge and training.

Supervision of any activity in an aquatic environment requires the use of one or more lifeguards. For multiple-user activities, the general ratio of lifeguards to swimmers is 1 to 75. This ratio is not written in stone; the number of lifeguards should be the number necessary to maintain a safe and healthy environment.

One or more lifeguards should be on duty any time the facility is open and available for use. Most states require pool operators on site while a facility is open (again, this is not universal, so knowledge of your municipal codes is essential here).

Lifeguards must be in complete charge and have the authority to enforce all rules and regulations pertaining to safety and sanitation. Policies and procedures must be understood by all employees in the facility (even nonaquatics staff) and the patrons in the facility. Other requirements are as follows:

- *Certifications.* Each lifeguard should possess a current American Red Cross or equivalent lifeguard certification, as well as first aid, AED, and CPR certifications that are immediately available to show to any enforcing agency.

- *Maturity or age.* Lifeguards should have mature judgment. They should be a minimum of 18 years of age at the time of employment (see figure 7.1).

- *Skills.* Lifeguards should be capable swimmers, competent in lifesaving methods, and able to perform artificial respiration and CPR, provide basic first aid, and use an AED.

- *Uniforms.* Lifeguards should wear appropriate swimsuits or uniforms with a distinguishing emblem or design so they are easily recognizable in a crowd by those using the aquatic facility or by personnel responding to an emergency situation.

- *Duties.* Lifeguards assigned to patron surveillance should not be subject to other duties that would distract their attention from proper observation and supervision or that would prevent them from providing immediate assistance to people in distress. Remember that the safety of the patrons is the number one priority of the aquatics staff.

- *Skills training.* Lifeguards should successfully complete an on-site **in-service training** program and attend monthly (or weekly) in-service training programs to prepare and train for actual emergencies (or as required by municipal codes; always go with the most frequent training requirement). In-service training topics may include:

  o Begin with a 500-yard timed swim and record the times. The Cooper swim test can be used to gauge condition.

  o Staff may break out into stations (10 to 15 minutes per station).

  Suggested Stations

  Spinal injury management (shallow water)

  Spinal injury management (deep water)

  AED skills

  CPR (adult skills)

  First aid skills

  Active victim rescue

  Kayak roll drills

  Rescue of a scuba diver

  Passive victim rescue

  Scenarios for dealing with problem patrons

  CPR (child and infant skills)

- *Physical training.* Lifeguards should successfully complete an on-site physical training program. For example, each lifeguard may be required to accumulate 500 points per week from the menu shown in figure 7.2, of which half the points must be from swimming. Other aquatics professionals should also participate in this program to keep their skills up to date.

Aquatics Program Instructors

The change in the purpose of an aquatic facility from the Roman bath to, well, an aquatic facil-

Lifeguard Preemployment Skill Assessment

Candidate name: _____   Test date: _____

Test facility: _____

Evaluator name: _____

Directions: Circle the appropriate score for each skill; tally on the last sheet.

500-yard swim (swimming pools only). Candidate must swim 500 yards on a marked course. Candidate may use any stroke or combination of strokes. Excessive stopping results in disqualification.

4	10 minutes or less
3	12 minutes or less
2	15 minutes or less
1	20 minutes or less
0	Greater than 20 minutes or does not finish

Spinal injury rescue skill assessment (deep water). Candidate must perform a spinal injury rescue of a victim facedown in deep water. Method used must be a skill recognized by a national certifying agency.

4	Uses recognized method. Holds victim securely. Easily treads with victim at surface. Victim can breathe freely.
3	Uses recognized method. Holds victim securely. Has trouble treading with victim at surface.
2	Uses a recognized method, but does so poorly. Does not hold victim securely, or victim periodically goes underwater.
1	Does not use recognized method. Cannot turn victim over or cannot keep victim above water.
0	Does not attempt skill.

Spinal injury rescue skill assessment (shallow water). Candidate must perform a spinal injury rescue of a victim facedown in shallow water. Method used must be a skill recognized by a national certifying agency.

4	Uses recognized method. Holds victim securely. Victim can breathe freely.
3	Uses recognized method. Does not hold victim securely.
2	Uses recognized method, but does so poorly. Does not hold victim securely, or victim periodically goes underwater.
1	Does not use recognized method. Cannot turn victim over or cannot keep victim above water.
0	Does not attempt skill.

Rescue of active victim, entry from lifeguard stand. Candidate must enter the water from the facility lifeguard stand (or deck if the facility does not have a stand) and perform a rescue of an active victim in deep water with available rescue equipment (rescue tube).

4	Performs safe entry from stand. Performs appropriate approach stroke. Performs appropriate rescue from rear. Tows victim to side and removes victim from water.
3	Performs safe entry from the stand. Performs appropriate approach stroke. Performs appropriate rescue from rear. Tows victim with difficulty and/or has difficulty removing victim from water.
2	Performs safe entry from stand. Performs appropriate approach stroke. Unable to perform successful tow and/or removal of victim from water.
1	Cannot perform effective entry from stand, or does so inappropriately. Unsure of how to tow or remove victim.
0	Does not attempt skill.

From NIRSA, 2008, *Campus Recreation: Essentials for the Professional* (Champaign, IL: Human Kinetics). © NIRSA.

Figure 7.1   Lifeguard preemployment skill assessment.

ity, has resulted in the need for a broad base of programming. Remember, the broader the programming base is, the more patrons you will attract (correspondingly creating greater revenue). This increase in programming comes with a price, though: You will need specifically trained instructors to plan, implement, and supervise the programs. An increasing number of organizations provide those certifications, including United States Water Fitness Association (USWFA), National Recreation and Park Association, American Council on Exercise (ACE), and American Fitness Association of America (AFAA). The list

continues to grow, but suffice it to say that the certification and organization should be researched before committing a facility to the programs it offers. Once the program is accepted, there are a few guidelines to follow:

- *Certified instructors* can supervise their own group activities, unless they will be in the water with the class. In that situation, an additional lifeguard should be required on the deck for supervision.

- *Aqua fitness instructors* and *aqua swimming instructors* in any aquatics program are required to have current certifications in lifeguarding and the American Red Cross Community Water Safety Program (or its equivalent). These certifications should be kept on record for viewing as required by all aquatics staff. Aquatics instructors should receive proper training from an appropriate, recognized agency; be trained and familiar with the facility in which the program or class is held; and have CPR and first aid certifications that are up-to-date.

Budgets and Revenue Generation

One of the major tasks of aquatics managers and directors is to generate sufficient revenue to cover the high costs of maintaining a natatorium. To best achieve this goal, they must know what their constituents want and need. A program that works at one facility will not automatically enjoy the same success at another. It is essential that aquatics directors do research (surveys, questionnaires, polls) to find out what the patrons want and need and then research the potential expenditure versus the potential revenue to make sure that the program is feasible. Safety, of course, is the top concern at all times. Any event that requires special consideration should be properly planned, and it should always be made clear that

Sample Physical Training Menus

Swimming 50 yards (any stroke)	25 points
Jogging 1 mile	100 points
Cycling 1 mile	50 points
Weight training (1 hour)	100 points
Aerobics fitness class	100 points

Figure 7.2   Sample physical training menus.

the aquatics professional is the final authority in all matters of arbitration or difference.

Renting the aquatic space to outside groups can help generate revenue. Outside groups can range from small-scale events such as birthday parties to larger-scale events such as competitive swim and dive meets. Because these events can infringe on paying members, however, they should be planned carefully. In addition, these groups will have special needs, and these must be delineated before the event occurs.

The primary method of generating revenue is to offer various aquatics programs that will meet the needs of the customer segments (Tobin, 2004). Aquatics sustainability relies on the provision of multigenerational activities that will in turn generate sufficient programming revenue (Quay & Dunn, 2004).

It should also be noted that an aquatic facility is not a monolith. The swim team can be practicing in the lanes while swim lessons take place in the shallow end, deep water aerobics are going on in the deeper water, and a lifeguard training class is meeting in the wet classroom. You should view your facility with the idea of generating revenue from every square foot individually, not from the space as a whole.

Programming

Aquatics programming choices are constantly evolving and expanding. When making an informed decision about the activities to offer patrons, aquatics professionals should take into account the changing nature of recreation and aquatic facilities, increasing number of aquatics standards and program providers, and changing populations (Reister & Cole, 1993). Not only do modern aquatics professionals deal with a finite and expensive asset, but they face the additional challenge of designing programs under the special concerns of liability, risk management, and safety in the water environment (Martin, 2002).

Policies and Procedures

Before establishing any aquatics program, professionals should seek legal consultation regarding record keeping and legal liability, among other things. Such consultations should be done on a continual basis to ensure that changing demands and requirements are met. This benefits the facility as well as every aquatics staff member and helps to set policies and procedures that are in line with the program's mission statement.

Policies need to be enforceable; policies that the program has no intention or ability to enforce will only lessen the efficacy of the other policies and procedures and will result in a complete destruction of staff morale. All aquatics staff personnel should be included in policy and procedure development. Lifeguards know what they need to do their jobs, as do other employees.

Once policies and procedures (for both patrons and employees) have been decided, they must be enforced evenly and fairly. There should be no exemptions from these ideals. Enforcement should also be codified to maintain support at all levels of enforcement and to ensure that enforcement cannot be abused (this will ensure legal protection as well).

Access to any program should be controlled by the participation policies and procedures of the institution. These procedures should also be followed when dealing with any patrons determined to be in a high-risk environment. Because safety is always a consideration, participation requirements for all activities must be clear and understood by both participants and supervisors alike.

The appropriate institutional waiver or medical screening forms should be used (see the discussion of the PAR-Q in chapter 5). Use of such forms should be considered during any legal consultation (see chapter 13, Risk Management).

Current Aquatics Industry Standards

Aquatics programming must adhere to health, professional, state, federal, and legal requirements. Programs should reflect the standards set by the sponsoring agency (i.e., American Red Cross, YMCA). Depending on the types of activities offered, the associations and agencies responsible for establishing standards of practice, instruction, and care should be consulted before establishing a program activity. These standards can be found by contacting the agencies themselves (e.g., the American Red Cross, the United States Water Fitness Association, the National Recreation and Park Association, the YMCA of the USA).

Aquatics programs should do the following:

- Provide a variety of aquatic sports and disciplines for patrons to participate in at their own pace.

- Maintain and instill in participants the idea of aquatic safety. All participants should learn and develop a feel for the water, and they should be taught the proper methods to ensure safety in any aquatic environment.

- Provide opportunities and assistance to participants at all levels who want to be involved with the aquatic environment.

- Recognize and provide a balanced, varied, and controlled program of activities as individuals or groups seek new sports or disciplines in the aquatic environment.

- Accommodate beginning, intermediate, and advanced participants, as well as those with varying levels of knowledge and expertise.

- Effectively instruct all levels of participants, provide as much self-direction as possible, and provide appropriate challenges when applicable.

- Offer voluntary programs that develop leadership skills and provide learning opportunities, fitness, and cardiorespiratory training.

Supervision

To be effective, all aquatics programs must have guidance, supervision, and a regular schedule.

Aquatic programs offering cardiorespiratory training activities can also incorporate fun and competition—for example, inner tube water polo.

William A. Cotton, Colorado State University.

Aquatics participants tend to be routine oriented. Sessions should be under the supervision of a lifeguard, unless the session instructor (or an instructor aide) is a lifeguard and remains on the deck, dock, pier, or shore at all times. The supervision chain for outside events should always end with the aquatics professional or representative of the aquatics department, who has the ultimate authority. Many times an event or group supervisor does not have the same primary goal as the aquatics supervisor (safety).

Scheduling

Although programs are a priority in aquatic facilities, times and locations should be set aside for self-directed activities such as recreational swimming and lap swimming. To meet the needs of these participants, facilities, equipment, and other necessary items should be coordinated and available. Providing equipment as a facility rather than having individual activities provide their own equipment helps ensure that it is in proper condition, thus reducing the potential for an incident or litigation.

Communication With Patrons

Communication with patrons is a crucial part of a successful aquatics program and facility. The facility should keep patrons informed on all pertinent policies and conditions. Pool closures and upcoming pool events that may alter their activities while at the pool can easily turn into a problem if patrons are not informed of these changes. Remember, pool patrons need time for planning any deviations from their routine. Facilities can use a variety of resources to alert their patrons of these events: Web site, scoreboards, posted signs at desks and locker rooms, and sandwich display boards. The greatest resource, however, is the lifeguards on the deck; they can answer questions pertaining to the change of routine.

Types of Programs

With the wide array of aquatic facilities out there, the ability to generate revenue from the aquatics area is endless. Following are the basic classes for most aquatics instructional programming:

- Learn to swim and dive
- Lifeguard training
- Masters swimming
- Scuba

- Water aerobics
- Water safety instructor

Instructional classes are the base of any revenue-generating aquatics program. For additional information on water depth, target markets, and equipment for programs, see table 7.1. Knowing these facility and space guidelines is critical when programming for a given population. Safety will dictate which is appropriate for each patron (e.g., a program for beginning swimmers should not be located in the 12-foot-deep diving well).

Aquatic Therapy Programs and Adapted Aquatics

Therapeutic and adapted aquatics programs cater to those with specialized requirements, in particular, seniors and patrons with disabilities or in need of therapy. Not only does this type of programming increase a facility's service to its community while creating a favorable public image, but it also decreases "dead water time" while catering to the increasing segment of older members of the population who, according to Martin (2002), will outnumber young people by the year 2050. Aquatic therapy is among the oldest healing interventions and is currently being used to assist senior patrons, swimmers with disabilities, and accident victims in various ways. Programs include arthritis patient therapy, stroke victim therapy, traction techniques, therapeutic massage, Watsu, tai chi, and adaptive swim lessons for developmentally disabled swimmers (Carter, 1998; Tobin, 2004).

Aquatic therapy programs have a number of special requirements that often require extensive planning and investment. These requirements vary with the type of program; for example, water temperatures may need to be above the temperature preferred by the majority of patrons (perhaps as high as 92 °F). Some pools have wheelchair access ramps and mechanical chairs if there are no therapy-specific pools within the facility. (This is standard in new facilities; retrofitted products are on the market to bring older facilities into ADA compliance.)

Generation X and Y Users

The rapidly growing programming segment for generation X and Y users caters to the sports minded. Emerging alternative sports such as underwater hockey and underwater rugby, water basketball, and volleyball are becoming increasingly popular and necessary in the standard aquatics sport program (Martin, 2002; Tobin, 2004). The attitude of this generation is, If you can do it on land, you can do it in the water (though it may not be practical). Programming is limited only by the imagination when it comes to these adaptations.

Recreational and Lap Swimming

Although recreational and lap swimming do not generate substantial revenue, they are an expected component of any aquatics program. Thus, facilities and equipment and other necessary items should be coordinated and available to meet the needs of these participants. Programs can increase this component by providing workouts in a structured or unstructured format for people to use at their own pace. These workouts should be customized to meet several levels of skill (bronze, silver, or gold or some variation of this type of theme).

Swimming for Fitness

Aqua fitness or water aerobics classes became popular after the national campaign to improve aerobic fitness throughout the United States during the 1970s. Aqua fitness remains popular today and appears as part of the standard activities offered by most aquatic facilities and recreation centers that feature a pool (Tobin, 2004). The style of class being offered by different facilities varies, but generally includes the more traditional water aerobics classes combined with modern variations such as aqua yoga, aqua jogging, pool spinning (with underwater bikes), and pre- and postnatal classes.

Swimming Instructor, Water Safety Instructor, and Lifeguard Training

Aquatics staff holding various certifications can allow the program to become self-sufficient and generate what it needs to maintain or even increase programming. At the same time staff certification is a great way to generate positive PR for the facility and showcase what the program does best (not to mention generating a little revenue in the process).

Community Water Safety Programs, Swim Lessons, and Coaching

Community water safety programs, swim lessons, and coaching teach adults and children as young as six months water-familiarization skills, basic aquatics skills, and water safety. The American

Table 7.1 Aquatics Programming

Program	Target market	Benefits	Facility factors	Equipment needs	Comments
Adapted aquatics	· People with disabilities · Pre- and post-surgery patients · Older adults	· Physical strength, endurance, and flexibility · Cardiorespiratory fitness · Social involvement · Psychological well-being · Fun	· ADA access · Safe access · Warmer water · 84-88 °F preferred · Accessible dressing area · Shallow water for teaching	· Flotation devices · Resistive equipment · Equipment for personal comfort · Mats · Lifts	
Community water safety courses	· Anyone (all ages, interests, and abilities) · Church groups · Families · Campers · Boaters · Day care providers · Scout groups	· Increased knowledge of safe practices in, on, and around the water · Recognition of dangerous situations and environments · Improvement in the quality of life around the water	· Some course content does not require a pool. · Immersion skills are limited but can be taught in water less than 5 ft deep.	· Reaching and throwing rescue devices · Throw bag · Personal flotation device	· Understand the needs of the customer and tailor the information to meet their needs
Competitive swimming	· Age group 5 to 18 years · Collegiate sport club · Intramurals · Masters	· Improvements in all dimensions of fitness · Opportunities for competition or social involvement · Opportunities to travel	· Minimum depth of 4 ft, 6 ft preferred · 75 × 45 ft for competition · Minimum deck space 10 ft on the sides and 25 ft on the ends · Water temperature 78 to 82 °F	· Lane lines · Starting blocks, stanchions · Flags · Recall rope · Lap counters · Whistle · Starting pistol · Stopwatches · Automated timing system is preferred.	· Starting blocks must be located in the deep end of the pool. · For competition, refer to the governing organization for rules.
Inner tube water polo	· All levels of swimmers · Church leagues · Scouts · Intramurals	· Social appeal · Recreational appeal · Competition	· Any size playing area, depending on number of players · Two teams of seven players	· Numbered water polo caps · Standard automobile size inner tubes · Referee flag stick, water polo goals, or orange safety cones to mark goals · Dividers at 2 m, 4 m, and mid-pool	· Can be played with mixed levels, coed · Nonswimmers may participate wearing life jacket.
Kayak	· Adventurers or extreme sports enthusiasts	· Core body workout	· Appropriate depth to practice water exits	· Kayak, kayak skirt, paddles, helmets, and life jackets	

(continued)

Table 7.1 *(continued)*

Program	Target market	Benefits	Facility factors	Equipment needs	Comments
Leisure or recreational swim	· Families · Elementary or middle school parties · Church groups · Scout groups · General users	· Social and recreational appeal · Opportunities for family interaction, relaxation, and fitness · Opportunities to reduce stress and improve skills	· 0 to 4.5 ft depth · Maximum bather load not to exceed 15 sq ft per user	· Equipment not needed but could enhance enjoyment · Sprays · Fountains · Small slide · Dive rings · Inner tubes · Balls of assorted sizes	· Older facilities may purchase large inflatable squeeze toys. · Have areas for small rental groups. · Provide theme day activities.
Swimming lessons	· Minimum six months to all ages	· Personal safety · Enhanced enjoyment of other aquatic activities	· 0 to 4.5 ft depth · Minimum of 9 ft to teach diving · Teaching area 45 × 45 ft	· Some programs require kickboards, life jackets, and reaching equipment.	· Market to Boy Scouts for swimming merit badge, day care centers, youth camps.
Swimming instructor or water safety instructor	· Participants must be 17 years old and have good swimming skills. · Education	· Job skills · Ability to analyze stroke mechanics · Professional development	· Yes, depending on the agency	· Yes, depending on the agency	· Market for adult education, continuing education.
Lifeguard training	· Teenagers, a minimum of 15 years old · Competitive swimmers · Boy and Girl Scouts	· Improved confidence around the water · Improved decision-making skills · Critical thinking · Maturity · Job skills	· Depending on the program, a minimum depth and distance for required skills	· Rescue tubes · Backboards · Head immobilizers · Reaching pole · Throwing device · Breathing barriers · Others, per agency	· Need classroom and VCR
Lifeguard instructor	· Usually late teens, early 20s · Lifeguards	· Job skills	· Minimum depth required	· Rescue tubes · Diving bricks · CPR mannequins · VCR/TV · Backboards	
Scuba	· Tend to be more affluent · Popular among young professionals	· Recreation · Possibly job skills	· Desired depth of at least 12 ft	· Dependent on tank, fins, weight belt, mask	
Small craft	· All ages and skill levels · Families · Scout groups · Church groups · Hunters · Fishermen	· Recreation · Safety	· No other programs should be scheduled in the facility unless a bulkhead is used.	· Life jackets · Boats · Paddles or oars	

Program	Target market	Benefits	Facility factors	Equipment needs	Comments
Springboard diving	· Age group 5 to 18 years · Club · Masters	· Opportunities for competition · Improved confidence · Improved self-worth · Strength · Coordination · Balance · Grace · Flexibility	· Consult NCAA and FINA standards	· Diving stand · Diving boards	· Introductory clinics · Competition · Demonstrations
Synchronized swimming	· Participants from swimming lessons · Competitive and recreational swimmers of all ages	· Conditioning · Balance · Grace · Flexibility · Strength · Enjoyment	· Minimum depth of 7 ft · Minimum competition area of 45 × 50 ft	· Adjustable lighting · Underwater lights · Underwater sound system · Locker room with more than one entrance preferred	· Incorporate synchronized skills into swim lessons. · Market pool to a local team for practice. · Offer clinics. · Collaborate with a dance company.
Underwater hockey	· Skilled swimmers · Competitive age group teams · Lifeguard teams · Intramurals	· Increased strength, endurance, and breath-holding capacity · Fun · Competition · Social involvement	· Official playing area is 22 × 25 m · Minimum depth of 2 ft · Maximum depth of 4 ft · Center spot in the middle of the playing area	· Mask · Fins · Snorkel · Official goal or markings on the pool wall · Hockey stick 11 in. long with a wrist strap · 3 in. diameter puck of protective rubberized material	· Has been an Olympic demonstration sport · Six players per team · Inexpensive work gloves coated with hot glue over the knuckles are recommended.
Water fitness	· Athletic teams · After-school teen programs · Adults and people with orthopedic limitations	· Improvements in all dimensions of fitness · Social interaction · Relaxation · Fun · Psychological benefits · Rehabilitation · Ease of progression	Shallow: · 3.5 to 4.5 ft maximum · Minimum 25 sq ft of surface area Deep: · Minimum depth of 5.5 to 6 ft · Minimum 36 sq ft of surface area	· None required but many types may enhance enjoyment and benefits · Resistive equipment · Buoyant equipment · Clothing for warmth · Shoes for foot protection	· Certifying agencies include AEA, USWFA, YMCA, local Red Cross units, AAHPERD.
Water polo	· Skilled swimmers · Competitive age groups · Lifeguards · Intramurals	· Improvement in every aspect of swimming fitness · Competition · Recreation · Strategy · Problem solving	· Rectangular playing area · Minimum size 75 × 45 ft · Constant water depth a minimum of 2 m (6.5 ft)	· Water polo ball · Numbered water polo caps · Water polo goals	

William A. Cotton, Colorado State University.

Alternative sports like water basketball are expanding standard aquatics sport programs to meet the needs of sports-minded generation X and Y participants.

Red Cross, YMCA, and other agencies sponsor and sometimes offer these classes.

Aquatic Sport Clubs

All aquatic facilities should accommodate sport clubs that provide competitive and semicompetitive activities for their members. The aquatics professional must keep in mind that each of the sports and activities in the following list requires special supervision and in many cases unique safety rules and guidelines. These should be made clear to the head of the organization, each participant, and the aquatics supervisors on duty during the activity. The aquatics professional on duty during the event or practice has the last word regarding rules and policy interpretation. Traditional aquatic sports are as follows:

- Board diving
- Kayaking

- Rowing
- Scuba diving
- Skin diving
- Swimming
- Synchronized swimming
- Water polo
- Waterskiing

Evaluating and Assessing Aquatics Programs

Evaluations play an important role in any program. There are four forms of evaluations:

1. Participant evaluations are a key way to find out whether your programs are meeting users' needs.

2. Self-evaluations give instructors the opportunity to assess how they have contributed to the program's mission and to its users.

© Eyewire/Photodisc/Getty Images

Aquatic sport clubs focus on a number of different recreational activities, with kayaking among them.

3. Supervisor evaluations allow employees and supervisors to discuss employees' performance.

4. Staff evaluations of their supervisors provide feedback and an outlet for any concerns.

Pool and Spa Facility Maintenance

In a swimming pool environment, the quality of the water and other factors are controlled directly by state or municipal health codes. These codes reflect minimum standards; however, individual facilities can always do more. If aquatics professionals decide to hold their facilities to higher standards, they should make sure they can do so cost effectively and that they will be able to maintain those standards. Lowering standards once they have been set can be problematic. Professionals should look at the standards of other facilities; they might be liable to meet those standards, even if the standards exceed the state codes.

Staff Training for Pool Quality

All aquatics staff members should play a key role in pool maintenance by knowing when to test water, how to treat water, and how to accurately monitor water chemistry trends. Tobin (2004) suggested that properly trained and certified aquatics staff who possess baseline knowledge of pool maintenance and operations form the front line of successful pool maintenance and operations. Aquatics professionals should check the test results of staff members at an in-service or randomly throughout their employment. The numbers on the test comparator can be interpreted 10 different ways by 10 different people. It is important to know this when looking at the records. It might explain why chemical problems occur every Friday night but not on Saturday morning!

Many U.S. states require that facilities with aquatic features and programs have at least one staff member educated as a certified pool operator (CPO), aquatic facility operator (AFO), or pool operator by a nationally recognized organization such as the YMCA (Anderson, 2003).

Daily Pool, Spa, or Facility Maintenance

The natatorium is often the highlight of the community or recreation center. However, maintaining public swimming pools and spas at an acceptable standard is a massive task for the aquatics manager. Proactive and preventative maintenance is vital to avoid problems.

Aquatics programs must be offered in an environment that is clean, safe, and conducive to participation, while also meeting the unique requirements placed on aquatic facilities. Several aspects must be required:

- The construction, maintenance, and quality of care provided in an aquatic facility are directly related to the respective state health and safety codes for swimming pools.

- The aquatics professional must maintain a copy of these codes, and the guidelines should be followed in their entirety.

- The blood-borne pathogens programs of the **Occupational Safety and Health Administration (OSHA)** should be considered for all aquatic facilities because of the possibility of injury and contamination of surfaces in aquatic environments. Many states require that all aquatics personnel have hepatitis B vaccinations.

- All aquatics personnel must receive training in OSHA programs to ensure that they never compromise their safety unknowingly by performing a task that is in violation of the OSHA directives.

- The aquatic facility should be kept clear of all obstructions to patron traffic and allow for respective state fire codes to be upheld.

- Maintenance inspections should be conducted on a regular basis for elements of the facility that are not on the daily inspection list (e.g., pump bearings, fuses, chemical feed lines).

- Equipment for aquatic facilities should have properly secured storage areas.

The difficulty of coping with the wide scope of maintenance and operational responsibilities is confirmed by the findings of a recent national study undertaken by the U.S. Centers for Disease Control and Prevention (CDC). Data collected from more than 22,131 pool inspections across the United States revealed that more than 50 percent of all pools investigated had one or more violations, and 8 percent of all violations were considered serious enough to warrant immediate closure of the pool. Over 75 percent of the violations recorded

Courtesy of University of Alabama.

Swimming pools must be maintained at an acceptable standard so that aquatics programming can be offered in a clean, safe environment.

were either water chemistry or filtration and water recirculation violations (CDC, n.d.).

Water Chemistry and Quality

"Water chemistry involves maintaining proper levels of sanitizers to kill bacteria and oxidize organic matter (like algae) and sustaining proper water balance" (Tobin, 2004). A solid pool maintenance regime requires a balance of proper water chemistry, filtration, and circulation.

Maintaining water quality and water chemistry is a concern for all aquatics staff. It requires consistent monitoring of pH balance, chlorine, and other chemical levels according to local and state government regulations (National Spa & Pool Institute, 2004). Recommended ranges for chemical levels vary depending on state and local government guidelines. Chemicals are necessary to ensure a sparkling clean pool with clear water. Such water quality makes the pool attractive to users and is a major factor in disease and drowning prevention.

The acceptable levels of chemicals vary slightly from organization to organization. For example, the U.S. Centers for Disease Control and Prevention (CDC) recommends the following:

Optimal levels for pH	7.2-7.8
Alkalinity levels	80-120 ppm
Calcium hardness levels	200-400 ppm

See also tables 7.2 and 7.3.

If pool operators and aquatics staff continually allow their pools to have high pH levels, chlorine may become ineffective as a disinfectant, increasing the risk of disease outbreak.

Filtration and Circulation

Water is treated and cleaned in two ways: chemically and physically. When water chemistry is poor, everyone can see that the water is cloudy or has a horrendous odor. The physical treatment of the water is known as filtration. Poorly functioning filtration and circulation systems may lead to cloudy water, making it difficult for lifeguards to see swimmers in distress.

The pump is the heart of the system, moving water from the pool shell into the pump room where the water is cleaned (filtered), heated, and then chemically treated (adding an oxidizer and pH adjuster). As stated earlier, the modern aquatic

Table 7.2   Ideal Water Quality

Water quality	pH
· Poor chlorine disinfection · Eye irritation · Skin irritation	8.0
· Most ideal for eye comfort and disinfection	7.8
	7.6
	7.2
· Eye irritation · Skin irritation · Pipe corrosion	<7.0

Source: www.cdc.gov/healthyswimming.

facility must coordinate several elements and procedures into one system. This systems approach means that all elements must function together, or the whole suffers. Circulation and filtration are the means of achieving this. Modern pools move all of the water in the pool (gallonage) past the filter every six hours (older pools do so every eight hours). Specialty pools (spas, hot tubs, and so on) can move the pool capacity past the filter in as little as 10 minutes. This is how the water is cleaned and sanitized. You can measure this

with the flow meter (located on a long, straight run of pipe in the pump room—usually located just before the water goes back to the pool).

Most of the chemical and physical work of the pool mechanics is done in the filter room and circulation system. Access should be limited to those people who are trained in using and maintaining the equipment located there.

Handling and Storing Chemicals

The National Spa & Pool Institute (NSPI) has a number of additional recommendations regarding both the handling and storing of chemicals.

Handling Chemicals

The aquatic environment is filled with a host of chemicals that are toxic and environmentally unfriendly. It would be impractical to list all of the chemicals at a pool and how to handle them (chlorine alone comes in liquid, gas, and solid forms—the solid of which occurs in five different forms). Protocols for handling chemical spills should be set in accordance with state and federal regulations. These regulations are generally available from chemical providers. Chemical storage and usage should follow the material safety data sheets (MSDS) provided by the chemical supplier; these sheets

Table 7.3   Factors Necessary to Calculate Water Quality

TF		CF		AF	
Temperature (Fahrenheit)	Factor	Calcium hardness	Factor	Total alkalinity	Factor
32	0.1	5 ppm	0.3	5 ppm	0.7
37	0.1	25	1.0	25	1.4
46	0.2	50	1.3	50	1.7
53	0.3	75	1.5	75	1.9
60	0.4	100	1.6	100	2.0
66	0.5	150	1.8	150	2.2
76	0.6	200	1.9	200	2.3
84	0.7	300	2.1	300	2.5
94	0.8	400	2.2	400	2.6
105	0.9	800	2.5	800	2.9
128	1.0	1000	2.6	1000	3.0

Substitute the pool test results.

Saturation index: pH + TF + CF + AF – 12.1

Example: ph 7.4, temperature 76 °F, calcium hardness 100, total alkalinity 50

S.I. = 7.4 (pH) + 0.6 (TF) + 1.6 (CF) + 1.7 (AF) – 12.1

The result is a saturation index of –0.8

Index results between –0.5 and +0.5 indicate balanced water.

Index results above +0.5 result in scale forming.

Index results below –0.5 result in corrosion.

should be available at the storage site and also in a safe and secure (but accessible) location.

When using pool chemicals, staff should always read the labels and directions carefully. Following are additional safety procedures to follow that apply to *all* chemical handling at an aquatic facility:

- Keep all chemicals out of the reach of children.
- Never mix two chemicals together.
- Never add chemicals to the pool when swimmers are in the water.
- Only add chemicals to the water; *never* add water to chemicals.
- Never reuse old chemical containers.
- Replace chemical test reagents used with test kits at least once a season or more often as required.

Storing Chemicals

Wet and dry chemicals should be stored separately, if at all possible in different rooms. Material safety data sheets (MSDS) should be located with the chemical and in an office (safe and accessible). Chemical safety designation signs (combustible diamond) should be posted on the door of any room where chemicals are stored. Proper ventilation should be maintained in all storage rooms, and staff should never venture into a chemical room alone. They should always use the buddy system and have someone outside the room when they enter (or at least make sure that someone knows where they are and checks up on them after a short interval). Here are some general chemical storage guidelines:

- Close all lids tightly.
- Never remove the label from a chemical storage container.
- Store chemicals in an area that is cool, dry, and well-ventilated.
- Store liquid chemicals away from flammable items.
- Wash hands thoroughly after using chemicals.

Additional Maintenance Strategies

A number of additional strategies are also necessary to ensure the smooth running of an aquatic facility. These include maintaining sufficient funds in reserve to address any unforeseen maintenance and operational issues, regularly using checklists, performing pool audits, and offering regular training.

Safety and Risk Management

Injury prevention in the aquatic setting must be part of the facility's risk management program. Because risk management is largely about prevention, it should involve identifying the conditions and behaviors that may lead to injuries and the steps that need to be taken to eliminate them wherever possible (American Red Cross, 2001). The management of risk in aquatic settings is increasingly important for aquatics professionals in light of increasing litigation and soaring insurance costs, not to mention the potential outcomes of serious aquatic incidents.

Clearly, not all injuries are preventable, and accidents will still happen. The key for aquatics and recreation managers and professionals is to identify potentially dangerous scenarios and the circumstances that contribute to these situations so managers and staff can be reasonably prepared to deal with them as they arise. One way to identify problems is to have all aquatics personnel vigilantly use a monthly facility checklist to spot loose ladder handles, any standing pools of water, slippery decks, unsecured drain covers, and so on. Every staff member should know that he or she is responsible for safety and reporting any potential dangerous areas. See also chapter 13 for legal issues regarding risk management.

Types of Risks

The most significant of risks is drowning, and it is a leading cause of accidental death in the United States (especially for children under the age of five years). Drownings occur in both natural settings such as oceans and lakes and swimming pools (see the National Spa & Pool Institute's Web site at www.nspi.org). According to the U.S. Centers for Disease Control and Prevention (CDC), in 2004, 3,308 people drowned in the United States, averaging nine people per day (this does not include those who drowned in boating-related incidents) (U.S. Centers for Disease Control and Prevention, 2006).

For every child who drowns, five receive emergency department care for nonfatal submersion injuries. More than half of these children require hospitalization (U.S. Centers for Disease Control and Prevention, 2006). Nonfatal incidents can cause brain damage that results in long-term disabilities ranging from memory problems and learning disabilities to the permanent loss of basic functioning (i.e., permanent vegetative state). Although this number includes those who drowned in all aquatic settings, it clearly illustrates the magnitude of the problem.

Lachocki (2004) listed the following potential risks common to aquatic facilities:

- Cuts and abrasions
- Diving injuries
- Electrocution
- Hair entanglement and entrapment
- Hazardous chemical exposure
- Neck and spinal injuries
- Recreational water illness outbreaks
- Paralysis
- Slips and falls

Prevention and Proactive Risk Management

Aquatic facilities usually pose the biggest risk in any recreation center, which is why so much of the aquatics literature focuses on risk management (Lachocki, 2004). Thus, aquatics professionals must be especially vigilant when developing a risk management program to ensure the safe operation of their facilities. Risk management practices should begin with the construction phase of the facility. Architects and builders should have knowledge of recreation facilities and the particular risks and regulations pertaining to these facilities. Proactive risk management can be greatly enhanced through the careful planning of the facility. It is never too early to plan for safety and risk management.

There are many elements to risk management, and when outlined, most are common sense. The following steps may be included in a risk management plan:

- *Identify the risks.* Is equipment damaged or faulty in any way? Is there a hole in the middle of the playing field? Is the equipment being used properly by the participant?

- *Evaluate the risks.* Predicting how severe an injury might be and how often an accident might happen helps to evaluate the risk. If severe injury or death is a possibility—even if it were to happen only once—it would be a high risk. If the injury is more likely to be a sprained ankle—but a sprained ankle that could happen over and over again—that is also a red flag.

- Address the risks as follows:
  - *Avoidance* is one course of action. Eliminating the facility, equipment, or activity may remove the risk.
  - *Reduce the risks* by posting applicable use and safety signage, instructing participants on the proper use of the equipment or the proper way of performing an activity, and ensuring that well-trained staff are on duty.
  - *Doing nothing* is an option if the accident or injury were the result of the carelessness of the injured party or an act of God.
  - *Transfer the risks.* The most common way to do this is to purchase liability insurance. Many public agencies, including state schools, are self-insured. However, campus recreation programs and facilities are often considered auxiliary services, with private sources of funding (such as student fees and program income, for example). To look into the insurance options that are available, seek guidance from the university's risk management department.

- *Implement the risk management plan.* Based on the information gathered while assessing the risks, develop a plan and put it into action. It is often worthwhile to work in conjunction with the university's risk management team to develop the plan.

Educating Patrons: Facility Rules and Procedures

Rules must be enforced at all times—no exceptions. Pools are fun, but rules are there to maintain a safe aquatic environment. Although each facility is unique and has its own rules, the following is a list of general rules:

- Shower before entering the pool.
- Proper bathing attire is required.
- No running on the deck.
- Patrons must obey the lifeguard on duty and all facility signage.
- No swimming under the bulkhead.
- Children under the age of eight must be under the direct supervision of a parent or guardian.
- Infants and toddlers not toilet trained must wear disposable swim diapers or plastic pants.

Sample Facility Safety Checklist

	Yes	No	Action taken	Date of safety check	Action needed
DECK					
Safety equipment in good condition					
Rescue tubes and straps in good condition					
Backboards with head immobilizers and straps readily accessible					
First aid station clean					
First aid equipment (AED and oxygen equipment) accessible; supplies accessible and well stocked					
Telephones working properly					
Deck not slippery and in good condition					
Deck clear of patrons' belongings					
All equipment used by patrons stored properly					
Lifeguard stands clean and in good condition					
Deck clear of standing water					
Deck clear of glass objects					
POOL					
Ladders secured properly					
Ladder handles clean and rust free					
Steps not slippery and in good condition					
Ramp not slippery and in good condition					
Drain covers secured properly					
Drain covers clean					
Lifelines and buoys in order					
Water color satisfactory					
Pool free of debris					
Gutters clean					
Water temperature in pool satisfactory					
Water temperature in spa satisfactory					
LOCKER ROOMS					
All areas clean and free of algae					
Floors clean and not slippery					
Showers in good condition (no drips)					
Soap available					
Drains clean					
Wastebaskets empty					
Drinking fountains and sinks clean and in good working order					

From NIRSA, 2008, *Campus Recreation: Essentials for the Professional* (Champaign, IL: Human Kinetics). Reprinted, by permission, from Oregon State University.

Figure 7.3 Facility safety checklist.

Use of Checklists

One of the keys to developing a successful risk management strategy to ensure a safe environment for participants is the use of checklists. Anderson (2003) suggested that "Checklists are ideal for translating operations and maintenance manual recommendations into the needed schedules that keep facility components looking and operating at their peak" (p. 19).

Daily, monthly, and annual checklists can and should be used by the facility and aquatics professionals (see figure 7.3). A checklist may be used in the annual inspection. An audit of the aquatic facility area by an outsider would help to bring a different perspective into the review of the facility. Checklists should include the following:

- Listing the needs of bigger projects that may require time to complete and are best done during shutdown
- Checking the AED (automated external defibrillator) for function
- Ensuring the correct positioning of rescue equipment
- Evaluating the position of the lifeguard stations
- Checking first aid equipment
- Checking equipment used by patrons (fins, pull buoys, kickboards, flotation belts)

Guidelines for Providing a Safe Aquatic Environment

· Conduct regular and thorough facility inspections (including pool, pool deck, rescue equipment, lifeguards, diving boards, and locker rooms).

· Ensure that the facility has sufficient and clear signage regarding pool and facility rules and regulations and potential risks.

· Ensure that all staff members are aware of and practice the maintenance and operation techniques necessary to ensure the smooth running of the pool (i.e., water quality and testing; pool temperature, chemistry, and filtration).

· Provide good aquatic rescue and maintenance equipment appropriate to the facility.

· Ensure that all aquatics staff members are trained and certified by nationally recognized organizations such as the American Red Cross or the YMCA of the USA.

· Ensure that all staff members are familiar with their respective roles in the event of an emergency.

· Contact **emergency medical services (EMS)** and identify the best entrance and exit they can use in an emergency. Rehearse using them.

· Post a drawing of the entrances EMS should use, with EMS phone numbers, so all staff give them the same directions.

· Provide adequate supervision for the facility.

When developing checklists, aquatics directors should ensure that they are consistent with both the guidelines of the facility and all relevant local, state, and federal regulatory bodies (Tobin, 2004). Some national associations, including the Fédération Internationale de Natation (FINA), the National Spa & Pool Institute, USA Swimming, and the National Aquatic Coalition, offer checklist guidance.

Emergency Action Plans

Staff should be prepared for emergencies. An **emergency action plan (EAP)** tells the employee what to do during an emergency. Because each facility is different, those who manage several facilities may have to train their staff on several different EAPs. The plan must cover non-life-threatening and life-threatening emergencies. Each employee should be trained on the emergency action plan during initial training and annually thereafter.

EAPs should be reviewed and updated if necessary on an annual basis and should be uniform within multiuse facilities. To create the best EAP, aquatics professionals should involve the staff in its development and review. Remember, they will be working with it constantly, and they will know what is best for them to keep the environment safe.

All aquatics staff members should be reminded that emergencies can occur at anytime. Having a sound and proven EAP in place is crucial to ensuring the successful resolution of the emergency situation. An EAP must address all potentially relevant categories of emergencies and risks pertinent to the facility (American Red Cross, 1997).

The American Red Cross (1997) provides a useful template to use to develop a comprehensive EAP that may be easily adapted to any program in any type of facility and to all relevant categories of emergencies (see figures 7.4 and 7.5).

There are three major components to an emergency action plan (see also figure 7.6):

1. Before the emergency:

   - All staff should have the necessary training and certifications (lifeguarding, first aid, CPR, use of the AED).

   - All staff members should have a working knowledge of the facility's emergency action plan and understand their particular role in it.

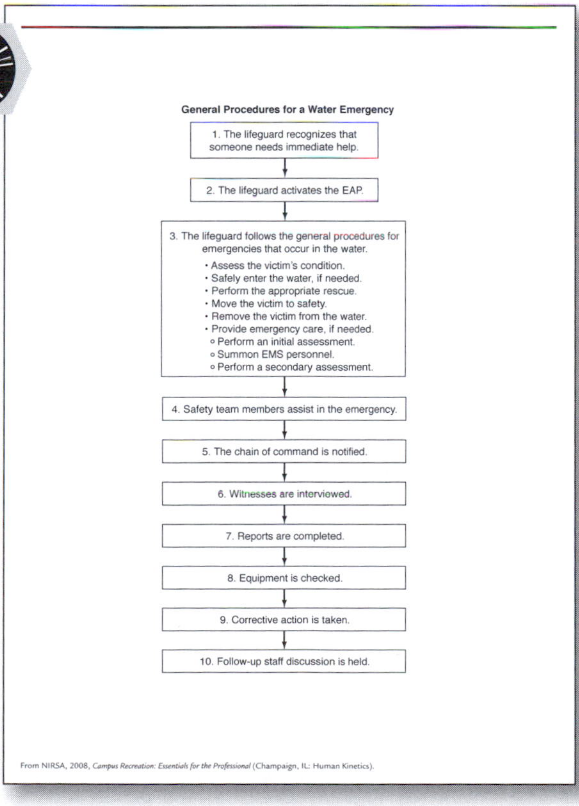

Figure 7.4 General procedures for a water emergency.

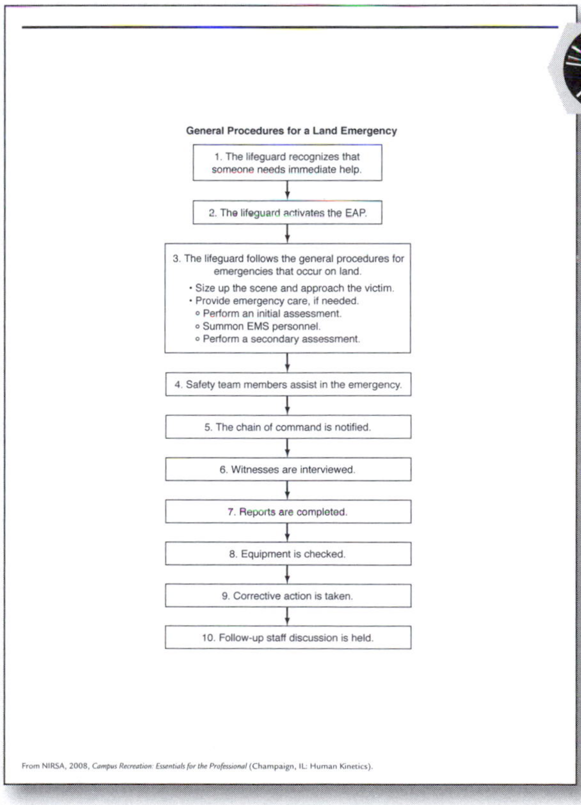

Figure 7.5 General procedures for a land emergency.

- Ensure that all emergency equipment is ready to use.
2. During the emergency:
   - Activation of EAP
   - Crowd control, if necessary
3. After the emergency:
   - Postincident cleanup
   - Accident report and incident forms and any additional paperwork
   - Analysis of policies and procedures
   - Postincident debriefing and counseling, if necessary

Accident Report Form and Record Keeping

There are various ways to ensure sound record keeping in the case of an emergency; an accident report form is commonly used (see figure 7.7). These forms are critical parts of facilities' EAPs and are often the key documents in the case of litigation. Sperling (2001) suggested that the incident or accident report form can either protect an organization or bring about its downfall, depending on how it is completed.

Aquatics professionals and management must ensure that all aquatics staff do the following:

- Fill out the form completely and correctly.

- Understand the significance of asking the right questions.

- Respond to incidents.

It is imperative that staff use accident report forms to collect detailed and accurate information pertaining to the incident as soon as possible after the incident or emergency. The following information should be recorded:

- Details of the care given and the time and location of the incident

- Details of the injury

- Personal details of the injured party

- Subsequent treatment provided

Conclusion

Aquatic facilities have an important role to play in offering users a unique and fun venue in which to exercise and enjoy their leisure time. This form of recreation has a long history that dates

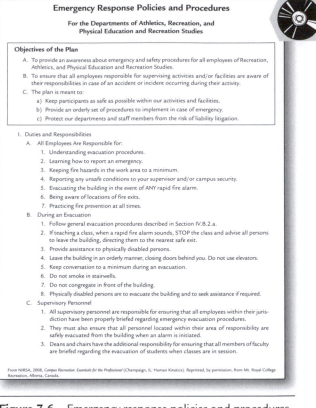

Figure 7.6 Emergency response policies and procedures.

Figure 7.7 Aquatic facility accident report form.

back to the Roman baths of antiquity. The aquatic facility has become an intricate web of systems that, when woven tightly enough, form a safe and healthy fabric capable of supporting the needs of a population that is becoming more diverse each year. The need to generate revenue and provide a greater variety of activity choices has spurred the industry and profession to creative endeavors that will continue into the foreseeable future. It is the job of the aquatics professional and the aquatic facility to meet this challenge and, if possible, to anticipate its outcome. This can be done if all components (chemistry, filtration, risk management, training, programming, communication, and planning) are applied. Perhaps the most important thing to maintain is humility. This is a form of recreation that has existed for over 2,000 years, and there are many aquatics professionals that have come before who can inspire; yet there are also just as many out there now who can assist.

Resources

Risk Management

American Society for Testing and Materials
www.astm.org

Fédération Internationale de Natation
www.fina.org

National Spa & Pool Institute
www.nspi.org

USA Diving
www.usadiving.org

USA Swimming
www.usswim.org

U.S. Centers for Disease Control and Prevention
www.cdc.gov

Rescue Equipment, Training Programs, and Education

American Red Cross
www.redcross.org

American Safety and Health Institute
www.ashinstitute.org

Aquatic Partners
www.aquaticpartners.com

Aquatic Safety Research Group
www.aquaticsafetygroup.com

Jeff Ellis & Associates, Inc.
www.jellis.com

National Recreation and Park Association
www.nrpa.org

National Swimming Pool Foundation
www.nspf.com

Lifesaving Society
www.lifesaving.org

YMCA
www.ymca.net

References

American Red Cross. (1997). *Lifeguard training manual.* Yardley, PA: Staywell.

American Red Cross. (2001). *Lifeguard training manual.* Yardley, PA: Staywell.

Anderson, K. (2003, April). Keeping up appearances. *Recreation Management,* 14-22.

Carter, M. (1998). Aquatics: HPERD linkage to health and human services. *Journal of Physical Education, Recreation and Dance, 69*(3), 6.

Lachocki, T. (2004, September). Public health. *Recreation Management,* 10-11.

Martin, M. (2002, January/February). Pool your resources. *Recreation Management,* 24-31.

National Spa & Pool Institute. (2004). *Children aren't waterproof.* Alexandria, VA: Author.

National Sporting Goods Association. (n.d.). 2004 survey. Retrieved from www.nsga.org/public/pages/index.

Quay, B., and Dunn, J. (2004, July/August). All purpose solution. *Aquatics International,* 62-66.

Reister, V., & Cole, A. (1993). Start active in the water. *Journal of Physical Education, Recreation and Dance, 64*(1), 52-54.

Sperling, J. (2001, November/December). Reporting for duty. *Aquatics International,* 16.

Tobin, K. (2004, April). Safe and swim: The best risk management practices for pool and water park safety. *Recreation Management,* 20-27.

U.S. Centers for Disease Control and Prevention. (2006). Water-Related Injuries: Fact Sheet. Retrieved from www.cdc.gov/ncipc/factsheets/drown.htm.

U.S. Centers for Disease Control and Prevention. (n.d.). Retrieved from www.cdc.gov/mmwr/preview/mmwrhtml/mm52a1.htm.

Glossary

automated external defibrillator (AED)—A device designed to administer a controlled shock to a pulseless victim.

certified pool operator (CPO)—A certification offered by the National Swimming Pool Foundation. May also refer to a person responsible for swimming pool maintenance in a recreation facility.

emergency action plan (EAP)—A comprehensive plan for responding to emergencies at a given facility.

emergency medical services (EMS)—The prehospital response, normally an ambulance and crew that are in the community.

in-service training—Regular or topic-specific training given to staff by their employer, that is designed to maintain currency of specific job-related skills.

natatorium—An aquatic facility.

Occupational Safety and Health Administration (OSHA)—The federal agency responsible for the development, administration, and enforcement of employment-related health and safety regulations.

CHAPTER 8

Outdoor Recreation

Erin Rausch, MS, Director, Center for Community Involvement, University of the Pacific
Nicole Olmeda, CRSS, MEd, Assistant Director, Division of Recreational Sports, The University of Texas at Austin
Josh Norris, CRSS, MA, Coordinator, Climbing and Adventure Education, Oregon State University

> Life is either a great adventure or nothing.
>
> *Helen Keller*

The role of outdoor recreation programming in a campus recreation department has grown over the years. Trips and equipment rentals have been a staple of outdoor recreation programs for decades, and climbing walls and challenge courses are becoming standard options as well. As the programs and facilities expand, outdoor recreation continues to be a vital component of campus recreation departments.

No matter what type of activities are offered, common elements are consistently found in outdoor recreation programs across the country. In this chapter we discuss some of these common program administration and operational elements, including the following:

- Philosophy and theory
- Legal issues and risk management
- Activity space and facilities
- Equipment
- Personnel
- Marketing
- Budgets

In addition to program administration and operations, the area of outdoor recreation involves many facets of both facility and program management. The components of the programs vary greatly depending on the institution's geographic location, size, organizational philosophy, and available resources. The following are typical outdoor recreation program components:

- Adventure trips
- Climbing wall
- Equipment rental
- Instructional clinics and workshops

Additional components might also include the following:

- Ropes or challenge course
- Facilities such as marinas and retreat centers
- Family and youth programs
- Camps

Outdoor professionals have career choices to consider as well as professional associations to help guide them. These are discussed at the end of the chapter.

Program Administration and Operations

The specifics of each university's administrative policies will vary, but some of the underlying elements that go into the decision-making process are presented here.

Outdoor Recreation Philosophies

The foundation of any campus outdoor recreation program is the program's philosophy or mission statement. Following a clearly defined philosophy will assist the primary administrator in short- and long-term goal setting and in establishing a direction for the programs and the activities offered. Whether an outdoor program is recreation or education based makes a tremendous difference in how it is managed and developed. Programs with foundations in recreation have an emphasis on fun and enjoyment, whereas programs with education as a fundamental purpose might lean more heavily toward instructional components, skill development, and environmental issues.

The purposes of outdoor programs can be as varied as the opportunities they provide, and many outdoor programs serve several purposes, as well as a diverse clientele. Students often participate in outdoor activities to increase their knowledge or skill in a certain area or because they are seeking a particular experience. Colleges and universities often desire and value outdoor programs as part of a comprehensive campus recreational sport department because they add an additional avenue for the pursuit of well-rounded and healthy lifestyles, and this generally supports the mission and vision of such organizations.

Although outdoor programs are often part of larger campus recreation efforts at colleges and universities, most maintain a unique philosophy that is derived from the cross-sections of university life and outdoor culture.

The outdoor industry itself, of which college and university outdoor programs are a small part, has many unique qualities. Compared to industries that revolve solely around business, the outdoor industry revolves around recreation, outdoor spaces, and the people who use those spaces. Few enter the industry with the intention of getting rich, and many do so to further something they are passionate about.

The "playing field" for outdoor recreation is a lot more varied and uncontrolled than that of the other program areas within campus recreation.

This "field" could be the wilderness, the mountains, a lake, an ocean, a trail, or even the air. For this reason it is critical to be aware of how our actions affect the field that we use. As more people begin to use outdoor spaces, we realize how this use affects the very spaces we visit. The Leave No Trace movement was born out of this realization.

Leave No Trace

There are seven **principles of Leave No Trace** (see figure 8.1). These principles are not a set of hard-and-fast rules governing people's actions in the field. Rather, they suggest behaviors and actions that reflect a genuine respect for the resource and an understanding of how behaviors affect that resource. The Leave No Trace principles are not a list of dos and don'ts, but rather a set of guidelines to help people understand their actions with respect to the resource. This is central to the philosophy of Leave No Trace; a list of rules cannot replace sound judgment and a true understanding of an environment with so much variation.

The Leave No Trace Center for Outdoor Ethics builds greatly needed environmental programs that teach awareness and respect for our country's natural areas. This nonprofit organization works with diverse populations to integrate a nationally recognized set of skills that help outdoor enthusiasts recognize and reduce their impact on the natural environment. Leave No Trace provides specific training and educational materials that take basic messages and techniques and apply them to our country's varied ecosystems and the multitude of outdoor activities in which people participate.

Why Leave No Trace?

We all have taken a pinecone, veered off the trail, or left an apple core behind. Although these actions seem harmless at the time, until we learn to reduce our impact, the quality of our outdoor experiences, vegetation, and wildlife habitat are at critical risk. Also at risk is our continued access to wildlands because land agencies must take restrictive action to protect the resources they manage. The Leave No Trace Center for Outdoor Ethics believes that although these impacts are widespread and the causes are complex, the solution is simple: "Change behavior through partnership, research, and education, one person at a time" (Leave No Trace Center for Outdoor Ethics, n.d.).

Risk Management

The arenas for outdoor recreation activities are often fundamentally less controlled than our daily living spaces. As such, they carry **inherent risks**, or risks that, if removed, would fundamentally change the activity at its core. For example, climbing would not be climbing without the inherent risk of falling.

Outdoor programs are often closely tied to these risks, relying on them as vessels for core program philosophies. To participants, all risks feel the same once they are cognizant of them. To an administrator, however, there is a huge difference between real risks and perceived risks. Indoor rock climbing offers a good example of the difference between these two types of risk. When we are high off the ground, our bodies and minds tell us we are in danger of falling a great distance and impacting the ground. Statistically, we know there is a very remote possibility of this actually happening. Yet, even with this knowledge, when we begin to climb to height, our pulse increases, our respiration becomes labored, and we ponder an unfortunate, though unlikely, outcome. This is an example of a risk that is more perceived than real. A converse example would be crossing a glacier on a rope team; in this case our fears or perceptions of risk may indeed be very real. Both are effective in providing the experiences programs strive for. Removing many of these real risks would be as seemingly ridiculous as removing a baseball from a baseball game so participants are not exposed to a high-velocity encounter with the ball.

Outdoor recreation often provides more perceived and real risks associated with the environment and groups than other types of programming areas. Being near hazardous terrain but distant from advanced emergency health care facilities is a distinct characteristic of outdoor pursuits. Some of these risks are easily mitigated; others are not. When it comes to outdoor programming, a comprehensive risk management philosophy and plan are requisite.

An organization needs to address five main concepts when developing an effective outdoor recreation risk management plan:

1. Protection of the university, its assets, and its employees (see chapter 13)

2. Emergency or incident response plan specific to the activities and areas used

3. Accident, injury, and near miss reporting and review

Principles of Leave No Trace

1. Plan ahead and prepare.
   - Know the regulations and special concerns for the area you'll visit.
   - Prepare for extreme weather, hazards, and emergencies.
   - Schedule your trip to avoid times of high use.
   - Visit in small groups. Split larger parties into groups of four to six.
   - Repackage food to minimize waste.
   - Use a map and compass to eliminate the use of marking paint, rock cairns, or flagging.
2. Travel and camp on durable surfaces.
   - Durable surfaces include established trails and campsites, rock, gravel, dry grasses, and snow.
   - Protect riparian areas by camping at least 200 feet from lakes and streams.
   - Good campsites are found, not made. Altering a site is not necessary.
   - In popular areas:
     - Concentrate use on existing trails and campsites.
     - Walk single file in the middle of the trail, even when wet or muddy.
     - Keep campsites small. Focus activity in areas where vegetation is absent.
   - In pristine areas:
     - Disperse use to prevent the creation of campsites and trails.
     - Avoid places where impacts are just beginning.
3. Dispose of waste properly.
   - Pack it in; pack it out. Inspect your campsite and rest areas for trash or spilled foods. Pack out all trash, leftover food, and litter.
   - Deposit solid human waste in catholes dug six to eight inches deep at least 200 feet from water, camp, and trails. Cover and disguise the cathole when finished.
   - Pack out toilet paper and hygiene products.
   - To wash yourself or your dishes, carry water 200 feet away from streams or lakes and use small amounts of biodegradable soap. Scatter strained dishwater.
4. Leave what you find.
   - Preserve the past: Examine, but do not touch, cultural or historic structures and artifacts.
   - Leave rocks, plants, and other natural objects as you find them.
   - Avoid introducing or transporting nonnative species.
   - Do not build structures or furniture, and do not dig trenches.
5. Minimize campfire impacts.
   - Campfires can cause lasting impacts to the backcountry. Use a lightweight stove for cooking and enjoy a candle lantern for light.
   - Where fires are permitted, use established fire rings, fire pans, or mound fires.
   - Keep fires small. Use only sticks from the ground that can be broken by hand.
   - Burn all wood and coals to ash, put out campfires completely, and then scatter cool ashes.

(continued)

Figure 8.1 Participants in and employees of outdoor programs need to be aware of the principles of Leave No Trace.

Reprinted, by permission, from Leave No Trace. Available: www.lnt.org/programs.lnt7/index.html.

6. Respect wildlife.

  · Observe wildlife from a distance. Do not follow or approach them.

  · Never feed animals. Feeding wildlife damages their health, alters natural behaviors, and exposes them to predators and other dangers.

  · Protect wildlife and your food by storing rations and trash securely.

  · Control pets at all times, or leave them at home.

  · Avoid wildlife during sensitive times: mating, nesting, raising young, or winter.

7. Be considerate of other visitors.

  · Respect other visitors and protect the quality of their experience.

  · Be courteous. Yield to other users on the trail.

  · Step to the downhill side of the trail when encountering pack stock.

  · Take breaks and camp away from trails and other visitors.

  · Let nature's sounds prevail. Avoid loud voices and noises.

Figure 8.1   *(continued)*

---

4. Consideration of industry standards

5. Accident prevention (arguably the most important concept)

The best plan for preventing accidents is to have properly selected and trained staff; appropriate activities, areas, and terrain; and correct and well-maintained equipment and facilities. Tending to these areas will minimize or even prevent the need to implement other aspects of the risk management plan (such as the emergency response plan).

Administrators must also think about and plan for a variety of participant issues. An outdoor recreation program must have an appropriate response plan for all situations, and all leaders should be trained and empowered to handle difficult situations whether they are technical, medical, or interpersonal.

For example, if someone behaves inappropriately in an intramural game, there is a set and standard way to handle the situation. In the worst cases, the player is thrown out of the game, security is called, or both. If a similar transgression occurs in the outdoor field 20 miles from the trailhead, 100 miles from the nearest town, and another 300 miles from the school, a different response is required. Plans for such situations must be in place before a trip begins.

Activity Space and Facilities

The spaces that outdoor programs use for activities are quite diverse. In other campus recreation program areas, activity space varies generally between indoor and outdoor spaces on campus, but in outdoor programs, activity space is infinitely diverse and uncontrolled. This space ranges from an indoor pool for kayaking lessons to a trail in the remote wilderness and all the places in between.

We share our outdoor spaces with multiple types and quantities of users. These spaces are often used for multiple purposes including recreation. The same section of public land could be used for logging, research, hunting, bird-watching, and hiking. Because of the variety of spaces used, gaining access to these spaces often involves obtaining permits and researching appropriate use of the areas in conjunction with public and sometimes private land and water managers. Permit and access guidelines should be foremost in the minds of outdoor programmers. Along with issues involving access and land use, participants in outdoor recreation need to be good stewards of the areas they use by adhering to the principles of Leave No Trace and modeling this behavior for other users.

Outdoor facilities can include climbing walls, equipment rental and storage areas, challenge and ropes courses, campgrounds, and picnic areas. It is particularly important that outdoor recreation staff perform regular inspections of all facilities, especially equipment storage facilities, climbing walls, and outdoor challenge course areas. Understanding outdoor program activity space in broad terms helps administrators comprehend the various challenges to the "facilities" used in outdoor programs.

Making regular inspections of outdoor facilities is vitally important, particularly for the safety and maintenance of equipment storage areas, climbing walls, and challenge courses.

William A. Cotton, Colorado State University.

Outdoor Equipment

Equipment is categorized by sport or sport environment, such as land based or water based. Some equipment can be used in multiple arenas. Occasionally, rental facilities and trip organizers can share equipment.

Following are core pieces of land-based equipment:

- Backpacks
- Cook kits
- First aid kits
- Ground pads
- Sleeping bags

- Stoves
- Tents

Following are core pieces of water-based equipment:

- Boats
- Dry bags
- Paddles
- Personal flotation devices (PFDs or life jackets)
- Trailers

Downhill skiing is an example of a sport-specific grouping. A downhill ski program would require the following equipment:

- Boots
- Helmets
- Poles
- Racks
- Ski tuning equipment
- Skis

Outdoor programs often begin acquiring land-based equipment first. When considering what kind of equipment to purchase, consider how it will be used. Whether you choose to purchase 40-degree sleeping bags or −10-degree bags depends on the location of the activity and the intended uses for the bags. Asking yourself the following questions before purchasing equipment will help in your decision-making process. The sidebar on gear basics on page 160 provides a specific evaluation of a backpack purchase.

Questions to Consider Before Purchasing Equipment

- How much space is needed to accommodate the equipment?
- How will the equipment be stored to maximize equipment longevity and space?
- What features are you looking for?
- What are the trade-offs among weight, ease of use, and additional features?
- How durable are the materials? (Some companies manufacture gear that is designed to be used by commercial guide companies. This equipment is usually heavier, but may be worthwhile for the durability trade-off.)
- How often and under what conditions will this equipment be used?

Courtesy of University of Alabama.

Outdoor equipment is categorized based on whether it is used on land, in water, or in a specific sport.

- How easy is it for participants to use the equipment? (This usually involves tents and stoves. Equipment that is difficult to use will be more easily broken or misused, leading to a shorter life span.)

If you have not used the product yourself, take the time to try it out or order samples. Check the equipment warranties and vendor repair policies to make sure these policies apply if the product is used in an institutional setting. Determine under which circumstances the manufacturer will replace or repair gear. Some manufacturers are willing to replace gear even if the damage is considered normal wear and tear.

Many equipment manufacturers want their products introduced to the market of young, emerging outdoor enthusiasts and are willing to help campus recreation programs access their equipment at substantially reduced rates. Depending on the manufacturer, discounted equipment is also a benefit you may be able to offer your student employees.

It is difficult to justify purchasing equipment that will be used infrequently. Often equipment is available for rent or to borrow from other university outdoor recreation programs. Such a collaboration is ideal.

Once you have purchased equipment, you should develop a plan for distributing, using, and maintaining it. Storage areas should be clean, accessible, and well ventilated. Establish a regular maintenance schedule to inventory equipment and clean used equipment, as well as procedures for the proper use of each piece of equipment. You should also have a plan for the purchase of new equipment and the replacement of used equipment.

Personnel

As with any campus recreation program, the specific aspects of the program cannot be administered or implemented without good personnel. An outdoor recreation program may employ trip leaders, equipment checkout and maintenance personnel, challenge and ropes course facilitators, and activity instructors, among others. Whether these employees are part-time students, graduate assistants, full-time professionals, contracted employees, or a combination thereof depends on the policies and procedures of the college or university and the goals of the program.

Marketing

Every outdoor program should develop a sound publicity and promotions plan. This plan should involve developing methods for marketing services to the targeted populations, including the use of flyers, posters, and other handouts.

Web sites are another marketing method that provides a central location where participants can find up-to-date information on rental rates, trip locations, and climbing wall class schedules.

Other methods of generating interest in adventure trips include the following:

- Pretrip slide shows and information sessions
- Campus tables and displays
- Ads in the campus newspaper

Budget Management

Budget management can be a substantial component of administering a campus outdoor recreation

Gear Basics: Backpack

Consider the purchase of a backpack to include with your outdoor programming equipment. First you must ask yourself how this pack will be used. The following are some additional questions to ask.

Volume Questions

> What is the longest time that you anticipate your program to be out with this piece of equipment?
>
> Will the pack be used exclusively for weekend program trips?
>
> Will you need the capacity to carry supplies for a week?

These considerations all affect the volume (measured in cubic inches) of the ideal pack. Backpacks come in a variety of sizes. Some are designed for a long day of summiting a peak; others are designed to carry a week's worth of supplies. Many packs are designed with a volume range to accommodate a load window. Aiming for this window is essential because overstuffed packs do not carry well and underloaded packs may not distribute the weight appropriately.

Structural Design Questions

> Will this pack be used in warm or cool environments?
>
> In what type of terrain will the pack be used?

These considerations affect the structural design of the pack. Backpacks are generally considered to have internal or external frame designs. Presently, internal frame packs are more popular and help effectively connect the load to the body. While traveling unstable terrain or when performing difficult maneuvers, internal frame packs provide superior load transfer. External frame packs offer better ventilation because they do not come into contact with the surface of the entire back. In hot, arid climates the opportunity for evaporative cooling can be essential. Additionally, external packs are generally less expensive than internal packs.

Weight Questions

> How frequently and in what contexts will this pack be used?
>
> Is this pack going to be rented out or used exclusively during programmed trips?

These considerations affect the weight of the pack versus its features and durability. Generally, the more features a pack has, the heavier it is (some empty packs weigh as much as seven pounds). Interchangeable hip belts can assist in fitting packs to a diverse group of participants. Removable hoods that act as detachable daypacks can be very convenient for program trips, but can add to the dry pack weight. Features can be nice if people know what they are used for, but often renters do not fully use complex features. Pack construction and materials also factor into use. Lighter materials are available, although durability and affordability are often compromised.

Storage Questions

> Where will participants travel with this pack, and how will the pack be transported?
>
> Is this pack going to be used for international travel or air travel?
>
> Will it be transported stacked with other packs in the back of a vehicle, in a trailer, or on a roof rack?

If the pack will be used for air travel, is there a way to secure the straps and suspension, or is another bag needed to enclose the pack for checking? If so, is the pack easily removable, to conserve space?

Budget Questions

> How much money do you have to spend on this pack?
>
> When will you be able to replace the pack?
>
> Do you have the funding to purchase multiple types of packs for distinct purposes, or are you purchasing the best "all-around" pack for a variety of programs?

These considerations affect how many and what kinds of packs you are able to purchase. Considerations should be made for replacement and time until replacement. Cost considerations should also be made for repair costs. You must decide whether you are investing in a "universal" pack or several types of more specialized packs.

program. Unlike many other university or college departments, outdoor recreation programs often charge for rentals and trips, which can be expensive. Those managing the budget of outdoor campus recreation programs will need to consider the following:

- Cash advances
- Cash-only outfitter charges
- Check requests
- Late fees
- Reimbursements
- Rental charges
- The U.S. Forest Service steel campground post. (Users deposit their registration forms and money, but are not issued a receipt.)
- Trip payments

Money-handling issues can be further complicated if the program sends participants outside the United States or uses student trip leaders and relies on reimbursement methods to pay them back. Revenue and expenses can be easily tracked by diligently using spreadsheets; however, these skills need to be developed. Budget management issues, concerns, and policies vary from institution to institution. Because of the diversity of money-handling challenges, it is important to establish guidelines specific to your institution.

Outdoor Recreation Program Components

As mentioned earlier, a comprehensive outdoor program will most likely offer adventure trips, a climbing wall, equipment rentals, and instructional clinics and workshops. These are discussed in more detail in this section.

Adventure Trips

Adventure trips are the core of many outdoor recreation programs. This section addresses the following components of adventure trips: staff training, skills, facilitation, supervision, participants and eligibility, program activities, and trip equipment. This is not meant to be an exhaustive list of components, but rather a good place to start.

Staff and Trip Leader Training

Staff training is an essential part of responsible leadership and staff development. Every outdoor recreation program should develop procedures for the recruitment, selection, and training of trip leaders.

A trip leader is defined as the individual(s) responsible for planning, organizing, directing, conducting, and evaluating the group activities. Leaders must have experience, possess the necessary skills to lead outdoor activities, and hold appropriate certifications. They should possess good interpersonal skills and the ability to articulate ideas clearly to both individuals and groups. Finally, they should be familiar with the waivers, release forms, and permission forms required for each trip.

Leaders should have the skills and knowledge to minimize the group's impact on the environment. They should practice proactive supervision to avoid dangerous situations and be aware of events that might lead to emergency situations.

Leaders should be trained in both the technical skills required for the activities they are leading and in the facilitation skills needed to manage the unique dynamics that occur when groups of people are in close proximity over time in potentially uncomfortable situations. Training should include actual outings to take part in the activities they will be leading. In addition, for any outdoor recreation staff member, gaining experience in some aspect of program management can be a great asset and lead to professional growth (figure 8.2).

Professional Outfitters

An outdoor recreation administrator may choose to use a professional outfitter to conduct an adventure trip when appropriate staffing cannot be obtained or when specific equipment is difficult to acquire. In many cases, entering into a contract with a professional outfitter shifts part of the liability from the outdoor recreation program and the university to the outfitter. (See the discussion of contracts in chapter 4.)

The outfitter should be reputable and able to provide documentation of previous trips. It should provide evidence of the following:

- A good safety record
- A list of well-maintained equipment available for use by participants
- Detailed trip plans for each outing, including what the outfitter will and will not provide
- Appropriate safety measures
- Liability insurance
- Staff training

Young Professional Skills Checklist

☐ Is involved in the creation of a marketing plan

☐ Creates a marketing piece including print design

☐ Is part of a departmental hiring and interview process (including your own)

☐ Directly supervises other student staff members (including addressing inconsistencies with staff) and elicits feedback regarding needed changes

☐ Researches a risk management issue and presents a solution and procedure to handle this issue

☐ Creates a program budget (including projections)

☐ Elicits bids for construction and large purchases and decides whom to hire

☐ Creates a plan for revenue generation

☐ Chairs a meeting that has a set agenda and ensures that minutes are taken and distributed

☐ Creates written policies and procedures for a program area

☐ Elicits sponsorship for an event (may need to work with development office if at a university)

☐ Experiences a full-scale performance review

☐ Is involved in any aspect of the construction, renovation, or expansion of a recreational facility (even if it isn't directly related to area of responsibility)

☐ Serves on a company or university committee

☐ Makes a presentation to or sits in on a directors, regents, or board of directors meeting

From NIRSA, 2008, *Campus Recreation: Essentials for the Professional* (Champaign, IL: Human Kinetics).

Figure 8.2   Professional skills checklist.

Technical Skills

Outdoor recreation staff should have and maintain the technical skills appropriate for the activity areas in which they work. Depending on the proximity to health care, current wilderness first aid certification and wilderness first responder certification are becoming industry standards for staff working in the field (see the section Professional Associations and Certifying Agencies at the end of the chapter). Additionally, current standard CPR certifications are the norm. Staff should be able to demonstrate any requisite technical skills and maintain documentation of their technical experience.

Facilitation Skills

Facilitation skills are the set of interpersonal and group management skills required to manage groups in the field. As with technical skills, the level and type of facilitation skills needed in outdoor recreation depend on the type and purpose of the activity. For example, on one end of the spectrum, a group of unrelated participants may gather to go on a rafting trip for the purpose of experiencing a river purely for recreation. On the other end of this spectrum, a group that works

together and is looking to deepen their level of trust with each other may go on a rafting trip on the same river. These are examples of what are often referred to as expedition goals. At a minimum, it is the guide's fundamental responsibility to be aware of the emotional, social, and physical safety needs and well-being of all participants at all times.

Supervision

In addition to the challenges connected with training and qualifying staff, supervisors of college outdoor recreation staff may encounter a few additional supervisory functions. Primarily, a lot of training is needed to prepare students for trip leader roles. The very nature of the collegiate experience causes challenges with staff turnover. Evaluating the trip leaders presents another staffing challenge. The supervisor is often not present on the trip to observe trip leaders directly. Although they are leaders, student trip leaders are also peers with participants.

Participants and Eligibility

Campus outdoor recreation programs should have written policies regarding eligibility to participate. These policies should be in accordance with the eligibility regulations of the institution. Initially participants should provide proof of medical insurance or the equivalent; health and allergy information; and the phone numbers of family, guardians, and physicians.

To understand and accept the assumption of risk, each participant should review and sign a waiver before participating in an outdoor program. Students who have doubts about their medical eligibility should consult their physicians.

Outdoor recreation programs should make reasonable accommodations to allow disabled participants to participate. The Cooperative Wilderness Handicapped Outdoor Group (C.W. HOG), which was established to provide recreation opportunities to people of all abilities, may have some suggestions. Visit their Web site at www.isu. edu/departments/cwhog.

As with all offerings (intramurals, sport clubs, aquatics, fitness classes), campus recreation departments should determine who is eligible for participation in the campus outdoor recreation program. Constituent groups may include the following, with various fees, rules, and risk management strategies applied to each group:

- Faculty and staff
- Friends and spouses

- Minors
- Students
- University affiliates

Program Activities

Trip programs can include a diverse grouping of activities and sports. Following is a list of typical trips offered by campus outdoor programs:

- Backpacking
- Canoeing
- Hiking
- Mountain biking
- Rock climbing
- Sea kayaking
- White-water rafting

Nontraditional activities may include surfing, hang gliding, stargazing, and even geocaching. In addition to this variety of activities, outdoor programs take trips to locations ranging from regional areas such as local mountain biking trails to large-scale international trips to India or New Zealand.

An activity that is gaining popularity is "adventure orientation," in which incoming students participate in outdoor experiences with a small cohort of other new students. The purpose is to bring arriving students together in a way that helps orient them to their new collegiate environment in a unique and exciting way.

Trip Equipment

Outdoor recreation programs commonly choose to maintain their trip and rental equipment separately. This is largely because equipment is used for different purposes in different environments. Tents, sleeping bags, and sometimes stoves used in trip programs are kept separate to prevent the damage they often receive in rental programs. Programs may also choose not to rent equipment that requires specific training for proper use or an understanding of special protocols, such as an avalanche beacon. Programs should keep first aid kits specifically for their trips, and these kits should be thoroughly checked before each trip. Upon return, the kits should be restocked immediately.

Preparation and Follow-Through

Once the other components are in place, planning and carrying out the trip is the next step (see figure 8.3). Initially, staff should research the location and feasibility of the program. This phase involves scouting locations for the suitability of terrain and researching expected weather and environmental conditions. It also includes creating a proposed budget.

After deciding to do the trip, the staff must address the **logistics of the excursion.** This includes making reservations, being familiar with the emergency action plan, going over transportation details, and looking into permits. As mentioned earlier, permitting may need to happen in the research phase. If the permits for a specific area are difficult to acquire, leaders may want to put other details on hold until they obtain the necessary permits. Along with addressing logistics, staff need to make recruitment and marketing efforts to attract participants to the adventure.

Once the participants are enrolled, the process of orienting them to the experience begins. This may include a pretrip meeting or a series of meetings, skill builders, or training for specific activities. Participants should also receive an environmental briefing that includes a verbal explanation of the risks involved, a description of the environment they are likely to encounter, and any safety concerns.

Adventure Trip Programming Time Line
Trip Time Line and Checklist

Date complete		Finished by (*initials*)
	Trip proposal complete—All information in hand	
	BEGINNING OF SEMESTER	
	Make reservations and payment arrangements	
	Campground, backcountry sites	
	Guides	
	Van reservation	
	Recreation truck	
	FINISHED ONE MONTH PRIOR TO TRIP	
	Promote trip (banner in building, flyers, etc.)	
	FINISHED THREE WEEKS PRIOR TO TRIP	
	Confirm all reservations	
	Travel request paperwork complete and submitted to recreation accountant by 5 p.m. Thursday (include list of participants thus far)	
	FINISHED TWO WEEKS PRIOR TO TRIP	
	All participant add-ons submitted to recreation accountant by 5 p.m. Thursday	
	FINISHED ONE WEEK PRIOR TO TRIP	
	Call about pretrip meeting time and place (talk with everyone in person)	
	Pretrip meeting packet complete and ready for proofreading	
	Emergency action plan complete	
	Confirm van reservation, drivers, special requests	
	Contact school newspaper about upcoming article	
	Travel request: List of participants, ID numbers, trip location, departure and arrival times	
	PRETRIP MEETING	
	Itinerary, what to bring, food, etc.	
	Determine leave time (overnight trips leaving on Friday must leave by 5 p.m.)	
	Drug and alcohol policy (read and sign)	
	Release/blue forms (check that all are properly filled out)	
	Insurance information/yellow forms	
	Front side: name, insurance/credit card confirmation, allergies and medications, emergency contact information	
	Back side: signature and date	
	Final updated list of trip participants to recreation accountant before leaving for the night	

From NIRSA, 2008, *Campus Recreation: Essentials for the Professional* (Champaign, IL: Human Kinetics).

Figure 8.3 Adventure trip programming time line.

Additionally, the orientation phase involves the following:

- Gear preparations, including what participants should be prepared to bring
- Issuance of equipment
- Explanation of trip expectations
- Details such as food, logistics, and schedule
- Discussion of any relevant environmental impact issues the group should be aware of, such as Leave No Trace issues or safety issues

This phase may occur at a meeting or a series of meetings and skill sessions. During this time participants will have the opportunity to get to know the leaders and other participants who will be sharing this adventure experience.

The trip is then executed. All institutions have policies and procedures for travel during outdoor recreation trips. Appropriate insurance should be required for individuals, equipment, and vehicles. Verification of insurance should be kept on file. Vehicles being used should have current registration and a roster of authorized drivers with appropriate state licenses.

Upon return, a trip evaluation should be conducted along with other posttrip paperwork. A revised budget should be completed to reflect the actual expenses incurred. Finally, all leaders and the program administrator should take part in a debriefing of the experience.

Climbing Wall

Another common component of an outdoor recreation program is the climbing wall or gym. Whether indoors or out, these facilities can be exciting components of any recreational sport program. This section addresses the facilities, programs, and operations involved with climbing walls.

Facilities

A climbing wall program is more than the physical structure. Nevertheless, the structure, or facility, is obviously requisite. Administrators of outdoor campus recreation programs will need to address both the construction and maintenance of climbing walls.

Construction Climbing wall construction is usually completed by a professional climbing wall manufacturer or vendor. However, plenty of existing facilities have been built by campus services, general contactors, and even volunteers. The deci-

sion about whom to enlist in the construction of a climbing wall is based on several factors:

- Construction materials
- Existing space
- Geographic location of the program
- Program mission
- Project budget
- Specifications
- Student population
- Vendor selection
- Wall design

Programs planning to incorporate climbing walls into new facilities should include climbing wall vendors in the planning from the beginning. Doing so can minimize costs, ensure the safety of the wall, and help to assure that the structure will be consistent with industry trends well into the future.

Maintenance Climbing walls, like other facilities and structures, require regular maintenance and

Courtesy of University of Alabama.

Indoor and outdoor climbing walls are becoming standard options in recreational sport programs.

care. This can include route setting, gear replacement, and inspections. **Route setting** (designing and implementing specific climbing routes via holds and wall features) for artificial climbing surfaces involves moving modular climbing holds into various positions on the structure. Like choreographing different dances, good route setting ensures that regular users have an opportunity to work on various moves, develop new muscle groups, and learn new techniques.

Route setting often begins with taking all of the modular holds off the climbing surface and washing them and the climbing surface. Then the route setter envisions a new sequence of holds, moves, and techniques.

Gear replacement is inevitable and necessary. Like other consumable goods, ropes, holds, harnesses, anchors, and almost everything else used in and on a climbing wall have life spans and will wear out. The climbing wall staff must be familiar with the signs of wear and guidelines for the appropriate replacement of this equipment.

There are two types of inspections for artificial climbing structures, and both are important. The first is internal, meaning that the staff of the facility inspect the structure themselves. The second is independent, or external. This is normally done by a climbing wall manufacturer at regular intervals (often annually). Most manufacturers recommend an inspection interval at the completion of construction. As with many campus recreation facilities, the preventative and regular maintenance of climbing walls often saves resources and ensures that participants have the positive experience they deserve.

Programs

Other important areas of discussion concerning climbing walls are the types of climbing and programming. There are three general types of indoor climbing:

1. **Top rope.** Top rope climbing involves the climber being protected from above, generally minimizing the fall potential.

2. **Lead.** Lead climbing requires the climber to establish a line from the ground upward, thus generally increasing the fall potential.

3. **Bouldering.** Bouldering is ropeless and generally occurs only a short distance off the ground. It requires a pad and partner spotting.

It is important that the programs associated with a climbing wall be appropriate for all levels, including participants who have never climbed before. There are two general types of programs: informal and instructional.

Informal, or drop-in, recreation—depending on the facility or the types of climbing—may or may not require supervision. Although, a few facilities currently host unsupervised bouldering, almost all climbing gyms require adequate supervision.

Instructional programs require a higher level of expertise and teaching by staff. Although many users of college and university climbing walls have climbed before, it is not uncommon for there to be a very large beginner population. An indoor facility may offer the first climbing experience many students have.

Many climbing wall programs involve an orientation or skills check class in which staff verify that each participant possesses the necessary skills to climb safely. Instructional classes allow beginners to learn the fundamentals and more experienced climbers to further develop their techniques. Classes can focus on any of the following:

- Belaying
- Equipment
- Knots
- Leading
- Movement
- Technique

Once the participants have either received instruction on the fundamentals or have proven their knowledge of basic belaying skills, typically they are ready to use the facility. Depending on how the climbing wall budget is maintained, using the climbing wall may either be free on a drop-in basis or involve a monthly or semester fee. Some facilities rent climbing equipment such as climbing shoes, harnesses, and belay devices.

Operations

The last general area concerning climbing gyms is operations, which includes staffing, equipment, and policies and procedures.

Staffing   Staff help control access to a climbing facility, ensuring that only those with the required skills use the facility. They also supervise and monitor the facility, ensuring policy compliance and helping to remind participants of techniques to use to prevent mishaps.

Often, staff members also provide instruction in various skills, monitor the issuance of gear, and work on route setting. Staff members who serve in these roles should possess both interpersonal and technical skills. They should be able to judge a person's skills and abilities based on perceptions and evaluations. Their focus should be on ensuring and maintaining a safe, yet enjoyable climbing environment.

Equipment General rock climbing equipment includes, but is not limited to, the following:

- *Harness.* Climber and belayer's point of attachment to the belay system
- *Rope.* Line used to catch falls
- *Carabiners.* Metal clasps used to link parts of a climbing system
- *Anchors.* Life-bearing attachment points on the structure
- *Belay devices.* Mechanisms used to apply friction or any other mechanical advantage that enables a partner to arrest a fall

In addition to general rock climbing equipment, climbing walls need a healthy supply of climbing holds. These movable, modular hand- and foot-holds made from wood, plastic, fiberglass, and a variety of polymers come in an almost infinite number of shapes and sizes.

Policies and Procedures A well-defined set of policies and procedures is a key component to operating a successful climbing wall facility. A comprehensive list of rules provides all participants with a clear understanding of the policies specific to the facility. Staff must then consistently enforce these policies and procedures for the sake of all participants.

Outdoor Equipment Rental and Resource Center

An outdoor equipment rental and resource center is often part of a comprehensive outdoor program. While developing the equipment rental component, administrators should use bulk purchasing arrangements to lower the start-up costs. Many manufacturers offer schools discounted rates on their equipment in an effort to gain brand recognition among new, young outdoor enthusiasts. The selection of gear for the outdoor program will depend on the location of the activities, as well as the interests of the participants it serves. Rental equipment varies from a full ski shop to surfboard rentals.

Equipment Rental Policies

Once the equipment is in place, a checkout structure should be created that includes policies on the following:

- Fees, if any
- Deposit amount
- Necessary paperwork such as rental agreements, damage waivers, and release of liability during equipment use
- Reservations
- Late returns
- Equipment condition (upon checkout and return)
- Training on use of equipment

Equipment Maintenance

After the equipment program is operational, equipment maintenance is the next largest concern. Equipment should be inspected both at checkout and upon return to ensure that it is in proper working order. Because of the nature of the activities, a certain amount of wear and tear is expected. Equipment may need to be repaired after a certain number of uses or a finite amount of time. An accurate inventory and tracking system is necessary to determine when equipment needs to be retired, especially within larger rental operations.

In many programs, the equipment used on trips is kept separate from the equipment used in rental programs. Trip programs may choose to retire their equipment to rental programs. Once equipment is ready to cycle out of rental, programs may hold a gear sale or swap to raise funds for the programs or staff. Because of the expense of acquiring equipment, depending on the funding structure of the organization, administrators must determine equipment replacement schedules. Some programs purchase a few pieces of every type of equipment annually. Others replace all equipment annually.

Resource Center

The resource center should be designed to complement equipment rentals, to help clients get out on their own without participating in formal programs. Resource centers support rental centers by providing information on the surrounding areas as well as sport-specific information. Resource centers may provide the following:

- Boards to post activity buddies
- Books on the local area

- Computer kiosk
- Information on equipment maintenance or purchasing
- Instructional and outdoor sport videos
- Map printing
- Maps
- Outdoor cooking resources
- Pamphlets
- Personal equipment sales
- Ride shares
- Ski area information
- Staff with local knowledge
- Trip files from past adventure trips

Outdoor Instructional Clinics, Workshops, and Special Events

Instructional clinics and workshops complement other areas of outdoor recreation programs. Special events may be considered part of instructional clinics and workshops because the purpose and content often overlap. Instructional clinics and workshops are shorter events, often lasting a few hours to a whole day. Examples of such programs are Dutch oven cooking, Leave No Trace training, bike and ski maintenance, injury prevention, and skill-specific rock climbing activities like bouldering and rappelling. Other special events may include slide shows, film festivals, and climbing competitions. These events often have ties to marketing efforts. Some programs even hold annual campouts on campus.

Reality Check: Working as a Campus Outdoor Professional

Many people become excited when they realize they can turn what they do for fun into something they can get paid to do. Whether you first found the field because of your interest in camping or through an experience on a climbing wall, interesting employment opportunities exist within outdoor recreation.

There are great benefits and challenges to working in this field. In most cases, working as a campus outdoor professional requires a balance of administrative and outdoor skills. Many professionals spend more than half of their weekday work time in the office and additional time in the field on weekends. Working in the campus setting often includes collaborative work on university-wide projects and time dedicated to committee work.

Opportunities in the field of campus outdoor recreation require various levels of education, training, and experience. Most often a bachelor's degree is required, although a master's degree is preferred. Employers place a heavy emphasis on experience in the field, as well as trainings and certifications. Outdoor skills are difficult to evaluate from a piece of paper, and sound judgment is developed through experience. Training and certifications assist in guaranteeing a minimum proficiency in a given area, but they do not make up for time in the field. Additionally, administrative skills and experience in areas such as marketing, budgeting, and supervision are often desired. In many cases, the program administrator is directly responsible for managing these aspects of the program.

Professional Associations and Certifying Agencies

A number of professional associations are available to those working in the campus outdoor recreation setting. Decide which associations are most relevant to the type of program you work with. Not only do these associations provide an active body of knowledge, both current and about changing trends, but they can also offer opportunities to network in this relatively small field.

The general field of outdoor recreation is so diverse that most people choose to specialize in a limited number of areas. Some associations and their conferences provide opportunities to learn more about new areas or to complete necessary certification or recertification courses; other benefits include learning about locations, trails, and so on.

Professional Associations

National Intramural-Recreational Sports Association (NIRSA) (www.nirsa.org)

Association of Outdoor Recreation and Education (AORE) (www.aore.org)

Wilderness Education Association (WEA) (www.weainfo.org)

Wilderness Risk Management Conference (WRMC) (www.nols.edu/wrmc/index.shtml)

Association of Experiential Education (AEE) (www.aee.org)

Additionally, outdoor agencies provide opportunities to learn professionally recognized skills and obtain practice-based certifications. These types of certifications are generalized into two categories: wilderness medical certifications and outdoor skills–based certifications.

Nationally Recognized Certifying Organizations in Wilderness Medicine

Wilderness Medical Institute (www.nols.edu/wmi)

Wilderness Medical Associates (www.wildmed.com)

Stonehearth Open Learning Opportunities (www.soloschools.com)

Outdoor Skills–Based Certifying Agencies

American Mountain Guide Association (AMGA) (www.amga.com)

American Canoe Association (ACA) (www.acanet.org)

Rescue 3 International (www.rescue3.com)

Leave No Trace (www.lnt.org)

National Association for Search and Rescue (NASAR) (www.nasar.org)

Association of Canadian Mountain Guides (ACMG) (www.acmg.ca)

Conclusion

The benefits of a well-planned outdoor program are as numerous as the activities it might include. Participants can develop leadership and communication skills as well as a sense of stewardship, both locally and globally. Finally, a diverse program can give participants the opportunity to develop skills that provide a lifetime of enjoyment and healthy living. Well-informed, trained administrators; qualified staff; proper equipment; and good programming are all essential components to providing these benefits in a reasonable and professional manner.

Resources

Leave No Trace Center for Outdoor Ethics
P.O. Box 997
Boulder, CO 80306
Web site: www.lnt.org

Stiehl, J., and Ramsey, T. (2005). *Climbing Walls: A Complete Guide.* Champaign, IL: Human Kinetics.

References

Leave No Trace Center for Outdoor Ethics. (n.d.). The solution. Retrieved from www.lnt.org/main.

Glossary

bouldering—A type of climbing that is ropeless and generally occurs only a short distance off the ground. It generally requires a pad and partner spotting.

facilitation skills—The set of interpersonal and group management skills required to manage groups in the field.

inherent risks—Risks that, if removed, would fundamentally change an activity at its core.

lead—A type of climbing that requires the climber to establish a line from the ground upward, thus generally increasing the fall potential.

logistics of the excursion—Making reservations, being familiar with an emergency action plan, going over transportation details, and looking into permitting if necessary.

principles of Leave No Trace—A set of guidelines that help outdoor users understand their actions with respect to resources.

route setting—Designing and implementing specific climbing routes via holds and wall features.

top rope—A type of climbing in which the climber is protected from above; this generally minimizes the fall potential.

CHAPTER 9

Sport Clubs

Thomas M. Roberts, CRSS, MSPE, Director of Recreation and Wellness, University of Richmond

> Tell me and I will forget, Teach me and I will remember, Involve me and I will learn.
>
> *Benjamin Franklin*

"Involve me and I will learn," wrote Benjamin Franklin. Sport clubs support the overall mission of colleges and universities by involving students in learning. Participation in sport clubs is a learning experience for the members through their involvement in administration, organization, budgeting, scheduling, fund-raising, and public relations, as well as the development of skills in their particular sport. Involvement in a group and team situation helps enhance students' overall education while living in a university or college setting.

The sport club program serves individual interests in various sports and recreational activities. These interests can be competitive, recreational, or instructional in nature. The role of the university is to provide encouragement, offer support and guidance, assist with the coordination of financial resources and facilities, and provide leadership training to the officers. The success of sport clubs depends on many variables, including student involvement, availability of facility space, volunteer coaches and advisors, educational opportunities, and most important, effective student leadership.

This chapter provides recreation professionals with information about the effective administration of sport club programs. Many ideas, guidelines, and strategies used at colleges and universities in the administration of sport club programs are included. Currently, there are no established industry standards for the administration and organization of sport clubs. The administrative responsibility for and philosophy of sport club programs can vary significantly; therefore, colleges and universities should select the most appropriate course of action for their individual program and circumstances.

Definition of Terms

A **sport club** is defined as a group of students (and if the institution allows, faculty, staff, and community members) who voluntarily organize to further their common interests in a sport through participation and competition. Sport clubs are strictly voluntary. Although some institutions refer to them as club sports, for the purpose of this publication, *sport clubs* will be used.

Sport clubs should not be confused with varsity sports administered by the athletics department. Varsity teams must follow NCAA rules and regulations, are usually fully funded, have paid coaches and athletic trainers, have mandatory practices and competitions, and usually require a full-year

commitment. Sport clubs often compete against clubs of other universities but are not affiliated with the NCAA. The majority of their funds are self-generated, coaches are often volunteers, and the organization and administration of the club is determined by the club officers. Sport clubs typically operate within the student development and campus recreation programs and report to a sport club administrator.

Program Philosophy

The philosophy and key to the success of the sport club program is the emphasis placed on student leadership and participation. The clubs should provide a learning experience for the members through their involvement in every aspect of the organization and administration of the clubs. Club officers should always be active participants in the leadership, responsibility, and decision-making process of the club.

The philosophy of sport clubs is to be inclusive and provide opportunities to the entire university community. Membership and participation within sport clubs must be free of discrimination based on race, religion, sex, age, national origin, or disability. Clubs are discouraged from having tryouts and making cuts to restrict the number of people allowed to join. Although this is a guiding principle, some factors may be out of the control of the club officers. Limitations on practice times or the use of facility space, for example, may require clubs to impose membership limits.

Sport clubs usually practice one of three philosophical administrative models. At one extreme, a **"hands-on" approach,** club activities are part of the institution. A coach, recreation director, or student affairs director plans and supervises team activities as an agent of the school. Club staff keep records and documents. The school is responsible for team activities and risks through its employees. The team leadership is covered by the institution's liability insurance policies.

At the other extreme, a **"hands-off" approach,** clubs are independent from the educational institution. Under this approach, sport clubs are contracted independent organizations. Contracted independent organizations are not agents, servants, or employees of the university, but rather are independent contractors that manage their own affairs. Club activities are run by students who are not working on behalf of the school for liability and insurance coverage purposes. Faculty and staff are removed from sport club activities, even in an advising capacity. Faculty and staff who observe unsafe conduct do not intervene unless the conduct will harm the school or its resources. Although teams are permitted to play on school property and receive financial support through a student government, this alone does not create an obligation for the school to supervise daily team activities, prevent injury, or assume the team's operational risks.

In the middle of these two extremes is more of an **"arm's-length" approach**. Students operate teams that are independent from the institution, but a coach or faculty advisor employed by the school provides education and guidance. The students are not agents of the school, but the coaches and faculty advisors are and can create liability for the institution.

The philosophy and administrative model are often determined by the availability of staff and resources. If sufficient staff and resources are available, then perhaps the "hands-on" approach is the best model to use to "control student clubs" and may be in the best interest of the students and institution. Unfortunately, many institutions do not have the staff and resources and have no choice but to use a "hands-off" approach.

Regardless of the philosophy and administrative model, every administrator, and perhaps more important, every coach, should keep in mind that a sport club is first and foremost a student organization. As such, the student representative must serve as the liaison between the club and the university.

Purpose

The purpose of sport club programs is to offer competitive, instructional, or recreational activities to any student who has the desire to partici-

Sport clubs provide students with the opportunity to stay in good physical condition and develop their skills in a specific sport while competing against students from other colleges and universities.

William A. Cotton, Colorado State University.

pate. They provide students with opportunities to participate and compete in a sport or activity on an extramural level, to develop skills in specific sports, and to socialize with other students around common interests.

Benefits

University administrators are beginning to understand the value of sport clubs and the many contributions they provide students. As mentioned earlier, sport clubs support the overall mission of universities by providing educational, recreational, and social programs. Sport club participation increases student satisfaction and plays an integral role in the recruitment and retention of students.

Kerr & Downs Research conducted a study to examine the value and contributions of recreational sports to participants. The results were as follows:

Students who participated in recreational sport programs and activities identified recreational sports as one of the key determinants of college satisfaction and success. . . . Among

171

all students, recreational sport programs and activities ranked higher than internships, cultural activities, part-time or full-time work, student clubs and organizations, shopping, entertainment, restaurant options in the community, the chance to study abroad, community service opportunities, watching varsity sports, participating in varsity sports, and sororities and fraternities as determinants of college satisfaction and success. . . . Heavy users of recreational sport programs and activities were similar to other students in the importance they placed on the quality and range of courses, the quality of professors, and graduate school and job prospects as determinants of college satisfaction and success. In other words, heavy participants in recreational sports were serious students concerned about the same academic standards and quality of education as other students. (Downs, 2003, pp. 9-10)

Universities invest significant resources in their efforts to increase diversity and recruit and retain students. Sport clubs have an impact on the recruitment and retention of students and contribute to diversity. The opportunity to participate in sport clubs should not be the number one reason a student selects a university, but it may have an influence on his decision. Sport clubs offer a variety of activities that provide a greater interaction with diverse groups of people and help make students feel like a part of the campus community and connect with others who share a similar interest. Universities also invest significant time and resources in addressing the emotional and behavioral issues of students. Participation in sport clubs can be a preventive approach to help students reduce stress and improve emotional well-being and happiness, build character, and improve self-confidence.

It's also important to mention the benefits of being approved and officially recognized by the college or university as a student organization and sport club. This will help the club officers and coaches perceive the sport club administrator and staff as friends and allies. The most obvious and essential benefits to most clubs are funding, facilities, and equipment. Some other noteworthy benefits include use of the university name and logos, access to office equipment and supplies, access to equipment storage space, assistance with fund-raising, access to alumni lists, tax exempt status, use of university legal counsel, and general liability insurance coverage. The sport club staff can also assist a club and its members by providing training programs for club officers, facility arrangements, special events and competitions, and financial assistance with budget preparation and fiscal management.

Levels of Participation

Varying levels of participation and degrees of interest must be considered within a sport club program to meet the desires of various groups. Care should be taken to meet ADA (Americans with Disabilities Act) requirements so that all people have access to sport club opportunities.

There should be at least three classifications for clubs within the program (National Intramural-Recreational Sports Association, 1996):

- *Social.* The social aspect should incorporate a variety of participation opportunities, including regular club meetings, clinics, practices, informal gatherings, and philanthropic functions.

- *Instructional.* The instructional component could be the primary element that attracts membership and aids in retention. Instruction should cover the necessary physical and mental safety prerequisites for participation, as well as the strategies, rules, and skills of the sport. Instruction should be provided for all levels of skill, from beginner to advanced, in order to provide appropriate skill development opportunities. Guidance in the use and role of an instructor should be provided.

- *Competitive.* The intensity of participation may vary depending on the interest and desires of its members. Some clubs have competition as their main purpose. The level of intensity should be controlled by the club membership. Sound tournament structuring should be taught to the leaders of clubs. Guidance in the use and role of coaches should be provided.

Starting a New Club

On many college campuses, sport club programs seem to be increasing in number and variety to meet the diverse needs of students. The inspiration to start a new club should come from the students. Students interested in initiating a new sport club should meet with the appropriate university administrator to discuss the feasibility. Special consideration should be given to student interest and the availability of resources, specifically funds and facilities. Universities can establish guidelines that give students the opportunity to request or petition the university to add a club at any time. Groups desiring recognition or renewal as a sport club may need to complete a form providing the administration start-up information (see figure 9.1). They should also satisfy several criteria, including the following:

- Proof of membership interest
- Formation of a written constitution or bylaws
- Submission of a financial budget
- Availability of facilities for practice and competition
- Availability of collegiate and extramural competition

The approval process varies and may involve many other formal councils and committees. There may also be a requirement for the group to be recognized as a student organization. Probationary periods with restricted resources and privileges are also not uncommon for new organizations and clubs. Once approved, club members may be required to complete a membership form (see figure 9.2) and sign a club roster (see figure 9.3). Clubs are typically required to go through a renewal process each year and remain active or be in jeopardy of losing their sport club status.

The final acceptance or rejection of the sport club is a university decision. Although the application of Title IX to athletics has gained the greatest public visibility, the law also applies to sport clubs in any educational program or activity that is a recipient of federal funding. Title IX states:

> No person in the United States shall, on the basis of sex, be excluded from participation in, be denied the benefits of, or be subjected to discrimination under any education program or activity receiving Federal financial assistance.

Compliance with Title IX is a requirement, but it has not been an issue for sport clubs because decisions to start new clubs or drop existing clubs are driven by student demand and interest. The result is usually a proportionate number of men's and women's clubs and equal levels of participation and resources for men's and women's programs. Many sport clubs are corecreational, which provides a healthy avenue for students of different genders to interact and socialize.

Washington State University
Sport Club Federation

Fall Semester Start-Up Information

Year ____

Club ____

President ____ Phone # ____ Student ID # ____

Address ____

E-mail ____

Other Officers:

Name and title of officer ____ ID # ____

Phone # ____ E-mail ____

Name and title of officer ____ ID # ____

Phone # ____ E-mail ____

Name and title of officer ____ ID # ____

Phone # ____ E-mail ____

Advisor's name ____

Phone # ____ E-mail ____

Club Web Site URL: ____

Club Meetings (regularly scheduled)

Date ____ Time ____ Location ____

Try-Out Dates

Date ____ Time ____ Location ____

Practice

Date ____ Time ____ Location ____

Number of members starting out with club ____

Does your club belong to a national organization? ☐ Yes ☐ No

If yes, please list the full name of the organization(s) ____

Individual membership dues? $ ____ Group membership dues? $ ____

Contact ____

Address ____

Phone # ____ E-mail ____

Figure 9.1 Start-up information.

The University of Texas at Austin
Division of Recreational Sports
Gregory Gym 2.200 471-3116

UTSCA Club Member Information Sheet

To be completed by all club members.
Participants in The University of Texas Sport Club Association should be **aware of the possible risks** that are inherent in the nature of some of the activities. These risks include, but are not limited to, the **potential for accidents or illness while traveling to and from events, as well as participating in the various club activities.** Every attempt is made to minimize the existing risks through the use of proper sports equipment, safe facilities which are under the Division of Recreational Sports' control, and sound safety practices. However, participants should realize these risks cannot be eliminated completely. If participants meet **minimum physical and mental conditioning and follow safety procedures,** the potential for accidents may be reduced. The Division of Recreational Sports strongly recommends that each club member have an **annual physical examination and personal medical and accident insurance.**

Notice Concerning Your Information

The Texas Public Information Act, with a few exceptions, gives you the right to be informed about the information that The University of Texas at Austin collects about you. It also gives you the right to request a copy of that information and to have the university correct any of that information that is wrong. You may request to receive and review any of that information, or request corrections to it, by contacting the university's Public Information Officer, Office of Financial Affairs, P.O. Box 8179, Austin, Texas 78713 (e-mail: cfo@www.utexas.edu).

Print Last name ____ First name ____ Sport club ____

Signature ____ Date ____ E-mail address ____

Local address ____ Apt. # ____ Zip ____ Local phone/cell phone ____

Permanent address ____ City, State ____ Zip ____ Permanent phone ____

UT EID ____ Date of birth ____

TX DL # ____

***If you are planning to drive on any sport club trip, you must be an authorized and appointed driver. See sport club handbook for details.**

Are you covered by a personal medical insurance plan? ☐ Yes ☐ No

This includes if you are covered by your parent's medical insurance plan or if you have purchased medical insurance from the Student Health Center. If you are not covered by any medical insurance plan, you must check No. If you checked Yes, a copy of your insurance card must be on file in the sport club office.

Gender: ☐ Male ☐ Female
Status: ☐ Student # hours enrolled currently ____
☐ Faculty/staff Department ____
☐ Coach

Do you give permission to have the above information released? ☐ Yes ☐ No

Figure 9.2 Membership form.

University of Richmond
Sport Club Membership Roster

Sport club: _____

Semester: _____

I understand that my signature on this membership roster authorizes release of my academic records for purpose of verifying team eligibility.

Print full name	Signature	Social Security #	Phone	Academic year

From NIRSA, 2008, *Campus Recreation: Essentials for the Professional* (Champaign, IL: Human Kinetics). Reprinted, by permission, from University of Richmond.

Figure 9.3 Membership roster.

Administration

The key to the success of the administration of a sport club program is finding a philosophical balance that encourages student leadership and involvement without compromising the established policies and procedures of the university or adding unnecessary risk or liability to participants or the university. Providing clearly written duties and responsibilities for each person with administrative responsibility may prevent conflicts from arising, thus allowing students more opportunity to determine their own club's destiny.

Club Officers

The success or failure of a club is often a reflection of its student leaders. Because clubs are student run and self-administered, the management of club business is the responsibility of the officers. The institutional administrator should provide ongoing officer training programs to review policies and procedures and risk management plans; involve other campus and community resources such as the safety officer, campus police, athletic trainers, and student health department; keep an open line of communication with club officers;

and encourage officers to notify the administrators of any potentially dangerous situations and to stay within the limitations of their knowledge and ability. Each club should identify the responsibilities of its officers. The following is a list of suggested club officers and leaders and their primary duties.

President

- Serves as liaison between the club and the club administrator
- Is knowledgeable of all sport club policies and procedures and ensures that the club is in compliance
- Attends club officer meetings as a representative of the club

Vice President

- Conducts club business in the absence of the president
- Assists the president

Courtesy of University of Alabama.

Sport clubs are increasing both in number and variety on many campuses in order to meet the diverse needs and interests of students.

Secretary
- Records club meeting minutes
- Coordinates club correspondence

Treasurer
- Develops and monitors the annual budget
- Collects dues and keeps record of all financial transactions

Scheduling Manager
- Coordinates and schedules club practices and competitions
- Completes and submits travel itineraries

Equipment Manager
- Oversees the purchase and inventory of all equipment
- Repairs and maintains all equipment and ensures that it meets all safety standards

Safety Manager
- Completes any required risk management training and certification
- Ensures the health and safety of all participants

A club officer has a tremendous amount of responsibility and is expected to know and understand lengthy university and departmental policies and procedures. Although officers receive officer training whenever possible, most of what they learn they learn on the job. Therefore, clubs should schedule officer elections at a time that will allow an opportunity for officer training and transition. This gives the newly elected officers ample time to learn the policies and procedures and ease into the position, get some practical experience, resolve any unfinished business, and consult with previous officers before they leave the club and the university. The successful transition from outgoing to new club leadership is vital to the continuing successful operation and existence of the club.

Coach

Sport club coaches come from the ranks of undergraduate students, graduate students, staff members, alumni, faculty members, or often the local community. Most club coaches are either volunteer or nominally paid; they donate their time and services because of a genuine love of and interest in the promotion and perpetuation of a particular sport.

Many sport club coaches believe that their coaching responsibilities are similar to those of varsity athletic coaches, including administering the budget, securing facilities, scheduling contests, and arranging for travel. However, most sport club programs are designed to allow students to handle these facets of the club's activity. Coaches should restrict their contributions to coaching and should minimize active involvement in club management. A sport club is first and foremost a student organization, and as such, the student representative, not the coach, must serve as the liaison between the club and the university. Coaches may need constant reminders that the philosophy and key to the success of the sport club program has been the continued emphasis placed on student leadership and participation.

Sport Club Administrator

Universities support clubs by providing administrators for assistance and guidance with clubs' organization and administration. The sport club administration acts primarily in an advisory capacity and is available to provide support in the areas of scheduling facilities for practice and competition, managing and developing budgets, arranging for the inventory and storage of equipment, providing risk management expertise, offering fund-raising advice, and helping with organizational management. The philosophical administrative model of the university will determine the extent to which the sport club administrator is involved in the business affairs of the club.

Faculty Advisor

Most universities require student organizations and clubs to have a faculty or staff advisor. The faculty advisor may oversee the club members on academic matters, advise club leaders, and maintain communication with the sport club administrator. They serve as an information source and a liaison between the club and the university or college. Faculty advisors are seldom paid and do not receive a reduced workload for their services. As a result, faculty members may be reluctant to become involved with sport clubs because of the time and commitment.

Sport Club Council

Many universities establish a sport club council composed of representatives from each of the sport clubs to assist in the administrative affairs of the program and represent the different facets of the sport club program. Council meetings are typically held once a month and serve as an opportunity for the administration to conduct business and convey information about policies and procedures, upcoming schedules of important deadlines and dates, financial reports, and funding distribution. In addition, these meetings give the sport club council representatives the opportunity to discuss items concerning the sport club program and to coordinate projects and programs cooperatively and efficiently. Guided by established policies, procedures, and by-laws, and with the sport club administrator advising, the sport club council makes recommendations concerning matters such as the following:

- Club approval
- Budget approval and allocation
- Disciplinary actions
- Sport club policies
- Related appeals and petitions

National Governing Bodies

At the national level, the majority of sport clubs have national governing bodies (NGBs) that work in partnership with regional and local leagues. National governing bodies make strategic decisions for the benefit of their sport to provide standards of competition and safety guidelines. They sometimes connect a club with other university and college groups that are actively pursuing similar goals, thus creating a network and support system for clubs. Representatives of national governing bodies work cooperatively with sport club administrators and the National Intramural-Recreational Sports Association to discuss opportunities for improvement in the administration of the programs and to support regional and national sport club championships.

Policies and Procedures

Sport clubs should develop policies and procedures that can be managed and enforced, and even more important, they should enforce all policies and procedures. Club officers should find the policies and procedures easy to understand and follow, and sport club administrators should find them realistic and manageable. A handbook or manual outlining policies and procedures for all clubs is often designed and available in hard copy or online as a reference guide for members,

officers, and coaches. The handbook can also outline and explain the services available on campus and how to make the most of those services. Club officers are expected to become familiar with and be in compliance with the procedures and policies in the handbook. Sport club administrators should periodically review and update the handbook and policies and procedures as needed.

Conduct

Participants in sport clubs assume an obligation to conduct themselves in a manner compatible with the university's mission as an educational institution. Administrators should provide written expectations for how club members and coaches should act when representing the college or university and these expectations should be included in the sport club policies and procedures. Self-governance is an important aspect of the sport club experience, and therefore students and the sport club council should be involved in the development and enforcement of policies and procedures. Sport club administrators should establish disciplinary procedures for individuals and clubs that violate rules and regulations, tarnish the image of the university or club, or put an individual or the university at risk of injury or litigation.

Simply by competing in a club event, an individual is agreeing to represent the sport club and the university in a manner that does not detract from the reputation of the university. Every club is responsible for the actions of its members and it is the club's responsibility to discipline members for any problems that may arise either on or off campus. Sport clubs or individual club members may face disciplinary action for inappropriate behavior while participating in any sport club–related activity.

"**Hazing** is an intentional action taken toward any student, on or off campus, by a student organization or any of its members to produce humiliation, physical discomfort, bodily injury or ridicule or to create a situation [in which] humiliation, physical discomfort, [or] bodily injury occurs" (James Madison University, n.d.). The definition of hazing is vague and varies with state laws. Hazing is defined in Virginia as "activities for the initiation or induction into an organization which include: calisthenics or other strenuous physical activity; exposure to inclement weather, consumption of any food, liquid, beverage, drug or other substance; confinement in any room or compartment; spraying, painting, or pelting with any substance; burying in any substance; burning, branding, or tattooing or any other activity which may result in physical injury or endanger the health or life of the individual being hazed" (James Madison University, n.d.). Many states have laws declaring hazing illegal, with established conditions for civil and criminal liability, and outline penalties for being found guilty of hazing.

Prohibiting and avoiding alcohol use in sport club activities decreases liability and helps build a positive reputation for the club and university. Clubs should be discouraged from taking part in sponsorships, advertising, or fund-raising activities involving alcohol or any illicit drug on or off campus.

Facility Scheduling

Scheduling policies and procedures must be available for sport club officers. These should address practice times, special club events, meets, proper sanctioning methods, tournament structuring, cost, and facility use. Prioritizing events based on club purposes facilitates scheduling. The administration should develop a system for facility priorities and communicate this information to club officers. The use of outside facilities should be considered when facilities are limited or when other groups are using the facility. Administrators should consider all club needs and requests regarding existing facilities, hours of possible use, priority of use, and the size and nature of events. Distributing home and away events evenly provides a well-rounded program (National Intramural-Recreational Sports Association, 1996).

Sport clubs may submit requests for facility use for the following:

- Meetings
- Practice
- Competition
- Equipment storage
- Social events

Clubs should be required to submit all requests for practice and competition space in writing on request forms (see figure 9.4). Facilities must receive requests in advance to ensure enough time to line the fields and reserve the facilities. When hosting regular competitions, tournaments, or special events, each club is expected to represent the university in a positive manner. It is also the club's responsibility to ensure that participants and spectators abide by university policies.

If staff and resources are available, athletic trainers should be available for club practices

Figure 9.4 Practice facility request form.

and competitions. Unfortunately, the majority of programs do not have the resources available to provide this level of medical attention. Another, more practical option is to assign a member of the club the responsibility of ensuring the health and safety of the members during practices, competitions, and travel. This person is often recognized as the club's facility or risk manager. She may be required to maintain current CPR certification from the American Red Cross or another nationally recognized organization; attend all practices and competitions; and comply with departmental policies, procedures, and emergency action plans.

Travel

Recent travel-related tragedies involving student organizations and sport clubs have required administrators of sport club programs to evaluate travel policies and procedures and respond to the need for improved transportation safety regulations. Travel requirements vary from college to college. Although most schools have stipulations that their traveling teams, individuals, or clubs must follow, each school determines the extent of the guidelines covering travel. Each club must abide by institutional policies and procedures for travel. Each institution, in working with sport clubs, should have policies and procedures for travel, and clubs should consult these before initiating a trip. When making arrangements for travel, all details regarding the trip should be taken into consideration, including housing, meals, registration, and the chaperone or person in charge. Vehicles being used should have current registrations and a roster of authorized drivers with appropriate state licenses inside the vehicle.

In May 2006 the American Council on Education, the National Collegiate Athletic Association, and United Educators Insurance completed a joint project on transportation safety. The report, "Safety in Student Transportation: A Resource for Colleges and Universities" (United Educators, 2006) does not intend to offer professional guidance, but instead offers many examples of programs, policies, and practices that institutions have developed to fit their specific travel needs. Following are some examples of transportation practices:

- Photocopy the driver's license for record keeping to show that the driver has a license.
- Require a certain number of years or miles of driving experience.
- Check the driver's motor vehicle record.
- Require training in defensive driving, van handling, trailer towing, accident protocols, or other topics.
- Limit the distance, number of hours, or number of passengers that students, or students under a certain age, may drive.
- Prohibit students, or students under a certain age, from driving campus-owned vehicles.
- Prohibit students from using personal vehicles on institution-related trips.
- Notify drivers of personal vehicles that their own auto liability insurance pays out first in the event of an accident.
- Prohibit students from driving large vehicles or any vehicles with passengers.
- Require drivers of vans to hold commercial driver's licenses.
- Post notices in vehicles about safe driving, seat belt use, and other key topics.
- Install electronic tracking or sensing equipment that monitors or corrects problems.

It is also recommended that a travel itinerary (see figure 9.5) be required for all club travel. A minimum notice of five days should be given to the recreational sport department when a club is planning to travel. The itinerary should include the names of club members traveling, a summary of the travel plans, and emergency contact information.

Funding

As a general principle, the members of sport clubs make every effort to support programs through their own resources, which may come from dues, fund-raising projects, and special events. Clubs are strongly encouraged to keep all of their funds on account with the university or college. Proper accounting practices must be followed with respect to all financial activities. Funding mechanisms for sport clubs may vary from institution to institution; however, several sources of funding may be available to each club: self-generated funds, institutional support, sponsorships, gifts, and commercial funds. Institutional guidelines for the use of funds should be available along with an appropriate management system to record all transactions. Clubs should be required to develop

University of Richmond
Sport Club Travel Itinerary

Club name: ____________ Date: ____________
Club contact: ____________ Phone: ____________
Campus address: ____________ E-mail: ____________
Travel destination: ____________ Type of competition: ____________
Departure date and time: ____________ Return date and time: ____________
Facility manager: ____________
Phone: ____________
Campus address: ____________ E-mail: ____________
Overnight lodging: ____________ Dates: ____________
Phone: ____________
Club members traveling: ____________

Mode of transportation (please circle):

Private vehicles Rental vans University vans Air travel Other ____________

Emergency Action Plan:

1. Perform resuscitation and/or first aid as needed.
2. Contact local emergency numbers.
3. Contact University of Richmond Police (804-289-8711) to report accident or injuries. University police will then notify parents and appropriate university personnel.
4. Immediately after the incident, sit down with all involved and fill our accident reports. Take written and signed reports from all witnesses.

Club contact signature: ____________ Date: ____________
Campus recreation director: ____________ Date: ____________
Office manager: ____________ Date: ____________

From NIRSA, 2008, *Campus Recreation: Essentials for the Professional* (Champaign, IL: Human Kinetics). Reprinted, by permission, from University of Richmond.

Figure 9.5 Travel itinerary.

and submit summary budgets (see figure 9.6). Fiscal management should be covered in training sessions for officers and key club members. The accountability of funds should fall within the purview of club leadership under the institutional policies and procedures. Each club must recognize its institution's system and abide by those guidelines.

The two most common forms of funding for sport clubs are dues and fund-raising; both are typically the responsibility of the club officers. The majority of universities provide some form of annual funding to sport clubs. Careful consideration should be given to how these funds are distributed. A funding system should involve the sport club council and club representatives to encourage participation, motivate the club to follow policies and procedures, and ensure that funding is allocations are based on the needs of the club.

Following are some methods of funding distribution:

- *Annual funds.* Some clubs receive annual funds, which are commonly distributed by the university through the sport club council or a similar administrative source. Any clubs receiving

funds must meet the eligibility criteria, submit a new budget summary for each academic year, and submit a report providing compelling justification.

- *Matching funds.* Using matching funds is a popular way to give sport clubs the incentive to raise funds. The sport club council allocates the matching funds to reward clubs that have successfully raised funds. Depending on the funds available, clubs may receive funds matching the amount they raised or a portion of the funds available to all clubs. When limited funds are available, all funds raised by clubs are totaled, and each club receives a proportionate percentage of the funds available.

- *Incentive program.* Incentive programs reward clubs for complying with policies and procedures and good behavior. Clubs can be financially rewarded for such things as attending sport club council meetings, submitting forms in a timely manner, and participating in community service projects.

- *Classification system.* Perhaps the most recent and increasingly popular method of distribution of funds is the classification, or tier, system. Tiers may range from tier 1 to tier 5, with tier 1 receiving the highest student fee allocation. Clubs are classified into tiers based on their level of competition, level of involvement, and number of players. The larger, more competitive clubs that have a need for more funds, and can justify that need, receive more funds.

Fund-Raising

Fund-raising has become one of the most important responsibilities of sport clubs. Because the majority of clubs receive only a portion of their total budgets from the university, they rely heavily on membership dues and fund-raising efforts. The opportunities to increase clubs' budgets are many and limited only by the degree of club members' dedication. Fund-raising projects involving direct solicitation may need to be approved by the university department responsible for fund-raising. Sport clubs can collaborate with this department to establish some general guidelines for planning fund-raisers.

Some university departments responsible for fund-raising prohibit solicitation of donations, whereas others encourage and assist clubs in soliciting from various resources including parents, alumni, and local businesses. Universities also differ in their attitude toward corporate sponsorships.

University of Richmond
Sport Club Summary Budget

Club _____   For academic year: _____

Summary prepared by: _____   Phone number: _____

Anticipated Expenses (used to see how much each club needs)

1. Equipment (any new equipment your club will be purchasing)
   New equipment: _____
   Uniforms: _____   Subtotal _____
2. Travel
   Fuel costs: _____
   Lodging costs: _____
   Rental costs of vehicle: _____
   Food costs: _____   Subtotal _____
3. Officials: _____   Subtotal _____
4. Awards/entertainment awards: _____
   Other social functions (describe): _____   Subtotal _____
5. Miscellaneous
   A. _____
   B. _____   Subtotal _____

Revenue

1. Membership dues: _____
2. Sport club council funding: _____
3. Fund-raising: _____
   A. _____
   B. _____
   C. _____
4. Other (describe): _____
   _____
   _____
   _____
   _____

   Revenue total: _____

From NIRSA, 2008, *Campus Recreation: Essentials for the Professional* (Champaign, IL: Human Kinetics). Reprinted, by permission, from University of Richmond.

Figure 9.6   Summary budget.

Corporate sponsorships can benefit clubs by providing funding to assist with the operation of the club or to cover direct costs for items such as uniforms and equipment. Sponsors benefit by being publicly acknowledged at activities and being able to display products and logos on printed materials, equipment, and uniforms.

Equipment

The purchase and maintenance of good recreational equipment is essential in providing effective programs. Ideally, the administrative office that supports the club should provide all sport club equipment. However, because of financial constraints, the club or its individual members generally purchase some equipment. Any recreational sport office that commits itself to a sport club program has an obligation to see that good equipment is available to club participants. All equipment must be purchased and maintained according to applicable institutional policies and procedures. The institution should have safe, secure, and clean facilities in which to store equipment. All purchasing and inventory procedures should be included in the program manual. The institution should state whether club-owned equipment is considered institutional equipment or private club equipment. Records regarding the purchase, use, and maintenance of equipment should be kept current. Club officers and members should be responsible for controlling the use of equipment through a checkout system.

To ensure that institutional purchasing policies are adhered to and proper equipment is received, sport clubs should follow specific and detailed university purchasing instructions. Any equipment purchased with institutional dollars remains the property of the institution for use by the club. Equipment purchased by the individual club members should remain the property of those members unless they donate it to the club. Once donated, the ownership transfers to the institution. If a club disbands, any equipment purchased with funds raised by the club becomes the property of the institution for safekeeping. If the cost to provide adequate, safe equipment is beyond the means of the department, the club, or its members, then the club should not be recognized until such time as equipment needs can be met. Using substandard equipment is unacceptable.

Improperly maintained sport club equipment not only shortens its useful life, but also creates unsafe situations. As a trained professional, it is imperative for the sport club administrator to take steps to reduce potential liability, as well as extend the life of the equipment. A person from each club should be designated to serve as the equipment manager. This person acts as a liaison between the club and the campus recreation office and is responsible for the annual inspection, maintenance, and inventory of all club equipment.

Risk Management

The administration of a sport club program requires a proactive approach to risk management. This kind of approach provides a safe environment for participants and reduces the likelihood of injury and litigation. Many sport clubs operate with a fair degree of autonomy. However, because clubs are usually deemed to be part of the college or university, the sport club administrator is ultimately responsible for club activities. Hence, the campus recreation department should maintain control over sport clubs to minimize the risk of participant injury. For both legal and financial reasons, the sport club administrator should be knowledgeable about the legal risks associated with sport club participant injuries and rights and have all club members complete an assumption of risk and release of liability form. The prudent administrator does the following:

- Stays within the limitations of staff knowledge and ability
- Develops policies and procedures that can be enforced
- Enforces all policies and procedures
- Reviews policies and procedures on an annual basis
- Allows and requires members of the club to be responsible for the leadership and direction of the club
- Provides ongoing officer training programs
- Requires club officers to sign written statements acknowledging and accepting their roles and responsibilities
- Informs participants of the inherent risk involved and requires participants to sign written statements acknowledging the risk of injury by the nature of sports
- Seeks legal advice and becomes familiar and knowledgeable regarding legal issues and current events

For information about writing waivers, assumption of risk, or release of liability documents, see chapter 13.

Although no organization can protect itself completely from lawsuits, sport clubs that have well-trained staffs, safe and well-maintained facilities and equipment, and carefully planned and executed risk management plans reduce the likelihood of injuries and avoid legal entanglements. More important, they provide participants with safe facilities and programs.

Most universities and colleges strongly encourage and often require participants who are practicing, participating in scheduled club events, and traveling with the club to carry adequate health and accident insurance coverage. Adequate insurance should include coverage for injuries incurred while practicing for, participating in, and traveling to club-related activities. The majority of colleges and universities do not assume responsibility for the cost of medical care given to participants in connection with injuries sustained while participating in sport club activities or while traveling for sport club purposes.

Discipline

Inevitably, club officers and coaches unintentionally and intentionally fail to follow policies and procedures. Sport clubs should have discipline procedures in place for when this occurs. Because self-governance as an important aspect of the sport club experience, students and the sport club council should be involved in the development and enforcement of disciplinary procedures. Such procedures should be used when members or clubs violate rules and regulations resulting in damage to the image of the university or club or an increased risk of injury to an individual or litigation for the university.

Disciplinary actions range from verbal warnings to club probations and suspensions. Verbal and written warnings are effective, gentle reminders for members and clubs that may have overlooked a minor or commonly misunderstood policy or procedure for the first time. Probationary status is for more serious violations or for a second offense and can include limitations or loss of funding, use of facilities, and voting privileges on sport club council matters for a period of one month to one year. Repeated and blatant disrespect for the policies and procedures may result in the suspension of a club. Suspension can be for any recommended length of time and typically indicates that the club is inactive and forfeits all privileges of a sport club; it may even affect the club's student organization status.

Conclusion

Sport clubs have been a cornerstone of campus recreation programs for more than a century, yet they continue to be one of the best kept secrets on campuses. For years university administrators have underestimated the value and benefits of recreational sports and specifically sport club participation. Today's administrators are becoming keenly aware of the magnitude of sport club programs and are beginning to recognize the value and benefits of participation as well as the impact sport clubs have on the recruitment and retention of students. For over a century there has been a dynamic and continuing growth of sport clubs on college campuses. As students become less interested in being spectators and more interested in being participators, and as administrators provide greater support and resources, the future of sport clubs looks promising.

References

Downs, P.E. (2003). Value of recreational sports on college campuses. *Recreational Sports Journal, 27*(1), 5-64.

James Madison University. (n.d.). *Sport club program manual 2006-2007*. Retrieved from http://orgs.jmu.edu/scc/2006-2007%20Folder/InfoPageContent/Manual.06-07.doc.

National Intramural-Recreational Sports Association. (1996). *General and specialty standards for collegiate recreational sports*. Corvallis, OR: Author.

United Educators. (2006). Safety in student transportation: A resource guide for colleges and universities. Retrieved from http://admin.ue.org/documents/Safety%20in%20Student%20Transportation.pdf.

Glossary

arm's-length approach—Adminstrative model for sport clubs in which students operate teams that are independent from the institution, but a coach or faculty advisor employed by the school provides education and guidance. The students are not agents of the school, but the coaches and faculty advisors are and can create liability for the institution.

hands-off approach—Administrative model for sport clubs that are independent from the educational institution. Under this approach, sport clubs are contracted independent organizations. Contracted independent organizations are not agents, servants, or employees of the university, but rather are independent contractors that manage their own affairs. Club activities are run by students who are not working on behalf of the school for liability and insurance coverage purposes. Faculty and staff are removed from sport club activities, even in an advising capacity.

hands-on approach—Administrative model for sport club activities that are part of an educational institution. A coach, recreation director, or student affairs director plans and supervises team activities as an agent of the school. Club staff keep records and documents. The school is responsible for team activities and risks through its employees. The team leadership is covered by the institution's liability insurance policies.

hazing—An intentional action taken toward any student, on or off campus, by a student organization or any of its members to produce humiliation, physical discomfort, bodily injury or ridicule or to create a situation [in which] humiliation, physical discomfort, [or] bodily injury occurs (James Madison University, n.d.).

sport club—A group of students (and if the institution allows, faculty, staff, and community members) who voluntarily organize to further their common interests in a sport through participation and competition.

CHAPTER 10

Facilities

Peter D. Schaack, CRSS, MS, Associate Director of Facility Operations, Division of Recreational Sports, The University of Texas at Austin

A doctor can bury his mistakes, but an architect can only advise his clients to plant vines.

Frank Lloyd Wright

Today's university recreation centers facilitate more than basic individual or group play; they also foster social interaction and the building of community on campus. These facilities can and should be the social hub of the campus. When they convey warmth and allow activities to be viewed as soon as one enters the front doors, they promote the social and active concepts desired in today's recreation venues.

Campus recreation departments design, construct, manage, and schedule a wide variety of both indoor and outdoor facilities. Many constituencies use these facilities: members of recreational sport programs, students from kinesiology and physical education programs, athletes from intercollegiate athletic programs, and outside or off-campus user groups.

Given the heavy demands placed on recreation facilities, administrators must give the utmost thought and care to the design, material selection, construction, and scheduling of their recreation venues. They must also consider not only the specific recreation activities that occur inside the facilities, but also the lounge, the ancillary spaces, and the exterior landscaping so that students, faculty, staff, and other members are drawn to the recreation center. Strictly utilitarian recreation facilities, although functional, do little to attract visitors.

Heating, ventilation, and air-conditioning systems should be engineered to provide ample air changes within each activity area to create enjoyable and inviting environments. Walkways and corridors should be designed for simple access and furnished with comfortable, inviting seating. Natural light, bright colors, plants, and other materials should be considered to create a warm and appealing ambiance. With facility life spans sometimes exceeding 75 years, careful planning is absolutely necessary and will yield extended facility life and an increased number of users.

Today's campus recreation centers are more than the activities that take place within them. This chapter provides a brief overview of the traditional types of indoor and outdoor facilities that have been built across the country. It also addresses a few of the less traditional and more cutting-edge facilities managed by today's recreation departments. Limited but specific design criteria for each type of facility are suggested. In addition, this chapter includes information and advice on how to schedule, maintain, and staff these facilities.

Indoor Facilities

The construction of indoor recreation facilities, especially since the 1980s, has had a huge impact, both socially and economically, on recreation departments across the country. This construction boom has helped to move recreation departments to the forefront of campus student affairs agencies, especially in terms of recruitment and retention of students.

Gymnasia

Often considered the cornerstones of recreation centers, gymnasia come in all shapes and sizes. Traditional uses include basketball, volleyball, and badminton. Court lines for these activities can be superimposed to maximize space and scheduling possibilities. Courts used for informal or intramural recreation or in physical education classes do not necessarily have to meet standard lengths and widths. Courts used for NCAA competition, however, will need to have specific dimensions.

Gymnasium floors are often constructed of maple to maximize performance and appearance. However, synthetic materials, either rolled or poured, are also used. Basketball goals may be wall mounted, ceiling hung, or portable. Portable units can be hydraulically or electrically operated and allow the most space flexibility, but they are expensive and can be time-consuming to set up and take down. Ceiling and wall-hung systems can be designed with hoist systems to maneuver backboards out of the way of other activities. Backboards should be made of glass with the bottom edge padded for player protection. Breakaway rims should be installed to prevent the shattering of backboards.

Advance planning should be given to placing sleeves for badminton and volleyball standards during the construction or renovation of a recreation facility. Determining precisely where court lines will be placed will allow standard canisters to be installed where they are out of play and far enough off the sideline to prevent injury. Net standards can be portable, but the preferred method is to use floor plate systems.

In addition to the more standard sports of basketball, volleyball, and badminton, gymnasium spaces are increasingly designed with indoor soccer and floor hockey in mind. Divider curtains can be lowered, and removable walls with rounded corners can be installed.

When designing gymnasia, recreation administrators should consider alternative special event

Safety, performance, appearance, and versatility are primary considerations when gymnasium floors, ceilings, and wall-hung systems are designed and constructed.

William A. Cotton, Colorado State University.

Racquet Courts

Handball, racquetball, and squash courts are generally arranged together in recreation facilities. Floors are typically constructed of maple and are finished much like basketball courts, although finish is not always applied to squash court floors. Walls are made of plaster, laminated panels, or tempered glass. The areas of the ceiling that are "in play" should be constructed of the same materials as the walls to mimic ball reflection. Lighting should be flush with the ceiling, and heating and ventilation supply grills should located out of the field of play.

The design of squash courts is determined by the particular brand of squash played: The international game is played on a slightly larger court with a softer ball; the North American game is played on a narrower court with a harder ball. The North American game is on the decline, and in all likelihood most new squash courts will be designed for the international game. Many campus recreation departments are converting racquetball courts to international squash courts by installing glass walls eight feet into the court, adding the telltale and appropriate lines, and sanding the floors to bare wood. Although this leaves converted courts one foot narrower than the preferred international size, sanctioned squash tournaments may take place on these courts. Obviously, unfinished squash court floors require special care and maintenance, because any type of spill will stain the floor.

Multipurpose Spaces

Recreation administrators in charge of scheduling understand the need for large open spaces that can accommodate a variety of activities. Well-lit rooms with high ceilings, uninterrupted floor space, mirrors on the walls, high-quality sound systems, and plenty of **air changes** can support a variety of activities, including aerobic dance, archery, table tennis, fencing, and various martial arts.

uses for the gym space, such as commencement exercises, large banquets, and concerts. Installing a floor cover to protect the floor will allow the gym to accommodate these types of events. With the floor cover in place, tables, chairs, stages, light stands, and sound mixing equipment can be placed without fear of damaging the floor. Such flexibility increases the gymnasium's potential as a revenue producer and can aid in placing the recreation department at the center of the academic mission of the university.

Maple floors add desired performance characteristics and scheduling flexibility to multiuse areas; however, synthetic surfaces are a viable alternative. Obviously, if the room is used as an archery range, a divider curtain should cover the area behind the targets to protect the wall and prevent arrows from being broken. All doors and windows should be located behind the shooting line.

Determining the type of mat to be installed is probably the most difficult design decision associated with martial arts rooms. Different forms of martial arts favor different types of mats, with the main criteria being the size and density of the mat. Mats can be installed as sheets or in roll goods. If martial arts groups will be the primary users of a multipurpose space, then adding wall pads should be a consideration.

Weight Rooms

The popularity of weightlifting and cardiorespiratory training continues to grow, and as much square footage as possible should be devoted to these activity spaces. The design of these spaces is influenced by many factors. Will free weight equipment, powerlifting equipment, and cardiorespiratory machines be grouped together in one room or located separately? Are there sufficient electrical outlets to power the desired cardiorespiratory machines? Are cable TV outlets available if integrated televisions are desired for the cardiorespiratory equipment? Because weight rooms, especially those with free weights, are typically supervised, designers should also consider the locations of supervisor stations.

Sufficient space must be provided for lifting areas and traffic flow. Different amounts of space may be necessary for different pieces of equipment. Participants should be able to move about the weight room without getting in the way of lifters. Mirrors should be affixed to walls high enough so that they are not in danger of being broken by weight plates. Storage racks and lockers help keep weight training areas clean and free of trip hazards.

Because weight rooms can be particularly noisy, sound absorption is critical. Rubberized floors provide cushioning and help absorb sound. Locating the weight room on the bottom floor of the facility will lessen the chance of disturbing other activities. Weight plates with rubber coatings or molded plastic plates will also help with noise abatement.

Purchasing the proper cardiorespiratory and machine weight units is critical to the success of the weight room. Companies with solid reputations for good equipment and service should be at the top of the purchasing list. Also, an in-house or maintenance service contract should be considered for upkeep of the weight room. See also chapter 5.

Climbing Walls

Indoor climbing walls continue to be a popular interest and are frequently included in the construction of new recreation facilities and the renovation of existing ones. These walls allow instruction to take place in a safe and controlled setting and are often centrally located in new facilities because they attract attention. Typically, climbing walls are designed with soft, cushioned floors and built-in anchors allowing for top rope climbing. Careful design consideration is necessary to ensure that support walls are engineered to carry the load of the framing, climbing wall material, and climbing holds. Recreation departments, architects, and general contractors typically subcontract with specialty climbing wall manufacturers to design and construct climbing walls. See chapter 8 for more information on climbing walls.

Jogging Tracks

Indoor jogging tracks are often elevated or suspended above a gymnasium to maximize the use of space. The length of the track will depend on the space available within the envelope of the gymnasium. However, designs with long straightaways and few curves are preferred. The track surface should have adequate cushioning properties and can be installed as tiles or rolled goods or poured in place. The installation of synchronized pace clocks should be considered when designing or renovating indoor tracks. A stretching and user storage area should be designed adjacent to the track.

Natatoria

Natatoria are typically thought of as conventional, rectangular competition pools. However, an increasing number of natatoria are being designed with free-form leisure pools that include rather exotic features such as current channels, waterfalls, fountains, lazy rivers, and other inviting water play features. Although these elements are commonly associated with private or municipal pools, campus recreation departments are increasingly adding them in the design of their pools. Recreation departments considering such features

Indoor jogging tracks are frequently elevated above a gymnasium to maximize the use of space, and they often feature designs with long straightaways and few curves.

must give careful consideration to the long-term popularity and construction, operational, and personnel costs associated with them.

Very specific dimensions are required for lap pools and diving wells that are used in competition. This is not the case for pools used primarily for recreational lap swimming. Health department codes, however, do require depth markings and minimum water depths for diving.

The lighting of the natatorium environment should be in the forefront of the design process. Fixtures should be designed so they shine light indirectly, not into the eyes of backstroke swimmers.

Ancillary Areas

Though not found in every recreation center, **ancillary areas** such as cafés, concession areas, and wellness centers are worth considering. These additional areas help to "round out" recreation centers, insuring a wide range of services and bringing in clients who may not typically use recreational sport venues.

Checkout Areas

Most recreation centers maintain equipment checkout areas near the front entrance. In most facilities, users present institutional identification cards to check out equipment such as basketballs, footballs, racquetball and squash racquets, table tennis paddles, and billiard balls and cues. The size of the area will depend on many factors, including the overall square footage of the facility, the number of activity areas within the facility, and the philosophical view of the recreation administration as to what equipment to provide to participants and what equipment participants should bring themselves. Equipment checkout areas should be clearly marked with signage and have computer terminals available for checkout and record-keeping purposes and cash registers, if necessary.

If the facility provides a towel service, it is usually located in the equipment checkout area. Checkout areas with towel services may require additional square footage depending on where and whether the laundry equipment is located within the facility.

Locker Rooms

Locker rooms should be centrally located within the recreation facility, preferably on the same level as the natatorium. Because locker rooms serve a variety of functions, including dressing, personal hygiene, and storage, careful thought must be given to planning locker room layouts. Dividing wet areas (showers, steam rooms), toilet areas, and dry areas (dressing, locker storage) makes facilities comfortable for users and easy to maintain. Finishes and materials selected for locker rooms should be considered first and foremost for maintenance ease and care. Locker room environments can be one of the most difficult areas in the recreation center to keep clean and maintain.

Cafés

A recent trend in recreation center construction is to include cafés and food service support near the front entries to both attract and serve clientele. A recreation department can choose to operate the café itself or subcontract with an established food service provider. A thorough knowledge of state and local health codes is necessary before designing a café. An inventory of appliances needed should be completed to ensure adequate electrical

William A. Cotton, Colorado State University.

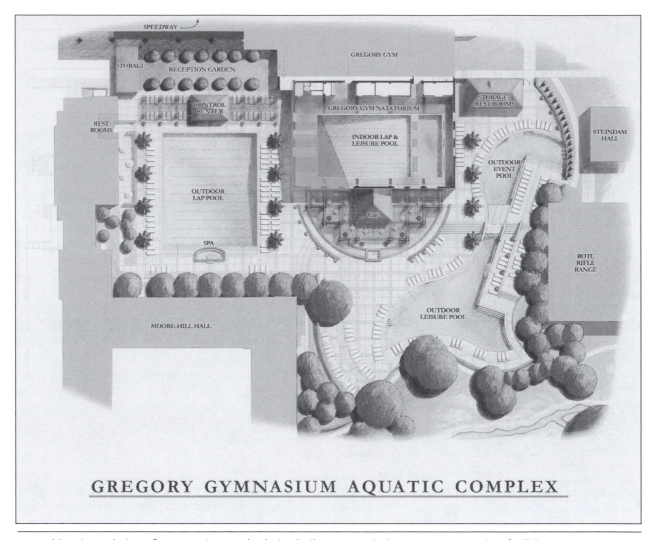

An architect's rendering of an aquatic complex being built next to existing campus recreation facilities.

Reprinted, by permission, from University of Texas at Austin.

power. Easy-to-clean floors and adequate counter space are necessary for any cafe operation to be successful.

Determining the café menu before construction will help with the design. Cafés serving cooked or fried foods, for example, will need grease traps, the installation of which should be incorporated into the design before construction begins. Another advantage to considering the café menu early is that administrators can think about the food odors that may waft into the facility; some of them may not be desirable.

Concession Areas

Concession areas located near gymnasia or multipurpose areas allow recreation departments not only to sponsor special events but also to sell merchandise to those attending the events. Like cafés,

concession areas should have easy-to-clean floors, adequate plumbing and electrical fixtures, and plenty of counter space to dispense product.

Wellness Centers

There is a movement by colleges and universities to provide faculty, staff, and students with wellness programs that match those found in corporate recreation. As a result, more recreation centers are being designed or retrofitted with **wellness centers.** In the past, these campus wellness centers were operated by kinesiology or health departments, but increasingly they are being managed by the recreation administration. Wellness centers included in recreation facilities should have enough private and semiprivate consultation rooms to conduct health checks, massages, manicures, and so on. A lobby or waiting area is also necessary; it should contain educational materials in paper, CD, or DVD formats. A kitchen, either in the wellness center or nearby, should be available for healthy eating workshops. Classroom space should be available for conducting wellness workshops.

The walls of wellness centers should be insulated to eliminate noise and provide privacy. Floors are generally carpeted for sound absorption. The centers should be close to the recreation activity areas so that aerobics rooms, pools, and tracks can be shared. Electricity should be available to provide power for treadmills, computers, refrigerators, and perhaps washers and dryers.

Outdoor Facilities

The desire among many people for a healthy and balanced lifestyle and a better quality of life has led to an increasing demand for outdoor facilities managed by recreational sport departments.

Field Sports

Popular field sports found at most outdoor areas managed by recreation departments include softball, flag football, soccer, lacrosse, rugby, and field hockey. Field lines for these activities, including softball, can be superimposed to maximize space and scheduling possibilities. They should be oriented so that play is in a north–south direction to prevent the sun from glaring into players' eyes. Softball fields can also be positioned with backstops adjacent to each other so that they are essentially in a quadrant.

The popularity of a given outdoor sport will dictate the number of fields devoted to it. For example, intramural departments do not typically offer rugby as a sport, but many recreation departments have rugby sport clubs. Therefore, one or two rugby fields may meet the needs of the recreation department, whereas many soccer and softball fields will be necessary because of the vast number of intramural, club, and informal recreation participants in these activities.

Much like indoor flooring, no one outdoor playing surface will completely meet the needs of the outdoor sports noted earlier. Each sport or activity has its own characteristics that lend themselves to different surfaces. Climatic conditions and construction costs also influence the surface design. However, natural grass continues to be the preferred surface because of its appearance, resiliency, footing, and cushioning capability. Other possible surfaces are exposed soil, synthetic turf, and aggregates.

Backstops for softball fields may be portable or permanent. Portable backstops provide field setup flexibility but can be difficult to move and store. The same advantages and disadvantages apply to portable or permanent soccer, rugby, and lacrosse goals. Lighting will add to the time the fields can be used, but lighting fixtures are expensive to install and operate. Metal halide lamps are usually preferred because of their "clear" color and directed concentration of light. Lighting levels must be high enough to allow players to safely see the activity objects (softballs, lacrosse balls, soccer balls). Typically, field complexes that support a variety of activities have 25 to 30 foot-candles of light spread evenly across all playing areas.

Popular recreational field sports include softball, flag football, soccer, lacrosse, rugby, and field hockey.

Track

Free-form tracks are often located around the field sport complex to accommodate recreational jogging. The track surface may be composed of an aggregate composition or a synthetic material that is typically poured in place with ultraviolet ray retardants.

Court Sports

Popular court sports found at most outdoor areas managed by recreation departments are basketball and tennis. However, many departments now use these courts for additional activities such as in-line skating and roller hockey. Subsurfaces for tennis and basketball courts can be made of asphalt, but concrete is preferred. Post-tension concrete will help prevent cracking and add service life to the courts. Top surfaces can made of interlocking plastic tiles or poured-in-place acrylic.

Court sports lines should be oriented so that play is in a north–south direction.

Ancillary Areas

Recreation departments are often charged with managing green space areas that are used for a variety of outdoor recreation activities. These areas can be located on or near campus, but are often located miles from the main campus. These green space areas might be designated as camps, ropes courses, or waterfront facilities. Outdoor recreation activities might include organized camping; high- or low-element ropes courses; climbing walls; canoeing; kayaking; and sailing, water skiing, fishing, snorkeling, scuba diving, and other water-related activities. Specific amenities will dictate what outdoor activities can be offered. Accessories such as docks, floats, and marinas will influence the types of boating and swimming activities offered. The size of a body of water will influence what boating activities are available. Larger bodies of water will allow for motorboating, canoe races, sailboarding, waterskiing, and so on. The quantity of open space will determine the availability of low- and high-element ropes courses, archery ranges, outdoor climbing walls, and tent or trailer camping spaces.

Ancillary outdoor areas may be managed by the facility operations area of the recreation department or may fall under the auspices of the outdoor recreation areas in which they are located.

Facility Scheduling

Recreation departments may have the best indoor and outdoor facilities available, but if the department cannot provide these areas to individuals and groups in an orderly fashion, they will have failed in their ultimate mission. Facilities need to be available for reservation and for drop-in, or informal, recreational use. It is up to recreation departments to ensure this availability.

Rules and Regulations

Given the ever-increasing inventory of high-quality facility space, it is no surprise that recreation professionals are bombarded with facility requests for their space. Because of this demand, the paper-and-pencil method of reserving space has quickly given way to proprietary and off-the-shelf computer programs for scheduling. However, before using these scheduling programs, recreation departments must establish a philosophy and a set of guidelines on which to base their reservation priorities. Before establishing a scheduling set of guidelines, administrators must research and understand all of the institutional rules and regulations that affect institutional facilities. For example, some institutional rules prevent recreation administrators from reserving space for groups outside the university. Other institutions allow outside groups to reserve on-campus space as long as a campus department sponsors them. Institutional rules governing the distribution of food or alcohol must also be thoroughly understood.

The facility-scheduling rules and regulations established by recreation departments should address the following:

- Permanent time blocks
- Informal recreation schedule
- Scheduling priorities
- Scheduling procedures

Permanent Time Blocks

As a result of high demand and limited space, recreation departments often restrict **permanent, or standing, blocks of time** to a few primary users. Typical primary users are the programs sponsored by the recreational sport departments (i.e., intramurals, fitness classes, sport club events and practices), physical and health education departments, and athletics departments. Primary users who are permitted to reserve time blocks typically do so on a semester or quarter basis. Because of reduced facility hours, and to allow for maintenance projects and other demands, permanent time blocks are generally kept in effect only while official university classes are in session.

Informal Recreation Schedule

Once permanent time blocks have been established, an **informal, or open, recreation schedule** can be created around the permanent time blocks. Informal recreation is defined as the drop-in use of a range of recreation activities at recreation facilities. For example, an informal recreation schedule might indicate that a gymnasium is available for drop-in use for basketball every Tuesday from 6 p.m. to 10 p.m.

In establishing the informal recreation schedule, administrators need to determine the popularity of specific activities and their specific use patterns to optimize the use of the informal recreation space. It makes sense to offer more informal recreation hours to popular activities such as basketball and soccer and fewer hours to less popular activities. Informal, or drop-in, users typically account for the largest participant constituency within the recreation department. A sample informal recreation schedule is shown in figure 10.1.

Scheduling Priorities

To meet the varied educational and recreational needs of the campus, a scheduling priority system should be established and disseminated so that all departments and groups able to reserve space understand the priorities. For the sake of efficiency, primary users often channel all requests through one department designee. Different facilities may have different scheduling priorities based on their intended use and funding base. Following is a sample priority list:

Priority 1: Programs administered through the recreation department

Priority 2: Academic classes and professional programs conducted by the physical education or kinesiology department

Priority 3: In-season practices for intercollegiate athletic teams

Priority 4: University tournaments and special events, defined as programs sponsored and conducted by and for university departments or registered student organizations

Priority 5: Sponsored tournaments and special events, defined as programs sponsored by

university departments or registered student organizations but open to nonuniversity participants

Scheduling Procedures

Deadlines for requesting recreation facilities should be established and made available to the campus community. For example, events occurring during a fall semester (September 1 to December 31) may have a deadline of April 1 for first-review consideration. October 1 might be the deadline for spring semesters, and January 1 for summer semesters. Requests received after preestablished deadlines are typically handled on a first-come, first-served basis as long as space is available.

Scheduling Decision Guidelines

The following criteria can be used in rendering decisions to approve or deny scheduling requests:

- Impact to existing programs and available spaces
- Scope and nature of the event (Does it conform with all system, university, and division regulations?)
- Appropriateness of the activity or event
- Compatibility of the activity and the facility in which it will be conducted
- Previous experiences with similar events
- Group's ability to meet all requirements relative to usage policies and procedures, facility usage, and event management charges
- Availability of required personnel

Space Requests

Groups or departments requesting facility space from the recreation department should complete a request form that contains the following:

- Department or group name
- Department or group contact information
- Facility space desired
- Appropriate signatures
- Policies and procedures that must be followed

The request form should be available on the recreation department's Web site. A sample request

Informal Recreation Schedule

Facility Abbreviations

AHG: Anna Hiss Gym	GRE: Gregory Gym	TSC: Texas Swimming Center
BEL: Bellmont Hall	PNK: Penick Allison Tennis Center	WF: Whitaker (Intramural) Fields
CLK: Clark Field	RSC: Recreational Sports Center	WT: Whitaker Tennis Courts

Activity	Facility	Monday–Friday	Saturday	Sunday
Badminton	BEL 528	5:30 p.m.–7 p.m. (T, Th)	10:30 a.m.–3 p.m.	12:30 p.m.–3 p.m.
		7 p.m.–9:45 p.m. (M)		
		5:30 p.m.–9:45 p.m. (F)		
Basketball	AHG 133 and 135 (half court only)	4 p.m.–10 p.m. (M, T, Th, F)	Closed	Closed
	CLK	12 p.m.–10 p.m. (M–Th)	12 p.m.–8 p.m.	12 p.m.–8 p.m.
		12 p.m.–8 p.m. (F)		
	GRE arena	6 a.m.–1 p.m., 6 p.m.–1 a.m. (M–Th)	8 a.m.–10 p.m.	10 a.m.–1 a.m.
		6 a.m.–1 p.m., 6 p.m.–10 p.m. (F)		
	RSC 2.200	6 a.m.–11 p.m. (M–Th)	8 a.m.–8 p.m.	10 a.m.–11 p.m.
		6 a.m.–8 p.m. (F)		
Dance/aerobics	GRE aerobics rooms	9 p.m.–1 a.m. (M–Th)	8 a.m.–10 p.m.	10 a.m.–1 a.m.
		7 p.m.–10 p.m. (F)		
	RSC 1.104 or 1.106	2 p.m.–5 p.m.	8 a.m.–8 p.m.	12 p.m.–11 p.m.
Dodgeball	AHG 133	4 p.m.–10 p.m. (W)	Closed	Closed
Faculty/staff	**HB/RB/SQ courts**			
Priority hours	BEL	12 p.m.–2 p.m.		
	GRE	12 p.m.–2 p.m.		
	RSC (four RB courts/two squash courts)	12 p.m.–2 p.m.		
	Basketball			
	GRE annex (two courts)	11:30 a.m.–1 p.m.		
	Volleyball			
	GRE annex (court 1)	12 p.m.–1 p.m.		
	Weight training			
	BEL 348	11 a.m.–2 p.m., 4 p.m.–7 p.m.		
Field sports	CLK Turf	6:30 a.m.–10 p.m. (M–Th)	8:30 a.m.–8 p.m.	10:30 a.m.–8 p.m.
		6:30 a.m.–8 p.m. (F)		
	WF	3 p.m.–10 p.m.	8 a.m.–6 p.m.	10 a.m.–6 p.m.

Handball/racquetball	GRE	6 a.m.–12 p.m.	8 a.m.–9 a.m.	10 a.m.–11 a.m.
		12 p.m.–1 a.m. (M–Th)	*9 a.m.–10 p.m.*	*11 a.m.–1 a.m.*
		12 p.m.–10 p.m. (F)		
	RSC	6 a.m.–12 p.m.	8 a.m.–9 a.m.	10 a.m.–11 a.m.
		12 p.m.–11 p.m. (M–Th)	*9 a.m.–8 p.m.*	*11 a.m.–11 p.m.*
		12 p.m.–8 p.m. (F)		
	Note: Courts may be reserved during *italicized* times. Please see front page for details.			
Jogging	GRE track (indoor)	6 a.m.–1 a.m. (M–Th)	8 a.m.–10 p.m.	10 a.m.–1 a.m.
		6 a.m.–10 p.m. (F)		
	CLK track (outdoor)	6:30 a.m.–10 p.m. (M–Th)	8:30 a.m.–8 p.m.	10:30 a.m.–8 p.m.
		6:30 a.m.–8 p.m. (F)		
Martial arts	AHG 39 or 134	6 p.m.–10 p.m.	Closed	Closed
Soccer (indoor)	BEL 528	7 p.m.–10 p.m. (W)	3 p.m.–6 p.m.	Closed
Squash	BEL	11 a.m.–12 p.m.	10 a.m.–11 a.m.	12 p.m.–1 p.m.
		12 p.m.–10 p.m.	*11 a.m.–6 p.m.*	*1 p.m.–6 p.m.*
	GRE	6 a.m.–12 p.m.	8 a.m.–9 a.m.	10 a.m.–11 a.m.
		12 p.m.–1 a.m. (M–Th)	*9 a.m.–10 p.m.*	*11 a.m.–1 a.m.*
		12 p.m.–10 p.m. (F)		
Swimming	**GRE aquatic complex**			
	Natatorium: lap pool	6 a.m.–9 a.m.	10 a.m.–2 p.m.	10 a.m.–2 p.m.
		12 p.m.–2 p.m.		
		5 p.m.–7 p.m.		
	Natatorium: leisure pool	6 a.m.–9 a.m. (M–F)	10 a.m.–2 p.m.	10 a.m.–2 p.m.
		1 p.m.–2 p.m. (M, W)		
		12 p.m.–2 p.m. (T, Th, F)		
		5 p.m.–7 p.m. (M–F)		
	Outdoor complex			
	August 30–October 31			
	Outdoor: lap pool	7 a.m.–10 p.m.	11 a.m.–8 p.m.	11 a.m.–8 p.m.
	Outdoor: leisure and event pools	11 a.m.–10 p.m.	12 p.m.–8 p.m.	12 p.m.–8 p.m.
	Children's hours	5 p.m.–10 p.m. (Friday only)	10 a.m.–2 p.m.	10 a.m.–2 p.m.
	November 1–December 8			
	Outdoor: lap pool	11 a.m.–2 p.m.	12 p.m.–5 p.m.	12 p.m.–5 p.m.
		5 p.m.–9 p.m.		

Figure 10.1 Informal recreation schedule.

(continued)

Informal Recreation Schedule *(continued)*

Activity	Facility	Monday–Friday	Saturday	Sunday
Swimming *(continued)*	**GRE aquatic complex** *(continued)*			
	Outdoor: leisure and event pools	Closed	Closed	Closed
	TSC	12 p.m.–2 p.m.	Closed	Closed
		5 p.m.–8 p.m.		
Table tennis	GRE stage	6 a.m.–1 p.m., 6 p.m.–1 a.m. (M–Th)	8 a.m.–10 p.m.	10 a.m.–1 a.m.
		6 p.m.–10 p.m. (F)		
	RSC 2.112	6 a.m.–5 p.m., 8 p.m.–11 p.m. (M–Th)	8 a.m.–8 p.m.	10 a.m.–11 p.m.
		6 a.m.–8 p.m. (F)		
Tennis	PNK	11 a.m.–1:30 p.m., 5:30 p.m.–10 p.m.	8 a.m.–10 p.m.	8 a.m.–10 p.m.
	WT	9 a.m.–10 p.m.	8 a.m.–10 p.m.	8 a.m.–10 p.m.
	Note: Whitaker courts can be reserved. Please see front page for details.			
TV/games Lounge	GRE games room (Billiards)	6 a.m.–1 a.m. (M–Th)	8 a.m.–10 p.m.	10 a.m.–1 a.m.
		6 a.m.–10 p.m. (F)		
	RSC 2.104	6 a.m.–11 p.m. (M–Th)	8 a.m.–8 p.m.	10 a.m.–11 p.m.
		6 a.m.–8 p.m. (F)		
Volleyball	GRE annex	11:45 a.m.–1 p.m. (faculty/staff only)	8 a.m.–10 p.m.	10 a.m.–1 a.m.
	GRE arena	6 a.m.–9 a.m., 6 p.m.–1 a.m.	8 a.m.–10 p.m.	10 a.m.–1 a.m.
	RSC 2.200	6 a.m.–11 p.m. (M–Th)	8 a.m.–8 p.m.	10 a.m.–11 p.m.
		6 a.m.–8 p.m. (F)		
Wallyball	GRE	12:15 p.m.–12:45 a.m. (M–Th)	*9:15 a.m.–9:45 p.m.*	*11:15 a.m.–12:45 a.m.*
		12:15 p.m.–9:45 p.m. (F)		
	RSC	12:15 p.m.–10:45 p.m. (M–Th)	*9:15 a.m.–7:45 p.m.*	*11:15 a.m.–10:45 p.m.*
		12:15 p.m.–7:45 p.m. (F)		
	Note: Wallyball is available by reservation only (courts can be reserved during *italicized* times). Please see front page for details.			
Weight training and conditioning	BEL 348	6 a.m.–10 p.m.	10 a.m.–6 p.m.	12 p.m.–6 p.m.
	GRE exercise lounge	6 a.m.–1 a.m. (M–Th)	8 a.m.–10 p.m.	10 a.m.–1 a.m.
		6 a.m.–10 p.m. (F)		
	GRE F/S weight room	6 a.m.–1 a.m. (M–Th)	8 a.m.–10 p.m.	10 a.m.–1 a.m.
		6 a.m.–10 p.m. (F)		
	GRE powerlifting room	6 a.m.–8 a.m., 12:05 p.m.–4 p.m., 6 p.m.–1 a.m. (M, T, Th)	8 a.m.–10 p.m.	10 a.m.–1 a.m.
		6 a.m.–8 a.m., 12:05 p.m.–1 a.m. (W)		
	GRE weight room	6 a.m.–8 a.m., 12:05 p.m.–1 a.m. (M–Th)	8 a.m.–10 p.m.	10 a.m.–1 a.m.
		6 a.m.–10 p.m. (F)		

Figure 10.1 *(continued)*

form from the University of Texas at Austin and its applicable policies and procedures are shown in figure 10.2.

Request Confirmations

Replies to facility requests should be prompt and verify that the facility space has been reserved. They should include the date and time of the reservation, personnel or facility costs associated with the reservation, and any special instructions that the requestor must follow. Confirmations should outline the guidelines groups are expected to follow while using the space. Following are some examples of usage guidelines:

- Recreation space is reservable for tournaments and events only; ongoing, permanent reservations are restricted to primary user departments.
- The premises must be returned in the same condition as when taken. The group is responsible for all damage to the premises and will be expected to reimburse the university for any damage. Willful destruction or abuse of university property will result in the forfeiture of the facility use privilege and in other university disciplinary action, if appropriate.
- Groups collecting money for tickets, donations, concessions, membership dues, or other purposes must do so in accordance with established university regulations.
- Smoking is permitted in designated areas only. Controlled substances are strictly prohibited; special permission must be obtained to consume alcoholic beverages within recreation facilities.
- Food and drink are not permitted in activity areas; prior approval is required for the sale of concessions.
- All advertising and the posting of ads must be approved by the recreation department.
- Any groups with an approved reservation that fails to honor or cancel the reservation within 24 hours, thereby denying others' use of the space, will be placed on "probation" and given limited future privileges.
- Special restrictions apply to specific sport facilities (e.g., footwear, use of equipment, and so on) and must be adhered to.
- The use of facilities is a privilege, and participants are expected to be good citizens and respect the rights of others. Responsible conduct is expected and required. Individuals who engage in unacceptable behavior may have their access to facilities revoked or modified or be subject to disciplinary action.
- The university reserves the right to make judgments concerning facility usage and cancel events that are deemed dangerous or are not in compliance with university regulations.
- Neither the university nor the recreational sport department is responsible for injuries sustained or property lost or damaged while using its facilities.

Rental Rates

Rental rates can help recreation departments offset the soaring utility and maintenance costs necessary for the upkeep of facilities. Many recreation departments establish rate schedules in which student and on-campus groups pay a lower hourly

The University of Texas at Austin
Division of Recreational Sports
GRE 2.202 FAX # (512) 232-4286
Facility Request form

Date submitted: ______

General Information

Organization/department: ______

Event title: ______

Description: ______

Authorized representative: ______ Telephone: ______

E-mail address: ______ UT EID: ______

Event coordinator: ______ Telephone: ______

E-mail address: ______ UT EID: ______

Facilities Requested

Anna Hiss Gym	☐ Room 133 (gym) ☐ Room 135 (gym)	☐ Room 136 (multipurpose) ☐ Courtyard
Bellmont Hall	☐ Room 302 (fencing multipurpose) ☐ Room 502A (dance) ☐ Room 528 (multipurpose) ☐ Room 902 (martial arts)	☐ Handball (# of courts: ______) ☐ Racquetball (# of courts: ______) ☐ Squash (# of courts: ______)
Clark Field	☐ Basketball (# of courts: ______)	
Gregory Gym	☐ Classroom ☐ Concourse ☐ Aerobic room (north or south) ☐ Games room ☐ Games room kitchen	☐ Basketball (# of courts: ______) ☐ Volleyball (# of courts: ______) ☐ Handball (# of courts: ______) ☐ Racquetball (# of courts: ______) ☐ Squash (# of courts: ______)
Gregory Gym Aquatic Complex	☐ Indoor lap pool (# of lanes: ______) ☐ Indoor leisure pool ☐ Outdoor lap pool (# of lanes: ______)	☐ Reception garden ☐ Outdoor event pool ☐ Outdoor event deck
Recreational Sports Center	☐ Room 1.104 (aerobics) ☐ Room 1.106 (aerobics) ☐ Room 1.138 (martial arts) ☐ Room 2.104 (games room) ☐ Room 2.104 (kitchen) ☐ Room 2.112 (multipurpose)	☐ Room 2.114 (multipurpose) ☐ Basketball (# of courts: ______) ☐ Volleyball (# of courts: ______) ☐ Handball (# of courts: ______) ☐ Racquetball (# of courts: ______) ☐ Squash (# of courts: ______)
Whitaker Fields	☐ Football (# of fields: ______) ☐ Soccer (# of fields: ______) ☐ Softball (# of fields: ______)	☐ Ultimate (# of fields: ______) ☐ Cricket (# of fields: ______) ☐ Other (# of fields: ______)
Whitaker Tennis	☐ (# of courts: ______)	

Dates and Times Requested

Day:	Date:	Set-up time:	Event start:	Event end:	Event strike:
Day:	Date:	Set-up time:	Event start:	Event end:	Event strike:
Day:	Date:	Set-up time:	Event start:	Event end:	Event strike:

Alternate Date

Day:	Date:	Set-up time:	Event start:	Event end:	Event strike:

From NIRSA, 2008, *Campus Recreation: Essentials for the Professional* (Champaign, IL: Human Kinetics). Reprinted, by permission, from The University of Texas at Austin, Division of Recreational Sports.

Figure 10.2 Facility request form.

Facility Usage Fees
(All rates are hourly.)

	User	University	Sponsored
Entire building	$600	$825	$1,100
Gymnasium: whole—social event	$410	$550	$775
Gymnasium: whole—sporting event	$250	$300	$450
Gymnasium: one court	$115	$160	$220
Meeting room	$35	$45	$70
Meeting room with kitchen	$60	$70	$115
Handball/racquetball/squash court (each)	$12	$18	$25

Note: All fund-raising events will be charged at the sponsored rates.

Definitions

- *User.* Programs administered through the Division of Recreational Sports, academic classes, intercollegiate athletics practices and events.

- *University.* Events sponsored by and conducted for university departments, registered student organizations, or both.

- *Sponsored.* Events sponsored by university departments or registered student organizations, but open to nonuniversity participants.

Figure 10.3   Sample rate schedule.

or half-day rate than off-campus groups. A rate schedule is shown in figure 10.3.

Facility Staffing

An entire chapter could be devoted to the staffing patterns used by recreation administrators in managing their facilities. What follows is a brief discussion of some of the key points of these philosophies and patterns.

Full-Time Versus Part-Time

A large number of institutions mandate that a full-time staff member must be on site during all operational hours of the recreation facility. Other institutions schedule a full-time staff member to be "on call" during operational hours, and others manage their facilities using a trained, part-time staff at all times. Still other institutions make use of graduate assistants to monitor facilities outside of normal business or office hours. Whatever philosophy is used as a basis for staffing, administrators should contact the institution's legal services department to be sure they are following institution-wide policies and procedures.

Part-Time Staff Positions

The number of part-time staff used to manage recreation facilities also varies widely. However, typically, a lead student oversees the other part-time staff working in the facility. These positions usually have titles such as facility coordinator, building coordinator, or building supervisor.

Most institutions have a variety of people reporting to the lead part-time supervisor. These include people checking out equipment, checking in racquet court reservations, checking IDs if an automatic scanning system is not used, selling pro shop items, and selling memberships. Most institutions staff their weight rooms at all times with a part-time staff member, especially if there are free weights. This weight room supervisor often reports to the lead student supervisor; however, a recent trend is to have this person report to the fitness director.

Recreation departments with aquatic complexes need a variety of lifeguards to supervise pools. The number of lifeguards needed depends on the number of pools, their size and shape, and local and state bathing codes. The number of field staff also varies widely depending on the size, shape, hours of operation, and activities offered.

Maintenance Staff

Many recreation departments hire their own maintenance staff to make general facility repairs and maintain the department's cardiorespiratory and weight training equipment . The maintenance staff typically reports to the assistant or associate director in charge of facility operations. Other institutions prefer to contract with outside agencies to maintain their equipment and facilities. Many institutions rely on their physical plant maintenance staff to care for their facilities and equipment.

Conclusion

The challenges facing recreation administrators in charge of facility design, construction, supervision, and scheduling can appear daunting. However, with well-thought-out preparation and plans given to facility design and construction; the hiring of competent, well-rounded student and full-time staff; and sound philosophical scheduling guidelines, administrators can meet these challenges. Recreation facilities that are well planned, designed appropriately, and constructed of good materials can be scheduled and supervised easily and efficiently. Such facilities also promote the recreation center as a hub on campus where genuine community building can occur.

Resources

Athletic Business
www.athleticbusiness.com

National Basketball Association
www.nba.com

National Collegiate Athletic Association (NCAA)
www.ncaa.org

National Federation of State High School Associations
www.nfhs.org

National Intramural-Recreational Sports Association (NIRSA)
www.nirsa.org

USA Swimming
www.usaswimming.org

USA Badminton
www.usabadminton.org

USA Rugby
www.usarugby.org

USA Fencing
www.usfencing.org

USA Racquetball
www.usra.org

US Squash
www.us-squash.org

Glossary

air changes—The total volume of air in a room that is turned over in one hour.

ancillary areas—Subordinate areas that help to "round out" recreation centers, insuring a wide range of services and bringing in clients who may not typically use recreational sport venues.

informal, or open, recreation schedule—A schedule outlining the drop-in use of a wide range of activities offered by recreation departments.

permanent, or standing, blocks of time—Periods of time that are reserved, usually on a semester or quarterly basis, for recurring events.

wellness center—In recreation facilities, an area devoted to providing individuals the opportunity to learn how to prevent illness and prolong life and to make choices that lead to better physical and mental health.

PART III

Operations and Management

CHAPTER 11

Writing a Business Plan for a Campus Recreation Department

Paul R. Milton, PhD, Assistant Professor of Sport Management, Ashland University

Once you think you've arrived, you are already apostate.

Anonymous

Because of the seemingly exponential explosion of facilities, staff, and budgets in campus recreation departments, such departments are operating more and more like businesses. Furthermore, legislators, the public, and their other constituents expect institutions of higher education to be more genuinely accountable than they have been in the past, particularly in their planning efforts. It is critical, therefore, that campus recreation administrators understand business processes, especially the planning process. This chapter provides the campus recreation administrator with a set of guidelines and concepts to aid in the long-term planning for a campus recreation department. Using the headings and subheadings listed in this chapter as an outline for a business plan is a valuable beginning toward this critical long-term planning process.

Writing a Business Plan

The **business plan** provides a campus recreation department with a blueprint for achieving fiscal self-sufficiency, stability, and success. Among other things, the plan provides specific fee increase requirements, revenue targets, and operating cost projections for the identified fiscal years, as well as long-range facility repair and replacement schedules. The plan also can identify department strategies to implement and goals to attain that will foster fiscal stability and success. The plan reinforces a campus recreation department's philosophical foundation of providing outstanding recreational and wellness opportunities. The plan also provides a set of specific recommendations that includes time lines, responsible people and groups, and potential net revenues and expenditures. A business plan for a campus recreation department, like any formal report, has the following three divisions:

1. The beginning includes the following:
   - Introduction
   - Department overview
   - Business description
   - Vision and goals
   - Description of management
2. The middle section, or heart of the plan, includes the following:
   - Summary of financials
   - Expense projections

- Revenue projections
- Capital reserve and requirements
- Discussion of the "bottom line"
3. The final section includes the following:
   - Highlights
   - Recommendations
   - Summary
   - Appendixes

A university budget director was once heard to say, "The only thing you know for certain about any short- or long-term business projections is that once they are made, they are wrong" (Armul, 1998). Nevertheless, it is critical in this age of increasing accountability and decreasing funds that appropriate short- and long-term planning occur. A campus recreation department should write its business plan for three to five years into the future.

Beginning Section

A business plan can be divided into three distinct sections. The beginning of the plan consists of the introduction, overview, business description, vision and goals, and management.

Introduction

The initial section of the business plan introduces the plan and outlines the general direction and purpose. The introduction should include, but is certainly not limited to, the following:

- Executive summary
- Letter from the director or person primarily responsible for the compilation of the plan
- Acknowledgments
- Purpose of the plan

Executive Summary

The **executive summary** is a one- to two-page condensed version of the plan. It captures the essence of the plan and includes only the most general and important concepts contained in the plan. Often written after the plan is complete, or near completion, the executive summary might emphasize general statements about programs, facilities, participation, budget, and staff—in other words, the primary items that are discussed in detail in the plan itself. This portion of the plan serves as an attention-getter, provides a frame of reference, and begins to create an ownership in the plan among the readership.

Director (Primary Author) Letter

The **director (primary author) letter** is a one-page letter from the person who leads the campus recreation program; it is generally addressed to his or her supervisor. It is part of the body of the plan and contains language that conveys to the immediate supervisor, as well as the entire institution, that the plan is complete and that suggestions, feedback, and input are welcome and encouraged. It contains statements that reiterate the purpose of the plan, along with the hope that the plan will serve the department as a business model well over the time of its intended duration.

Acknowledgments

Recognizing and thanking those who contributed to the research and writing of the business plan is important, as it is in any such undertaking. Although the **acknowledgments** section is not extensive (even a paragraph is appropriate), acknowledging those who were involved also sets up another level of buy-in, even accountability, for the contents of the plan.

Purpose of the Plan

The **purpose of the plan** is a succinct statement about why the plan was undertaken in the first place. Consider the following:

> The plan's major purpose is to provide for the [campus recreation department] to achieve fiscal self-sufficiency, stability, and success well into the initial decade of the twenty-first century. (Gosky & Milton, 2002, p. 7)

The purpose section declares in writing who is involved, why the plan was written, the direction the department will take, and the overall tone of the plan. Other items that might be included in this section are as follows:

- A statement about the flexibility of the plan (that it is not a static, inflexible rulebook)
- A statement to the effect that regular review and appropriate adjustments are required to keep the plan aligned with ever-changing internal and external factors
- More general, but revealing statements about what the reader can expect to see, such as fee increase requirements, revenue targets, operating cost projections, and

perhaps a long-range facility repair and replacement plan

The purpose of the plan is usually one page long. It can serve to reinforce the department's philosophical foundation. It might also include a specific set of recommendations including time lines, the people or groups responsible, and potential net revenues.

Overview

Whereas the introduction sets the tone of the plan, the **overview** sets the foundation. The overview section provides a perspective and justifies the direction of the plan. Each department writing a business plan needs to determine the areas it wishes to highlight in the overview. Although the overview can certainly include a variety of items, strong consideration should be given to the following:

- Mission statements
- Organizational values
- Department history
- Current status
- Organizational structure

Mission Statements

At this juncture of the plan, the mission statement of the campus recreation department should be included, as well as the mission statements of both the area to which the department reports and the institution itself. The goal is to provide a graphic depiction of how the department's mission is derived from the mission of its overall reporting unit, which is in turn derived from the mission of the institution. A discussion of how each emanated from the other should be included to ensure that the reader clearly understands the direct relationship of the missions. This should be brief, succinct, and even include bullet points instead of prose. Consider the following example:

> The mission of the Campus Recreation Department is derived from adherence to the mission of the University and the mission of the Division of Student Affairs, as well as an impetus to provide the highest quality programs and services to members and guests. The Department is an auxiliary operation housed in the Student Development area of Student Affairs. The Department strives to achieve an appropriate balance among quality services and programs, student development

concerns, and generally accepted business practices. (Gosky & Milton, 2002, p. 11)

Organizational Values

Often, campus recreation departments create a set of **organizational values** that describe what is important to the department. Following are some examples of organizational values:

- Creating and maintaining a diverse workforce
- Providing customer service
- Enhancing student development
- Providing the most up-to-date equipment
- Making use of the latest breakthroughs in technology

The list of organizational values is normally no more than one page long and can contain anywhere from 3 to 15 value statements. Table 11.1 shows what a list of organizational values might look like.

Department History

Few campus recreation departments maintain an account of the history of the department. However, most are able to piece together at least a brief synopsis of the milestone events that have occurred in the department during its existence. A **department history** in a business plan need be nothing more than such a synopsis.

Historical records to be included in a business plan should provide details on the following underpinnings of any recreational sport department:

- Philosophical
- Programmatic
- Staff
- Facility
- Financial

These significant reference points help the business plan writers develop the background of the department and the background for the business plan itself. They provide both the readers and the writers of the plan with ideas about where the recreational sport department has been and therefore help clarify and define its future direction.

A two- to three-page department history should discuss the following:

- Leaders of the department and the impact they had during their tenure
- Participation levels and trends
- Student involvement in the department, especially the impact of student advisory organizations

This section could also highlight any unique achievements the department has had, such as being the "first university building in the United States created solely to serve students' recreational needs" (Purdue University, 2001, p. 5).

Current Status

An important purpose of the overview portion of the business plan is to provide a present-time snapshot of the campus recreation department. The **current status** section summarizes the current state of the department.

Used to provide a synopsis of key areas of the department, the current status section might include categories such as the following:

- Advisory groups
- Equipment inventory
- Expenses
- Facilities
- Memberships
- Participation
- Staff
- Student fee revenues
- Technologies

Table 11.1 Organizational Values

Organizational value	The campus recreation staff
Commitment to mission	. . . has a personal belief in and focus on mission, creating a pride in, desire for, and commitment of action to achieve its goals and keep its promises.
Students first	. . . views students as the primary membership group, but is committed to providing all members and guests with the highest levels of service, courtesy, respect, and dignity.
Customer service	. . . is committed to consistently meet and exceed the expectations of our members and guests. We understand we exist because of the participants whom we are here to serve.

Reprinted, by permission, from Kent State University Department of Recreational Services.

The writer should select the categories carefully to ensure that the readers see the best key areas. Often, the current status section is used to make sweeping statements about the key areas that put the department in the best light possible and help draw the readers' attention. Consider this one:

The department oversees $30 million in physical plant, manages an inventory of equipment and supplies valued at over $2 million, and employs a staff of highly educated and skilled professionals of whom nearly 80 percent possess a Master's degree or higher. (Gosky & Milton, 2002, pp. 17-24)

An adequate current status section would be four to eight pages in length, depending on the number of categories identified for discussion. Some writers include charts, graphs, and tables in this section to augment the text provided in later sections. For example, a mere listing of the major holdings in an inventory, their individual worth, and a summation of their total worth may suffice when discussing the inventory portion. However, a bar chart comparing participation over the last five years may be the best way to enhance the participation section. Furthermore, with the advanced word processing technology of today, multicolored graphics can be easily added to professionalize the presentation of the business plan.

Organizational Structure

At this point in the plan, a graphic one-page depiction of the organizational flow chart of the campus recreation department should be included (see figure 11.1). It should be the most accurate and up-to-date listing of the staff. Most organizational charts include the following:

- Administrative positions
- Support positions
- Graduate student positions

Business Description

When writing a business plan, a campus department of recreational sports needs to describe its major business functions in detail. Writers should give considerable deliberation to how the philosophies, values, and priorities interact with and affect the program, facilities, and staffing of the department.

The **business description** section contains detailed descriptions of the major areas of a campus recreation department. This section can also be used to highlight any part of the department the writer chooses, so long as it describes a business function. The following items might be included in a business description:

- Department philosophy and priorities
- Description of the major areas of a department
- Participation levels
- Pricing strategies

Department Philosophy and Priorities

Unlike the philosophy outlined in the introduction section, the philosophy in this section describes the particular philosophical concepts that drive the business functions. Some specific examples may help clarify this distinction.

- *Students first.* Many campus recreation departments take the position that student participants are their primary, if not sole, user group. In their programming, customer service, staffing, resource allocation, and facility scheduling, such departments primarily emphasize student needs and interests. Departments with this philosophy place significant importance on student development. They may provide students with real-world and degree-related work experience through departmental employment in accounting, marketing, graphic design, fund-raising, sales, advertising, fitness, recreation, exercise physiology, facility management, first aid or CPR, education, human resources, technology, computer science, public relations, journalism, aquatics management, and physical education.

- *Effective programs and services.* The provision of high-quality, student-oriented recreation and fitness programs is a major part of the mission of virtually every campus recreation program in the nation. In the department philosophy and priorities section of the business plan, departments can reaffirm their philosophical, as well as practical, commitment to good programs and services.

- *Stewardship.* Because students at most institutions are the primary "payers" and "users" of recreational programs and services, departments should convey that they take the philosophical position of maintaining good stewardship of the resources under their purview. Furthermore, this provides an opportunity to express other concepts

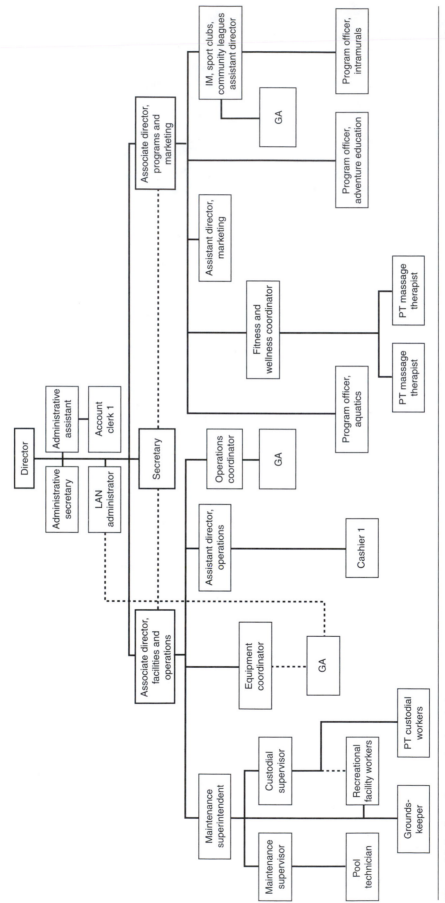

Figure 11.1 Sample organizational chart.

regarding stewardship, such as the position that students pay the lowest rates for programs and services. This section might be closed with a statement such as "The Campus Recreation Department remains committed to providing the highest-quality program of recreational services for the students at the lowest cost possible, while, of course ensuring fiscal solvency" (Gosky & Milton, 2002, p. 28).

- *Image building.* Most campus recreation departments are expected to enhance the positive image of their institutions. The department philosophy and priorities section of the business plan should emphasize that the campus recreation department provides a comfortable, friendly, enjoyable, clean, and safe environment for all participants. In addition, as an integral part of **image building,** most campus recreation departments are expected to play an ever-increasing role in the recruitment and retention of academically prepared and qualified students. The department should document its relationship with enrollment management efforts and the admissions area and collaborations with academic units in this section. In the business plan of one midwestern university, the following quote was used to highlight the importance of the existence of the new recreation center to the image of the institution: "This is the most important building on our campus in the last twenty-five years, maybe ever" (Gosky & Milton, 2002, p. 15).

Descriptions of Major Areas of the Department

This section of the business plan (from 2 to 10 pages long depending on the size and scope of the department) provides a detailed description of the major areas of the campus recreation department. It is a good idea to develop mission statements for each of these areas, if they do not already exist, as part of their descriptions.

In a way, these descriptions serve as "plans within the larger business plan" because each area description should begin with an overview, continue with a description of the mission, and include a philosophy statement. The plan then moves into more specific descriptions of the major functions of the area, finally ending with a summary of the goals and expectations. Following are examples of major areas of a department:

- Programs
- Facilities
- Member relations

- Guest relations
- Marketing
- Human resources
- Technology

Participation Levels

Participation has always served as an important benchmark of the success of, and satisfaction with, campus recreation departments. Until recently, **participation levels** were virtually the sole measure of the value of recreational sports on a particular campus. Recent researchers (Ellis, Compton, Tyson, & Bohlig, 2002), however, have begun to challenge this notion, suggesting that frequency of participation does not reflect program value.

Nevertheless, participation levels provide some evidence of trends, shifts in interests, and participant need, particularly if individual programs and facility use are tracked. Furthermore, frequencies and percentages, when considering certain demographics, can not only give clues to trends, but also provide impetus for further investigation.

Given these considerations, a business plan should include some indicators of participation levels and trends. One obvious demographic available to most campus recreation departments is gender; another is age or the traditional-aged student compared to the nontraditional-aged student. Many institutions track student participation by ethnicity and could easily report levels of participation using this category. Although frequencies and percentages are not significant in and of themselves, they can be windows of information that, when opened, can shed further light on participation.

Pricing Strategies

The business description portion of the business plan might seem like an unusual place to include a discussion of **pricing strategies.** Of course, each recreational sport department that undertakes the writing of a business plan must decide whether this is the right place to include it, just as it must make decisions regarding the placement, even the inclusion, of the categories suggested throughout this chapter. However, pricing is a critical component of the financial success of any department and therefore an important business function.

The pricing strategy section includes a brief recap of the philosophy of charging students for access, programs, and services. Any recent, positive trends should be noted here. Consider the following statement:

It is important to note that student fees for recreational sports have not increased in nearly five years, while expenses have increased along the lines of the Consumer Price Index over the same period. (Gosky & Milton, 2002, p. 51)

Such a statement may be included to indicate the need to increase student fees.

This section of the business plan should convey and justify, in written form, all price changes projected to occur during the life of the plan. Major sources of income such as the following should also be included:

- Day passes or passes of other duration
- Food sales
- Memberships
- New revenue ideas
- Pro shop merchandise
- Rentals
- Sponsorship pricing
- Student fees

Vision and Goals

To this point, little discussion has occurred regarding the **vision and goals** that a recreational sport department should convey in a business plan. This section of the business plan lists sustained operating and major departmental goals, program and facility guiding principles, and vision projects.

Sustained Operating Goals

One higher education accreditation organization defines goals as a more sustained, long-lasting set of ideal accomplishments (Smith, 2001). Goals should be based on the missions of the institution and the department and should, at least by this organization's definition, be general in nature. These sustained goals are operating parameters that will probably remain unchanged during the life of the business plan. They are the goals from which current major departmental goals emanate. A list of sample **sustained operating goals** follows:

- *Program and facility offerings.* Offer outstanding and diverse programs, facilities, and customer service that meet the changing needs of participants.
- *Effective workforce.* Build, maintain, and encourage a knowledgeable, friendly,

conscientious, and service-oriented workforce.

- *Sound financial management.* Implement sound financial and budgeting practices, including comprehensive planning and reporting.
- *Technology support.* Develop, implement, and maintain an efficient, adaptable, and inclusive technological support structure that will streamline procedures and enhance communication and customer service.
- *Mission adherence.* Create and consistently adhere to a shared vision derived from the mission statement of the Department of Recreational Sports (Gosky & Milton, 2002, p. 57).

Current Major Departmental Goals

As mentioned earlier, the **current major departmental goals** are derived from the sustained operating goals. They should be a series of actions that occur during the identified year and that serve to accomplish the sustained operating goals. These goals might look like the following:

- Provide diverse participation opportunities, superior service, and safe and clean facilities.
- Use technological advances to improve and streamline service.
- Continue to provide sound financial management, including the finalization of a five-year business plan.
- Continue to seek ways to generate increased income that do not have negative impact on existing use of programs and facilities (Gosky & Milton, 2002, p. 57).

Program and Facility Guiding Principles

Some campus recreation departments include a set of **program and facility guiding principles** as part of the departmental vision. These principles, according to Myers (1994, p. 3), inform readers and participants about such details as the following:

- Where the department receives its revenues
- That the programs and services are marketed aggressively to maximize facility usage and generate such revenues
- That the programs offered are intended to enhance the lives and lifestyles of the participants

- That policies regarding priority usage and access are established and agreed upon

The **priority usage** among major constituent groups should be identified and listed in this section of the business plan. Following is an example of a priority usage statement for a building that is exclusively devoted to recreational sports:

The recreational department reserves the right to prioritize space usage for the following categories based on need, usage patterns, and availability:

- Informal, walk-in recreation by students, other paying members, and guests
- Organized recreational sports, intramurals, sport clubs, and wellness programs
- Department of Recreational Sports noncredit instruction programs
- Special events organized by the Department of Recreational Sports

Again, the preceding list (Gosky & Milton, 2002, p. 59; Myers, 1994, p. 3) serves only as an example; individual departments must determine and list the priorities that are appropriate in their settings.

Department Vision

Most campus recreation leaders maintain a vision of what the future of their organizations will look like. Although not a part of every business plan, such a statement would be found in a department vision section. Determining a vision for the department can be an enjoyable exercise for the entire staff as it comes together to consider how the department might look in three to five years. It is important to put these things in writing so that both staff and the greater institution can see what the department has planned. Although areas considered for this section are limitless, they could include the following:

- Future staffing
- Facilities
- Revenue generation
- Reorganization or retooling
- Philosophical shifts
- Proposed moves to another reporting unit

Management

The business plan is often used to highlight or describe some part of the department that is positive or some accomplishment that the writers of the plan wish to emphasize to the public. This should occur in the **management section.** Many researchers report that it is incumbent upon leaders to commend staff at every opportunity (DePree, 1992; Kouzes & Posner, 1995), and the management section of the business plan is the perfect place to do so.

The management section also highlights specific hiring practices and philosophies. It should describe in great detail the type of employee sought by the department. Staff professionalism should be paramount in the discussion. This serves to express an overall appreciation for the qualifications and contributions of staff members. This section allows the department to parade outstanding qualities in front of the university and other constituencies served by the department.

Management Overview

The **management overview** section describes the meticulous, yet cost effective, hiring process. It should include a statement saying that the department takes great care in seeking and then selecting a highly educated, experienced, and diverse group of employees. In addition, this section can include the following:

- List of the highest degrees earned by administrative and professional staff
- List of the highest degrees earned by support staff
- Cumulative years of professional experience within the department
- Ethnic makeup of the department (in graphic or text form)

A brief discussion of the percentage of "homegrown" staff and those recruited from outside the institution might be included. Such a discussion provides insight into whether the staff reflects a sense of history, tradition, and stability while also experiencing a constant infusion of fresh ideas and new ways of conducting business (Gosky & Milton, 2002, p. 69).

Professional and Support Staff

This straightforward and utilitarian section has a biographical paragraph for each staff member that includes the following:

- Name
- Position title
- Years with the department
- Years in current position
- Degrees
- Majors
- Where degrees were earned
- Brief job description (five to six lines)

Middle Section

The second major section of the business plan is made up of the summary of financials, expense and revenue projections, capital reserve and requirements, and the bottom line. This is an extremely important part of the plan and is often the focus of an executive summary.

Summary of Financials

The **summary of financials** section is the heart of the business plan. Many readers turn first, if not exclusively, to this section because it provides intricate details of the financial side of the department.

Preface

The all-important summary of financials section is introduced with a statement of introduction, or preface. This two- to three-paragraph section summarizes the current financial situation of the country, state, institution, and department. It includes general financial forecasts (with the specifics to follow in greater detail) for the department and provides an opportunity to prepare the reader for what follows.

Consider the following summarizing statement at the end of the preface of a business plan for recreational sports:

> The applicability of [the plan's] stated assumptions, threats, targets, recommendations, and forecasts will, therefore, require regular review as national, regional, and local economic conditions shift. (Gosky & Milton, 2002, p. 77)

Financial Assumptions

It is critical to the success of any campus recreation business plan to consider the conditions under which that plan will succeed. The plan's writers should create assumptions about the financial climate and then develop the plan based on those assumptions. Following are sample assumptions to foster ideas on creating and writing financial assumptions:

- Student enrollment remains relatively constant throughout the duration of the business plan.
- Enrollment increases provide additional, unexpected income.
- Specific increases in student general fees and in fees charged for other services will be approved as proposed within this plan.
- An average annual inflationary cost factor of 3.0 percent is used for the duration of the plan. Thus, the compounded rate of increase in operating expenses (for five years) is estimated at 18.7 percent.
- Specific budget line exceptions to this 3.0 percent cost factor are noted in the financial forecasts section of this plan.
- The institution will renegotiate the debt retirement on the recreation center to reduce the annual debt; the estimated actual cost reduction is 3.0 percent of the current annual payment.
- Specific increases in fees and charges to institutional faculty and staff for use of the programs and facilities will be approved as proposed within this plan.

Of course, clearly, if even one of these assumptions is not met, the success of the plan is less certain. However, it is important that those who hold the campus recreation department accountable understand the assumptions well in advance, or the plan has little chance of being accepted.

Financial Threats

Following the financial assumptions section, the **financial threats** section responds directly to those assumptions by articulating what will happen if the department does not meet them. Each assumption should be addressed in a paragraph or two providing as much detail as possible. It is reasonable to discuss the impact that reductions in income and revenue would have on the department and even propose alternatives, if available.

Financial Forecasts

The **financial forecasts** section provides painstaking detail regarding expense and revenue projections for the life of the plan. Close attention should be paid to expense lines that are expected to exceed or fall below any across-the-board inflationary cost factor. The entire section could take as many as 20 pages.

Expense Projections

The **expense projections** section deals specifically with the expenses the department predicts it will incur during the duration of the plan. One practical method is to use the expense lines in the actual department budget and discuss how and why expenses are predicted to be what is itemized in the plan. Expenses might include, but are not limited to, the following:

- Personnel services (administrative, hourly, student), nonpayroll personnel services, staff benefits, employee fee waivers
- Current expenses, supplies, maintenance and repairs, rentals, travel, utilities, miscellaneous current expenses, purchases for resale
- Equipment
- Technology

This section should provide great detail about specific areas that would divert from the pro forma annual percentage increases established by the plan. For example, because utilities are so volatile and increase at rates much beyond the Consumer Price Index, a separate calculation should be made in this expense line, most likely based on historical spending. It should be notated as such in the business plan.

A detailed, columned table summary of this area that is easily understood at a glance can often put the reader's mind at ease about projected expenses. The following should be included:

- Predicted expenses from one fiscal year to the next
- Projected increases in expenses over the previous fiscal year
- Projected percentage increases from one fiscal year to the next

Revenue Projections

The revenue projections section deals specifically with the revenues the department predicts it will generate during the period of time covered by the plan. Graphs, tables, and charts can certainly help clarify revenue expectations and enhance the presentation. Revenue projections do the following:

- Identify and detail the major sources of revenue
- Tell what percentage of the total revenue each major area represents
- Describe increases or decreases predicted to occur in each area over the life of the plan

The specific sources of existing revenue, as well as proposed new revenue sources, should be discussed in detail. Typical existing sources include, but are not be limited to, the following:

- General student fees
- Membership and pass sales
- Pro shop sales
- Program revenue (should provide a breakdown of the revenue generated by each program area)
- Other revenue
- Any new sources of revenue agreed on by the department and the institution
- Any projected sources
- Specific price increases (This section announces the details of any specific price increases or user fee increases and lists what the expected increases might generate in revenue.)

A membership grid that indicates the specific increases in each of the membership and pass categories over the life of the plan can be helpful (see table 11.2).

Capital Reserve and Requirements

The **capital reserve and requirements** section of the business plan outlines plans to create and enhance capital reserve funds that are expected to pay for capital repairs and replacement of indoor and outdoor facilities. This is also an excellent place to identify specific facility items that will require repair, replacement, or renovation over the longer term—that is, to create a capital replacement schedule.

Capital Reserve

Although the name of the fund will vary from institution to institution (**capital reserve fund** is one example), it is highly recommended that a campus recreation department create and enhance

Table 11.2 Membership Grid

Membership category	Current	April 2002	April 2003	April 2004	April 2005	April 2006
Percent increase		10%	3.5%	3.5%	3.5%	3.5%
Student, less than 5 hours	$55.00	$60.50	$62.62	$64.81	$67.08	$69.43
Student, nonassessed: monthly	$30.00	$33.00	$34.16	$35.35	$36.59	$37.87
Student, nonassessed: semester	$80.00	$88.00	$91.08	$94.27	$97.57	$100.98
Student, continuing: summer	$40.00	$44.00	$45.54	$47.13	$48.78	$50.49
Student, spouse: monthly	$30.00	$33.00	$34.16	$35.35	$36.59	$37.87
Student, spouse: semester	$80.00	$88.00	$91.08	$94.27	$97.57	$100.98
Student, family: monthly	$60.00	$66.00	$68.31	$70.70	$73.18	$75.74
Student, family: semester	$200.00	$220.00	$227.70	$235.67	$243.92	$252.46
Student, dependent: monthly	$20.00	$22.00	$22.77	$23.57	$24.39	$25.25
Student, dependent: semester	$60.00	$66.00	$68.31	$70.70	$73.18	$75.74
Faculty/staff I: monthly	$30.00	$33.00	$34.16	$35.35	$36.59	$37.87
Faculty/staff I: semester	$80.00	$88.00	$91.08	$94.27	$97.57	$100.98
Faculty/staff I: annual	$180.00	$198.00	$204.93	$212.10	$219.53	$227.21
Faculty/staff II: monthly	$40.00	$44.00	$45.54	$47.13	$48.78	$50.49
Faculty/staff II: semester	$100.00	$110.00	$113.85	$117.83	$121.96	$126.23
Faculty/staff II: annual	$240.00	$264.00	$273.24	$282.80	$292.70	$302.95
Faculty/staff, couple: monthly	$70.00	$77.00	$79.70	$82.48	$85.37	$88.36
Faculty/staff, couple: semester	$180.00	$198.00	$204.93	$212.10	$219.53	$227.21
Faculty/staff, couple: annual	$450.00	$495.00	$512.33	$530.26	$548.82	$568.02
Faculty/staff, family: monthly	$100.00	$110.00	$113.85	$117.83	$121.96	$126.23
Faculty/staff, family: semester	$300.00	$330.00	$341.55	$353.50	$365.88	$378.68
Faculty/staff, family: annual	$750.00	$825.00	$853.88	$883.76	$914.69	$946.71
Alumni or spouse: monthly	$40.00	$44.00	$45.54	$47.13	$48.78	$50.49
Alumni or spouse: semester	$130.00	$143.00	$148.01	$153.19	$158.55	$164.10
Alumni or spouse: annual	$375.00	$412.50	$426.94	$441.88	$457.35	$473.35
Alumni, couple: monthly	$75.00	$82.50	$85.39	$88.38	$91.47	$94.67
Alumni, couple: semester	$235.00	$258.50	$267.55	$276.91	$286.60	$296.63
Alumni, couple: annual	$720.00	$792.00	$819.72	$848.41	$878.10	$908.84
Alumni, family: monthly	$130.00	$143.00	$148.01	$153.19	$158.55	$164.10
Alumni, family: semester	$400.00	$440.00	$455.40	$471.34	$487.84	$504.91
Alumni, family: annual	$1,000.00	$1,100.00	$1,138.50	$1,178.35	$1,219.59	$1,262.28
Community: monthly	$48.00	$52.80	$54.65	$56.56	$58.54	$60.59
Community: semester	$160.00	$176.00	$182.16	$188.54	$195.13	$201.96
Community: annual	$440.00	$484.00	$500.94	$518.47	$536.62	$555.40
Community, couple: monthly	$80.00	$88.00	$91.08	$94.27	$97.57	$100.98
Community, couple: semester	$300.00	$330.00	$341.55	$353.50	$365.88	$378.68
Community, couple: annual	$780.00	$858.00	$888.03	$919.11	$951.28	$984.57
Community, family: monthly	$150.00	$165.00	$170.78	$176.75	$182.94	$189.34
Community, family: semester	$430.00	$473.00	$489.56	$506.69	$524.42	$542.78
Community, family: annual	$1,100.00	$1,210.00	$1,252.35	$1,296.18	$1,341.55	$1,388.50
Nonprime: monthly	$35.00	$38.50	$39.85	$41.24	$42.69	$44.18
Nonprime: semester	$125.00	$137.50	$142.31	$147.29	$152.45	$157.78
Nonprime: annual	$375.00	$412.50	$426.94	$441.88	$457.35	$473.35
Dependent: monthly	$28.00	$30.80	$31.88	$32.99	$34.15	$35.34
Dependent: semester	$80.00	$88.00	$91.08	$94.27	$97.57	$100.98
Dependent: annual	$180.00	$198.00	$204.93	$212.10	$219.53	$227.21
Adult: day pass	$6.00	$6.60	$6.83	$7.07	$7.32	$7.57
Youth: day pass	$5.00	$5.50	$5.69	$5.89	$6.10	$6.31
Child: day pass	$3.00	$3.30	$3.42	$3.54	$3.66	$3.79
Adult: 10-punch card	$60.00	$66.00	$68.31	$70.70	$73.18	$75.74
Youth: 10-punch card	$50.00	$55.00	$56.93	$58.92	$60.98	$63.11
Child: 10-punch card	$30.00	$33.00	$34.16	$35.35	$36.59	$37.87

Reprinted, by permission, from Kent State University Department of Recreational Services.

a budgeted account whose purpose is to provide the necessary funding for immediate and long-term capital expenses on indoor and outdoor recreational facilities. Many campus recreation departments have such accounts and add to them through a variety of sources.

Occasionally, institutions permit campus recreation departments to generate interest income on the capital reserve account as a way to create a steady flow of additional funds. A recreational sport department that is designated as "auxiliary" by the institution is allowed to roll over any positive fund balance into the capital reserve fund at the end of the year.

Departments also enhance capital reserve funds through financial gifts from generous donors, often in exchange for naming rights of an area of a facility or the facility itself. A department may also be permitted to deposit a certain amount of its earned revenues each year to the capital reserve account, as though the transfer to the fund is an operating expense. A 30-year capital reserve fund with columns showing interest and transfers from revenue is shown in table 11.3.

Long-Term Capital Replacement Schedule

A campus recreation department responsible for the operation of a recreation center, and thus

Table 11.3 Capital Reserve Fund

Capital replacement fund as of	Balance	Fiscal year	Estimated expenses	Amount remaining	3.5% interest	Annual transfer in	Total fund balance at end of FY
6/30/2001	$884,174	2002	($25,000)	$859,174	$—	$100,000	$959,174
6/30/2002	959,174	2003	(25,000)	934,174	32,696	100,000	1,066,870
6/30/2003	1,066,870	2004	(56,100)	1,010,770	35,377	100,000	1,146,147
6/30/2004	1,146,147	2005	(43,500)	1,102,647	38,593	100,000	1,241,240
6/30/2005	1,241,240	2006	0	1,241,240	43,443	100,000	1,384,683
6/30/2006	1,384,683	2007	0	1,384,683	48,464	100,000	1,533,147
6/30/2007	1,533,147	2008	(48,200)	1,484,947	51,973	100,000	1,636,920
6/30/2008	1,636,920	2009	(25,000)	1,611,920	56,417	100,000	1,768,337
6/30/2009	1,768,337	2010	(103,000)	1,665,337	58,287	100,000	1,823,624
6/30/2010	1,823,624	2011	(39,400)	1,784,224	62,448	100,000	1,946,672
6/30/2011	1,946,672	2012	(18,400)	1,928,272	67,490	100,000	2,095,762
6/30/2012	2,095,762	2013	(20,400)	2,075,362	72,638	100,000	2,247,999
6/30/2013	2,247,999	2014	(59,186)	2,188,813	76,608	100,000	2,365,422
6/30/2014	2,365,422	2015	(61,275)	2,304,147	80,645	100,000	2,484,792
6/30/2015	2,484,792	2016	(84,600)	2,400,192	84,007	100,000	2,584,198
6/30/2016	2,584,198	2017	0	2,584,198	90,447	100,000	2,774,645
6/30/2017	2,774,645	2018	0	2,774,645	97,113	100,000	2,971,758
6/30/2018	2,971,758	2019	(34,000)	2,937,758	102,822	100,000	3,140,580
6/30/2019	3,140,580	2020	(97,000)	3,043,580	106,525	100,000	3,250,105
6/30/2020	3,250,105	2021	0	3,250,105	113,754	100,000	3,463,858
6/30/2021	3,463,858	2022	(136,000)	3,327,858	116,475	100,000	3,544,334
6/30/2022	3,544,334	2023	0	3,544,334	124,052	100,000	3,768,385
6/30/2023	3,768,385	2024	(1,538,000)	2,230,385	78,063	100,000	2,408,449
6/30/2024	2,408,449	2025	(86,500)	2,321,949	81,268	100,000	2,503,217
6/30/2025	2,503,217	2026	0	2,503,217	87,613	100,000	2,690,829
6/30/2026	2,690,829	2027	0	2,690,829	94,179	100,000	2,885,009
6/30/2027	2,885,009	2028	(127,700)	2,757,309	96,506	100,000	2,953,814
6/30/2028	2,953,814	2029	(1,197,900)	1,755,914	61,457	1,775,000	3,592,371
6/30/2029	3,592,371	2030	(466,200)	3,126,171	109,416	1,775,000	5,010,587
6/30/2030	5,010,587	2031	(1,603,000)	3,407,587	119,266	1,775,000	5,301,853
6/30/2031	5,301,853	2032	(1,755,000)	3,546,853	124,140	1,775,000	5,445,993

Reprinted, by permission, from Kent State University Department of Recreational Services.

for the repair, renovation, and replacement of the various components of its structures, must develop a **long-term capital replacement schedule.** This schedule identifies the replacement item, the predicted year for replacement, and the cost of the replacement based on an estimation for that predicted year. A figure of 3.5 percent per year is normally used to make this projection.

In compiling the information for the replacement schedule, the administrator should hold discussions with a variety of sources to create the most accurate list possible of actual items needing to be replaced and their accompanying cost of replacement. It is critical to include the cost of labor and shipping in those estimates. Contact sources could include, but are not limited to, the following:

- Manufacturers
- Other recreational sport departments with similar facilities
- Campus physical plant departments
- University architects

Even though a business plan may be written to encompass a five-year period, a long-term capital replacement schedule should be developed for as many as 30 years.

Tables 11.4 and 11.5 provide a replacement schedule of such duration, with a list of suggested replacement items, the year in which they are predicted to be replaced, and the associated costs, compounded at the suggested 3.5 percent rate.

Debt Service Requirements

Many campus recreation departments are not just building multimillion-dollar recreation and wellness centers; they are responsible for the debt incurred by the construction of such facilities. The **debt service requirements** section of the business plan includes a discussion of the annual payments on the debt, the point at which the debt is retired, and when the payments are due.

If the institution is considering refinancing the debt on recreation facilities, this should be mentioned and the following points included:

- Length of time it will take to retire the new debt
- What the annual payments will be for the new indebtedness
- What the new funds will be used for

Amortization Detail

Retiring the debt on recreation facilities is very similar to paying off a home mortgage, although on a much larger scale. A business plan should include a chart or table that lists the **amortization detail** on the debt. Most bond companies provide this for an institution that has taken on the debt incurred through the construction of recreation facilities.

Account Total: The Bottom Line

The **account total,** or bottom line, is a one-page summary of the financial forecasts section that puts the total picture in perspective by summarizing the key points articulated in the expense and revenue projections sections. A bar graph depicting revenues and expenses, side by side, year to year, will provide a practical, easy-to-follow graphic display of all projections. The major expenses and revenues should be shown separately on each bar to give the reader a clear picture of the projections for each area.

A **pro forma budget** over the proposed period is one of the most important, and most referred to, parts of a business plan. For five-year plans, the projected revenues and expenses should be listed line by line in columns per annum. This gives the reader a comprehensive record of all of the years of the plan and proposed revenues and expenses for each year. A sample of a pro forma budget is shown in table 11.6.

Final Section

The final section of the business plan provides the highlights, recommendations, a summary, and any appendixes. This section serves to reiterate the key points, pose recommendations and to some extent the proposed solutions to the recommendations, and present supporting documentation (appendixes).

Highlights

The **highlights** section is a recap of the major points of the plan and is an important section of the business plan. Usually one to two pages, it can be presented as a series of bullet points. It is a point-by-point list of the major tasks that a recreational sport department says it will accomplish during the life of the plan. It puts the major issues in a prominent position in the plan. When this section is included, there can be no doubt, institution-wide, about the major points of the plan.

Table 11.4 Long-Term Capital Replacement Schedule

Item	Qty.	2003	2004	2005	2006	2007	2008	2009	2010	2011	2012	2013	2014	2015	2016	2017	2018	2019	2020	2021	2022	2023	2024	2025	2026	2027	2028	2029	2030	2031	2032
Air handler AHU-1 33,000 CFM	1																						T								
Air handler AHU-2 37,000 CFM	1																						U								
Air handler AHU-3 30,000 CFM	1																						V								
Air handler AHU-4 15,000 CFM	1																						W								
Air handler AHU-5 3,000 CFM	1																						X								
Air handler AHU-6 3,000 CFM	1																						Y								
Boiler (gas-fired 175)	2																						Z						JJ		
Carpet (administrative offices, pro shop, seminar rooms)													K																		
Carpet (entry-level hallways, game room, vending areas)			A						F						M						R						EE				
Carpet (lower-level hallways, cardio stretching areas)				C					G					L					P					DD					KK		
Carpet (men's and women's locker rooms)			B				D				I				N				Q				AA				FF				OO
Chiller (steam absorption 390)	1																											GG			
Climbing wall	1																											HH			
Climbing wall floor	1																														PP
Exterior: building surface maintenance								E										O										II			
Floor: rubber (weight room)	1									H											S								LL		
Pool filtration system																															
Pool pak	2																														
Poured surface (multipurpose room)																							BB								QQ
Roof (over pool)																															RR
Roof (standing metal seam and flat section over pool)																														MM	
Security/entrance systems												J																		NN	
Track surface																															SS
Windows and entrance doors	250																						CC								

See table 11.5 for key to letters.

Reprinted, by permission, from Kent State University Department of Recreational Services.

Table 11.5 Capital Replacement Cost Estimates: FY2002 to FY2032

Reference	Estimated cost	Reference	Estimated cost
A		X	$21,250
B		Y	21,250
C	$43,500	Z	353,000
D	48,200	AA	28,000
E	25,000	BB	264,000
F	51,500	CC	318,500
G	51,500	DD	86,500
H	39,400	EE	95,800
I	18,400	FF	31,900
J	20,400	GG	630,500
K	59,186	HH	504,400
L	61,275	II	63,000
M	63,500	JJ	102,600
N	21,100	KK	102,600
O	34,000	LL	261,000
P	72,750	MM	156,500
Q	24,250	NN	38,000
R	78,000	OO	36,700
S	58,000	PP	56,000
T	147,000	QQ	1,100,000
U	170,000	RR	255,000
V	145,000	SS	344,000
W	70,000		

Refer to table 11.4 for specific capital replacement items.

Reprinted, by permission, from Kent State University Department of Recreational Services.

Recommendations

A complete business plan for a campus recreation department contains **recommendations** at various points in the text. The writers should also list these in a separate section so the reader may peruse them as a whole. In addition to listing the recommendations from the text, this section should also include any others that may arise. An effective method of presenting the recommendations is a table that includes a column for each of the following:

- Recommendations
- Area or people responsible for the completion of the recommendations
- Time line for the completion of the recommendations
- Revenues or costs of the recommendations

The recommendations section can be especially useful as the recommendations are accomplished during the duration of the plan. In updating the plan periodically, a new column should be added to the table that shows how and when the recommendations were accomplished or the reasons they were not accomplished according to the time line. The key is that these issues, and how the department responds to them, should be out in the open.

Summary

The **summary** section of the business plan is a two- to three-paragraph general recap of the plan's purpose that explains how it is both visionary and flexible. A few well-crafted sentences should solidify the department's position on important institutional issues. Following is one such concluding statement:

It is important for the Department of Recreational [Sports] to be able to maintain an appropriate balance between the expressed needs and expectations of its primary users—the students—and sound fiscal management. Often in university settings, student development is sacrificed for the bottom line, or vice versa. The five-year Business Plan offered by the department should provide optimal balance between these often-competing interests. (Gosky & Milton, 2002, p. 121)

Appendixes

Appendixes are used to provide details of items that are referenced in the text and to include items that augment the text. Following are examples of items that may appear in appendixes:

- Copy of the most recent year-end financial report of the department
- Program guide of departmental offerings for the most recent year
- Section that updates certain portions of the plan, especially the financial and recommendations portions
- Staff resumes
- Any audit reports or departmental reviews occurring within the last fiscal year
- Copies of evaluation forms used by the department
- Capital replacement schedule
- Most recent annual report of the department
- Pro forma budget projections for the duration of the plan

Table 11.6 Pro Forma Budget

	Proposed FY2002 ($)	Proposed FY2003 ($)	Proposed FY2004 ($)	Proposed FY2005 ($)	Proposed FY2006 ($)	Proposed FY2007 ($)
PERSONAL SERVICES						
Contract: administrative and professional	584,400	604,854	626,024	647,935	670,612	694,084
Hourly	447,183	462,834	479,034	495,800	513,153	531,113
Faculty	—	—	—	—	—	—
Summer program	—	—	—	—	—	—
Graduate assistants	41,575	43,030	44,536	46,095	47,708	49,378
Students	587,564	625,000	646,875	669,516	692,949	717,202
Nonpayroll services	13,000	40,000	41,400	42,849	44,349	45,901
Total personal services	**1,673,722**	**1,775,719**	**1,837,869**	**1,902,194**	**1,968,771**	**2,037,678**
STAFF BENEFITS						
Retirement (13.31%) (included in benefits pool)	137,122	141,921	146,889	152,030	157,351	162,858
Benefits budget pool	—	—	—	—	—	—
Group insurance (included in benefits pool)	196,984	203,878	211,014	218,400	226,044	233,955
Medicare (included in benefits pool)	—	—	—	—	—	—
Other staff benefits budget pool	15,965	16,524	17,102	17,701	18,320	18,961
Employee/department fee waiver (included in benefits pool)	44,000	46,640	49,438	52,405	55,549	58,882
Graduate staff tuition budget pool	26,670	28,270	29,966	31,764	33,670	35,690
Retirement buyout	—	—	—	—	—	—
Total staff benefits	**420,741**	**437,234**	**454,410**	**472,299**	**490,934**	**510,347**
CURRENT EXPENSES						
Travel	28,075	29,058	30,075	31,127	32,217	33,344
Entertainment	9,950	10,298	10,659	11,032	11,418	11,817
Supplies	163,896	190,000	196,650	203,533	210,656	218,029
Duplicating and printing	20,700	21,425	22,174	22,950	23,754	24,585
Telephone	31,050	32,137	33,262	34,426	35,631	36,878
Postage	13,250	13,714	14,194	14,691	15,205	15,737
Other information and communication	41,400	42,849	44,349	45,901	47,507	49,170
Maintenance and repairs	74,425	109,425	113,255	117,219	121,321	125,568
Rentals	9,550	40,000	41,400	42,849	44,349	45,901
Utilities	394,649	430,000	451,500	474,075	497,779	522,668
Miscellaneous current expenses	48,664	75,000	75,000	75,000	75,000	75,000
Purchases for resale	32,000	40,000	41,400	42,849	44,349	45,901
Total current expenses	**867,609**	**1,033,905**	**1,073,917**	**1,115,651**	**1,159,185**	**1,204,598**
Equipment	10,000	40,000	45,000	50,000	55,000	60,000
Technology	—	65,000	68,250	71,663	75,246	79,008
Special project technology upgrade	—	100,000	—	—	—	—
TOTAL EXPENSES	**2,972,072**	**3,451,857**	**3,479,445**	**3,611,807**	**3,749,135**	**3,891,631**

(continued)

Table 11.6 *(continued)*

	Proposed FY2002 ($)	Proposed FY2003 ($)	Proposed FY2004 ($)	Proposed FY2005 ($)	Proposed FY2006 ($)	Proposed FY2007 ($)
REVENUE						
FEE REVENUE						
Intramural fee	917,840	1,237,145	1,556,450	1,641,598	1,769,320	1,897,042
Student recreation and wellness center fee	2,360,560	2,360,560	2,360,560	2,360,560	2,360,560	2,360,560
Total fee revenue	**3,278,400**	**3,597,705**	**3,917,010**	**4,002,158**	**4,129,880**	**4,257,602**
OTHER REVENUE						
Operations: membership and pass sales	660,090	732,580	758,220	784,758	812,224	840,652
Operations: other	104,428	114,871	126,358	138,994	152,893	168,182
Programming	215,867	250,000	275,000	302,500	332,750	366,025
Total other revenue	**980,385**	**1,097,451**	**1,159,578**	**1,226,251**	**1,297,867**	**1,374,859**
Total revenue budget	**4,258,785**	**4,695,156**	**5,076,588**	**5,228,409**	**5,427,747**	**5,632,461**
Net operating budget surplus/(deficit)	**1,286,713**	**1,243,299**	**1,597,143**	**1,616,603**	**1,678,612**	**1,740,831**
TRANSFERS OUT						
Debt service	1,678,445	1,679,175	1,678,535	1,681,485	1,677,735	1,677,735
Contingency repair and replacement	100,000	100,000	100,000	100,000	100,000	100,000
Total transfers out	**1,778,445**	**1,779,175**	**1,778,535**	**1,781,485**	**1,777,735**	**1,777,735**
TRANSFERS IN						
Education and general	600,000	600,000	240,000	180,000	150,000	150,000
Total transfers in	**600,000**	**600,000**	**240,000**	**180,000**	**150,000**	**150,000**
Net increase/(decrease) in fund balance	**108,268**	**64,124**	**58,608**	**15,118**	**50,877**	**113,096**

Reprinted, by permission, from Kent State University Department of Recreational Services.

Conclusion

Each campus recreation department must write a business plan that is appropriate for its unique situation. The chapter offers many suggestions and includes some of the best elements of business plans from recreational sport departments; nevertheless, it is intended to provide assistance, even guidance, so that readers can develop the most effective plan for their settings. Simply using the headings and subheadings found within the chapter as an outline would be a substantial beginning to an effective plan.

Placing some of the more memorable quotes from the text of the plan in strategic positions throughout the plan helps add emphasis to both the information contained in the quote and the presentation of the plan itself. This gives the reader powerful statements at a glance and emphasizes the information immediately contiguous to the quote. Following is a quote from an existing plan:

It has been and continues to be the department's policy to offer students the lowest possible rates for all services, activities, and programs. This is reflected in both the fees that students pay each semester/quarter and in the prices students are charged for add-on services such as locker and towel service, climbing wall certifications, and outdoor trips. (Gosky & Milton, 2002, p. 28)

This statement shows that the department is committed to placing students at the focal point of its fees and charges philosophy. It also reflects the department's long-term commitment to the primary supporter of the campus recreation program: students.

Here is another:

Little or no need for additional staffing throughout the five-year life of the plan is anticipated. (Gosky & Milton, 2002, p. 83)

This message makes an authoritative statement about the department's intent regarding staffing, sending a clear message to the institution: Resources will not be tied up in new positions.

Finally, a business plan must make clear that continual reviews and revisions will occur during the life of the plan. The plan should be a blueprint for department action, but not so inflexible that it becomes the department rulebook. Indeed, if done right, the business plan should be the most useful document and reference point for the department for which it is written.

References

Armul, J. (1998, June). *Meeting*. Kent, OH: Kent State University.

DePree, M. (1992). *Leadership jazz*. New York: Dell Publishing.

Ellis, G., Compton, D., Tyson, B., & Bohlig, M. (2002). Campus recreation participation, health and quality of life. *NIRSA Journal, 26*(2), 51-60.

Gosky, J., & Milton, P. (2002). *Kent State University business plan 2003-2007*. Kent, OH: Kent State University.

Kouzes, J.M., & Posner, B.Z. (1995). *The leadership challenge*. San Francisco: Jossey-Bass.

Myers, S. (1994). *Miami University guiding principles*. Oxford, OH: Miami University.

Purdue University. (2001). *Division of Recreational Sports strategic plan 2001-2006*. West Lafayette, IN: Purdue University.

Smith, S. (2001, April). *AQIP*. Presentation at monthly meeting of the Council of Enrollment Management and Student Affairs, Kent State University, Kent, OH.

Glossary

account total (the bottom line)—A one-page summary of the financial forecasts section in a business plan that puts the total picture in perspective by summarizing the key points articulated in the expense and revenue projections sections.

acknowledgments—A statement in a business plan that recognizes and thanks those who contributed to its research and writing.

amortization detail—A chart or table in a business plan that lists the amortization details on the debt.

business description—A section of a business plan that contains a detailed description of the major areas of a campus recreation department: its participation levels, the philosophy that drives the business functions, its pricing strategies and priorities, and its values.

business plan—A comprehensive document that discloses the recent financial and operational history, the current operational and financial status, and the projected operational and financial outlook of a campus recreation department. It serves as a tool to emphasize campus recreation department accomplishments to the public and the institution, and it provides a blueprint for achieving fiscal self-sufficiency, stability, and success.

capital reserve and requirements—A section of a business plan that outlines plans to create and enhance capital reserve funds that are expected to pay for capital repairs and replacement of indoor and outdoor facilities.

capital reserve fund—A budgeted account whose purpose is to provide the necessary funding for immediate and long-term capital expenses on indoor and outdoor recreational facilities.

current major departmental goals—Goals derived from the sustained operating goals of a campus recreation department. They outline a series of actions to take to accomplish certain ends during the identified year.

current status—The section of a business plan that provides a current snapshot of key areas of the campus recreation department.

debt service requirements—The annual payments on debt incurred by a campus recreation department.

department history—A brief synopsis in a business plan of the milestone events that have occurred in the campus recreation department during its existence.

director (primary author) letter—A one-page letter from the head of the recreational sport program that is generally addressed to his or her supervisor as part of a business plan. It reports that the plan is complete and encourages suggestions, feedback, and input.

executive summary—A one- to two-page condensed version of the business plan that serves as an attention-getter and provides a frame of reference. It captures the essence of the plan and includes only the most general and important concepts, such as programs, facilities, participation, budget, and staff.

expense projections—The expenses a campus recreation department predicts it will incur during the period of time covered by a business plan.

financial forecast—A forecast of expense and revenue projections for the life of a business plan.

financial threats—Any impact reductions in income or revenue will have on the campus recreation department.

highlights (of a business plan)—The major points of a business plan, usually presented as a bulleted list in the plan.

image building—A campus recreation department's efforts to enhance the positive image of the institution and increase recruitment and retention of academically prepared and qualified students by providing a comfortable, friendly, enjoyable, clean, and safe environment for all participants.

long-term capital replacement schedule—A schedule that identifies any items that will need replacing, the predicted year for replacement, and the predicted cost of the replacement (usually 3.5 percent per year).

management overview—A section of a business plan that describes the hiring process; lists the highest degrees earned by administrative, professional, and support staff; and lists the cumulative years of professional experience within a campus recreation department.

management section (of a business plan)—A section of a business plan in which positive aspects of the department are highlighted and staff are commended for their work.

organizational values—What is important to a campus recreation department.

overview—The part of a business plan that provides a perspective and justifies its direction.

participation levels—A benchmark of the success of, and satisfaction with, campus recreation departments. These provide some evidence of trends, shifts in interests, and participant needs, particularly when individual program and facility use are tracked.

pricing strategies—How a campus recreation department charges participants for access, programs, and services.

priority usage—A statement about the priority for the use of indoor and outdoor campus recreation facilities. The campus recreation department reserves the right to prioritize space usage based on need, usage patterns, and availability.

pro forma budget—A budget that lists projected revenues and expenses for each year of a business plan.

program and facility guiding principles—Principles on which a campus recreation department proposes to operate in regard to revenue generation, marketing practices, lifestyle enhancement, and priority usage and access.

purpose of the plan—A succinct statement describing why a business plan was undertaken, who was involved in the writing, why it was written, the direction the department will take as a result, and the overall tone of the plan.

recommendations—A section of a business plan that lists the plan's recommendations and provides a time line for their completion, the area and people responsible for their completion, and a list of revenues or costs.

summary—A recap of a business plan.

summary of financials—The heart of a business plan that provides intricate details of the entire financial side of a campus recreation department.

sustained operating goals—Unchanging, general, long-lasting goals that are based on the missions of the institution and the campus recreation department.

vision and goals—A section of a business plan in which the campus recreation department lists operating principles, purposes, and program-user priorities.

CHAPTER 12

Marketing

Evelyn Kwan Green, MBA, MS, Instructor, Tourism Management, The University of Southern Mississippi

Aaron Hill, BA, Graduate Teaching Assistant, The New School, New York City

A campus recreation department must market itself as primary to the mission of the institution. Can your operation afford *not* to have a marketing professional?

Sid Gonsoulin, Associate Vice President, Student Affairs, The University of Southern Mississippi; NIRSA Past President (2004)

Marketing has been a part of trade and commerce systems for centuries. Some marketing scholars date the practice of marketing back to the ancient Greek philosophers Plato and Aristotle (Shaw & Jones, 2005). Today we mostly think of marketing as a highly evolved practice that fuels the corporate economy. Increasingly, the science of marketing is being applied to nonprofit and cause-driven organizations, including those that provide campus recreation programs and services.

This chapter begins with a discussion about hiring a marketing professional and the structure of the position. Next, we present the fundamentals of program promotion. This is followed by a pragmatic approach to constructing a marketing plan. We then outline the approach for seeking sponsorship funding. Finally, we present the strong new role of technology in marketing and discuss emerging trends.

Job Description and Specifications of a Campus Recreation Marketing Professional

Before setting out to hire a marketing professional, campus recreation administrators have many things to consider. The first is whether they truly need one. Once that determination has been made, many other job functions need to be considered before the right professional can be chosen. This section will address these considerations.

Does Your Department Need a Marketing Professional?

Before developing a job description and specifications for the position of a full-time campus recreation marketing professional, campus recreation administrators must first assess the need for one. Assessment factors (Green & Gonsoulin, 1995) should include, but need not be limited to, the following:

- Funding status of the program
- Comprehensiveness of the program
- Complexity of income production activities, programs, and services
- Percentage of revenue to be generated from additional sources
- Availability of funds

Campus recreation programs that are fully funded by the institution and student recreation fees would have a lesser need for a full-time marketing professional. On the other hand, a profit-centered campus recreation program would need a full-time marketing professional to create and implement strategic marketing planning to ensure that income-generating activities are well executed and resources are optimally used.

The size of the student population also dictates whether the program needs a full-time marketing professional. The larger the student population is, the more likely it is that the campus recreation program is extensive and varied in its programming and service offerings. Likewise, the greater the complexity of income production activities, programs, and services, the greater the demand for a professional who can conduct the market research necessary to put together a well-coordinated and integrated marketing plan.

Can Your Department Afford a Campus Recreation Marketing Professional?

The additional level of income to be generated and the availability of funds must be assessed to determine the feasibility of hiring a full-time marketing professional. Campus recreation departments must recognize that marketing professionals generally command higher salaries than other campus recreation professionals. According to the American Marketing Association's *Compensation Survey of Marketing Professionals 2006* (Aquent/American Marketing Association, 2006), the median salary for an entry-level marketing position in education is $40,600. A midlevel marketing position in education commands a $52,740 median salary. The median salary for a top-level marketing position in education is $80,000. These salaries are relatively higher than those of campus recreation professionals; new graduates can expect to earn an annual salary of approximately $25,000 (entry level) in most municipal and not-for-profit organizations. Private agencies or for-profit organizations typically offer higher entry-level salaries of $30,000 or more (North Carolina Central University, 2005).

The discrepancies in salary between a marketing professional and a campus recreation professional can potentially create resistance in the staff. To facilitate a smooth transition, campus recreation administrators must help their staff to adjust to and accept the notion of recruiting a marketing professional to coordinate the department's marketing plan. Campus recreation administrators must be able to clearly define the changes, identify possible resistance to change, plan the change, and implement the change (Green & Gonsoulin, 1996). For example, if the introduction of the marketing position would eliminate the need for individual programming directors to develop their own promotional plan and materials, administrators must be prepared to address the issue of ownership, or "turf." They must be able to articulate the benefits of the new infrastructural change to existing staff (e.g., more time to focus on programming needs) to gain buy-in for the new plan. Without the support of their campus recreation programming colleagues, marketing professionals will encounter issues of "not fitting in," which can potentially sabotage their efforts.

Whom Should You Hire?

Hiring the right person for the right job directly affects the productivity of the department and the organization (Lussier, 1994). Campus recreation administrators should first identify and determine the department's needs and match those needs to the professional whose strengths match the highest-priority needs of the department (Green, Gonsoulin, & Nordin, 1997). Campus recreation administrators must conduct a job analysis (see figure 12.1) to determine remuneration and needs and to serve as a basis for evaluating job performance (Lussier, 1994).

Job Description and Specifications

According to Sperling (1983), a **job description** must address the function and primary objective of the position and accountabilities. The role of the position within the organization and its relationships with and dependence on other functions and jobs must also be defined. The scope of control, the major areas reporting to the person in this position, and the balance between authority and responsibility must be accurately defined to avoid staff conflicts, job dissatisfaction, and over- or underhiring situations. External relationships and interaction needs must also be clearly identified. The significance of the job's impact within and outside of the department must be carefully evaluated to justify the salary compensation. The dollar amounts in terms of budget, assets, and income incurred or generated by this position must also be considered to justify the hire. Campus recreation administrators must perform the previously mentioned tasks to fully assess the feasibility of hiring a campus recreation professional and to develop an idea of the personality, technical, managerial, communication, and people skills required by the job.

Key Function Areas for a Campus Recreation Marketing Professional

Generally, the key areas of responsibility for a campus recreation marketing professional include promotion of campus recreation programs, marketing management, sponsorship solicitation, market research, public relations, and sales. See table 12.1.

Promotion of Campus Recreation Programs

Before the 1990s, "marketing" campus recreation primarily involved promoting individual campus recreation programs. The key promotional activities were the creation and distribution of programming flyers, brochures, and calendars of events. However, with the expansion of programming variety and depth, the growing popularity of the Internet, and increasing competition, promotional planning and activities must be more innovative. Without proper planning, innovative programming, and timely promotion, campus recreation programs may not be able to keep up with the ever-changing needs of today's stakeholders as

The University of Southern Mississippi
The Department of Human Resources
Job Analysis Questionnaire

(Revised: December 2000)

Date: ____ / ____ / ____

Job title: ______________________ Level: __________

Department: ______________________

Location: ______________________

Completed by (print clearly): ______________ Phone #: __________

Basis for job knowledge: ☐ Hold job now ☐ Supervise job ☐ Previously held job

☐ Other, explain: ______________

General Purpose of the Job. Please summarize the position, describing the main function and purpose of the position in general terms. This summary will be used in future job postings. Use no more than three sentences, if possible.

Essential Duties and Responsibilities. List the job's essential duties, tasks, and responsibilities. Limit the number of essential duties, tasks, and responsibilities to a maximum of 15. Please use the following rules when writing task statements for consistency of job description format:

a. Task statements typically begin with an action verb (examples: Types, Directs).
b. Be specific in writing duties and include all relevant aspects of the task. Use specific verbs to clearly convey the tasks performed on the job. For example, the task statement "stamps, sorts, and distributes mail" would be preferable to "handles the mail."
c. Focus on the purpose of the task rather than the manner in which the task is performed. For example, the job may require that instructions be given to subordinates. There is more than one way to give instructions, e.g., verbally or in writing. Unless there is some reason that verbal or written instructions are required, the task statement "provides instructions to subordinates" would be preferable to "provides verbal instructions to subordinates."
d. Avoid vague terms such as "many" or "relatively easy." Be concise and consistent in writing task statements. Spell out abbreviations the first time they are used.

Figure 12.1 Job analysis questionnaire.

Table 12.1 Marketing Professional Key Function Areas

Job description	Job specifications
Promotional activities · Creates and distributes program brochures, flyers, and calendars of events · Writes press releases · Contacts media for coverage · Evaluates the effectiveness of promotional activities and makes the necessary adjustments	**Knowledge, skills, and experience** · Marketing · Promotional planning and strategies · Media relations · Communication · Writing · Editing · Creative thinking and innovative · Critical thinking · Graphic and Web-authoring software · Print media specifications · Organization and time management · Campus recreation programming · Print media specifications · Software: Dreamweaver, Photoshop, Word®, Access®, Excel® · Supervisory skills
Marketing management · Develops a marketing plan to serve as a blueprint for the entire organization · Assists departmental heads with the planning process · Develops and manages milestones for accomplishments of tasks, objectives, and goals · Analyzes, evaluates, and revises the plan · Stays abreast of trends (internal and external) and makes necessary adjustments	**Knowledge, skills, and experience** · Leadership · People skills · Visionary · Critical thinking · Marketing planning · Market research · Organization and time management · Project management · Critical thinking · Software: Word, Excel, project management software
Sponsorship solicitation · Calculates and assesses the cost value of the program · Identifies potential sponsors · Sells sponsorships · Maintains and cultivates sponsorship relationships · Negotiates media services and rates · Evaluates the effectiveness of the sponsorship campaign and makes adjustments if necessary	**Knowledge, skills, and experience** · Financial management · Cost accounting · Negotiation · Communication · Writing · Sales · Marketing · Creative thinking and innovative · Critical thinking · People skills · Software: PowerPoint®, Word, Excel
Market research · Assesses the appropriate types of research needed · Develops, distributes, collects, analyzes, and evaluates survey instruments · Writes research reports and provides recommendations · Implements necessary changes	**Knowledge, skills, and experience** · Market research · Communication · Writing · Statistical software · Statistical analysis · Project management · Organization and time management · Presentation (oral and software) · Software: Access, Excel, PowerPoint, Word · Critical thinking · Supervisory skills

Job description	Job specifications
Public relations	Knowledge, skills, and experience
· Serves as a spokesperson for the department · Writes and distributes press releases · Cultivates and maintains media, industry, alumni, university, and community relations · Maintains and updates media information · Maintains alumni database · Writes and maintains alumni and/or staff newsletter · Analyzes the effectiveness of the public relations efforts and makes necessary adjustments	· Media relations · Communication (speech and writing) · Managing databases · Creative thinking and innovative · Critical thinking · People skills · Professional appearance · Print and Web-based publications · Software: Access, Excel, Word, PowerPoint, Photoshop, Dreamweaver · Time and project management · Supervisory skills
Sales	Knowledge, skills, and experience
· Develops sales strategies and generates membership sales · Establishes and manages the point-of-sale (POS) system to integrate with campus IT and credit card systems · Develops customer service and POS training materials and conducts training · Develops bookkeeping and audit procedures · Develops and executes shift change procedures · Develops and maintains sales reports · Serves as a liaison with the campus finance office and internal auditor	· Sales management · Customer service · Staff training · Bookkeeping · POS and credit card authorization systems · Organization · Detail oriented · Spreadsheet development and maintenance · Writing · People skills · Supervisory skills

options for their time and attention increase. Marketing professionals must be able to conduct creative thinking, or brainstorming, sessions, generate creative solutions, and implement effective promotional strategies.

Marketing Management

Marketing management is the analysis, planning, implementation, and control of programs designed to create, build, and maintain beneficial exchanges and relations with target markets for the purpose of achieving organizational objectives (Kotler, 1984). The **marketing plan** is the blueprint for marketing management. The development, implementation, and management of a marketing plan require skills that entry-level marketing professionals may not have. If marketing management is a high-priority need, campus recreation administrators must be willing and able to hire experienced marketing professionals who can coordinate the marketing planning and implementation process. Marketing management requires people skills to solicit buy-in from all involved. Besides knowledge of the marketing planning process, a campus recreation marketing professional must also possess organizational, planning, time and project management, market

research, evaluation, and critical thinking skills to properly manage the marketing plan cycle.

Sponsorship Solicitation

Sponsorship contributes significantly to the delivery of program and special events; without it, many department budgets may not be able to support such activities. Sponsorship is an important revenue source, particularly for profit-centered campus recreation departments. To develop and successfully solicit sponsorship, a campus recreation marketing professional must be able to calculate and assess the cost value of the program or activity and conduct the necessary market research to sell the sponsorship benefits to potential sponsors. The campus recreation marketing professional must also be strong in communication, writing, and selling skills to put together an attractive solicitation package. The marketing professional must also understand and appreciate the value of postsponsorship relations.

Market Research

The ability to conduct market research is a critical job specification for the campus recreation marketing professional position. **Market research** is key to successful sponsorship solicitation, justification to upper administration for funding support, and programming success. Sponsors and upper administration expect statistical, or hard, evidence of facts and figures to substantiate a sales pitch and budget requests. Programming directors need to know what their customers want in order to package programs attractive to their target markets. Such information can be generated via market research activities such as attendance reports, target market segmentation reports, and customer satisfaction surveys.

A campus marketing professional should minimally possess research skills including but not limited to survey questionnaire development, testing, distribution, data collection, data analysis, and report writing. A knowledge of basic statistical and data software such as Access® or SPSS is needed to perform data collection and analysis. The campus recreation marketing professional must also know various methods of market research and the appropriate use for each method (e.g., how to establish and conduct a focus group and when it is appropriate to use a focus group versus an e-questionnaire). Generally speaking, candidates with graduate degrees such as MBAs are more likely to possess market research skills.

Public Relations

Effective **public relations** is more than writing press releases and publishing newsletters. A campus recreation marketing professional must actively network with the local media and within the industry, the university community, and the community in which the university does business to establish the department's presence and value to these entities. Serving on the NIRSA marketing committee, serving on local community service boards such as Boys and Girls Clubs, and being a member of the university wellness council are examples of how a campus recreation marketing professional can develop and grow the relationships necessary to connect the department to these entities. To be successful in building business relationships, a campus recreation marketing professional must possess personal communication and creative thinking skills to identify relationship-building opportunities.

The marketing professional's ability to manage a database, such as an alumni mailing list in Access or Excel®, will enable the department to maintain updated networking information. Accurate database information will save the department money in postage and help project professionalism.

Effective public relations professionals understand the most effective means of distributing information in a timely manner. Competency in electronic media (e-newsletters and Web site development, maintenance, and management) is an asset to look for in today's campus recreation marketing professional who has public relations responsibilities. Project management skills and a good understanding of graphic design and publication processes and procedures will help the marketing professional coordinate the production of public relations materials on a timely basis.

Sales

Most justifications for and decisions in hiring a marketing professional are based on the need to generate membership sales to supplement student recreation fees. It is reasonable to expect a marketing professional to be able to develop selling strategies, but not all marketing professionals can manage a sales office. To manage a sales office, a marketing professional must be able to understand the **point-of-sale (POS) system** and its integration with the campus finance office and credit card authorization system. The marketing professional must be able to develop and implement sound bookkeeping procedures and checks and balances, and to manage personnel. Customer service and POS training must also be conducted to ensure performance efficiency.

Program Promotion

Promotion is a catchall phrase that has become popular as one of the "four Ps" of marketing. **Promotion** is "the persuasive flow of marketing communication," including advertising, sales and sales force, promotions, public relations, publicity, packaging, point-of-sale displays, and brand name or identity (Green, Miller, & Cook, 1999). Before the introduction of the marketing concept in campus recreation, many campus recreation professionals equated promotion with marketing. In reality, *marketing* is the umbrella that covers promotion as well as place, price, and product. Together, these four variables make up the marketing mix, which is commonly referred to as the four Ps (Borden, 1965). Alternatively, the marketing mix can be addressed as the four Cs—communication, convenience, cost, and customer needs and wants (Lauterborn, 1990).

Product Versus Market Orientation

Without market research, campus recreation departments often develop a program, event, or

Placing a recreational department logo on a prominent structure such as a climbing wall is an effective way to publicize the department's identity.

activity first and then decide how to market or promote it. This is a product-oriented approach in which advertising and promotions are used to stimulate "wanting" in the market (Green et al., 1999). Before the acceptance and proliferation of campus recreation marketing, most campus recreation departments were dependent on this less-than-effective and -efficient approach. The introduction of marketing professionals in campus recreation enabled campus recreation departments to evolve their promotional efforts from a product orientation to a market orientation. In the market-oriented approach, the department first determines its market's needs and wants *before* developing the program, event, or activity (Green et al., 1999).

Marketing Planning Cycle

Under the market-oriented approach, a marketing professional implements a planning cycle to determine the market's needs and wants. The **marketing planning cycle** involves analysis, research, plan development, implementation, and evaluation (see figure 12.2).

SWOT Analysis

Marketing analysis involves analyzing the department's strengths, weaknesses, opportunities, and threats (SWOT). Factors in a **SWOT analysis** could include student wages, office technology, and facility or equipment upgrades.

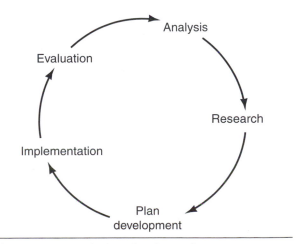

Figure 12.2 Marketing planning cycle.

PEST Analysis

In addition to analyzing its internal environment, the campus recreation department must also perform a **PEST analysis,** a macroanalysis of external factors that can potentially affect the success of its operation. This macroanalysis includes political, economic, social, and technological factors (PEST). For example, an economic crisis may force students to choose part-time jobs instead of participating in intramurals. The increasing popularity of Web sites such as You Tube and My Space may keep students on their computers instead of on the treadmill.

Target Audience

Before promotion can take place, the department needs to identify its **target audience.** *Target audience* is defined as the market for whose needs and wants the program or service is developed. The identification process should also involve the study and consideration of the other marketing variables (the four Ps) that can affect the success or failure of the program or service promotion. For instance, belly dancing may be identified as a fitness activity the students want (product or customer wants or needs). The effectiveness of the belly dance class promotion (communication) can be diminished if the class schedule (taking into account both place and convenience) or cost (of giving up a part-time job) is not evaluated for feasibility.

Current Audience

Marketing from the inside out means taking care of current customers before reaching out to prospective customers (Green, 2000). If a campus recreation department is unable to meet the needs of its current customers, it is unlikely to find success in attracting new customers. Moreover, it makes economic sense to focus the department's efforts and resources on customers who are already sold on the programs and services. The goal is to retain their patronage by continuing to meet their needs and wants. The higher the retention rate of current customers is, the less pressure there is to attract new ones.

Program or Service Life Cycle

Every program or service has a life cycle. The cycle begins with the introductory phase, followed by growth. Once a program or service reaches the peak of its growth phase, it has reached maturation. At maturation, a program or service can potentially plunge into a state of decline, or it can be rejuvenated into a new program or service life cycle (Green et al., 1999). The campus recreation marketing professional plays an important role in helping the department track a program's or service's life cycle. The marketing professional has to observe the cycle and use SWOT and PEST analyses to identify positioning or differentiation opportunities during the maturation phase in order to revitalize the program's or service's appeal to current and target customers.

Promotional Strategies for Campus Recreation Programs and Services

The staple programs and services offered by a typical campus recreation department are intramural sports, sport clubs, fitness, wellness, outdoor adventure, aquatics, and special events. The promotional strategies differ for each type of program and service. The one-size-fits-all approach is not appropriate for promotional efforts. Following are some of the most common promotional strategies used by campus recreation departments:

- *Printed media.* These include flyers, brochures, and calendars. Printed media can be expensive and wasteful. The development of printed media is also time consuming and requires computer skills and print media knowledge.

- *Banners.* Banners are relatively expensive because they are seldom recyclable—they contain event dates. However, banners hung in strategic locations are highly visible, which appeals to sponsors.

- *Electronic signage.* Before the Internet, electronic signage was the extent to which technology was integrated into the campus recreation arena. Because of the high cost of electronic signage and the technology skills required to properly operate the system, most electronic signs were brought onto campuses via sponsorships. Because of the high level of skills and knowledge required to maintain electronic signage, this tool was revered more as a status symbol than an effective promotional tool.

- *Vending machines.* Soft drinks, energy drinks, and bottled water companies are often interested in exchanging sponsorship dollars for the right to place their vending machines in strategic locations within campus recreation facilities and across campuses. This promotional strategy is often a win–win situation for both the department and the sponsor.

- *Press releases and publicity.* This promotional strategy is often the cheapest yet most credible form of promotion. The marketing professional should possess the communication and public relations skills to consistently promote the department's programs and services to its target community.

- *Advertising.* This is the most costly form of promotion, which few campus recreation departments can afford. Most advertisement is derived from sponsorships solicited from the department, such as a campus recreation department logo on Greek life rush T-shirts.

- *Promotional items.* Campus recreation is a key consumer of promotional items, ranging from intramural T-shirts (see figure 12.3) to pens displaying the department's contact information. Such items are mobile forms of promotion as they are worn or used by stakeholders. Promotional items can be expensive, but most campus recreation departments budget for them. These are also popular sponsorship assets.

- *Vehicle signage.* Signs on golf carts and department vans optimize the use of department vehicles. The mobility of the vehicles makes this promotional strategy a highly visible one.

- *Electronic media.* In the 21st century, the ubiquity of the Internet has resulted in electronic media (Web sites, e-mail marketing, podcasting, online reservations) becoming the most popular form of promotion for campus recreation departments. The medium itself is usually free. However, it takes technological skills and Web site marketing knowledge to develop and launch an effective Web site. For electronic promotional strategies to be effective, the department needs to ensure that the person or people given the responsibility have both technology and marketing knowledge, plus the skills to make this promotion avenue an efficient and effective one. Web site loading speed and search engine optimization are just a couple of issues that a department must know how to address. Therefore, using graduate assistants with only rudimentary skills to handle electronic media promotion can prove costly in the long run. The lack of continuity caused by graduation can also interrupt the consistency in communication and promotion delivery.

Marketing Plan

What is a marketing plan? And why do you need one? This section looks at the practical applica-

tion of a proven marketing strategy to guide you through the process of developing a marketing plan.

Although marketing is commonly viewed as an "art"—with accoutrements such as creative posters, new media, and colorful communications—the practice of marketing is actually quite scientific and analytical. The process of creating a marketing plan allows an organization to really flush out its goals and objectives and examine how they relate to program issues of marketing concern,

Marketing Plan Defined

A marketing plan is a detailed road map for the planning and supervision of all marketing activities for the following year. It addresses the four basic questions in planning: (1) Where are we now? (2) Where do we want to go? (3) How do we get there? and (4) Are we there yet?

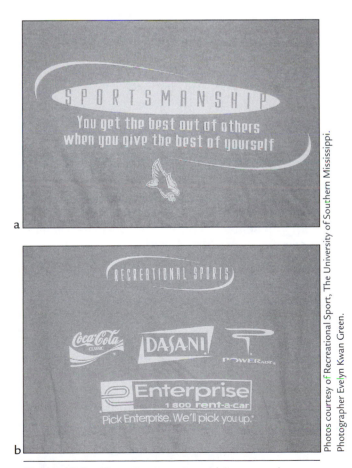

Figure 12.3 Corporate-sponsored intramural sports championship T-shirt: *(a)* front, *(b)* back.

Photos courtesy of Recreational Sport, The University of Southern Mississippi. Photographer Evelyn Kwan Green.

such as participation rates, revenue from fee-based opt-in programs, and the program's public image on campus and in the community.

Preparation for Creating a Marketing Plan

The process of creating a marketing plan is iterative and comprehensive. If done well, it should take about a year to complete. But don't be overwhelmed by this; the outcome of all that work is extremely valuable. When broken down into manageable steps, the process should go smoothly and efficiently. Why does it take so long? Consensus building can be slow, but it is absolutely necessary to the success of the marketing plan as a living document. The plan must be embraced by all staff—not just the marketing staff.

The marketing plan is created in seven steps:

1. Explain why you have decided to create (or update) a marketing plan.
2. Define your environment.
3. Perform a situational analysis and conduct research.
4. Identify your central goals and issues.
5. Develop tactics and strategies.
6. Write the plan.
7. Evaluate the plan.

Step 1: Explain Why You Have Decided to Create (or Update) a Marketing Plan

This first step involves explaining the broad goals and major desired outcomes that your plan will help you achieve. Following are some common goals:

- *Participation in programs.* Do you desire an increase in program participation rates or facility visitation frequency? By how much? By when?
- *Revenue-based programs.* Often, programs and facilities are included in a student fee that is paid as part of tuition. However, niche programs and services, or those provided outside the student base, are paid for by fees. What are your goals for these revenue-based services? Are there new revenue-based services you are considering?
- *Facilities.* How are usage rates? Could they be improved? Alternatively, are facilities stretched too thin? Do you need to evaluate the possibility of new facilities?
- *Image.* How are you viewed by students? The administration? Other departments? Are you merely a "program" or "facility," or does the university see you as integral to its mission—fulfilling other broad goals such as recruitment, retention, and student development?

Step 2: Define Your Environment

There are three main ways to define your environment.

- *Structure.* Take the time to define your situation thoroughly and exhaustively. How is your department structured internally? How is it structured within the university system? Who makes final decisions? How are those decisions reached?
- *Processes.* Create flow charts for common interactions with your customers (see figure 12.4 for an example). This will help illustrate these interactions and will allow for easier identification of improvements and collaboration as the plan is developed.
- *Institution direction.* What are the priorities of the institution? Increased enrollment? Student safety? Define these, and begin to look for places where your programs might complement or enhance them.

Step 3: Perform a Situational Analysis and Conduct Research

This step allows you to use the information gained in the previous step to expand on the definition of your situation. Using qualitative analysis, map out specific parallels to similar departments within your institution, similar departments at other institutions, and the overall trends in the field (i.e., NIRSA committees). This step involves a lot of benchmarking research—capturing what others are doing and how that relates to what you want to do.

Following are some tools for this step:

- SWOT analysis (strengths, weaknesses, opportunities, and threats)
- PEST analysis (political, economic, social, and technological)
- Table of key players
  - Decision makers and allies
  - Competitors and critics

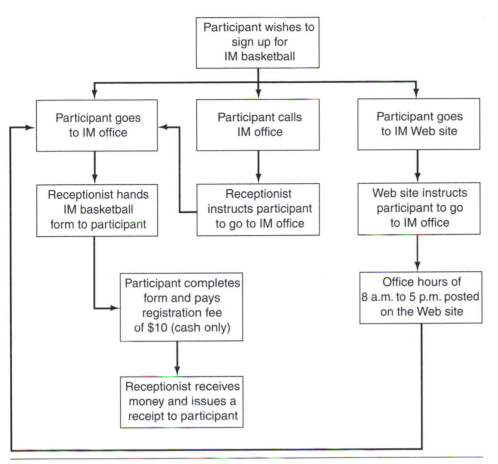

Figure 12.4 Sample customer interaction flow chart.

ing them on exercise benefits and instilling practices that will establish lifelong good habits. Strategy: Reach every student with a strategic message of healthy living on campus and beyond.

Step 5: Develop Tactics and Strategies

The tactics and strategies developed in this step stem from the central goals and issues developed in step 4. It is also a consensus-building step. To reach consensus, the best approach is systematic. First, spend a half day transcribing *all* ideas by participants—taking care not to judge any of the ideas. Next, decide which criteria will be used to judge the ideas. Following are some suggested criteria:

- *Mission.* Complements the mission and agenda of the department and the institution.
- *Feasibility.* Could be reasonably implemented.
- *Cost.* Is within the ability of the department to afford, or is worthy of pursuing additional funding.
- *Image.* Enhances the department's image in the eyes of participants and the administration. Does not create political animosity.
- *Equality.* Reaches out to minority populations.

Systemically compare all ideas against the criteria and project outcomes. Table 12.2 demonstrates this process.

Step 6: Write the Plan

At this step, you should have captured almost everything you need to create a single, cohesive document that will serve as your final marketing plan. The structure should resemble the following outline:

Step 4: Identify Your Central Goals and Issues

Throughout the process of the previous three steps, the most prominent themes will have begun to emerge. In this consensus-building step, the senior staff of your department should work together. This is best achieved during an off-site, day-long retreat, whereby the agenda is strictly oriented toward working together to narrowly define the marketing-related central goals and issues. These statements should include the broad context as well as specific, measurable goals. Following are two examples:

- Participation in campus recreation programs is linked to greater satisfaction with the overall college experience. Satisfaction among students increases the university retention rate, which is a priority of the institution. Strategy: Increase overall student participation in campus recreation programs from 66 to 75 percent by 2010.
- The department mission includes enhancing the lifelong health of young people by educat-

Table 12.2 Criteria and Outcomes Matrix

| Ideas | Criteria | | | | |
	Mission	Feasibility	Cost	Image	Equality
Place full-page ads in newspaper for intramurals	+ Intramural sports are important part of mission	+ Good relationship with newspaper	– More than budgeted; takes away from other programs	+ Would enhance our brand	+ Reaches all students
Build outdoor pool	+ Great recreation	– This is Michigan	– No capital allocations	– May seem extravagant	– Benefits only summer students
Offer free personal training session to all students	+ Great for educating for good habits	– Not nearly enough staff	– Would be extremely costly	+ Great outreach	+ Great for those who can't afford to pay
Have residence hall competitions	+ Outreach	+ Good relationship with residence life	+ Could get grant from residence hall	+ Campus outreach	– Misses off-campus students

1. Central goal or issue

  1.1. Strategy (and assessment measure)

    1.1.1. Tactic

      1.1.1.1. Plan for implementation

An example:

1. Our department mission includes enhancing the lifelong health of young people by educating them on exercise benefits and instilling practices that will establish lifelong good habits.

1.1 Reach every student with a strategic message of healthy living on campus and beyond. (Success will be measured by the total percentage of students who receive exposure to this message on an annual basis.)

1.1.1. Integrate a campus recreation presentation into the new student orientation process.

1.1.1.1. Meet with admissions staff (director, by 1/31/08).

1.1.1.2. Create presentation (assistant director for marketing, by 2/28/08).

1.1.1.3. Deliver presentations (alternating programming staff, summer 2008).

1.1.2. Offer a free personal training session to all freshmen.

1.1.2.1. Create a structure for free session (fitness director, by 4/30/08).

1.1.2.2. Create signage for recreation facility (assistant director for marketing, by 5/31/08).

1.1.2.3. Create a sign-up process (facilities manager, by 6/30/08).

Step 7: Evaluate the Plan

The evaluation of every element of the marketing plan on an annual basis is essential. The marketing plan should be a living document, and changes in course should be easily decided and made based on evaluation and assessment results. (See chapter 14 for a description of an assessment strategy.)

In addition to assessment, the data you collect will be valuable for structuring your intelligence about how marketing strategies and tactics should evolve. Every interaction with a participant is an opportunity to collect quantitative data about his or her experience (keeping in mind that overassessment should be avoided too; there is a limit to participants' willingness to complete surveys).

Following are sources for data collection:

- Evaluation survey (after the program or experience)
- Random sampling techniques to get broader data from fewer participants
- University databases

This process is an undertaking for sure, but the value of the result is tremendous. A successful plan culminates from an analytic framework and involves the entire department staff and allies in its creation. Although the process can take a full year—or sometimes longer—it can be broken down into manageable pieces. In measuring outcomes, it is helpful to "quantify" as much as possible (e.g., although "satisfaction" is abstract, it can be measured on a 10-point scale).

Sponsorship Solicitation

Sponsorship is cash or in-kind fees paid to an organization in return for access to the target audience of the program, event, or activity whose commercial potential appeals to the sponsoring organization (Green, Miller, & Cook, 2000). At the University of Southern Mississippi's Payne Center fitness lounge, the Coca-Cola Bottling Co. of Hattiesburg sponsored the Club Natural High. In exchange for including the campus recreation's Club Natural High logo on all Dasani vending machines across campus, the Coca-Cola Bottling Co. of Hattiesburg was allowed to place its Dasani vending machine in the fitness lounge (see figure 12.5). The fitness lounge is strategically located outside the high-traffic fitness area. In this section we discuss why campus recreation departments need sponsorships and the sponsorship development process.

Why Do Campus Recreation Departments Need Sponsorships?

Campus recreation departments, particularly those that are profit centers, often rely on income to defray the costs of putting together a campus recreation event, program, or activity. Sponsorships—especially blue-chip sponsors such as Dasani and Nike—increase the visibility and credibility of an event, program, or activity. Sponsorships also create relationship-building opportunities within the corporate community and sometimes create networking and placement opportunities for students.

Sponsorship Development Process

Sponsorship development requires careful market research, marketing planning, personal selling, negotiation, implementation, and follow-through to ensure the success of both the sponsor and the department.

Market Research

Market research is critical to understanding the potential and value of the sponsorship package to the sponsor (Green et al., 2000). To prepare a sponsorship package, the department must know the target audience for the event, program, or activity

in terms of demographics, psychographics, and attendance levels. **Psychographics** describe the target audience's lifestyle, education, approximate income, types of careers, leisure activities, reading habits, and so on. Target audience data are important to the sponsor in terms of commercial potential and establishing a marketing database for future opportunities. Businesses are willing to pay for data that have strong commercial potential. A target audience database, for example, is a campus recreation department's asset that should never be shared with sponsors. However, providing statistics summarizing the demographics and characteristics of the target audience to the sponsor is a way of sharing valuable data without jeopardizing the integrity of the database and trust of the audience. Therefore, it is critical for a campus recreation department to have the expertise to carefully research and analyze its assets and the commercial value of its assets (e.g., target audience statistics) to potential sponsors.

Photo courtesy of Recreational Sport, The University of Southern Mississippi. Photographer Evelyn Kwan Green.

Figure 12.5 Dasani vending machine at The University of Southern Mississippi's Payne Center fitness lounge, featuring the Southern Miss Recreational Sports "Club Natural High" logo.

Marketing Planning

The sponsorship package is the tangible outcome of the marketing planning step in the sponsorship solicitation process. As mentioned earlier, the campus recreation department must first identify its assets and their commercial value to potential sponsors. Assets in campus recreation and their value to sponsors (Green et al., 2000) include but are not limited to the following:

- Marks and logos (promotional rights, official sponsor designation)
- Participating audience, spectators, staff (access for sales, sampling, surveying)
- Talent (athletes, staff, appearance, ID on uniform)
- Vehicles (ID and signage)
- Equipment, scoreboards, message boards, Web sites (ID, signage, Web banner, or tile) (see figure 12.6)
- Venues or facilities (naming rights, signage, display, sampling, sales)
- Publications, collateral materials, Web sites (guaranteed exposure, impressions, visibility)
- Media buy (guaranteed impressions)
- Passes, event tickets, facility rentals (client, customer, employee entertainment)
- Mailing list (sales, promotional, marketing database)
- Special events and programs (propriety platforms, sense of ownership)
- Cosponsors (cross promotions, business-to-business relationships)
- Participant or audience survey (market research)
- Merchandise (sales, ID, or promotional use)
- Broadcast and Web package (advertising rights)
- Web site (ID, banner ads or links, special programs)

Once the department has identified and valued its appropriate assets, the department should identify potential sponsors. Sponsor identification should not be limited to the obvious, such as soliciting Powerade to sponsor an intramural event. The campus recreation marketing professional should use outside-the-box, creative thinking to uncover unique or niche sponsors that may not ordinarily be considered.

Sponsorship Proposal Package

The department should package its assets into sponsorship opportunities and benefits that are customized to meet targeted sponsors' goals and priorities. A proposal that is well crafted demonstrates professionalism and promotes efficiency in the solicitation process (Green, 2000). The components of a sponsorship proposal should minimally consist of a cover letter, a list of sponsor opportunities and benefits, event or asset details, the sponsorship contract or options for customization, and additional information to further illustrate the merits of the proposal. Additional information could include a media buy schedule,

Photo courtesy of Recreational Sport, The University of Southern Mississippi. Photographer Evelyn Kwan Green.

Figure 12.6 Scoreboard sponsored by the Coca-Cola Bottling Co.

press releases or coverage of a previous event, and photos of sponsorship exposure at previous events. The cover letter should include a statement of invitation to participate and follow-up contact information. Sponsorship opportunities could include niche marketing, cross promotion, market research, sales rights, exposure via signage and collateral materials, point-of-sale promotions, client entertainment, and employee benefits. Media exposure, increased visibility, positive image building, blue-chip cosponsors, and—most important—brand awareness building are always high priorities for potential sponsors.

Event details must be included to allow the potential sponsor to gauge the feasibility of sponsorship. Timing is key to successful sponsorship solicitation. Most corporations and organizations have their annual budgets planned and earmarked three to four months before the beginning of the fiscal year. A good marketing professional will stay abreast with potential sponsors' corporate fiscal years and ensure that solicitation takes place during the budgeting period. Sponsorship opportunities and benefits are best presented in levels of options to allow for sponsorship flexibility. For instance, if a sponsor is not in the position to commit at the level desired by the campus recreation department, the availability of other sponsorship levels can help avoid a total loss of sponsorship.

Personal Selling

A well-created sponsorship proposal is useless unless personal selling is involved to close the deal. Sponsorship solicitation often fails from lack of personal follow-through and failure to close the sale. The campus recreation marketing professional must arrange for face-to-face meetings to address any concerns a sponsor may have that could jeopardize the solicitation process. The marketing professional must be able to convey the benefits to the sponsor—making sure the benefits exceed the cost of sponsorship. The meeting also serves as an opportunity to close the sale by having the sponsor sign the contract. Commitments should be solicited while the excitement and enthusiasm are still fresh in the sponsor's mind.

Implementation of Contractual Terms

Once the sponsorship contract is signed, the marketing professional must execute the terms and conditions of the contract. Tangible outcomes such as press releases, advertisements, and photos of past sponsors' exposure at the event must all be documented as proof of contract delivery. Nondelivery of contractual items not only reflects negatively on the department but may also jeopardize future sponsorship opportunities.

Because most sponsored events, programs, and activities are handled by graduate assistants and students, the campus recreation marketing professional must pay close attention to details, including overseeing and supervising the implementation of all contractual items. For example, the display of sponsor banners and mentions of the sponsor during speeches must be done to the sponsor's satisfaction.

Follow-Through

Upon the completion of the event, program, or activity, the campus recreation marketing professional must compile all tangible outcomes of the sponsorship (e.g., media coverage, photos, T-shirts with the sponsor's name) and present them along with a letter of appreciation to the sponsor. In the same letter, the sponsor should also be asked to commit to the following year's event, if it is an annual event. By asking for a commitment immediately after a successful event, the department is more likely to get a recommitment from the sponsor. Additionally, the early commitment will allow the sponsor enough lead time to set money aside in its next budget.

Weighing the Decision to Pursue Sponsors

Solicitation of sponsors to supplement revenues is a strategic decision not to be taken lightly. Ultimately, departments are using the equity of a strong image to sell the right to directly market to students and customers. First and foremost, a campus recreation department should only participate in sponsorships that truly add value to its mission, programs, and services. Equally important, sponsors should closely align with the department's mission and goals. Finally, students and customers should be considered. If they believe that programs and services have used invasive marketing techniques, they will likely resist. Participating only in sponsorships that make sense will prevent such a backlash. Before embarking on any sponsorship partnership, administrators should ask the hard questions and make sure it will truly add value for students and customers.

E-Marketing

The Internet offers opportunities to market to more customers than ever before through banner ads, sponsor logos, and so on. A campus recreation department can use the Internet as a communication tool, registration tool, and revenue-generating tool.

With wireless modems, laptops give students access to the Internet wherever they go. Accessibility and instant gratification are the expectations of the "Net generation." With the introduction of Internet access via cell phones, text messaging, instant messaging, and iPods, the student population is constantly connected to the Internet. Web sites such as My Space and You Tube have totally captured the attention of students to the point that they are on the Internet at every opportunity.

The constant-connectivity trend is a positive one for campus recreation because promotion on the Internet is relatively affordable compared to printed media and other traditional forms of communication and advertisement. The Internet is available anytime and anywhere, and campus recreation departments can capitalize on this convenience. Intramural calendars, fitness class schedules, and facilities' operation hours can all be posted online. This reduces the phone traffic to the department and consequently labor costs. The convenience also helps improve the perception of good customer service.

Online registration can also be offered on the department's Web site. Once again, the convenience makes the registration process more attractive and user-friendly. The ease of changing information on the Web allows the department to be more responsive and up-to-date with its information sharing. For example, intramural results can be posted on the Web site shortly after the games have been played. Also, constant connectivity to programs and services encourages greater participation.

Most important, the campus recreation department Web site is an attractive promotion and marketing outlet for both the department and its sponsors. Advertising banners or tiles or sponsor logos can be sold or offered as part of a sponsorship package. The department can use data mining (careful analysis to glean important facts from your data) to assimilate market research data that can be useful to the department in the solicitation of advertisers and sponsors.

Trends in Campus Recreation Marketing

New technologies should continue to improve the efficiency of campus recreation departments,

helping to keep costs under control. To use these new technologies, though, campus recreation personnel will need training. The new technologies will provide new job, training, marketing, sales, and promotional opportunities for the department. A dedicated Web portal can be used for student staff attendance and training purposes. A portal is generally a password-protected Web site used to access relevant information and educational materials about a particular topic.

Technology—the Internet in particular—will continue to compete with campus recreation for students' attention. The Internet is now the primary source of media and entertainment among college students (Gordon, 2006). Campus recreation professionals will have to determine how to integrate the Internet into its programs and service offerings, hence providing its customers with the best of both worlds. For example, a campus recreation department may offer a video segment or a video game on mountain climbing on its Web site to promote its outdoor adventure program or lessons in mountain climbing. The fitness department may offer belly dancing tips on the same Web page as its registration or fitness class schedule.

As college students' use of Web sites for purchases and entertainment increases, corporate partners and sponsors will be interested in campus recreation Web sites as an alternative marketing medium. Campus recreation departments should make Internet marketing a priority and capitalize on the new revenue and reach potential of their Web sites. Campus recreation departments can negotiate for reciprocal links, banner exchanges, sponsorships, and banner or tile advertisements with corporate partners.

Branding is an advertising method that has served collegiate athletics well throughout the years. Branding is used to increase awareness and customer loyalty through cumulative impressions and positive reinforcements. Campus recreation departments can take advantage of the rapid growth of consumerism to open stores in which to sell campus recreation merchandise. They can team up with corporations that share the same target audience to manufacture campus recreation merchandise. For example, a campus recreation department can team up with a clothing line to manufacture T-shirts and fleece jackets that brand the campus recreation logo.

Campus recreation departments can also approach their drinks sponsor to manufacture bottled water branding the campus recreation logo. Local businesses looking for promotional opportunities are also viable partners for departments, when pursuing national corporations is not a feasible option. A campus recreation and a local restaurant may partner to create and brand a healthy menu. Branding and campus recreation merchandise not only represent a viable revenue source, but they also serve to increase the department's visibility on and off campus.

Conclusion

A campus recreation department must proactively market itself to run a successful program. A strategic marketing plan serves as a blueprint to guide the department in achieving its marketing goals and objectives. Before the development of a marketing plan, a campus recreation department must first assess its marketing needs to determine the level of marketing skills needed to implement a marketing plan. The department must create a job description and specifications to identify its marketing needs and determine the feasibility of hiring a full-time marketing professional to oversee and ensure the success of its plan.

The marketing planning cycle involves conducting SWOT and PEST analyses and research and then developing, implementing, and evaluating the marketing plan. Key job functions for a marketing professional include program promotion, development and maintenance of a marketing plan, sponsorship solicitation, market research, and electronic marketing development and management. To efficiently manage its program, a campus recreation department must also be aware of trends affecting campus recreation. These include new technologies that can help with staff training and membership management; the increasing popularity of e-commerce that can potentially turn a campus recreation Web site into a new sponsorship revenue source; Web sites such as You Tube and My Space that compete for students' time; and the potential of branding as a lucrative and effective method of gaining customer awareness and loyalty.

Resources

NetMBA Business Knowledge Center
www.netmba.com/marketing

Content: The marketing concept, the marketing mix, marketing definition, situation analysis, market segmentation, and target market selection

www.netmba.com/strategy

Content: The strategic planning process, SWOT, and PEST analysis, and competitor analysis

U.S. Small Business Administration
www.sba.gov/gopher/Business-Development/Business-Initiatives-Education-Training/Marketing-Plan

Content: Marketing Your Business for Success Workbook

About.com
http://marketing.about.com

Content: Marketing topics, including Internet marketing and brand marketing

ChiefMarketer.com
http://chiefmarketer.com/disciplines/branding/brand_marketing_trends_11102006

Content: Marketing trends for 2007

http://chiefmarketer.com/Channels/online/interactive_marketing_trends_08252006/index.html

http://chiefmarketer.com/Channels/online/future_online_trends_09092006/index.html

Content: Future Trends in Interactive Marketing (and the Future Is Now)—Part 1 and Part 2

References

Aquent/American Marketing Association. (2006). Compensation survey of marketing professionals. Retrieved from www.marketingsalaries.com/aquent/Report.form.

Borden, N.H. (1965). The concept of the marketing mix. In G. Scheartz, *Science in marketing* (pp. 386-397). Chichester, UK: Wiley.

Gordon, K. (2006, November 24). 10 marketing trends to watch in 2007. Retrieved from www.entrepreneur.com/marketing/marketingcolumnistkimtgordon/article170208.html.

Green, E. (2000). From the marketing perspective: Marketing from the inside-out. *REC Connections, 5*(2), 3.

Green, E., & Gonsoulin, S. (Eds.). (1995). Marketing professional: Can your operation be successful without one? *Proceedings from the 46th NIRSA Annual Conference.* Corvallis, OR: National Intramural-Recreational Sports Association.

Green, E., & Gonsoulin, S. (Eds.). (1996). Expectations of the marketing professional: Dos and don'ts. *Proceedings from the 47th NIRSA Annual Conference.* Corvallis, OR: National Intramural-Recreational Sports Association.

Green, E., Gonsoulin, S., & Nordin, C. (Eds.). (1997). Marketing, sales, and public relations: Your winning trifecta. *Proceedings from the 48th NIRSA Annual Conference.* Corvallis, OR: National Intramural-Recreational Sports Association.

Green, E., Miller, J., & Cook, J. (1999). Marketing up close and personal: Learn to make cows fly (a preconference workshop). 50th NIRSA Annual Conference, Milwaukee, Wisconsin.

Green, E., Miller, J., & Cook, J. (2000). The price is right: How to create a successful sponsorship proposal (a preconference workshop). 51st NIRSA Annual Conference, Providence, Rhode Island.

Kotler, P. (1984). *Marketing management: Analysis, planning and control* (5th ed.). Englewood Cliffs, NJ: Prentice Hall.

Lauterborn, B. (1990). New marketing litany: Four Ps passe: C-words take over. *Advertising Age, 61*(41), 26.

Lussier, R. (1994). *Supervision: A skill-building approach* (2nd ed.). Burr Ridge, IL: Richard D. Irwin.

North Carolina Central University. (2005, January 10). Campus recreation management. Retrieved from www.nccu.edu/artsci/pe/sptmgt.html.

Shaw, E., & Jones, D.G. (2005). A history of schools of marketing thought. *Marketing Theory, 5*(3): 239-281.

Sperling, J. (1983). *Job descriptions in marketing management.* AMACOM Special Projects Division, American Management Association.

Glossary

branding—An advertising method that repetitively exposes the brand or logo of an organization in order to establish widespread recognition of the brand or logo and thus recognition of the organization it represents.

job description—A written description of a position of employment that addresses the function and primary objectives of the position and accountabilities.

market research—To analyze data pertaining to a target audience in order to glean information that may be relevant for program planning, sponsorship sales, or assessment.

marketing management—The analysis, planning, implementation, and control of programs designed to create, build, and maintain beneficial exchanges and relations with target markets for the purpose of achieving organizational objectives.

marketing plan—A detailed road map for the planning and supervision of all marketing activities for the following year. It addresses the four basic questions in planning: (1) Where are we now? (2) Where do we want to go? (3) How do we get there? and (4) Are we there yet?

marketing planning cycle—A continuously reoccurring cycle of planning that involves analysis, research, plan development, implementation, and evaluation.

PEST analysis—An organizational analysis of political, economic, social, and technological factors.

point-of-sale (POS) system—A sophisticated computer system to manage and record sales transactions.

promotion—"The persuasive flow of marketing communication," including advertising, sales and sales force, promotions, public relations, publicity, packaging, point-of-sale displays, and brand name or identity (Green et al., 1999).

psychographics—Statistics that describe a target audience's lifestyle, education, approximate income, types of careers, leisure activities, reading habits, and so on.

public relations—Management of relationships with media outlets and the general public to strategically communicate information about an organization, program, or event.

SWOT analysis—An organizational analysis of strengths, weaknesses, opportunities, and threats.

target audience—The market for whose needs and wants the program or service is developed.

CHAPTER 13

Risk Management

Ian McGregor, PhD, President, Ian McGregor & Associates Inc.

A policy or procedure without implementation is a liability gallows.

Joe Risser; Director, Risk Management; Cal Poly, San Luis Obispo

Life is full of risks. Changing careers, getting married, crossing the street, and playing tennis all involve some element of risk. In the sport and recreation setting, the specific concern is risk of injury. Eliminating the risk of injury in physical activity programs is impossible. However, it is possible to minimize that risk. In today's litigious society, sport and recreation administrators must manage risk in the same way they manage other functions within their departments. For example, the marketing function within campus recreation must be actively managed to ensure effective program advertising and promotion.

Across North America, campus recreation departments typically report to student affairs and student services departments, along with other units such as residence life, student unions, and student clubs. All of these units plan and organize events, all of which involve some element of risk. Hence, the need for risk management is obvious. The principles and planning tools outlined in this chapter apply equally to campus recreation and all student organizations involved in running events.

Laws constantly change, and legal rulings vary from one state or province to another. The purpose of this chapter is not to provide legal advice but rather to provide general guidelines and tools to assist in the development of a risk management plan. Because of the uniqueness of each campus or recreation department, plans should always be customized to specific situations. Safety is everyone's concern. Implementation of a comprehensive risk management plan can help ensure a safe playing environment in which the risk of injury (and the possibility of a negligence lawsuit) is minimized.

The basic principles used to govern the required level of safety in athletic and recreational sport programs are not complicated legal doctrines. Rather, they are the simple principles of common sense, reason, and foresight. You do not have to be a legal wizard to implement a sound risk management program. It is important, however, that everyone involved in the execution of the risk management plan have a basic understanding of the law as it applies to negligence liability in the athletics and recreational sport settings.

What Is Negligence?

Negligence is the unintentional harm to others as a result of an unsatisfactory degree of care. It occurs when a person does something that a rea-

sonably prudent person would not do, or when a person fails to do something that a reasonably prudent person would do. Negligence is, therefore, the failure to use reasonable care. In a negligence lawsuit, the person who is harmed—the **plaintiff**—brings about legal suit claiming the person being sued—the **defendant**—acted negligently.

During the lawsuit, the courts will consider four issues:

1. Was the defendant negligent?
2. Who is liable for that negligence?
3. Can the defendant escape that liability?
4. What damages does the defendant have to pay?

Was the Defendant Negligent?

For a legal claim of negligence to be successful, all four of the following must be demonstrated:

1. The defendant owed the plaintiff a duty of care.
2. The defendant breached a reasonable standard of care affecting the plaintiff.
3. The plaintiff suffered actual harm on which a value can be placed.
4. The defendant's carelessness was the proximate (direct) cause of harm to the plaintiff.

Duty of Care

An individual does not owe a **duty of care** to everyone, only to those for whom harm could reasonably have been foreseen. The key here is reasonability, and a court of law has to decide whether an incident that caused harm could have been foreseen.

Standard of Care

Although the duty of care is often clear, the **standard of care** is a more complex issue. In a negligence suit, the court will be required to establish a minimum standard of care (i.e., how careful is careful enough) and determine whether the defendant breached that standard. Generally, courts base their decisions on the following:

- The facts of the case
- The "reasonable person" test: What would the average reasonable person have done in the same circumstances? What would the average, reasonable lifeguard, instructor,

coach, or administrator have done in the same or similar circumstances?

- Professional standards: What are the normally accepted practices in this field? Expert witnesses often testify to help define professional standards.

Actual Harm

In a court action, the plaintiff sues the defendant to receive monetary compensation for **actual harm** or loss. Damages can be assessed for the following:

- Harm to or loss of property
- Medical expenses: past, present, and future
- Loss of income: past, present, and future
- Pain and suffering: past, present, and future
- Extended care

The plaintiff can also be shown to have been negligent. In some states or provinces, the degree to which the plaintiff's own negligence contributed to the damage can directly affect the amount of damages payable by the defendant (see the section Contributory Negligence on page 243).

Proximate Cause of Harm

To prove **proximate cause of harm,** the plaintiff must show that the harm caused was the direct result of the carelessness or negligence of the defendant. The courts must identify how the injury occurred. Was it the direct result of the defendant's carelessness? If the defendant had acted differently, would the injury still have occurred? If the answer is yes, then there is no proximate cause. If the answer no, then there is proximate cause.

Is the Defendant Liable for the Negligence?

After establishing negligence, the courts must next decide who is liable for the negligence. This means that the courts must determine who is to be held responsible and accountable for the negligent behavior. In the sport and recreation field, liability for negligence is assigned to the following categories:

- Personal liability
- Vicarious liability
- Products liability
- Premises liability

Personal Liability

When a person acts outside the scope of his or her employment, that person may be held personally liable for damages caused, and the employer may not be held vicariously liable. **Personal liability** also applies to situations in which damage is caused by an employee's deliberate or intentional attempt to injure someone.

Vicarious Liability

Organizations such as colleges and universities generally function through the actions of their employees, agents, and officers. The action of the employee is considered the action of the organization under the following circumstances:

- The person is acting as an agent or employee of the organization.
- The person is performing the assigned duty or duties reasonably expected in the type of employment.

In this situation, the employee is, or should be, covered by the university's general liability insurance policy and will not be held personally liable. Hence, if an employee is found negligent, then the university or organization is held vicariously liable for the employee's negligence.

Note that the actions of a person or lesser organization working for the larger organization are not considered the actions of the larger organization if the person or lesser organization is operating as an independent contractor. Consider the case of an independent fitness instructor operating within a recreation facility. If an accident that caused harm occurred because of the fitness instructor's negligence, then the recreation facility administration cannot be held vicariously liable. Because the fitness instructor was acting as an independent contractor, she is liable for the negligence. Obviously, in this situation, the fitness instructor should carry appropriate liability insurance coverage.

In a lawsuit, the plaintiff generally sues everyone in the organization: the university board of governors, the director of athletics and recreation, coaches, trainers, and the like. Subsequently, the courts may assign liability at any level.

Products Liability and Occupiers (Premises) Liability

In some negligence cases, liability can be established without having to prove the four elements of negligence described earlier. **Products liability** and **occupiers (premises) liability** refer to situations in which injury has occurred as a result of some defective or hazardous aspect of the premises (occupiers liability) or piece of equipment (products liability). Both of these issues represent specialized areas within the law. Although their complexity prohibits detailed discussion, it is important to understand their significance within the sport setting.

Products Liability   The concept of products liability is based on the notion of **relative knowledge.** Those responsible for manufacturing and selling a product are expected to know more about that product than those who use it. Because users expect safe equipment, it is the duty of those who manufacture, sell, rent, or loan that equipment to do everything reasonably possible to make sure the product is safe. Thus, duty of care may mean the following:

- Designing hazard-free products
- Using nondefective materials
- Ensuring good workmanship
- Warning of potential hazards or problems

Users of equipment can ensure product safety by doing the following:

- Buying safety-approved products from reputable manufacturers and installing it properly (it is best to have the manufacturer do the installation)
- Implementing comprehensive inspection and maintenance programs
- Using the product only the way it was designed (e.g., do not use a bicycle helmet for ice hockey)
- Adapting its use only after consulting the manufacturer

Occupiers (Premises) Liability   As with products liability, occupiers liability is based on the notion of relative knowledge. In other words, the occupier is in a better position to know about a hazard than a visitor is. Occupiers are not necessarily the owners of the property. Liability will depend on whether the owner or the occupier is in the best position to detect and deal with a hazard.

Many states and provinces have clearly set out the duties of an occupier in a statute that is generally called the Occupiers (Premises) Liability Act. Although variations exist among provinces and states, the principles are the same.

The duty and standard of care owed by an occupier is essentially to make the premises safe for the people entering them by taking reasonable precautions to protect such people from foreseeable harm. This duty applies to the following:

- Condition of the premises
- Activities on the premises
- Conduct of third parties on the premises

Leasing or renting space to outside groups is a common practice of sport and recreation departments. If a college leases its gymnasium for a weekend basketball tournament, and an injury occurs during that time, two things need to be determined:

1. Was the accident or injury on the premises caused by some hazardous or dangerous part of the facility or fixed equipment? If the answer is yes, then the occupier may be liable for these damages.

One way to ensure product safety is to use the product only in the way it was designed to be used.

William A. Cotton, Colorado State University.

242

2. Did the accident or injury result from the activity being undertaken on the premises? If the answer is yes, then the owner of the facility is not likely responsible, *except in situations in which the owner retains control over activities within its facilities.*

Departments involved in renting or leasing their facilities, or parts of their facilities, to outside groups should have a contract in place outlining the conditions of the rental or lease. In many cases, these contracts are administered centrally by the university. In any case, it is important that the university administration or legal counsel, or both, approve any contract language.

From a liability perspective, contracts should do the following:

- Require the renting group to purchase a comprehensive, general liability insurance policy in a form and with limits that are satisfactory to the university

- Require insurance coverage for bodily injury and property damage

- Outline adequate per occurrence coverage (as determined by the university)

- Name the university as an additional insured

- Require proof of insurance coverage

Defenses Against Negligence

The obvious way to escape or avoid liability is not to be negligent. Having stated that, the courts will decide whether any circumstances exist under which the defendant can avoid being held liable for negligence. Following are the most common defenses against negligence:

- Contributory negligence
- Voluntary assumption of risk
- Waiver forms and informed consent agreements

Contributory Negligence

If the plaintiff fails to exercise reasonable care for his own safety, it is then deemed that the plaintiff has contributed to the negligence. There will be a reduction in the damages awarded, or there may be no damages awarded whatsoever if the plaintiff is found to be more negligent than the defendant. Clearly, **contributory negligence** applies only to cases in which negligence has already been proven.

Voluntary Assumption of Risk

When people consent to participate in certain activities, such as contact sports like hockey or football, there is no liability if the harm is caused by normal hazards inherent to the activity. For example, if two participants collide when playing football during a normal sequence of events and one person suffers a broken arm, the injured person is deemed to have voluntarily assumed the risk inherent to the activity. Thus, there is no negligence and hence no liability. This situation can also apply to spectators. A foul ball that hits a fan attending a baseball game is considered a risk inherent to the activity.

However, although it is reasonable for participants to assume risks that are inherent in certain activities, it is not reasonable to assume risks not inherent in an activity (i.e., injuries caused by improper supervision or faulty equipment).

The use of the **voluntary assumption of risk** defense has enjoyed less success in recent

William A. Cotton, Colorado State University.

As long as the harm was caused by normal hazards inherent to the activity, there is no liability for injuries that occur while playing contact sports like hockey, because participants have consented to engage in that activity.

years—mostly because the courts are having difficulty distinguishing between inherent risks and hazards. One consequence of this is that waivers have become more popular—and more successful in the courts.

Waiver Form and Informed Consent Agreement

A **waiver** is the intentional or voluntary relinquishment of a known right. In recent years, there has been significant discussion regarding the following:

- Use of waivers
- Waivers' intended function
- Validity of waivers (by state)
- Limitations of waivers
- Value of waivers and how to evaluate and construct them

Because of the variance in a waiver's validity from state to state, its use in sport and recreation activities depends greatly on where it is being used. Clearly, a waiver may provide some protection, because many have stood up in court. However, a waiver, in and of itself, does not waive negligence, but only the rights of the plaintiff to sue if negligence occurs. In terms of providing protection to an organization, however, waivers are a critical component of a risk management plan.

Some sport and recreation organizations prefer to use informed consent agreements. Informed consent is an agreement to allow something to happen that is based on full disclosure of facts needed to make the decision intelligently—that is, knowledge of the risks involved and the alternatives. Although an informed consent form does not have the same legal clout as a waiver, institutions that do not want to use, or are uncomfortable with using, waivers may require informed consent agreements instead as a way of informing participants of the risks involved. Remember: Although valid waivers protect against negligence, informed consent agreements protect an organization only from inherent risks.

Waivers can work in at least 46 states if they are well written and meet court requirements in the particular state. The following are some of the key requirements when developing a waiver. (For a more in-depth discussion on waivers and how to construct them, consult Cotten & Cotten, which is listed in the Resources section at the end of this chapter.)

- The waiver should be specific; it should detail the risks involved in the specific activity in question.
- The wording should be clear, and the font size should be a minimum of 8 points (12 points or larger is better). (See the sidebar How to Write Effective Waivers.)
- The waiver should be a stand-alone document; it should not be part of another form such as a registration form.
- The waiver should cover all types of risk.
- The waiver should include all parties, such as staff, volunteers, coaches, and officials.
- The waiver should include all aspects of the activity, such as transportation to the activity.
- Participants signing the waiver must be of legal age; a waiver signed by a minor is not valid. Parents cannot sign away the rights of a minor.

Damages

The next and final stage in a negligence liability lawsuit is the determination of damages payable to the plaintiff. The calculation of the final settlement depends on the complexity of the case. For example, in the case of a person rendered quadriplegic because of a negligent act, the courts must calculate the cost of medical care for the remainder of the plaintiff's life. Other factors might also come into play, such as pain and suffering.

The court may also reduce the final settlement by an amount proportional to the extent of contributory negligence found by the court. For example, if the initial settlement is $5 million awarded to the plaintiff, but the court found that the plaintiff was 20 percent contributorily negligent, the final settlement would be reduced to $4 million.

Five Key Risk Areas Involving Negligence in the Campus Recreation Setting

It is useful to categorize the key areas in which campus recreation organizations are most vulnerable to negligence liability lawsuits because of injuries to participants. Understanding these "negligence hotspots" also provides a starting point in the development of a risk management plan.

How to Write Effective Waivers

Benjamin J. White, CRSS, Assistant Director of Recreational Sports, Bridgewater State College

Liability waivers are an important tool in managing risk as part of a larger risk management plan within a college or university recreation program. When written properly, waivers can provide a barrier to costly settlements resulting from lawsuits.

The primary purpose of a waiver is to help protect against negligence.

Document Separation

A waiver should be clearly distinguished from other parts of a document. Courts have invalidated waivers based solely on a failure of separation. A waiver should be a stand-alone document.

Proper headings should be used to label different parts of the waiver. The assumption of risk should be labeled as such and be easily distinguished from the waiver of liability. Both the assumption of risk and the waiver of liability are considered parts of the waiver form, however.

Readability

A critical aspect of a waiver is whether it is understandable. For a waiver to be effective, it must be written at a level that is comprehensible to the target audience.

The reading level or readability of a document is measured by grade-level equivalents. Reading levels start at first grade and go through the PhD level. For instance, to read and understand a form written at the 15th-grade level requires the reading skills equivalent to a third-year college student. People who can read at or above the fifth-grade level are considered literate. The average reading level for American adults is eighth grade. Furthermore, correlations between one's reading ability and educational attainment suggest that people usually read about three grade levels lower than their highest year of completed school. Thus, a typical college freshman may, in reality, read at about a ninth-grade reading level.

Reading Level

Although some research has found that it made no difference at what reading level forms are written, other research, as well as court cases, contradict these findings. For example, in a case brought before the Florida courts, three women involved in a medical study regarding pregnancy filed suit claiming that the waiver they signed before participation was unreadable. The participants did not contest that they or their unborn babies were harmed in any way during the study. Nor did they contest that they had not read and signed the waiver—they had. Their suit was based only on the assertion that the informed consent agreement and waiver of liability form used by the university researchers were written at a reading level higher than that of the average American adult. The case was settled out of court with a reward granted to the plaintiffs in the sum of $3.8 million. Because this case was settled out of court, it is not legal precedent; however, it does illustrate the point that readability is a major issue in writing waivers.

Sentence and Word Length

Sentence and word length contribute to the reading level of a document. The shorter the sentences and the smaller the words, the easier the document is to read. For example, the phrase "waive my right to bring legal action," might be replaced by the phrase "promise not to sue." The phrase "the undersigned," might be replaced simply with the word "I." Although sophisticated readability software is available for those seeking an accurate representation of the readability of their document, Microsoft Word® offers a readability function that, when enabled, provides an accurate assessment (see Tools, Options, Spelling & Grammar).

Font Size

In addition to reading level, courts have also determined that font size is a consideration. For a waiver to be effective, it should be written with at least a 12-point font.

The five key areas are as follows:

1. Emergency response plan
2. Supervision
3. Training
4. Facilities and equipment
5. Documentation

Emergency Response Plan

Given the certainty that accidents will happen in a campus recreation setting, the organization should have an **emergency response plan** in place to effectively deal with an accident or injury when it happens. Failure to address this adequately could lead to problems in court. The emergency response plan should do the following:

- Be documented.
- Address different emergencies (e.g., medical, fire, evacuation, missing persons, bomb threats). The plan should be customized to the institution and specific to its geographic location (e.g., some will address weather-related emergencies such as lightning strikes, tornadoes, earthquakes, and hurricanes).
- Indicate who should be trained in what.
- Detail how emergencies are communicated.
- Address emergency-related equipment and emergency rehearsals.
- Detail postemergency procedures (e.g., accident report forms, other follow-up procedures).

Supervision

Accidents caused by inadequate or improper supervision are the main reason organizations end up in court. Following are supervision situations that can cause problems:

- Inadequate supervision (i.e., too little, depending on the number of people participating, the risk level of the activity, or the age of the participant)
- Lack of established supervision ratios (supervisor to participant), particularly in higher-risk activities
- Improperly qualified supervisors (e.g., uncertified supervisors or supervisors not qualified to supervise or instruct activities)

- For higher-risk instructional activities, lack of lesson plans outlining teaching progressions

Training

It is reasonable to expect a campus recreation department to train all staff (full- and part-time) and volunteers adequately. This does not mean it must train everybody in everything, but that the essential people should receive training in appropriate areas. If there is a negligence liability lawsuit, the courts will want to see documented evidence that adequate training was addressed in the following areas:

- Emergency response training (i.e., procedures to deal with emergencies such as medical, fire, evacuation, weather-related emergency)
- Emergency skills training: first aid, CPR, AED, blood-borne pathogens
- In-service training (ongoing staff training)

Facilities and Equipment

Many accidents happen because of facility problems and equipment malfunctions. Facility problems (i.e., substandard rink ice quality or potholes in fields) may be caused by a lack of maintenance. Equipment breakdown may be the result of improper design, construction, or installation.

Organizations are responsible for ensuring that facilities and equipment are safe. To do so, they need effective inspection and maintenance programs. Hence, the courts will ask to see all inspection or maintenance records of a facility or piece of equipment that may have led to a participant injury.

The following four key issues must be addressed in this important area:

1. Inspection of facilities and equipment
   - Frequency of inspections
   - Documentation of inspections (i.e., use of checklists)
2. Maintenance of facilities and equipment
   - Frequency of maintenance
   - Documentation of maintenance (i.e., use of checklists)
3. Preinspection of facilities and equipment
   - Conducting inspections before starting an activity

William A. Cotton, Colorado State University.

To ensure that facilities and equipment are safe, effective inspection and maintenance programs must be followed.

4. Signage
   • Providing warnings, safety information, and instructions on the proper use of facilities and equipment

Some organizations contract out some facility and equipment inspections and maintenance, particularly for higher-risk facilities and equipment. The reason for this is twofold: (1) It uses professionals who may have more experience and knowledge in specific areas, and (2) it potentially passes on the liability to the organization conducting inspections and maintenance.

Documentation

In any negligence liability lawsuit, a key element in any defense is the existence of good documen-tation. It is important to show the courts that you are documenting your actions. This can involve the following:

• Documenting emergency plans
• Filing instructor certifications
• Using accident report forms
• Using equipment checklists

In all cases, producing these documentations clearly demonstrates to the court that the organization takes risk management seriously. In addition to the types of documentation listed, the following sections summarize other key areas in which documentation is important.

Waiver and Informed Consent Forms

The use of waiver and consent forms shows the courts that the organization is attempting to provide participants with sufficient information on the risk of an activity or activities, so that they can decide whether they wish to participate. Although a waiver may protect an organization from negligence, an informed consent agreement addresses only the assumption-of-risk issue.

Medical Screening Forms

If someone suffers a heart attack while participating in a program, the court may ask whether the participant was medically screened before participation. In other words, what attempts were made to determine whether the person was medically fit to participate?

Although it may not be practical or even reasonable to medically screen all participants, there may be some high-risk programs in which it would be prudent to determine whether there are any medical reasons to exclude a participant. For example, taking a scuba class requires a medical examination by a physician, yet many fitness programs rely only on a simple screening tool such as the PAR-Q (Physical Activity Readiness Questionnaire) (see chapter 5, p. 98).

Risk Information

Recreation organizations have a duty to inform people of the risks involved in physical activities. Providing this information allows participants to make informed decisions about whether to participate. There are many opportunities to provide risk information—from activity descriptions inserted in program brochures, to facility signage, to information provided in waivers and informed consent agreements.

Transportation

Transportation of participants is a major concern on campuses across North America—for good reason. It embodies all five of the key risk areas described earlier. Consider the situation of a rugby team traveling to play in a city several miles (or states) away.

1. *Emergency response plan.* Is there a plan in place to deal with a vehicular accident or a serious injury to a player on the field during the game or in the hotel? Is there a communication plan to implement if there is an accident? Are accident report forms used to report accidents or incidents?

2. *Supervision.* Is the coach accompanying the team properly qualified? Is the driver of the vehicle properly qualified to drive?

3. *Training.* Are there people traveling with the team who are trained to deal with an emergency? Is there a driver training program in place?

4. *Facilities and equipment.* Is the vehicle inspected before leaving? Does someone reputable maintain the vehicle?

5. *Documentation.* Are waivers required before participation? Does the rugby club require that participants be medically screened?

Transportation is a complex and worrisome issue, but it must be addressed. For more information on how to develop a comprehensive transportation plan, refer to McGregor's "Travel Trouble" article cited in the Resources section of this chapter.

Risk Management Planning

The five key risk areas mentioned earlier are the main issues to focus on when initiating a risk management plan. Obviously, there are many other safety issues to address, but developing a realistic plan within a realistic time frame means making priority decisions based on the identified key risk areas. By focusing (at least initially) on these key issues, administrators can prioritize their risk management efforts. High-risk programs, activities, or facilities that have a higher probability of a serious injury occurring (rugby, flag football, and rock climbing) should have a higher priority than low-risk programs or activities such as tennis or yoga.

Role of Insurance

Liability insurance is an integral component of an organization's overall risk management strategy. Insurance allows an organization to transfer to the insurer (for a price and under certain conditions) certain types of risks inherent in operating the organization. Although different kinds of insurance policies are available within the university setting (e.g., vehicle insurance, property insurance), liability insurance is of critical importance to campus recreation departments.

Campus recreation departments are usually covered for negligence liability under the university's general liability policy. What this means is that in the worse-case scenario (i.e., a department is found negligent by the court), the university's general liability insurance policy pays any damages awarded.

Although liability insurance provides the cornerstone and ultimate safety net for campus recreation departments, this does not mean that departments should rely on these insurance policies to protect them from lawsuits. It is the professional, and moral, responsibility of everyone working within a campus recreation department to take reasonable steps to minimize the potential for injury to participants. This is where effective risk management planning becomes essential.

Risk Management Planning Principles

Developing a risk management plan for recreation and sport programs can be approached in different ways. In some situations, a department may have to start from scratch. In other cases, the department may currently have a plan in place, and therefore any planning efforts focus on reviewing the plan and determining what changes or improvements are required. In either case, the approach is the same; it begins with answering the following five questions:

1. What is the problem?
2. What are you going to do about it?
3. Who is going to do it?
4. Who needs the training?
5. How are you going to communicate?

When reviewing programs and facilities, the department's risk management committee (or the director, if this committee does not exist) may decide that some activities are just too risky. If the organization believes it is unable to manage the risk of certain activities, those activities should be discontinued or sufficiently modified.

Risk Management Planning Process

Analyze	Conduct an audit
Plan	As a result of an audit, *what* needs doing?
	Who carries out the tasks?
	When are the tasks going to be done?
Execute	Implement the plan.
Control	Ensure that the plan is implemented; refine the plan.

Figure 13.1   The risk management planning process involves four steps.

Risk management planning is a process. The situations for fitness instructors, facility managers, lifeguards, coaches, and volunteer board members of sport associations are all different, and the risks and types of injury are unique. However, the process for managing those risks is the same. Figure 13.1 is the classic APEC approach to planning: analyze, plan, execute, control.

Audit or Risk Assessment

Before beginning any risk management planning effort, the first step is to get a handle on the status quo; that is, what are you currently doing (or not doing) to make your programs and facilities as safe as possible for everyone?

Conducting an audit (or risk assessment) of the whole operation, or a specific area within the organization, provides the data needed to initiate the development of risk management action plans. There are two approaches to developing audit questions:

1. The "off the shelf" approach involves implementing an existing audit document. For example, there is a comprehensive Web-based audit designed specifically for campus recreation programs. Recreation departments can complete this audit and receive a report detailing their risk profile. They can also see how their risk profile compares to that of other campus recreation departments across North America. It shows the areas of vulnerability from a negligence liability perspective and offers a series of risk management planning recommendations. Go to www.studentliferisk.com for details.

2. The "custom" approach involves developing your own risk assessment. The advantage of using the custom approach is that organizations are able to address all risk areas unique to their situation.

In developing a custom audit, start by referring to the five key risk areas outlined in this chapter. Ask questions to determine what needs to be done (i.e., what plans you need to put into place). See figure 13.2 for a sample audit.

Risk Management Plan

Based on the results of the audit, the organization can develop a risk management plan. In this phase, the objective is to develop an action

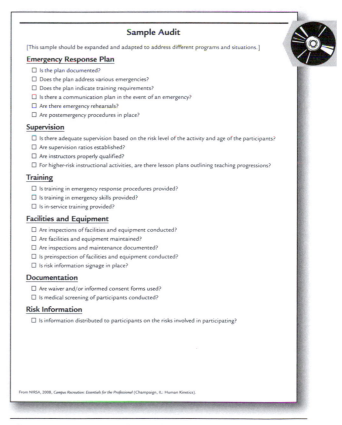

Figure 13.2   Sample audit. This audit should be expanded and adapted to address various programs and situations.

plan or series of action plans that address the following:

- What action are you going to take?
- Who is going to do the work? (This is discussed in the next section.)
- When will the work be done?

The list of tasks in the action plan may end up being quite long, depending on the size of the operation or the complexity of the activity. The type of work that needs doing usually falls into one of two categories: developmental work (e.g., policies and procedures) or day-to-day work (e.g., implementing checklists).

Some tasks are obviously more urgent than others. The highest-risk areas should be addressed first, and then responsibilities should be assigned and tasks should be time activated.

Implementation

It is neither reasonable nor fair for one person in the campus recreation department to assume the overall responsibility for risk management. Everyone is responsible for managing risk, from the director of campus recreation, to the arena manager, to the fitness coordinator. Clearly defined risk management responsibilities must be part of all job descriptions.

In smaller operations, the senior administrator may determine how to implement the plan. However, many departments (large and small) have gone the route of establishing a risk management committee. This group controls the risk management effort, including the performance and assignment of responsibilities. It is therefore important that the campus recreation director ensure that this committee is established, that it is structured appropriately, and that it has a clear mandate with realistic action plans and time lines.

Role of the Risk Management Committee

The risk manager (or chair of the risk management committee) is the key person in the implementation of a comprehensive risk management plan. This person provides the overall coordinating function and is responsible for ensuring the following:

- All safety policies and procedures are followed
- Checklists are completed, reviewed, and filed

- Safety and emergency response training is conducted

Although the risk manager provides the day-to-day leadership, the risk management committee functions as an invaluable resource group for the risk manager and the department. The committee may have responsibility for the following functions:

- Developing and conducting an audit
- Developing staff safety responsibilities for incorporation into job descriptions
- Reviewing and developing policies and procedures
- Conducting (and documenting!) regular risk management committee meetings

Perhaps the committee's most valuable role is helping to determine the standard of care in various situations. Often no guidelines are available regarding the level of safety in some programs and facilities. Because the committee may be called on to make a judgment in these cases, it is important that its membership be selected carefully and represent a cross section of knowledge and expertise. The committee should have broad departmental representation and be kept to a manageable size (usually no more than six people; others in the department can become involved in subcommittee work). Some organizations have adopted creative approaches to ensure a broad representation of skills and experience, such as enlisting a lawyer who is an active (off-campus) member of the facility.

Job Descriptions

As indicated earlier, taking risk management seriously means that everyone should be responsible for safety. It is important that these responsibilities be incorporated into formal job descriptions that state the specific risk management tasks that the staff member is required to perform as well as the limitations of the position. (This may become important later in establishing whether an employee was acting within the scope of the job description.)

In the implementation of an effective risk management plan, the risk management committee must set realistic goals. This means setting goals that are achievable in a designated time span. For example, a realistic goal for the risk management committee might be "to ensure that all program areas have a consistent emergency response plan in place within 12 months."

Risk Control

Once the risk management plan has been implemented, it becomes important to control the implementation effort by doing the following:

- Ensuring that identified tasks are completed
- Ensuring that time lines are followed
- Evaluating the plan

Conclusion

Generally, some programs within a campus recreation department manage risk better than others do. A key issue for most universities is the lack of consistency within program units. Therefore, the director needs to direct the risk management committee to review all program areas and develop plans to ensure that policies and procedures are consistent within all program units.

Any planning process is cyclical in nature. Thus, the risk management committee needs to evaluate the risk management plan on an ongoing basis and modify it where changes and improvements are necessary. Analysis leads to planning, execution, and control, which ultimately lead to further analysis. Risk management planning is never finished!

Resources

In developing a solid risk management plan, you do not have to start from scratch or reinvent the wheel. Some excellent resources are available to assist you. Also, contact other professionals in the field and ask what they have done in their risk management planning efforts.

People Resources

Professional colleagues

Experts in the field

Organizations

NIRSA (National Intramural-Recreational Sports Association)

NRPA (National Recreation and Park Association)

ACSM (American College of Sports Medicine)

Conferences

NIRSA (national and regional conferences and state workshops)

Athletic business conferences

Publications

American College of Sports Medicine. (2007). *ACSM health/fitness facility standards and guidelines* (3rd ed.). Champaign, IL: Human Kinetics.

Cotten, Doyice J., & Cotten, Mary B. (2005). *Waivers & releases of liability* (6th ed.). Statesboro, GA: Sport Risk Consulting.

McGregor, I. (2000). *SportRisk: The complete risk management planning & resource manual.* Blaine, WA: McGregor & Associates.

McGregor, I. (2000, March). Travel trouble. *Athletic Business,* 66.

McGregor, I., & MacDonald, J. (2000). *Risk management manual for sport and recreation* (2nd ed.). Corvallis, OR: NIRSA Publications.

Van der Smissen, B. (1990). *Legal liability and risk management for public and private entities.* Cincinnati, OH: Anderson Publishing.

Periodicals

Sports, Parks and Recreation Law Reporter (PRC Publishing, Canton, Ohio)

From the Gym to the Jury (Center for Sports Law and Risk Management, Dallas, Texas)

Athletic Business magazine

Videos

Core Concepts in Negligence and Legal Liability by Ian McGregor. Healthy Learning Videos (available through www.sportrisk.com).

Web Sites

www.studentliferisk.com

www.recsport.sa.gov.au

www.urmia.org

www.risksociety.org.nz

www.riskinbusiness.com

Glossary

actual harm—What the plaintiff suffered as a result of negligence, such as harm to or loss of property; past, present, or future medical expenses; loss of income; and extended care.

contributory negligence—Refers to conduct by an injured person who contributes to his or her injuries or damage by failing to take reasonable care for his or her own safety.

defendant—In a negligence lawsuit, the person sued for allegedly acting negligently.

duty of care—An obligation to protect someone from unreasonable risk of injury.

emergency response plan—A plan for dealing with a wide variety of emergencies.

negligence—The unintentional harm to others as a result of an unsatisfactory degree of care. It occurs when a person does something that a reasonably prudent person would not do, or when a person fails to do something that a reasonably prudent person would do.

occupiers (premises) liability—The responsibility of the owners to ensure that their premises are free of hazards.

personal liability—The liability that attaches directly to the individual who has been found negligent.

plaintiff—In a negligence lawsuit, the person who was harmed and who brings about legal suit.

products liability—The responsibility that applies when an injury was caused by some defective or hazardous aspect of a product or piece of equipment.

proximate cause of harm—A judgment made when evidence proves that the harm caused was the direct result of the carelessness or negligence of the defendant.

relative knowledge—The notion that a product manufacturer is expected to know more about a product than a consumer is expected to know, and an owner or occupier is expected to know more about a facility hazard than a user is expected to know.

standard of care—A determination made by the courts based on factors such as the nature of the activity and particular circumstances involved. The courts rely on published standards and current industry practices when deciding what the current standard is.

voluntary assumption of risk—When a person consents to participate in (or watch as a spectator) certain activities such as contact sports (hockey or football), there is no liability if harm is caused by normal hazards inherent to the activity.

waiver—An agreement between an organization (the service provider) and the participant by which the participant agrees to absolve the service provider of any fault or liability for negligence of the service provider or its employees.

CHAPTER 14

The Art of Assessment

Danell J. Haines, PhD, Director, National Research Institute for College Recreational Sports
  & Wellness, Department of Recreational Sports, The Ohio State University
Elizabeth A. Davis, CRSS, MA, Associate Director, Department of Recreational Sports,
  The Ohio State University

Without data, it is only an opinion.

Source unknown

Campus recreation assessment is an ongoing and dynamic process that involves gathering and examining data and information that is used for the promotion and improvement of campus recreation programs, facilities, and services. It also assists in forecasting future directions.

Accountability in higher education (i.e., the ability to justify dollars spent) is necessary to explain the rising cost of higher education. When budgets are strained, universities tend to redirect resources from nonacademic units such as campus recreation to academic units, as well as to drastically cut nonacademic areas. Within this environment, it has become increasingly important to defend the existence of some departments. Departments of campus recreation must show proof of the benefits they provide the campus population. In other words, there is a need to obtain valid data that confirm the critical role that campus recreation plays on college campuses.

An example of using data to support the need for campus recreation is the Kerr & Downs Report published in *The Value of Recreational Sports in Higher Education* (National Intramural-Recreational Sports Association, 2004). It concluded that campus recreation contributes significantly (and in diverse ways) to the college student's "out of classroom" learning experience. This report provided powerful evidence of the key role that campus recreation plays on college campuses.

This chapter illustrates the importance of implementing a campus recreation assessment program. With the goal of improving recreation facilities, programs, and services, it defines the role of the department mission, vision, values, goals, and objectives in the assessment process; provides examples of an assessment plan; defines valid and reliable methods of data collection and analysis; and emphasizes the need for data translation and application.

General and Specialty Standards

To ensure that campus recreation programs meet the needs of the campus population, a comprehensive assessment program is essential. The assessment programs begin with the establishment of standards and guidelines. Chapter 17 amplifies the role of standards and provides further explanation of the relevant standards and guidelines that form the foundation for campus recreation assessments.

Aims of an Assessment Program

Gathering data to support the existence of campus recreation is only one aim of a comprehensive campus recreation assessment program. As depicted in figure 14.1, the campus recreation assessment process should do the following:

1. Determine whether the campus recreation mission, vision, and values are being met

2. Determine whether specific program, facility, and service goals and objectives are being fulfilled

3. Determine whether specific questions about particular programs are being answered

4. Fulfill diverse evaluative needs that range from addressing strategic planning concerns to finding answers to specific program questions

The following scenarios illustrate the application of one aspect of an assess-

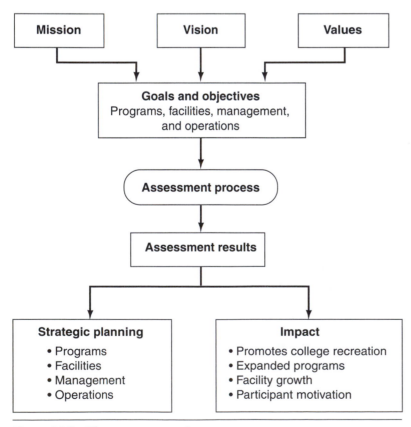

Figure 14.1 The campus recreation assessment process.

ment process. Specifically, the scenarios answer specific questions about particular programs. Additionally, the examples illustrate the need to understand when various assessment methodologies should be used. This chapter explores and describes various assessment methodologies that lead to data-driven services and decisions.

• *Scenario 1.* Because of changing trends, an indoor tennis, volleyball, and basketball facility manager wants to change the focus of offerings to include a fitness component. The facility is located close to the residence halls. Not knowing the types of fitness equipment students prefer, the manager conducts a survey to obtain feedback. The survey lists the choices of fitness and conditioning equipment, with respondents requested to indicate preferences. The data are analyzed and summarized, and the equipment is purchased based on the recommendations. The survey respondents are elated that their voices were heard and that equipment was purchased based on their recommendations. Consequently, facility usage and patron satisfaction improve significantly.

• *Scenario 2.* A fitness program manager routinely surveys group fitness participants to determine whether their fitness needs are being met. The survey questions pertain to the times that classes are offered—specifically, whether additional times need to be offered. There is an 80 percent return rate on the survey, and conclusions indicate that participants want a 6:00 a.m. aerobics class. When this class is offered, attendance is low, or no one shows up. To promote goodwill and give the patrons what they requested, the 6:00 a.m. aerobics class is continued. Then, in an attempt to increase participation, the manager recruits the best instructors to lead the classes, but attendance still does not improve. The survey conclusions indicating that a 6:00 a.m. aerobics class should be offered are puzzling and illustrate the need to understand assessment methods and the types of assessments.

In the second scenario, the fitness program manager needed a more thorough understanding of participants' desires and whether they would follow through with their requests. A focus group should have been conducted instead of a survey. This illustrates that employing the wrong assessment methodology or not asking the right questions will elicit data and information that is not applicable to the decision at hand.

Mission, Vision, Values, Goals, and Objectives

There is more to college recreation assessment than developing and administering surveys. An assessment plan should use the department mission, vision, and value statements, along with program, facility, and service goals and objectives. As shown in figure 14.2, the mission statement describes who you are and what you do. A mission statement does the following:

• Describes the overall purpose and intent of an organization
• Is used to guide the department's operation
• Guides policies and procedure development
• Aids in strategic planning and major decision making
• Increases the value to internal and external customers

A mission statement is designed to do the following:

• Improve organizational focus
• Ensure that the entire department is moving in the intended direction
• Foster a professional image within and outside of the organization

Developing a vision is another planning tool for organizational operation. A vision statement is a compelling and futuristic statement of a desirable state of reality made possible by accomplishing the mission in a way that is consistent with the values.

Value statements comprise the third portion that helps to guide the assessment process. Value statements express the core value of an organization in a powerful, brief, descriptive, and direction-oriented manner. They serve as routes on a map that guide organizations toward specific destinations. Although the destination changes constantly, the paths are consistent and reliable and yield the necessary results.

The values statements shown in figure 14.2 illustrate what is important, or valued, within an organization.

Once developed, the mission, vision, and value statements give direction to the assessment process, as illustrated in figure 14.1. The mission, vision, and values function codependently within an organization, each playing a vital role in creating a functional organization. Each component

Campus Recreational Sports

Mission, Vision, Values

Mission

We are committed to providing the finest programs, services, facilities, and equipment to enrich the university learning experience and to foster a lifetime appreciation of and involvement in wellness and recreational sports and activities for our students, faculty, and staff.

Vision

We will be a vital component of the university community.

Values

Diversity. Create an environment that values, embraces, and enriches individual differences by providing programs, services, and staff that reflect the diversity of the university.

Customer satisfaction. Consistently meet or exceed the needs and expectations of the university community and their families by providing an environment that values our customers. Develop a friendly and knowledgeable staff that anticipates changing needs and actively solicits and responds to input. Provide clean, safe, accessible, and attractive facilities that are user-friendly.

Mutual respect. Offer a welcoming environment that values, embraces, and enriches individual differences by providing programs, services, and staff that reflect the diversity of the university.

Tradition. Honor our tradition as the first formally organized intramural department in the United States. This compels and challenges us to maintain our national distinction of excellence and leadership in the field of collegiate recreation and intramural sports.

Development. Provide superior opportunities for students to evolve as leaders by recognizing and fully developing their talents. Offer all department members training, education, and opportunities. Encourage them to pursue responsibility and develop to their full potential while maintaining a balance between work and personal needs. Foster an enriching, participatory, and fun environment that encourages open communication among all staff.

Awareness. Develop a community-wide awareness of our programs and services to attract and invite new and current participants through aggressive, innovative marketing and promotional strategies.

Partnership. Build sustaining relationships with other units on and off campus to maximize the university's efforts in wellness, leisure time services, and facilities. Operate in a fiscally and ethically responsible manner. The results will strengthen the university's recruitment and retention of students, faculty, and staff. Our role both inside and outside the traditional academic setting as teachers and mentors will continue to enhance the education of the individual.

Innovation. Take advantage of cutting-edge technology and creative thinking to provide programs and services that are progressive and designed to meet the changing needs of the communities we serve.

Community support. Contribute exemplary leadership and assistance to efforts that enrich our communities and support our environment.

Figure 14.2 An example of a mission, vision, and values statement in one document.

should be well defined before implementing the assessment process. One phase of the assessment process is to determine whether the department is operating in accordance with the mission, vision, and values of the organization. Assessment results should be used during the planning phase.

To realize its mission, vision, and values, a campus recreation department must establish program, facility, and service goals and objectives that lead toward producing positive outcomes. The goals and objectives are considered steps, or tasks, that need to be completed to achieve a specific intent. A goal is a broad, clear statement of a vision, which is a general intention that is intangible and abstract and can't be validated. An example of a goal for student staff development within college recreation would be "The student

Program Assessment

Goal: To create and conduct a longitudinal study

Objectives:

- Conduct pre- and posttesting based on the construction of the new facility.
- The study will span eight years.
- Determine the effect that recreational facilities, programs, and services have on recruiting students to the college campus.
- Determine the role that college recreation facilities, programs, and services have on student recruitment and retention.
- Determine the role that college recreation facilities, programs, and services have on customer satisfaction.
- Establish an environment for enhanced student learning in and outside of the classroom.
- Partner and collaborate with departments, colleges, and offices on campus.

Goal: To conduct an assessment of each campus recreation component in established user profiles

Objectives: Complete assessments for each of the following areas:

- Fitness programs
- Intramural sports
- Sport clubs
- Aquatics
- Open recreation users of main and satellite facilities
- Outdoor facilities
- Family programming
- Adapted recreational programming
- Nonusers and nonparticipants

Goal: To establish student employee profiles for college recreation

Objectives:

- Gather data that justify needs.
- Define areas in which employees obtain useful skills and benefits.
- Define areas in which campus recreation employees require more training and plan training accordingly.

Figure 14.3   Examples of program goals and objectives.

staff will be certified in first aid and cardiopulmonary resuscitation."

Objectives, on the other hand, are behaviors that are narrow in scope, precise, tangible, and concrete; they can be validated. For example, to accomplish the preceding goal, the objectives might be as follows:

- To conduct quarterly first aid and cardiopulmonary resuscitation training for student-staff
- To create an incentive program to award students who are certified in first aid and cardiopulmonary resuscitation

Figure 14.3 lists some goals and objectives in the area of assessment.

Developing the Assessment Plan

An assessment plan provides organization to the assessment process. This section addresses the tangible components of the college recreation customer experience and describes five primary respondent groups from which to solicit data.

Campus Recreation Components

The first step in developing an assessment plan is to dissect the college recreation organization. In

257

its simplest form, college recreation is composed of four components that work dependently and independently within the organization:

- Programs
- Facilities
- Management
- Operations

As indicated in figure 14.4, there are subcomponents within each component. For example, programming subcomponents include the following:

- Adapted recreational sports
- Age group and camp programs
- Adventure recreation programs
- Intramurals
- Special events
- Fitness
- Aquatics

Conditioning and exercise are among the subcomponents of the programming component of a college recreation department.

William A. Cotton, Colorado State University.

- Open recreation
- Conditioning and exercise
- Sport clubs

Management refers to the professionals responsible for the programs, facilities, and operations and includes those in human resources, business, technology, scheduling, marketing and development, research and assessment, and risk management.

Operations of specific programs, facilities, and services are an integral segment of the organization, as are the facilities used by all programs and services within the department. Each component operates as its own entity but influences the others.

A campus recreation assessment should be planned for each calendar year. The campus community should be surveyed annually to determine the following:

- Campus recreation participation rate
- Campus recreation needs and whether those needs are being met
- Campus communities' overall perceptions of campus recreation programs, facilities, management, and operations
- Whether additional programs and facilities are needed

The campus recreation subcomponents need to be assessed at the conclusion of a program. For example, at the conclusion of the water polo club season, the participants should assess the program, its officials, the facility, the operation, and the administration. Additionally, the administration will assess the water polo club.

When developing an assessment instrument, it is important to answer these questions: What do I need to know? and, Why do I need to know it? For example, if a program is suffering from a lack of participation, what could be asked to determine ways to increase the number of participants? The following factors may influence attendance:

- Time the program is offered
- Skills of the instructor
- Ease of program registration
- Location of the class
- Available parking
- Quality of the facility

Knowing this, a survey could be administered to participants and nonparticipants that would

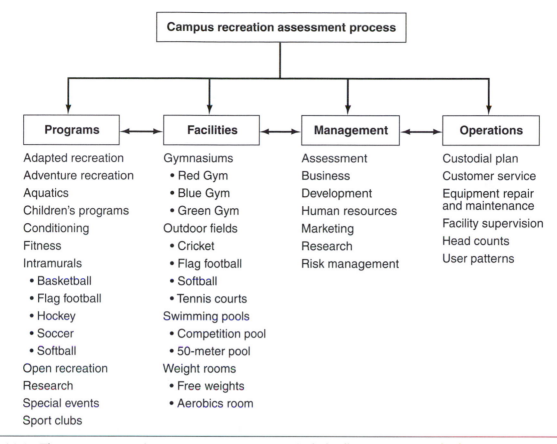

Figure 14.4 The campus recreation assessment process must include all components and subcomponents.

include sections that relate to the mentioned factors.

One section of an assessment survey should request respondents' demographics. The following information should be collected, at minimum:

- Age
- Gender
- Ethnicity
- Status (student, faculty, or staff)

A focus group (see Qualitative Assessment on pages 261-262) is another method of assessment that should be considered in this situation. As demonstrated, when conducting an assessment, it is important to include components that are pertinent to the area. For example, if intramural basketball is being assessed, questions about the facility and administration might be included.

Campus recreation assessment goes beyond the tangible components seen and experienced by the customer. The following assessment forms are not directly connected to the customer; however, the data obtained can be used to improve customer satisfaction:

- Staff evaluations
- Facility assessments
- Equipment inventory
- Event analysis

Employee evaluations (written records of employee performance) are essential in making recommendations regarding employee training, transfer, dismissal, or promotion. Staff evaluations should be based on the following:

- Department's mission, vision, and values
- Employee's job description
- Program policies and procedures

Facility assessment involves gathering information about existing facilities and facility needs and covers items such as the following:

- Cleanliness
- Equipment
- Event scheduling
- Heating
- Lighting

- Lockers
- Showers
- Towel service
- Ventilation

A system for reporting the condition of these areas should be developed. This documentation is needed not only for liability, but also for corrective purposes. The most efficient method is a checklist that includes all areas being assessed on a daily basis. For example, facilities can be checked daily to determine the following:

- Whether all of the lights work
- Whether the floor is clean
- Whether the trash is removed
- Whether the equipment is put away
- Whether any hazards exist

Equipment inventory can be a subcategory of the facility assessment form. Equipment needs to be checked to determine whether it is operational and whether safety concerns exist. For example, intramural fields need to be walked before use to check for broken glass or debris and to assess weather conditions. Just like the facility checklist, this information should be documented and filed.

Special events and facility rentals are common in campus recreation and can be lucrative. Before hosting an event, the event manager should complete a needs analysis. The specifics of the facility, equipment, and personnel requirements should be part of the analysis. At the conclusion of the event, a follow-up evaluation that reports the positive and negative aspects and what could be done to improve the event should be performed. This information is beneficial when planning subsequent events of the same nature.

Responders

Five primary groups help with campus recreation assessments by providing data. A comprehensive assessment program should include feedback from all five respondent groups as shown in figure 14.5 and listed here:

- *Program participants.* Participants are the customers. They participate in and provide first-hand information about programs and facilities. Participants provide important information about the quality of the programs, facilities, management, and operations.

- *Nonparticipants.* Nonparticipants do not participate in programs or use the facility; however, they should be involved in the assessment process. Nonparticipants answer the question, Why are you not participating in the programs or using the facilities?

- *Programmers.* Programmers are professionals who administer college recreational sport programs and have a global view of the department and campus. Programmers conduct facility assessments, provide head counts, and examine user patterns and demographics as they relate to their programs.

- *Administration.* The administration consists of the managers and programmers who evaluate personnel, determine trends, and make recommendations about future programs and facilities.

- *External evaluators.* External evaluators are campus recreation professionals who are not affiliated with the department being assessed. They provide an unbiased view of the department and can assist the department in critical decision-making processes.

Types of Assessment

Campus recreation data can be gathered using a variety of methods, including observation, questionnaires, interviews, and records.

Basically, assessment methods are classified as qualitative, quantitative, or a combination of the two. Qualitative methods permit the evaluator to study selected issues in depth and detail, include gathering data from interviews and observations, and require much smaller samples than quantitative methods. Quantitative methods, on the other hand, require the use of an instrument, such as a survey, and allow the evaluator to measure varying perspectives and experiences. These methods require much larger samples than qualitative methods. As a result, the information can be generalized from the sample to the population studied.

The assessment method depends on the purpose of the assessment, why and what is to be evaluated, the audience for whom the assessment is intended, and the resources available, including money, time, and personnel. For example, if the purpose of the assessment is to determine the demographics of those who use the recreation facility, the most efficient method is the quantitative method. However, to assess selected issues in depth and detail, such as lap swimming etiquette and whether slow and fast swim lanes should be enforced, a qualitative approach would be most advantageous.

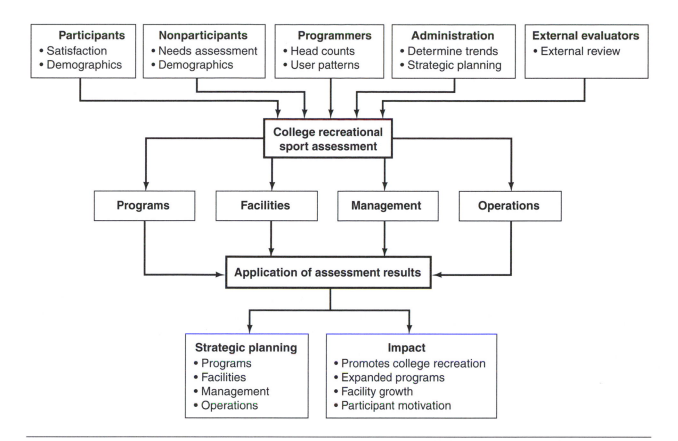

Figure 14.5 Recreational sport assessment model showing populations active in the assessment process.

Qualitative Assessment

Qualitative assessments include observations, case studies, one-on-one interviews, and focus groups. In college recreation, the most popular qualitative method is the **focus group.** Focus groups are group discussions used to generate a large amount of data in a short amount of time. The intent of a focus group is to focus in depth on a relatively small sample of people. The art of planning and conducting focus groups is well defined in qualitative research textbooks. Because of the value of focus groups in campus recreation, the following overview is provided.

A focus group begins with a question or problem that cannot be understood through numbers or statistics. As illustrated in scenario 2 (see page 255), a qualitative method would have been better than a quantitative method (survey) to determine whether participants would attend a 6:00 a.m. aerobics class.

The area of inquiry in a focus group is well defined. For example, using the scenario, the two questions would be, Do aerobics participants desire a 6:00 a.m. class? and, Will they participate? Fundamentally, focus groups give evaluators a chance to listen to people and learn from them. In so doing, they may be able to ascertain their attitudes, beliefs, experiences, feelings, and reactions.

Focus groups answer the question, Why? rather than, How many? By observing the discussions, evaluators obtain a better perspective on the opinions surrounding the issues.

The four basic steps to conducting a focus group are planning, recruiting, moderating, and analyzing and reporting.

During the planning step, questions such as the following may be asked:

Can the project be done in-house, or does it require outside experts?

Who should the focus group participants be, and what can be used to motivate them to participate?

What questions will be asked?

Will the discussions work better with smaller groups or a larger one?

Where will the focus group be conducted, and do we need a neutral site?

How will focus group notes be taken?

The next step is to recruit participants. It is important to devote enough time and effort to recruiting. Determine the target population, define segments within the target population, identify the best composition for each group, and determine how to ensure that participants will show up for the focus group.

In some cases the moderator is the person who needs the answer to the focus group question. In other cases it is a neutral person not associated with the college recreation department. Additional items that need to be determined are as follows:

- Role of the moderator
- Whether multiple moderators are needed
- Who will train the moderator in the correct way of asking the question
- Questions to ask during the focus group session

Even the simplest project produces a wealth of data that must be sorted and interpreted. This phase is known as analysis. During this phase the notes are organized, data are studied to determine the key conclusions, and the final report is written. From the report, recommendations concerning the programs, facilities, administration, or organization are made.

Other points that need to be considered when planning and conducting focus groups include the following:

- Focus groups demand resources—specifically, time, skills, and money.
- People who are willing to discuss the topic at hand should be recruited and incentives should be provided to encourage their participation.
- The amount of time needed to conduct the focus group is often underestimated.
- A focus group is led by a neutral moderator whose role is to facilitate the discussion, keep time, deliver the script, and establish a trusting relationship with participants.
- Questions should be pilot tested with professionals who are familiar with the program to learn whether the words flow smoothly or whether there are awkward questions.
- The moderator should ask questions in a conversational manner to create and maintain an informal environment. The wording of the question should be direct, comfort-

able, and simple. Effective questions are clear, brief, reasonable, and limited to a single topic.

Quantitative Assessment

Quantitative assessments include questionnaires, surveys, inventories, and census. The advantage to this approach is that it is possible to get feedback from a large number of people in a short amount of time. When respondents complete a survey online, the data can go directly to a data file, thus eliminating the tasks of mailing the surveys and entering the data.

Factors to consider when administering a survey are the return rate and the percentage of people who complete the survey. A high return rate is needed to help eliminate bias. The return rate should be included in the results of a survey.

Constructing an effective questionnaire is the first step to getting an appropriate response rate. Don A. Dillman (1978) provided the following suggestions for developing a mailed survey. These suggestions would also apply to an e-mailed survey.

1. Provide a brief, simple cover letter thanking the respondent and explaining the purpose of the survey, why that person was chosen to complete it, and why that person's participation is important.

2. The survey should be visually inviting and give respondents' clear instructions on how to complete the items. Consider including a correctly completed sample item.

3. Use the minimum number of questions needed to obtain the data desired, and resist the temptation to gather data not pertinent to the purpose of the questionnaire.

4. Identify problems with items or responses by pilot testing the survey with colleagues and respondents from the target audience. Pilot tests help identify redundant or poor questions.

5. Send a notice to the respondent five to seven days before sending the survey.

6. Send follow-up surveys to those who did not return completed surveys.

Standardized Instruments

A standardized instrument is an established, valid, and reliable tool that allows for comparisons among institutions and programs. The most common standardized instrument used in campus recreation to date is the *Quality and Importance of Recreational Services (QIRS)* (National Intramural-Recreational Sports Association, 2000). It was designed to help recreational sport professionals assess their services and establish standards. Results from the QIRS help to document the positive impact that college recreation, fitness, and wellness have on the recruitment and retention of students. A feature of this tool is that it can be customized to individual college recreational sport settings and lets evaluators make judgments based on the results from other institutions.

The assessment process at some institutions might involve assessing the physical activity habits or fitness levels of the campus community. Numerous standardized instruments are available to accomplish this phase of the assessment process and can be found in *Physical Activity Assessment for Health-Related Research* (Welk, 2002).

Tracking Participants

According to Mull, Bayless, and Ross (1987, p. 488):

> Traditionally, participant head-counts have provided the basis for determining the success in a given area of a program. These counts have been used to measure success in terms of quantity: attendance figures, frequency of participation, maximum use of facilities, percentage of participants returning, and number of events.

The head-count method of tracking participants is flawed, however. Head counts do not measure the quality of programs, only the number of people participating. High numbers do not indicate that a program is good, nor do low numbers indicate that a program should be dropped. A particular program may meet the needs of a diverse group of students, faculty, or staff. For example, head counts for cricket may be low compared to other programs. However, cricket meets the recreation needs of a particular group on campus.

Even though head counts should not be the primary assessment tool, they are valuable in the planning process. These numbers assist in determining whether additional space is needed or whether spaces that are not being used should be converted to usable space. For example, if racquetball head counts have progressively been dropping while weightlifting head counts have been climbing to the point where there is not enough facility space, one solution might be to convert racquetball

courts to weightlifting space. Head-count data will assist in justifying the facility conversion.

There are various methods of tracking head counts. Head counts can be taken manually by counting the number of participants who enter the facility. This count can be more detailed by counting the number of participants at each facility site (i.e., gymnasium, pool, weight room) on an hourly basis. These data can be analyzed to determine whether facility use is changing and whether additions or modifications are needed. Head counts can also be taken electronically by scanning users' cards. Each card is unique and is linked to the user's demographics in the computer system. Reports can be generated to show, for example, who used the facility during a given period of time, what their gender and ethnicity is, and what year of school they are in. This awareness will assist in determining whether programs and facilities are meeting the recreation needs of a diverse campus population.

Data Collection

This section details various methods of obtaining data and what to do when your population of participants and nonparticipants is too large to feasibly capture all of their feedback.

Sampling

Once it is determined that a survey will be administered as part of the assessment process, the next task is to decide whether it is feasible to survey all users of the facility or program being assessed. If not, then sampling is needed.

Sampling involves taking a portion of the population, collecting data on this group, and then generalizing the findings to the population. For example, rather than surveying all swimming pool patrons to determine their preferred water temperature, a predetermined portion of the swimmers is surveyed. This makes the process manageable and less costly and time-consuming.

When sampling, it is important that the sample represent the population. For example, if aquatic center users are 79 percent Caucasians, 18 percent African Americans, and 3 percent Asian Americans, the sample should include this breakdown. The same is true for a breakdown of faculty, staff, and students, along with a breakdown by the ages of respondents. These subgroups are noted as strata, and the process is called **stratified sampling**.

When the population consists of a number of strata that may differ in characteristics, stratified sampling should be used. For example, to ensure an equal representation of campus recreational sport users, a department may administer a survey to an equal number of students, faculty, and staff.

An advantage of stratified sampling is that it improves representativeness and enables the evaluator to compare differences that might exist among various subgroups. In this type of sampling, the evaluator may either take equal numbers from each stratum or select in proportion to the size of the stratum in the population. For example, if 10 percent of the facility users are retirees, then 10 percent of the sample of users to be polled would be taken from this stratum.

Systematic sampling involves systematically choosing samples from a list of the population. For example, if the recreation facility has 5,000 members and the sample size is 500, the evaluator would choose every 10th name from the list of members.

Sample Size

A common question is, How many people do I need in my sample? According to Ary, Jacobs, and Razavieh (1990, p. 178), "The size of the sample depends upon the precision the evaluator desires in estimating the population parameters at a particular confidence level." Algebraically, an estimation of required sample size can be calculated. It is determined using the variance of the population, the expected differences, and the desired probabilities. Statistics textbooks provide the steps needed to calculate a sample size.

The size of the sample depends on the homogeneity of the population from which it is to be selected. For example, for a survey of intramural basketball players at a large college campus, the sample size would be large because the population is diverse. On the other hand, for a survey of early morning lap swimmers, the group might be homogeneous; consequently, fewer completed surveys would be needed to draw conclusions. The sample size also depends on the issue being investigated and whether cross-tabulation of demographics is needed. According to Ary et al., (1990, p. 178), "The best answer to the question of sample size is to use as large a sample as possible. Other things being equal, a larger sample is much more likely to be representative of the population. Furthermore, with a large sample the data are likely to be more accurate and precise."

Randomization

It is often too time-consuming and expensive to ask each person in the population to complete the survey. For example, if the population of your facility users is 10,000, it may be inefficient to administer a survey to all 10,000. The solution would be to administer the survey to a **random sample.** The basic characteristic of a random sample is that all members of the population have an equal chance of being included in the survey.

Data Collection Methods

Campus recreation departments collect data in the form of observations, head counts, surveys, and employee evaluations. Data can be collected using a variety of methods. The "old-fashioned" method of collecting data is paper and pencil. This system is appropriate when there are numerous open-ended questions. However, when a survey has multiple response items, it is most efficient to use a bubble-dot form that can be scanned into a computer.

Another scale that has been widely used and is conducive to a bubble-dot form is a Likert scale. A Likert scale assesses attitudes toward a topic by asking respondents to indicate the degree they strongly agree, agree, are undecided, disagree, or strongly disagree with each statement on the survey.

In the age of electronics, companies sell software capable of creating electronic bubble-dot surveys that can be e-mailed; the results go directly into a data file.

Data Analysis

Data analysis is the process of examining quantitative information to extract meaning. This procedure has two main advantages:

- It assists in organizing, summarizing, and describing the data gathered.
- It helps to describe the population to determine whether the inference is valid.

Most recreational sport professionals can perform basic descriptive statistical analysis, such as computation of the mean, median, and mode and tabulation of data. Other computations such as standard deviation, t-test, chi-square, and analysis of variance (ANOVA) may require the use of a computer statistical program such as SPSS (Statistical Program for Social Sciences) or SAS (Superior Software and Services) or a statistical consultant.

SPSS is a comprehensive and flexible statistical analysis and data management system. SPSS can take data from almost any type of file, such as Excel, and use it to generate tabulated reports, charts, and descriptive statistics. The campus technology department may provide copies of statistical programs and statistical assistance at no cost.

Reporting and Using Assessment Results

Assessment data that are not reported or acted on have no impact. Nothing is more frustrating than conducting an assessment and then learning that decision makers tucked the results in a file drawer and failed to act on them. One reason program participants and nonparticipants participate in an assessment is that they believe their time and effort will be of good use and that the results will be put into action.

An assessment report should include the following:

- *Meaningful title.* The title of an assessment report alone may convince a potential reader to read or discard the report. The title should be eye-catching, yet specific and descriptive.

- *Executive summary.* The executive summary is the most important part of the report because it might be the only part that the busy administrator reads. This one-page section should provide important data along with a summary and recommendations of the findings.

- *Statement of purpose.* A statement of purpose explains why the assessment was conducted. Supplemental background information or a literature review is appropriate in this section. It is advantageous to write this section before conducting the assessment. If writing this section is difficult, maybe there is no need to conduct the assessment.

- *Assessment method(s).* The methods section of the report includes the design that was used in the assessment and why it was used. Instruments, interviews, sampling, data collection, and analysis should be included, as should the results of statistical analyses and their meanings. The section should begin by sharing the response rate and a description of the respondents' gender, age, ethnicity, and so forth.

- *Results.* Results should be reported as they relate to the purpose of the assessment.

- *Recommendations.* Finally, the report should include an explanation of the results—specifically, how they can be applied to present practices and operations. If these are expected to change as a result of the new knowledge, that should be stated. In this section, speculation of the reasons for the findings can be made. Suggestions for other assessments are also appropriate.

Once the report is written, a dissemination plan needs to be implemented. A frequent mistake is to consider the assessment process complete when the report is submitted to the appropriate people. Assessment results need to assist the strategic plan review and drive decision making, and in some instances, results need to be shared for "impact" purposes to promote college recreation, expand programs, advocate for facility growth, and motivate participants. Assessment results that lend themselves to these areas need to be shared with campus media, such as newspapers, alumni materials, and Web pages.

Conclusion

Campus recreation assessment is an essential component for providing the finest programs, services, facilities, and equipment to the campus community. The assessment process assures that campus recreation departments are acknowledging and addressing the needs of the patron. Assessment also helps to determine future needs. Moreover, the process provides the data needed to support the existence of campus recreation programs, facilities, and services.

References

Ary, D., Jacobs L.C., & Razavieh, A. (1990). *Introduction to research in education* (4th ed.). Orlando, FL: Holt, Rinehart and Winston.

Dillman, D.A. (1978) *Mail and telephone surveys, the total design method.* New York: Wiley-Interscience.

Mull, R., Bayless, K.G., & Ross, C.M. (1987). *Recreational sports programming* (2nd ed.). North Palm Beach, FL: The Athletic Institute.

National Intramural-Recreational Sports Association. (2000). *Quality and importance of recreational services (QIRS).* Champaign, IL: Human Kinetics.

National Intramural-Recreational Sports Association. (2004). *The value of recreational sports in higher education.* Champaign, IL: Human Kinetics.

Welk, G. (2002). *Physical activity assessment for health-related research.* Champaign, IL: Human Kinetics.

Glossary

data analysis—The process of examining quantitative information to extract meaning.

265

focus group—A group discussion used to generate a large amount of concentrated data in a short amount of time.

random sample—A sample in which all members of the population have an equal chance of being included.

sampling—Taking a portion of the population, collecting data on this group, and then generalizing the findings to the population.

stratified sampling—A system for choosing subjects based on their representation of specific demographics, such as year in college, gender, ethnicity, or income. Stratified sampling allows for comparison between various subgroups of a population.

systematic sampling—A system for choosing subjects from a population that involves drawing names from a list at a specific sampling interval, such as every second, third, or fourth name. The number of subjects needed must first be decided. Then the population of possible subjects is divided by the number of subjects needed. The answer to that equation becomes the sampling interval.

PART IV

Professional Aspects of Campus Recreation

CHAPTER 15

Ethics

Gerald S. Fain, PhD, Professor, School of Education, Boston University

Ethics is a branch of philosophy; it is *moral philosophy* or philosophical thinking about morality, moral problems, and moral judgments.

William Frankena, Ethics

Those directly responsible for campus recreation programs, facilities, and services have the responsibility of upholding standards and striving for ideals that require moral judgment. This is affirmed in the NIRSA code of ethics:

> An outstanding characteristic of a profession is that its members are continually striving to improve the quality of life for the populations they serve. In making the choice to affiliate with a professional association, individuals assume the responsibility to conduct themselves in accordance with the ideals and standards set by the organization. For NIRSA members, this means they will strive to uphold the Bylaws in a manner illustrated in the Code of Ethics. (NIRSA, Code of Ethics, Preamble)

Codes of Ethics

Codes of ethics are a necessary part of professional affiliations but nonetheless insufficient for ensuring trustworthiness. Edwin J. Delattre (1996), a philosopher and renowned authority on ethics and policing, wrote:

> Although persons in official life find guidelines useful, codes of ethics do not motivate people to behave well. They assist only people who already want to do so. Even when men and women are virtuous, even when they behave with high standards of conscience, they benefit from responsible supervision and instruction designed to help them become better. They deserve superiors and peers who assess their performance with care and make departmental expectations clear. If the leadership and the experienced personnel do not show that they take ethics violations seriously, their codes will be treated as worthless platitudes. (p. 33)

To be effective then, codes must be more than platitudes. If they are to be useful at all, they need to be clearly stated and accompanied with cases illustrative of current practice. When codes are used as the basis for ongoing instruction, beginning with the newly inducted, they can set the groundwork for personnel practices and the mission of a department. In contrast, codes unrelated to standards of practice can never be expected to exert a good influence.

One area of moral judgment commonly addressed in codes of ethics is confidentiality. Although the practical applications with respect to matters of confidentiality will necessarily vary from one group and setting to the next, all judgments of this kind should reflect a common sense of morality. The following case illustrates a practical example for professional development derived from another field of practice. Here, within the general category of confidentiality, the duty to warn is examined. This case influenced refinements to professional standards now common in higher education, thereby directly benefiting those who work in campus recreation.

In the 1976 *Tarasoff v. Regents of University of California* case, a voluntary outpatient told his therapist that he intended to kill Tatiana Tarasoff. Tarasoff was a student at the University of California at the time. The therapist believed that his patient was capable of killing her and informed the local authorities. Nonetheless, the outpatient killed Tarasoff. The California Supreme Court found the therapist liable for his failure to warn the victim or her parents (Nohe, 2000).

Prior to this case, therapists were taught that when they broke therapist–client confidentiality, they not only violated their obligation to clients, but they also put in danger the entire enterprise of counseling and psychiatric care. If patients believed that what they told their therapists would not be kept in strict confidence, they might not tell their therapists all of what they were thinking, thereby undercutting the very purpose of therapy.

The arguments in this case take most seriously the view that despite the therapist's belief that the outpatient intended to commit the murder, he did not do all that he should have to protect Tarasoff from harm. Had the outpatient failed to convince the therapist that his threat was genuine, then the therapist would not have had a duty to warn. It is commonplace for patients in treatment for mental illness to reveal troubling thoughts. To the extent possible, therapists are obligated to distinguish disclosures that threaten the welfare of others from those that do not.

The case illuminates an ethical problem that requires professional competence and good judgment. Because the death of Tarasoff was found by the court to be avoidable, the case does not present an **ethical dilemma,** pitting confidentiality against public safety. Dilemmas are moral problems in which, no matter what the agent does, the outcome remains unavoidable and unwanted. The agent has to choose between two or more undesirable actions. Ethical dilemmas are different from moral problems, in which the successful use of reason can prevent harm.

Applying these points to campus sport clubs, let us imagine a highly competitive game of intramural soccer. A player is humiliated on the field for making a mistake that costs his team the win. The player tells his coach he is going to "get the star player from the opposing team, once the game is finished." If the coach believes his player, he should do all that is reasonably possible to prevent the attack. Using *Tarasoff* as our reference point, we see that the coach would be obligated to do what he could to stop his player from carrying out the threat, including warning the coach and the player from the opposing team.

Campus recreation personnel do not typically know whether a student is receiving treatment for mental illness, has a criminal record, or has a history of violence. There is a certain tension here between the privacy of medical and juvenile criminal records and the duties of recreation personnel to protect the safety of others.

No code of ethics is useful without good judgment in the application of its precepts and principles. In *Tarasoff*, we can see how the fundamental principle "Do no harm" leads to the duty in practice, "Warn against harm."

Moral Philosophy

The study of moral philosophy would be incomplete without an introduction to the contributions of Socrates. The following passage is from William Frankena's *Ethics* (1973), which presents what is among the most often-studied contributions of Socrates, "the patron saint of moral philosophy." Here a classic example of moral deliberation illustrates the enduring **values** derived from learning how to reason well.

Suppose that all of your life you have been trying to be a good person, doing your duty as you see it and seeking to do what is for the good of your fellowmen. Suppose, also, that many of your fellowmen dislike you and what you are doing and even regard you as a danger to society, although they cannot really show this to be true. Suppose, further, that you are indicted, tried and condemned to death by a jury of your peers, all in a manner which you correctly consider to be quite unjust. Suppose, finally, that while you are in prison awaiting execution, your friends arrange an opportunity for you to escape and go into exile with your family. They argue that they can afford the necessary bribes and will not be endangered by your escaping; that if you escape, you will enjoy a longer life; that your wife and children will be better off; that your friends will still be able to see you; and that people generally will think that you should escape. Should you take the opportunity? (Frankena, 1973, p. 1)

Socrates was in conversation with his friend, Crito, who was trying to convince him to escape from jail and his impending execution. Socrates explained to Crito that even though others wanted him to escape, they might be wrong, and he must think this through on his own. In so doing, Socrates opened the door for civil disobedience. He explained that he has been convicted of breaking the law and was therefore morally obliged to accept the punishment imposed by his state even though he denied that he had actually broken the law. Socrates knew full well that he could have avoided trial and conviction by not displeasing his fellow citizens or by leaving Athens to begin with. But he decided instead to stay and challenge public opinion, because he believed it was his personal responsibility to do exactly that. To the very end, he remained faithful to the principles on which he based his life. He was not willing to violate those principles to save his life, for in so doing he would have surrendered his integrity as a person and a citizen. Socrates was teaching by example that a life dedicated only to self-preservation is without moral substance and therefore can never be relied on as a model of doing the right thing.

From Socrates on, moral philosophers have held for the primacy of reason over emotion. Moral decisions ought not to be made simply on the basis of what others want us to do or what is popular at the time. This dialogue with Crito makes clear that individuals are ultimately responsible for making their own decisions and leading moral lives. Striving to achieve justice by thoughtfully applying moral principles requires the will to sacrifice personal happiness when called on to do what is right. Doing right over time establishes habits that define one's character. In this dialogue, Socrates was not persuaded by the arguments of his friend, Crito; he stood for what he believed to the very end. The fact that beginning students of philosophy everywhere still read

Plato's account of Socrates and other works, as well as those of Aristotle, provides evidence of the enduring value of moral philosophy within and across cultures. Ethics is ethics.

Since the time of Socrates, the world has changed in many ways. Yet, the ancient works are still studied, because basic ethical principles are enduring across cultures. In many respects, being a good person today turns on the same basic habits of character that ancient Greeks respected.

Ethics and Justice

Ethics is a branch of philosophy that deals with judgments of obligation, value, and responsibility that are part and parcel of everyday life. It is common to observe young children become enraged when they sense an injustice. The feeling of not being treated fairly or with kindness, especially by those we respect, is deeply rooted. But as noted earlier, feelings about fair treatment are not the same as actually being treated fairly. As Plato's account of Socrates illustrates, feelings alone—love of family and friendship—ought never to overrule reason. Reasoning well, or applying ethics, is doing what is morally right. The fact that doing the right thing can make a person feel good ought not to be confused with feeling good for the wrong reason. People sometimes mistakenly think that love of family and friendship alone provides reason enough to act immorally. An example would be when a person lies about facts and injures a third party to protect a family member or friend. That person who lied knows it was wrong but may try to soothe his or her conscience by accepting that the protection from harm of a person they love or respect is morally superior to telling the truth. This is the sort of reasoning that describes gang loyalty when criminals flout the law. It also applies to professional misconduct when one colleague lies in a court of law, committing perjury while trying to protect another. In direct contrast are the lessons taught by Socrates, who lived a moral life distinguished by his love of reason. Believing that a person is acting morally only on the grounds of emotion and feeling is not the same as being moral. Both Plato and Aristotle after him were careful to acknowledge the legitimate roles of emotion and feeling, however—just not in the driver's seat.

Justice can be studied by using three distinct categories. The first concerns the fair distribution of goods, the second addresses retribution, and the third deals with receiving what is earned.

Distributive Justice

Distributive justice seeks to achieve the fair distribution of goods. Here the young child complains when everyone else has a bigger piece of cake: "That's not fair. I'm a person too and I should have just as much cake as anyone else." College students may complain that the recreation department is giving less than an equal share of resources to the programs they want most. The claim that every cause is deserving of an equal share is morally obtuse, as is the responsibility of a college to provide every student or program with an equal measure of resources on every count. What does matter is whether all students have reasonable access to the available recreation programs and facilities. The program at St. John's College in Annapolis, Maryland, and Santa Fe, New Mexico, illustrates this principle by assigning every entering student to a club—for life. This means that whenever her team plays, the student assigned to that team has the opportunity to play. "For life" means that the same right is extended to alumni as well. The purpose here is clear: Participation in sports is valued, every student is encouraged to play every sport, and assembling a winning team is of no particular importance.

Retributive Justice

Retributive justice is illustrated by the Biblical injunction, "an eye for an eye," moderating the still harsher code of King Hammurabi (1792-1750 BC) of Mesopotamia, whose laws listed 282 directives. Hammurabi's Code is the best organized and perhaps the most commonly cited example of retributive justice from that time. These laws gave the court clear direction on how to administer a system of justice comprehensible to the common citizen. It attempted to embody a higher standard of civic responsibility by arbitrating complaints among citizens and by overturning the conception that might makes right. Nonetheless, it was overly harsh by Biblical standards.

The usefulness of codifying principles of retributive justice lies in publicizing the consequences that violators can expect. Students may similarly expect that they will lose rights or privileges for failing to obey rules or for doing harm to others.

Commutative Justice

The third category is **commutative justice.** This is achieved by receiving what is earned. The fastest runner should get the gold medal. Not everyone can earn first prize in a competitive event. Trying hard, although an admirable character trait, is no substitute for an excellent performance. When students complain that teachers don't reward hard work with higher grades, they challenge the basis for commutative justice. Students who fail to understand the difference between doing one's best and being the best may never understand what it takes to reach high standards in anything. This is why teachers who knowingly give students higher grades than they rightly deserve are acting unjustly. By reporting an inaccurate assessment of student achievement, they fail to tell the truth. Doing this contributes to grade inflation and undermines the possibility of helping students appreciate what is required to achieve higher standards of performance.

Being treated unjustly may hurt our feelings, but far more important, it can ruin our lives and harm others. Adults with sufficiently formed character know the difference between those forms of injustice over which they have control and can try to correct and those that are either inconsequential or out of reach. Having trouble deciding on

Winning a hard-earned victory is an example of commutative justice.

© StockByte "Sport: The Will to Win" Royalty Free Images

the color of a new car does not present a moral problem. Knowing that children live in poverty and die from preventable illness is. Adults with good character stand for what they believe and take actions to address injustice appropriately. Studying moral philosophy may not lead to making better decisions in every instance, but at the very least, understanding the distinctions between decisions having moral weight and those that have none is within the purview of moral philosophy.

Virtue Ethics

Since happiness is an activity of soul in accordance with perfect virtue, we must consider the nature of virtue: for perhaps we shall thus see better the nature of happiness.

—Arisotle

It is in the Aristotelian tradition of ethics that we find the basis for an ethics of virtue. His *Nicomachean Ethics* in particular provides the foundation for virtue as the substance for the moral life. Here Aristotle is not arguing for a set of principles *per se,* or a theory of the moral life, but rather for cultivating dispositions of both action and feeling. Courage, for example, is a fixed disposition to meet challenges both actively and emotionally in ways that practical wisdom prescribes. The desire to be brave is insufficient by itself. Genuine courage requires knowing what the brave thing to do and the brave way to feel are. This knowledge, like the disposition, can only be developed over time, with reflective practice.

Campus recreation programs can help to cultivate these dispositions in students if the leaders understand what to do and how to feel. For example, coaches who emphasize developing character excellence in their players over winning at any cost exemplify the Aristotelian concept of virtue.

The Leisure Test

The leisure test offers the possibility of discovering what we are really like:

The kinds of people we are "really like" are revealed not so much in what we actually do as in what we like to do, and this is precisely what the leisure test is best at bringing out. In the course of discharging our personal and professional responsibilities we may actually do all sorts of things that we find positively distasteful. We neither like them for themselves nor find ourselves endorsing them as expressions of the kinds of people that we would really like to be. We wouldn't do them if we didn't have to. We like them only insofar as they are ineluctable constituents of the roles in life that we have decided to play. But in those moments when we are free of such responsibilities, when our settled dispositions—our virtues and vices—can be given free rein, and the lower thresholds of our strength and weakness of will become relevant, we show what we are really like by showing what we are most disposed to do, within the prioritizing limits of our wills. (Tigner, 1995, p. 17)

From Tigner's leisure test, a college student can acquire the self-knowledge to build good character. This fact alone provides sufficient justification for intramural sports and recreation on any campus. A college education lacking such opportunities may meet all academic requirements but fail to test for good character. When we are at leisure, our obligations to self are preeminent. Learning how to bring out the best in ourselves involves voluntary actions in which we learn what we value most and hope to become.

What students do with their free time during their college years does matter. Some students fill their time with overeating and gaining unwanted weight. Others overindulge in alcohol, narcotics, and sex. Some students die because they misjudge their limits or get infected with avoidable sexually transmitted diseases. Others, unable to cope effectively with the demands of college life or being away from home, become so emotionally distraught that they leave school. They fail the leisure test.

Friendships

After what we have said, a discussion of friendship would naturally follow, since it is a virtue or implies virtue.

—*Aristotle*

Genuine **friendships,** if nothing more, are morally pleasing. Unlike business partners, friends are together because they hold common values. Friends do not necessarily agree on every matter of moral importance, such as the laws governing the death penalty for capital crimes, abortion laws, or how best to eliminate poverty. But at the center of their friendship is a common agreement that the other person is admirable.

Social and commercial relationships vary in both moral importance and complexity. Aristotle described three basic types of friendship: friendships of utility, friendships of pleasure, and friendships of mutual admiration.

Friendships of Utility

Friendships of utility are those devoted to the task at hand, such as students undertaking a project together. Once the work is completed, there is no reason for them to continue to meet or work together, so they may drift apart.

Friendships of Pleasure

Friendships of pleasure are likewise formed for a purpose and then dissolved once the pleasure is satisfied. An example is students who play a recreational sport together and then find no reason to continue meeting after the last game.

Friendships of Mutual Admiration

A third, more perfect variety of friendship is embodying mutual admiration, respect, loyalty,

William A. Cotton, Colorado State University.

What we do when we are at leisure gives us the chance to discover what we value most and hope to become.

and a sense of moral kinship. These are friendships between people who don't care as much about what they do together as they do about being together. Such friendships are rare, and the reason some people never have them is the subject of countless self-help books. Yet, it is easy to see the connections between the first two types of friendships and the third. When students have opportunities to work and play together during their college years, it is not uncommon for those experiences to serve as the origin of more perfect friendships lasting long after school days have ended. In Book VIII of the *Nicomachean Ethics,* Aristotle also recognized friendships between equals and unequals. In this category is the memorable and lasting friendship between a staff member and a college student. Friendships of this kind can be the reason students are forever grateful for their undergraduate education.

Deontological and Teleological Theories

Taken together, moral theories touch every aspect of human experience. Although justice is one overarching theme, the work of philosophers concerns intellectual inquiry of virtually every kind, including the pursuit of happiness, the nature of evil, duties to self, duties to others, and so on.

Philosophy (from the Greek word meaning "love of wisdom") thrives on competing concepts. Although all philosophers share a common understanding of their discipline, their subjects of interests and methods of scholarship vary.

In an effort to sort effectively into categories the works of the great philosophers required for a comprehensive study of ethics, Frankena (1973) identified two types of theories. The first type is **deontology.** Deontological philosophers contend that

> it is possible for an action or rule of action to be the morally right or obligatory one even if it does not promote the greatest possible balance of good over evil for self, society, or universe. (p. 15)

A deontologist might therefore object on moral grounds to any action or rule that was wrong in a manner commensurate with the seriousness of that wrong. Such a person would stand for a principle even though it might mean offending or going against majority opinion. We find this illustrated clearly in Socrates' argument that it is

better from a moral point of view to be put to death than to abandon what he stood for and believed to be morally correct. This can be understood in instances in which a person insists on being jailed for breaking an unjust law or refuses to be a soldier in a war he believes to be morally wrong.

Deontological theories do not try to bring about the greatest good and least harm. Instead they are grounded in principles that should never be violated even if more harm may come from them. Examples would be a person who will not be corrupted for the sake of getting along with colleagues, or people who will not tolerate an injustice even when great harm to themselves may result. Such was the case for many who fought against the enslavement of Africans in this country. It did not matter whether abolishing slavery would hurt plantation owners—they believed that slavery was simply wrong. We also know that civil rights laws as well as laws concerning the rights of people with disabilities were enacted not in consideration of financial consequences, but rather on principles of equality inherent in this constitutional republic.

In the extreme, deontological theorists contend that rules alone should govern the moral life. For example, the rule not to kill another human being is invoked by the conscientious objector. Taken to its logical end, such people would not kill even to save their own lives or those of loved ones.

The second theory is **teleology.** Teleologists contend that in our action we are morally obligated to bring about the greatest good with the least amount of harm. These philosophers, taking into account the inevitability of good and bad consequences, argue for the rightness of actions that bring about the greatest balance of good over evil.

Ethical egoists are likewise interested in maximizing the good, but for themselves. This might explain the fact that some people care not for virtue, have little interest in nurturing the character of others, and seem satisfied just as long as they have their hefty share of whatever it is they want. Ethical egoists believe they have no moral obligation to others—only to themselves. If staying out of jail is in their best interest, they either obey the law or break it shrewdly. If keeping their jobs means following the wishes of their employers, even when they know that in so doing they are ignoring or violating the rights of others, they do what they are told. They do not see the merit in losing a job over a principle or in defending the rights of others.

The ethical egoist's point of view is easily confused with what is often thought of as prudent business practice. For example, firing some people to save a business may be morally justified on the grounds that the aim of the employer is to save as many jobs as possible. This might be advanced as a morally superior stand, because losing the business would result in an even greater loss of jobs and more harm to others. Ethical egoists would not follow that principle, favoring instead exclusive consideration of what is best for them. The more problems occur, the less effective their administration is, and the more likely they are to blame their subordinates. They credit the productivity and accomplishments of their staff to themselves and can easily demoralize those who report to them.

Call for Moral Leadership

Directors of campus recreation and physical education programs are the first-line defenders of ethical standards. College students push boundaries. Elvis Presley, rock and roll, the Beatles, Woodstock, and civil rights protests that took place in the past remind us of the transformative contributions of youth to culture. The college student of today is no different. We should not confuse body piercing, tattooing, and living in coed dormitories where there is easy access to music and video games with violations of civic virtue. Today's college students are probably just as difficult for some adults to understand as previous generations of college students were in their day. Still, pushing boundaries without regard to the rights and welfare of others should never be accepted in communities where respect for individual rights is more important than having fun. It is on this basis that the legal boundaries of civic life on the college campus of today have changed. For example, we now have laws addressing hate crimes, sexual harassment, and privacy protection that reflect the ethical standards of our times.

Recreation programs are affected by these changes in standards of conduct. Consider dress codes intended to hold the line on fitness equipment and in swimming pools. In response to such codes, a student might ask, "On what grounds do you have the right to tell me what to wear?" or, "I don't see why I'm not allowed to wear whatever I wish. I just came back from Europe, where people wear even less clothing when they exercise." It is, of course, more than dress codes that challenge boundaries of decency, respect for others, and the

chance to use recreation as a means to build and celebrate habits of strong character.

Long ago in this country, citizens openly enjoyed sports that are banned today. As early as 1618, when King James issued a pronouncement known as the Book of Sports, bear and bull baiting were common forms of entertainment (Dulles, 1965, p. 10). Bull fighting, permitted elsewhere, is illegal in the United States. Yet, we allow boxing, knowing the high risk to personal safety, which includes serious and lasting damage to the brain. Boxing is one of the few sports in which spectators might actually see a person killed by a deathblow.

On what moral grounds does anyone have the right to limit another person's right to the recreation of his or her choosing? What brings pleasure to one person may not do so for another. Isn't the purpose of recreation to make one happy and feel good? And isn't life filled with risk?

Perhaps the most helpful reply to those indifferent to the rights of others is simply "We don't do that here." Recalling the ethical egoist, it is easy to see how a fair rule strongly enforced can hold a boundary. For the student who really does want an answer, perhaps a lesson on toleration might be useful. In "A Letter Concerning Toleration," John Locke (1689) wrote that toleration means not interfering with something of which we disapprove.

At the founding of this country, religious freedom was based on toleration, meaning that my neighbor has the right to pray to a god that I think of as satanic, as long as his practices don't interfere with my right to pray to the god of my choosing. The letter from George Washington (1790) to the Hebrew Congregation in Newport, Rhode Island, likewise proclaimed religious freedom as a tenet of this democracy. But although toleration in matters of religion is well established, we find the same tenet problematic when applied to recreation. For example, the noise of a jet ski interrupts the quiet at the lakefront, and snowmobiles break the silence of a winter wilderness. Living well together may require toleration from time to time, but friendships do not arise between people who merely tolerate each other.

Acting in Good Conscience

One recreation director told of a time early in his career when the members of a traveling sport club stopped on their way home from an off-campus competition to buy several cases of beer. The staff from his department were on the trip and driving the two vans used to transport the team. Several of the students were under the legal age to drink alcohol. The recreation director learned of the incident that evening when one of the students who went on the trip called to tell him of his concern that the school policy governing student conduct had been violated.

The director immediately called his staff, and when he had confirmed the facts, he fired the staff responsible and sent the names of each of the students on the trip to the school's committee to review the cases of policy violation. The university stood behind his dismissal of the staff, and the dean of students took each of the student cases under due process review.

Among the students on the trip were several with parents who worked at the university, including the son of the university provost. The director told me that he did not flinch when it came to making these decisions. All he had on his mind was protecting the students from harm and upholding the university policies. His habit of reflective thought immediately went to the dreaded possibility of having to call parents to report that their son or daughter had been injured or killed in a drunk driving accident that had occurred on his watch. He said that he knew it was morally wrong to ignore the facts. Even if the university officials failed to do their jobs in upholding the university policy, he would do his.

He didn't need to refer to a code of ethics to make his decision, nor did he need to have completed an academic course of study in moral philosophy. Like others of strong moral fiber, he wanted to act responsibly, consistent with the trust the university placed in him as its director and consistent with his own sense of right and wrong. He also said that he was willing to lose his job over this, if the administrators he reported to failed to uphold the policies that supported his actions.

In a situation such as this, we would be right to take the word of the director. We would be right to believe that he is telling the truth, the whole truth, and that his "habits" of moral reflection are indeed virtuous. If we could not believe these things, that would indicate a lack of trust in the director, and raise the question of why anyone would choose to work under the supervision of such a person. This director followed university policies and prevailing state law without hesitation. In so doing, he demonstrated his leadership responsibility.

However, this may not be evidence of integrity. He might have made his decisions because it was in his self-interest to do so. Not doing what he did, ignoring university policy and Massachusetts state

law, might have put his job at even greater risk, and knowing that may have influenced his decision. What we can learn about the character of this director might be best derived from his staff. If he *is* a person of character, this will be revealed in his actions every day. If he is simply self-interested, that will also become apparent over time.

Those who study ethics can draw on their knowledge of ethics to sort out the differences in a case such as this. Administrators with a knowledge of ethics can teach it to subordinates as they make decisions. When that happens, codes of ethics are more than the "worthless platitudes" Delattre warned about (1996). Finally, ongoing discussions of ethics within a department are perhaps the best way to improve staff morale.

Risk Management and Campus Security

The job of recreation director has changed in recent years. Recreation centers have to be protected from sophisticated criminal organizations in this country, as well as terrorists from abroad. Ongoing and effective contact with local law enforcement is vital. Directors need to know about illegal activities on and off campus. Knowing about organized gangs, the selling of illegal narcotics, prostitution, possible kidnapping, and terrorist attacks is a moral responsibility.

Matthew Pantera and his students at Springfield College, Massachusetts, created a checklist for ensuring that campus facilities used by large numbers of people, and the people who use them, are protected. The checklist used for securing facilities during major spectator events reflects the best practices in use today. A growing number of professional sport organizations, as well as campus athletics departments, have adopted their Game Day Security Operations Checklist (Pantera et al., 2003). The campus recreation profession needs more work of this type to protect those who use recreation facilities from unreasonable risk.

The call for moral leadership in the conduct of campus recreation demands more than knowing how to tolerate what is otherwise disapproved. Recreation should be restorative, bring to mind past pleasures, and by drawing out the best in us, instill a properly measured sense of pride.

The Lyceum: Lost and Found

The lyceum of ancient Greece was a large open space for physical exercise and philosophical

Courtesy of University of Alabama.

A recreational festival on a college campus could be considered a modern equivalent to the lyceum of ancient Greece.

discussion and contemplation. It was an ideal place for scholars and students to congregate. Given the expansion of campus recreation facilities and programs in recent years, it is easy to imagine the modern university offering these same opportunities. Yet, when the task at hand is to earn a degree and defer the joys of tranquility, education becomes work and the concept of the lyceum is lost.

The following account of an undergraduate student who entered college in the fall of 1900 reminds us of the ongoing importance of campus recreation as a means for every generation to rediscover the ideal place for scholars and students alike:

I began my studies with eagerness. Before me I saw a new world opening in beauty and light, and I felt within me the capacity to know all things.

The lecture-halls seemed filled with the spirit of the great and the wise, and I thought the professors were the embodiment of wisdom.

But I soon discovered that college was not quite the romantic lyceum I had imagined. Many of the dreams that had delighted my young inexperience became beautifully less

and "faded into the light of common day." Gradually I began to find that there were disadvantages in going to college.

The one I felt and still feel most is lack of time. I used to have time to think, to reflect, my mind and I. We would sit together of an evening and listen to the inner melodies of the spirit, which one hears only in leisure moments when the words of some loved poet touch a deep, sweet chord in the soul that until then had been silent. But in college there is no time to commune with one's thoughts. One goes to college to learn, it seems, not to think. When one enters the portals of learning, one leaves the dearest pleasures—solitude, books and imagination—outside with the whispering pines. I suppose I ought to find some comfort in the thought that I am laying up treasures for future enjoyment, but I am improvident enough to prefer present joy to hoarding riches against a rainy day. (Shattuck & Herrmann, 2003, pp. 81-82)

Helen Keller passed the entrance examinations and began her college education at Radcliffe College in the fall of 1900. Her legendary life followed a childhood illness that left her both deaf and blind. She didn't learn language until she was seven, and just a few years after that was famous in this country and abroad. Her story is not simply about the remarkable accomplishments of one woman, for none of this was done without her teacher—the genius Anne Sullivan Macy. Her story continues to influence children around the world.

The passage from Helen's story teaches us what is humanly possible for children with life-altering disabilities, and more. In describing her education at Radcliffe, she joined with all other students who find college life packed with responsibilities that prevent reflective thought and leisure. Students who devote themselves intensely to studies often have little time left for recreation. They too hope, perhaps, to be "laying up treasures for future enjoyment" by getting good grades and completing their degrees in the normal time. They don't take a semester off, and they willingly sacrifice their health to study in order to earn degrees that might give them access to better lives.

Also present 100 years ago and today are students who want college to be filled with more than academics. Seeing the disadvantages to college that Helen did, but could not avoid, this second type of student is more likely to want an active social life along with college-sponsored opportunities for the performing arts, physical fitness, sports, and recreation. From their point of view, the "lyceum" is utopian in that it provides "the capacity to know all things . . . [with] lecture-halls . . . filled with the spirit of the great and the wise, and . . . professors embodied with wisdom."

This utopian ideal of the lyceum gives unbridled access to abundant, excellent intellectual works, creative expressions of every kind, and most important, the freedom to develop and pursue one's interests. Ideally, the college experience should be anti-utilitarian. Students should not have to worry about or be troubled by the routines commonly associated with the externally regulated life of the factory worker. Students can look forward to sleeping late into the day if they choose, they can stay up all night, and they can spend time in long conversations with no particular purpose in mind other than getting to know someone else. The hallmark of this utopia is the reflective life in which self-interest is taken seriously. It is the time to ponder and to act on vitally important questions: What will I do with my life? What will I become? What am I becoming? How can I best pursue my own happiness?

Like Helen Keller, many experience college life not as the utopian ideal, but rather as a way to meet one degree requirement after the next. In that case, the intended outcome of college is a job. A corollary to this position is the intention to earn enough money from work to retire at a young age, thereby turning life from that point on into one marked by leisure. Ironically, leisure as utopia is no more closely approximated in present American society than it is in the life of the undergraduate. It is simply there for the taking.

Conclusion

For some students, recreation and pleasure seeking are the same. Recreation programs offer students the chance to grow up in ways otherwise not present in college life. Taking the risk to join an exercise class, taking a turn at bat, or pushing hard to acquire a new skill can reveal immaturity and what more is needed to achieve adulthood. Recreation can make life better because there is much to be learned by doing what we think is in our best interest.

In the classic children's story, Pinocchio is made out of wood that Master Cheery gave to his friend, the carpenter, Geppetto. Master Cheery recognized this to be a special piece of wood when he drew it out of his pile. It had a voice and spirit long before Geppetto carved it into the boylike puppet Pinocchio. The original version of this children's story has 36 chapters (Collodi, 1946). The cricket, who in the two Walt Disney versions is the persistent voice of a caring mentor, doesn't make it past page 21. Because the talking cricket pitied Pinocchio for being a puppet and having a wooden head, Pinocchio killed him with one blow from a wooden hammer. This freed Pinocchio for adventure. A boy without a conscience (or in this case, the cricket) is bound to choose pleasure and self-interest over reason and virtue at every chance.

Perhaps this story has held its appeal across cultures for decades because it describes what is universally common among human beings. Loving parents suffer when their children misbehave, and they are grateful when their children become adults who strive to be virtuous. Parents know that undisciplined children don't want to work hard at anything. These children live for the moment with no realistic conception of the future. Pinocchio wanted to be a self-made person and learned with each adventure why it was better for him to moderate his pleasure seeking in favor of obeying his father's wishes.

Pinocchio learned, albeit the hard way, that his father Geppetto loved him. Trying to be a good son transformed him from a wooden puppet into a boy. This classic coming-of-age story has appealed to parents and children across cultures and over time. It makes clear one of the lessons to be learned from reading Socrates' dialogue with his friend, Crito: Children ought to respect their parents and teachers.

This story is also a reminder that good character is formed in childhood through parents and teachers. Geppetto did what any caring father would have done for Pinocchio, and he constantly worried for him. For Geppetto knew that even with the best of parents and teachers, there is no way to control moral luck.

Frederick Douglass was a man of excellent character who never had the advantages of sustained love from parents or formal education. Born a slave without the benefit of parents and teachers to guide him, his self-determination proved undeniable. His moral strength seems rather to have arisen first from that universal spark that commonly ignites the moral sense in children, a sense of unfairness and injustice in the way he was treated.

To be ethical is to be just, to do one's level best to lead a good life, fulfilling one's moral responsibilities to oneself and not harming others. These two principles—being the best person we can be and not harming others—are essential for a morally sound life. Imagine how much better the world might be if all adults lived every day with justice as their guide.

Appendix 15.1

NIRSA Code of Ethics

National Intramural-Recreational Sports Association Conflict of Interest Policy

Adopted by the Board of Directors on October 20, 2002

The Board of Directors of the National Intramural-Recreational Sports Association (the "Association") has adopted the following policy to ensure that the affairs of the Association are managed in an ethical manner, free from the temptations for personal gain which conflicting desires may provide. There are no exceptions to this policy.

The Association expects all employees, officers and directors to exercise good judgment and the highest ethical standards in their private activities outside the Association which in any way can affect the Association. In particular, every employee, officer and director has an obligation to avoid any activity, agreement, business investment or interest, or other situation which is in conflict with the Association's interests or interferes with the duty to serve the Association at all times to the best of the person's ability. To implement this principle and to establish clear guidelines, the following policy has been adopted:

No employee shall furnish services to, or seek or receive, for personal or any other person's gain, any payment, whether for services or otherwise, loan (except from a bank), gift or discount of more than nominal value, or entertainment which goes beyond common courtesies usually associated with accepted business practice, from any business enterprise which is a competitor of the Association or has current or known prospective dealings with the Association as a supplier, customer, lessor or lessee, except with the prior written approval of the Executive Director upon complete disclosure of the facts. If the matter involves a director or the Executive Director, then the director or Executive Director must first obtain the prior written approval of the Executive Committee of the Board of Directors upon complete disclosure of the facts.

No employee or director shall for personal or any other person's gain deprive the Association of any opportunity for benefit which could be construed as related to any existing or reasonably anticipated future activity of the Association.

No employee shall have any outside interest which materially interferes with the time or attention that the Employee should devote to the Association.

No employee or director shall have a direct or indirect financial interest in, or receive any compensation or benefits as a result of, transactions between any individual or business firm:

From which the Association purchases supplies, materials or property;

Which renders any service to the Association;

Which enters into leases or assignments to or from the Association;

To which the Association sells any of its products, materials, facilities or properties; or

Which has any other contractual relations or business dealings with the Association;

except with the prior written approval of the Executive Director upon complete disclosure of the facts. If the matter involves a director or the Executive Director, then the director or Executive Director must first obtain the prior written approval of the Executive Committee of the Board of Directors upon complete disclosure of the facts.

The financial interests mentioned above do not include interests in corporations listed on a national stock exchange or traded over the counter, providing the financial interest is one percent or less of said corporation's outstanding shares.

If any employee or director or member of his or her family has or is about to assume an interest or other outside relationship which might result in a conflict of interest, it is the employee's duty and responsibility to immediately give all the pertinent information to the Executive Director, who shall report all information to the President.

Article III, Section 15 of the Bylaws of the Association provides that a conflict of interest on the part of any director must be disclosed or known to the Board of Directors or a committee of the Board of Directors. Transactions in which a director has a conflict of interest may be approved and is not voidable if the transaction is fair to the Association. A conflict of interest may be approved by the Board of Directors as provided for in Article III, Section 15, of the Bylaws.

Appendix 15.2

American Society of Association Executives: Standards of Conduct

ASAE & The Center for Association Leadership's Standards of Conduct have been adopted to promote and maintain the highest standards of association service and professional conduct among Certified Association Executives (CAEs) and Association Chief Executive Members and Association Professional Staff Members of the American Society of Association Executives (ASAE) & The Center for Association Leadership. Adherence to these standards is expected from all CAEs and all Association Chief Executive Members and Association Professional Staff Members and serves to ensure public confidence in the integrity of these constituencies of the association management profession.

As a CAE and/or Association Chief Executive Member or Association Professional Staff Member of ASAE & The Center, I pledge to:

- Maintain exemplary standards of professional conduct.

- Actively model and encourage the integration of ethics into all aspects of management of the association(s) which employ(s) me.

- Pursue the objectives of the association(s) that employ(s) me in ways that are ethical.

- Recognize and discharge my responsibility and that of the association(s) that employ(s) me to uphold all laws and regulations in implementing the policies and conducting the activities of the association(s).

- Strive to continually advance my knowledge and achieve higher levels of excellence in association management.

- Maintain the confidentiality of all privileged information, except when so doing becomes an ethical or legal breach of conduct.

- Serve all members fairly, holding foremost the interests of the association that employs me and its industry or profession; faithfully executing my duties and never using my position for undue personal gain; and promptly and completely disclosing to appropriate parties all potential and actual conflicts of interest.

- Actively encourage all people qualified or eligible to be a part of the association(s) which employ(s) me to participate in the activities and leadership of the association as appropriate.

- Communicate all association internal and external information to the elected leadership(s) and membership of the association(s), which employ(s) me in a truthful and accurate manner to facilitate timely execution of their fiduciary responsibilities.

- Actively advance, support, and promote association membership and the profession of association management through word and deed.

Narrative Description of Standards of Conduct Provisions

Maintain exemplary standards of professional conduct. As with an elected official, an association executive's professional conduct is held up to public scrutiny due to the dual obligation to serve both the association's members' interests as well as the public's interests, requiring the association executive to be a leading citizen of the community. Maintenance of these standards of conduct requires an unwavering commitment on the part of the association executive to live a life above reproach.

Actively model and encourage the integration of ethics into all aspects of management of the association(s) which employ(s) me. Association executives fulfill an important leadership role. In this role, they have the opportunity to enhance the ethical awareness of their members. They have the obligation to actively apply ethics throughout the activities of the association, and simultaneously throughout the management of the association.

Pursue the objectives of the association(s) that employ(s) me in ways that are ethical. An association executive has a primary and fundamental responsibility to loyally serve the interests of the association and the members of the association. At the same time, however, the executive has a responsibility to operate in an ethical manner. Where an association executive believes that the direction of the association raises an ethical conflict, there is a responsibility to notify the governing body of the association of this opinion; and, should the conflict become irreconcilable, the executive has a responsibility to maintain individual integrity and act to preserve the highest ethical standards.

Recognize and discharge my responsibility and that of the association(s) that employ(s) me to uphold all laws and regulations in implementing the policies and conducting the activities of the association(s). An association executive has a responsibility to be familiar with the basic principles of law and regulation, which affect the association. As a leader of the association, the executive has a responsibility to help members understand the legal framework within which they operate in the association, and to make sure that all policies of the association are formulated, and all activities are conducted within this framework.

Strive to continually advance my knowledge and achieve higher levels of excellence in association management. Association executives have a responsibility to keep current with the best thinking in the field of association management and to apply their best management ability in all of the affairs of the association.

Maintain the confidentiality of all privileged information, except when so doing becomes an ethical or legal breach of conduct. Association executives frequently have access to privileged information, and are expected to exercise discretion in handling it. If association executives find themselves the recipients of information that potentially places the association and/or the association executive at risk legally, they should seek to protect the association and/or themselves while recognizing the confidentiality of the information.

Serve all members fairly, holding foremost the interests of the association that employs me and its industry or profession; faithfully executing my duties and never using my position for undue personal gain; and promptly and completely disclosing to appropriate parties all potential and actual conflicts of interest. By virtue of position, association executives may find themselves able to grant special favors to members, vendors, and others. Association executives have a responsibility to represent the interests of all members fairly and should avoid incurring an obligation to a single individual or some fraction of the membership.

Association executives also have a responsibility to make the best possible management decisions in the interest of the association without regard to personal gain. Therefore, executives should take special care to avoid either the fact or the appearance of personal gain in decision-making, and should never leverage their position to receive special favors, either as opportunities or gifts, for personal gain, that would also impact impartiality in decision-making for the association. To this end, association executives should always promptly and completely disclose all their potential and actual conflicts of interest to appropriate parties.

Actively encourage all people qualified or eligible to be a part of the association(s) which employ(s) me to participate in the activities and leadership of the association. Association executives have a unique opportunity to be a voice for inclusiveness, mentorship, and leadership development within the context of the association(s) which employ(s) them and there is an obligation for association executives to use this voice at every opportunity.

Communicate all association internal and external information to the elected leadership(s) and membership of the association(s), which employ(s) me in a truthful and accurate manner to facilitate timely execution of their fiduciary responsibilities. The essence of effective communication is credibility. The association executive has a responsibility to maintain credible lines of communication both within the association and between the association and its publics. All communications should represent honest, clear, and unimpeachable statements of fact, and recommendations and opinions when expressed should be clearly stated as such.

Actively advance, support, and promote association membership and the profession of association management through word and deed. Theodore Roosevelt said, "Every man owes a part of his time and his money to the profession which supports his way of life." Association executives who do not actively take part in the affairs of their own professional association are in a weakened posture to influence their own members to participate in their associations. Association executives should actively participate in the full spectrum of activities of their own professional association through the contributions of presence, time, and resources. They should also strive to build collaborative relationships with their association management colleagues and others for the advancement of the profession of association management and use every opportunity to improve public understanding of the profession and the positive impact of associations on our society.

www.asaecenter.org/AboutUs/content.cfm?ItemNumber=16007

References

Aristotle. (1980). *Nicomachean ethics* (Ross translation, revised by Ackrill and Urmson). New York: The Oxford University Press.

Collodi, C. (1946). *The adventures of Pinocchio*. New York: Grosset & Dunlap.

Delattre, E.J. (1996). *Character and cops* (3rd ed.). Washington, DC: The AEI Press.

Dulles, F. (1965). *A history of recreation: America learns to play*. New York: Appleton-Century-Crofts.

Frankena, W. (1973). *Ethics* (2nd ed.). Englewood Cliffs, NJ: Prentice Hall.

Locke J. (1689). A letter concerning toleration. (William Popple, Trans.). Retrieved from www.constitution.org/jl/tolerati.htm.

Nohe, C. (2000). Duty to warn: Who? When? Retrieved from www.ksbsrb.org/dutytowarn.html.

Pantera, M., et al. (2003). Game day security operations checklist, Springfield College, Massachusetts. Retrieved from www.thesportjournal.org/2003Journal/Vol6-No4/documents/Checklist-GameDaySecurity.pdf.

Shattuck, R., & Herrmann, D. (2003). *Helen Keller: The story of my life*. New York: Norton.

Tigner, S. (1995). Signs of the soul. In G. S. Fain (Ed.), *Leisure and Ethics*. Reston, VA: American Alliance for Health, Physical Education, Recreation and Dance.

Washington, G. (1790). A letter in response to Moses Seixas, the Hebrew Congregation in Newport, Rhode Island. Retrieved from www.tourosynagogue.org/GWLetter2.php.

Glossary

codes of ethics—Principles and standards voluntarily developed and agreed to by professionals for the purpose of protecting the public from harm. These codes are intended to secure the public trust and to be useful for the induction of new members of the respective profession.

commutative justice—The moral position that justice is achieved when one gets what one has earned. Students earn grades. Accordingly, it would be morally unjust for a teacher to assign grades without regard to merit.

deontology—Ethical theories that view moral obligation as duty without regard to its consequences. For example, one can take the moral position that capital punishment is wrong and sustain that position without qualification no matter what the circumstance or consequence.

distributive justice—The fair distribution of good and evil. According to this normative theory, equals deserve comparable treatment. While we distinguish between the punishment of juveniles and adults found guilty of crimes in our system of justice, we expect all juveniles to be treated the same, and likewise for adults. In the distribution of goods, the same idea applies—equals are entitled to their fair share.

ethical dilemma—A moral problem without a satisfactory solution—for example, having to make a decision that will result in harm.

ethical egoist—A person who believes that whatever is in his or her best interest is morally correct. These individuals may not break the law, simply because going to jail or having to pay a fine is not in their interest. At the same time, ethical egoists see no value in helping others unless they believe it is in their interest to do so. The ethical egoist does not believe in or practice altruism or beneficence.

ethics—Ethics is moral philosophy, a branch of philosophy concerned with reasoning, judgments, and thinking about moral problems. The philosophic study of morality.

friendship—An achievement between people that is freely formed for the sake of the other and without contractual obligations. There are various types of friendships. Aristotle distinguished between friendships that exist between superiors and subordinates, fleeting friendships of utility and pleasure, and the perfect and enduring form, where the moral excellence of the other is admired for its own sake.

justice—The equal treatment of equals, classically studied as being either commutative or distributive. Plato considered justice the central question for political thought.

retributive justice—Commonly understood as "an eye for an eye, and a tooth for a tooth," retributive justice is based on the moral defense of punishment as a means of balancing the consequences of harm. This position is in contrast to more forward-looking moral principles embodied in forgiveness, where resolution of an unjust act has to do with advancing the possibilities for moral enlightenment. For example, being sorry—having genuine feelings of guilt—can change the way a person reasons and behaves in the future and can justify forgiveness over retribution.

teleology—Ethical theories that view moral obligation as aiming for the greatest good. In contrast to deontological theories, consequences matter. The aim is to end up doing the least harm while achieving the greatest happiness.

values—Generally considered a common conception of what is good, useful, important, or desirable. A nonmoral value is in the utility of something, such as a "good" car. Moral values are good simply because they are moral.

CHAPTER 16

Sustainability: Road Map to Implementation and Practice

Anthony D. Cortese, PhD, President, Second Nature, Inc.
Julian Dautremont-Smith, BA, Associate Director, Association for the Advancement of Sustainability in Higher Education

> Today's problems cannot be solved by the same level of thinking from which they were created.
>
> *Albert Einstein*

This chapter explores the role of higher education in creating a healthy, just, secure, and sustainable society now and in the future, a defining challenge of this century. It outlines the dimensions of the challenge and the role of higher education in both creating the mind-set that has led society to this point in history and what it can do to meet the challenge. A road map for making sustainability a foundation of all education and practice is presented, as well as some of the more promising and exciting efforts by higher education institutions that model sustainability in activities and operations.

What Is Sustainability?

The literal definition of **sustainability** refers to the ability to maintain a positive status or set of conditions over time. In the past two decades, the concept of sustainability that has emerged as an aspiration for the direction of society evolved from the conclusions of the World Commission on Environment and Development (WCED) in its 1987 landmark report titled *Our Common Future.* Established by the United Nations, WCED examined the worldwide problems of environmental pollution, degradation, and destruction and their relationship to hunger, poverty, public health, and social and political structure. Contrary to conventional wisdom, traditional economic development was making all of these environmental problems worse. WCED called for a new kind of development—sustainable development—that meets the needs of the present without compromising the ability of future generations to meet their own needs (United Nations World Commission on Environment and Development, 1987). The WCED report led to the United Nations Conference on Environment and Development, popularly known as the Earth Summit, in Brazil in 1992. During this conference, 162 heads of state developed Agenda 21, a 21-point action plan for human progress in the 21st century. Agenda 21 set the international framework for sustainable development and international environmental treaties, and its definition of sustainable development became the most commonly accepted meaning for what is now called *sustainability.*

The purpose of the international commitment to Agenda 21 was to improve health for current and future humans; build strong, secure, and thriving communities; and provide economic opportunity for all by restoring and preserving the integrity of the life support system—the bio-

sphere. Sustainability is not just about protecting the environment; it is also about finding ways to meet the basic needs of all current and future generations. This can be done only by finding a better way for humans to live within the "cradle of life." The earth and its ecosystems provide all the resources and services that make life possible, including the conversion of waste products into useful substances. Humans can live about three minutes without breathing, three days without water, and three weeks without food. Food, shelter, fuel, pharmaceuticals, water, and all economic activity derive from the earth's biosphere. For these reasons, sustainability advocates have focused primarily on the environmental dimensions of sustainability. Unless we also simultaneously focus on the health, social, and economic aspects of sustainability, it is unlikely that we will achieve the desired result—a better life for current and future generations.

21st-Century Challenge

Notwithstanding the international agreements that emerged from the Earth Summit in 1992, humanity is still at a crossroads. For the first time in human history, the size and scale of the human population and its technological and economic prowess have made humanity a pervasive and dominant force in the health and well-being of the earth and its inhabitants. No part of the earth is unaffected by humans, and the scale of our impact is huge and growing exponentially. (The Inuit in Alaska have the highest level of the toxic chemicals **polychlorinated biphenyls** and **DDT** in their bodies in the world, despite being 1,000 miles from any industrial activity.) Despite all the work we have done on environmental protection, all living systems are in long-term decline and are declining at an increasing rate according to all international scientific, health, and policy organizations. And the challenge that will accelerate all of the negative trends is global warming, which is leading to unprecedented destabilization of the earth's climate.

Human progress has accelerated in the last 10,000 years during a time of a relatively stable climate. Global warming is now destabilizing the earth's climate in ways that threaten to reverse this progress and undermine the survival of millions of people now and in the future. The resulting climate disruption is real and is already affecting us; it is worse and happening faster than predicted by the most conservative scientists. This is happening with 20 percent of the world's population consuming 80 percent of the world's resources. How will we cope in a world that will soon have 9 billion people and that plans to increase gross world product by 500 percent by 2050? This is an awesome ethical responsibility for us, especially those of us in higher education. We can meet this challenge if we act rapidly and decisively to provide the necessary education and research and make higher education a model for sustainable living.

We need an unprecedented shift in the way we think and act. We currently view health, social, economic, political, security, population, environmental, and other major societal issues as separate, competing, and hierarchical when they are really systemic and interdependent. For example, we do not have environmental problems, per se. We have negative environmental consequences of the way we have designed our social, economic, and political system. *We have a de facto systems design failure.* The 21st-century challenges must be addressed in a systemic, integrated, and holistic fashion. *Sustainability requires that we focus simultaneously on systemic changes that improve health for current and future humans; build strong, secure, and thriving communities; and provide economic opportunity for all by restoring and preserving the integrity of the life support system.*

Higher education plays a unique and critical role, one often overlooked, in making this vision a reality. Higher education has been granted tax-free status, the ability to receive public and private funds, and academic freedom in exchange for educating students and producing the knowledge that will result in a thriving and civil society. It prepares most of the professionals who develop, lead, manage, teach, work in, and influence society's institutions, including the most basic foundation of K-12 education. Besides training future teachers, higher education strongly influences the learning framework of K-12 education, which is largely geared toward subsequent higher education. For the first time in U.S. history, 70 percent of children in the K-12 system intend to go to college. Moreover, given the need for a much more highly skilled workforce for the 21st century, lifelong education has become another critical role for higher education.

However, the current educational system is reinforcing the current unhealthy, inequitable, and unsustainable path that society is pursuing. The people who are leading most of society's institutions down this path are graduates of the best colleges, universities, and professional schools in the world. As David Orr (1994) said, the crisis humanity is facing is a "crisis of mind, perception and heart. It is not a problem *in* education; it is a problem *of* education" (p. 126). This is not intentional; it is a function of a worldview that is no longer suitable to create a world that works for everyone. Higher education, following and enabling this worldview, is generally organized into highly specialized areas of knowledge and traditional disciplines. Designing a sustainable human future requires a paradigm shift toward a systemic perspective emphasizing interdisciplinary understanding, collaboration, and cooperation that must be led by those in higher education.

Leading the Transition to a Sustainable Society

What if higher education were to take a leadership role, as it did in the space race and the war on cancer, in preparing students and providing the information and knowledge to achieve a just and sustainable society? The education of all professionals would reflect a new approach to learning and practice. A college or university would operate as a fully integrated community that models social and biological sustainability within itself and in its interdependence with the local, regional, and global communities.

In many cases, we think of teaching, research, operations, and relations with local communities as separate activities; they are not. All parts of the university are critical in helping to create transformative change in the individual and collective mind-set. Everything that happens at a university and every impact, positive and negative, of university activities shapes the knowledge, skills, and values of the students. Future education must connect head, heart, and hands. The educational experience must reflect an intimate connection between curriculum and (1) research; (2) understanding and reducing any negative ecological and social footprint of the institution; and (3) working to improve local and regional communities so that they are healthier, more socially vibrant and stable, economically secure, and environmentally sustainable (see figure 16.1).

Just imagine if in the 21st century the educational experience of all students were aligned with the principles of sustainability.

- The *content of learning* would reflect interdisciplinary systems thinking, dynamics,

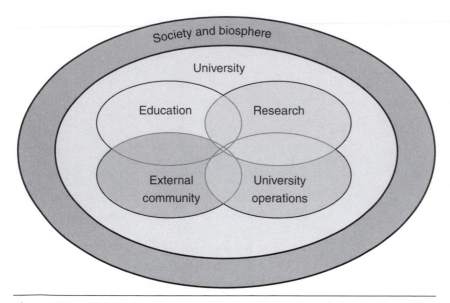

Figure 16.1 Higher education modeling sustainability as a fully integrated community.

efforts to the formal curriculum. The university is a microcosm of the larger community. Therefore, the way it carries out its daily activities is an important demonstration of ways to achieve environmentally responsible living and to reinforce desired values and behaviors in the whole community. These activities provide unparalleled opportunities for teaching, research, and learning.

• Higher education would form *partnerships with local and regional communities* to help make them healthy, socially vibrant, economically secure, and environmentally sustainable as an integral part of higher education's mission and the student experience. Higher education institutions are anchor institutions for economic development in most of their communities, especially now that the private

and analysis for all majors, disciplines, and professional degrees. Education would have the same rigor across disciplines as it has within disciplines.

• The *context of learning* would change to make human–environment interdependence, values, and ethics a seamless and central part of the teaching of all the disciplines, rather than isolated as a special course or module in programs for specialists. All students would understand that we are an integral part of nature. They would understand the ecological services that are critical for human existence, including how to make health, social, economic, and environmental impacts as positive as possible and *visible*. For example, most people do not know that it takes several thousand pounds of fossil fuels, metallic ore, and chemicals to produce a laptop computer. The energy and resource use, pollution, and waste that is incurred during the manufacture are invisible to the final consumer, especially because that impact typically occurs a great distance from where the product is finally sold.

• The *process of education* would emphasize active, experiential, inquiry-based learning and real-world problem solving on the campus and in the larger community.

• Higher education would *practice sustainability*. Institutions of higher learning would practice what they preach and make sustainability an integral part of operations, planning, facility design, purchasing, and investments, and tie these

Courtesy of Sonoma State University.

These tiles are made in the United States and are composed of over 55 percent recycled glass. Reusing recycled glass is an environmentally sound alternative to using raw materials.

sector moves facilities, capital, and jobs frequently as mergers, acquisitions, and globalization become the norm for corporations. The 4,000 higher education institutions in the United States are, themselves, large economic engines with annual operational budgets that totaled $317 billion in 2003. This is greater than the gross domestic product of all but 25 countries in the world.

Can Higher Education Meet This Challenge?

At issue is not the ability of higher education to take on the sustainability challenge, but rather the will and the time frame for doing so. Most of the world's major international governmental, scientific, and nongovernmental institutions, as well as many business organizations, agree that the changes needed in individual and collective values and action must occur within the next decade. If higher education does not lead the sustainability effort in society, who will?

Fortunately, there are hundreds of examples of changes in all areas of higher education activities that help students and the rest of the campus community understand and implement actions that align with the principles of sustainability, and the number is increasing exponentially. Following are some examples of the innovative actions being taken at U.S. colleges and universities. These lists are by no means exhaustive. They also do not cover the encouraging work of over 500 colleges and universities that grow their own food or purchase locally and organically produced food. A more extensive and growing list of examples is available through the American Association for the Advancement of Sustainability in Higher Education (www.aashe.org).

Institutionalizing Sustainability

The following institutions have achieved or pledged to achieve energy independence, reductions in greenhouse gases, or green building design.

- *Climate neutral commitments.* Four hundred college and university presidents have committed their institutions to achieving **carbon neutrality**—that is, no net emissions of carbon dioxide that cause global warming—and to providing the education and research for the rest of society to do the same (American College & University Presidents Climate Commitment, 2007). These small and large public and private institutions

from 47 states include Cornell, University of Pennsylvania, College of the Atlantic, Carleton and Oberlin Colleges, Arizona State University, Lane Community College, Cape Cod Community College, the Los Angeles Community College District, University of North Carolina at Chapel Hill, University of Florida, University of Colorado at Boulder, University of Idaho, and the entire University of California system.

- *Comprehensive policies.* The 10-campus University of California system passed a policy to meet 20 percent of its electricity needs from renewable sources by 2017, ensure that 10 percent of its energy comes from locally generated clean sources by 2014, reduce energy consumption by 10 percent by 2014, hold all new buildings and renovations to stringent efficiency standards, require that a percentage of university fleets be converted to low emissions or carbon-free vehicles by 2010, and implement a plan to track and reduce university-related personal vehicle trips. The 23-campus CSU system followed suit with similar policies mandating renewable energy purchase and installation, conservation, and green building (California State University Public Affairs Office, n.d.; California Student Sustainability Coalition, 2004; Renewable Energy Access, 2005; University of California, 2006).

- *Building policies.* The Los Angeles Community College District (2006), encompassing nine colleges that collectively educate over 130,000 students per year, is currently undertaking one of the largest public sector sustainable building efforts in the United States. More than 18 American colleges and universities have adopted LEED (Leadership in Energy and Environmental Design) building policies, and another nine have approved policies that require green design for all new buildings (Association for the Advancement of Sustainability in Higher Education, 2006). The improved performance of green buildings, coupled with cost savings, has prompted over 10 states to require all new state-funded or public buildings to comply with LEED standards (U.S. Green Building Council, 2006).

- *Carbon trading.* The Universities of Oklahoma, Minnesota, and Iowa, and Michigan State University have joined the Chicago Climate Exchange (CCX), North America's only legally binding greenhouse gas (GHG) emission registry, reduction, and **carbon trading** system. In joining, these institutions have committed to either reducing their GHG emissions each year beginning in 2003, or to buying **carbon offsets** from another member to bring them into compliance with CCX's membership terms. As member institutions continue to lower their emissions, they may benefit from the sale of their emission allowances through CCX (Chicago Climate Exchange, 2006; Tufts Climate Initiative, 2003).

• *Investing.* Harvard University's Green Loan Fund is an interest-free revolving fund that provides capital for projects that reduce pollution and resource and energy consumption. The fund is paid back with energy efficiency savings. This fund solves the common problem of separate capital and operating budgets, which creates a disincentive to invest in more efficient designs and technologies. The Green Loan Fund realizes a consistent return on investment of over 30 percent (Harvard Green Campus Initiative, 2006).

• *Student leadership.* Students at the University of Colorado at Boulder organized a vote increasing student fees ($1 per semester) to purchase the entire output of a wind turbine that produced 2 million kilowatt hours per year of energy.

They later voted to expand the wind purchase to 8.8 million kilowatt hours per year, reducing annual carbon dioxide emissions by 12 million pounds (University of Colorado Environmental Center, 2006). More than 25 additional institutions have approved similar renewable energy fees. Students at over 380 campuses have joined the Campus Climate Challenge to promote GHG reductions at their institutions (Energy Action Coalition, 2006).

Model Projects in Energy and Transportation

Some model projects include renewable energy, conservation, and transportation initiatives.

• *Renewable energy.* In 2004 Carleton College used money from its endowment to build a 1.65-megawatt wind turbine that produces enough electricity to supply 40 percent of the college's electricity use. With state financial incentives, the project's payback period is 10 years—providing 10

A south-facing lobby and no west-facing windows prevent excess heat in the building. Overhangs shade windows from high summer sun, but not the lower winter sun. Low-e glazing on all windows keeps a constant temperature inside the building by blocking heat but allowing light to enter.

Courtesy of Sonoma State University.

Skylights allow natural light to be used. This is the most energy efficient way to light any space.

Courtesy of Sonoma State University.

years of earnings on investment (Carleton College Facilities Management, 2006). Mount Wachusett Community College converted its electric heating system to a biomass hydronic district heating system, reducing its carbon dioxide emissions by 23 percent over four years and saving $300,000 in annual fuel costs (Mount Wachusett Community College, 2006). Napa Valley College installed a 1.2-megawatt photovoltaic solar array on its campus, saving the college $300,000 annually on its electric bills (De Leon-Menjivar, 2006). More than 130 campuses have on-site renewable energy generation capacity, collectively producing over 50 megawatts of clean energy. More than 70 educational institutions are buying renewable energy (U.S. Environmental Protection Agency, 2006b), with Bates, Bowdoin, and Colby Colleges; Evergreen State College; New York University; Western Washington University; University of Central Oklahoma; and College of the Atlantic powered 100 percent renewably (U.S. Environmental Protection Agency, 2006a).

- *Conservation.* At the State University of New York at Buffalo, students, faculty, and staff have practiced energy conservation through the university's Conserve UB program since the late 1970s. In 2003 the You Have the Power campaign saved the school $10,000 in energy costs *in a single day.* Documented energy savings are in excess of $10 million annually and $100 million since the beginning of the program (University of New York at Buffalo, 2006).

- *Transportation initiatives.* Cornell University has raised parking fees, redrawn parking systems to favor carpooling, integrated school transit systems with the city's, and given free public transit throughout the county to anyone who doesn't get a parking pass. These efforts have saved 417,000 gallons of fuel and 10,000,000 vehicle miles traveled annually, cutting costs by more than $36 million and reducing greenhouse gas emissions by 51,100 tons over 12 years (Cornell University, 2006). Several hundred colleges and universities are implementing plans to make their campuses more pedestrian and bicycle friendly, thereby saving money and reducing their ecological footprints.

Education for Climate Neutrality and Sustainability

Some institutions are already transforming education. Northern Arizona University and Emory University have implemented faculty development programs that have helped approximately 200 faculty revise 300 courses in virtually every discipline to make sustainability the context or the content of learning. These courses reach more than 15,000 students annually. The University of Georgia has made course work in environmental literacy a requirement for all graduates (University of Georgia, 2006); sustainability is the foundation of all curricula at the six members of the Eco League (2006). Cape Cod Community College is developing renewable energy education and training in collaboration with technical high schools and nonprofits.

Making sustainability one of its top priorities, Arizona State University in 2006 established the first School of Sustainability—a degree-granting unit fully dedicated to sustainability at the BS, MS, and PhD levels. The new school advances the scholarship of sustainability science and policy and facilitates the offerings of sustainability-focused degrees and minors in law, business, engineering, architecture, planning, and education. It hopes to eventually include all majors and professional offerings.

Sustainability in Athletics Programs

Other institutions are making efforts to achieve sustainability in their athletics programs.

- *Middlebury College ski facility and ski teams go carbon neutral.* Beginning with the 2006-2007 ski season, the Middlebury College Snow Bowl will be a carbon neutral ski facility (Middlebury College, 2006). The college is offsetting electric, gas, propane, diesel, and biodiesel usage, as well as skier transportation to and from the ski area. To achieve carbon neutrality, the college purchased carbon offsets for the ski area's 2006-2007 operations in the amount of $7,138 to compensate for a total of 679.9 tons of carbon dioxide emissions. The Middlebury alpine and nordic ski teams have also become carbon neutral by purchasing carbon offsets to compensate for the teams' carbon dioxide emissions related to everything from travel to the electricity used to power the coaches' offices.

- *Green design.* Haverford College's Douglas B. Gardner Athletic Center is among seven sport facility projects in the United States that were certified at the gold level by the U.S. Green Building Council for sustainable design. It is the only one to our knowledge at a college or university anywhere. In a May 31, 2006, *USA Today* article, Haverford's president Tom Tritton said,

"I believe educational institutions can be among the leaders in creating energy-efficient, environmentally-friendly and beautiful buildings on our campuses" (Ruibal & Upton, 2006). The University of Connecticut and Oregon State University have recently built athletic facilities that are in alignment with sustainability principles (Oregon State University, n.d.; University of Connecticut, n.d.).

• *Conservation and recycling.* The University of Michigan has had an active conservation and recycling program at its football games since 1995. In the seven games of the 2006 season attended by 770,000 people, 120 tons of mixed refuse were recycled and 76,000 gallons of water and 46,000 kilowatts of electricity were saved. Recycling of paperboard and paper saved 186 large trees (University of Michigan Plant Operation Division, n.d.). For the first time at an Auburn University football game, people will be encouraged to recycle their trash instead of littering or throwing it away. Under a new program, lucky football fans "caught" correctly using new recycling bins at the stadium will receive miniature helmets autographed by the head coach. Fourteen miniature helmets will be given away over the course of the season, with two being awarded during each home game (Auburn Plainsman, n.d.).

Conclusion

Broad transformative change and leadership in higher education have large implications for college and university directors of athletics and recreation. Taking the educational experience from a theoretical to a practical level will have an impact on the way institutions interact with external communities. This shift will certainly affect the leaders who are necessarily the most interdisciplinary and long-range thinkers and connected to the decision-making structure of higher education.

Making sustainability the lens through which colleges and universities view all of their actions will have major lasting benefits:

• Improve learning for all—inside and outside higher education
• Prepare students for citizenship and career
• Meet increasing student desires for sustainable living
• Increase external respect from alumni, businesses, and communities

• Attract students, faculty, and funding
• Reduce economic, social, and environmental costs
• Cooperation and satisfaction across the university
• Fulfillment of moral and social responsibilities

Finding a way for 9 billion people to live in harmony with each other and the natural world of which we are a part is the defining challenge of the 21st century, and higher education must lead the effort to address this challenge. What will society say about higher education if there is runaway climate change and those with the expertise and the mandate to create a thriving society didn't do everything they could to help society recognize the risks and find solutions to the challenge? Higher education could lose its lofty perch in society, which would be a tragedy for humanity.

We *can* provide this leadership in higher education by making ourselves fully aware of the impact of daily and long-term decisions and consciously teaching and modeling the behavior and actions that will lead to a healthy, just, and sustainable world.

References

American College & University Presidents Climate Commitment. (2007). Retrieved from www.presidentsclimatecommitment.org/index.php.

Association for the Advancement of Sustainability in Higher Education. (2006). Campus building guidelines and green building policies. Retrieved from www.aashe.org/resources/building_policies.php.

Auburn Plainsman, The. (n.d.). Retrieved from www.theplainsman.com/vnews/display.v/ART/43175e5a2029f.

California State University Public Affairs Office. (n.d.). CSU moves to greener policy. Retrieved from www.calstate.edu/pa/news/2005/green.shtml.

California Student Sustainability Coalition. (2004). Renew CSU news. Retrieved from www.renewcsu.org.

Carleton College Facilities Management. (2006). The history of Carleton's wind turbine. Retrieved from http://apps.carleton.edu/campus/facilities/sustainability/wind_turbine.

Chicago Climate Exchange. (2006). Members of the Chicago Climate Exchange. Retrieved from www.chicagoclimatex.com/about/members.html.

Cornell University. (2006). Transportation demand management. Retrieved from www.sustainablecampus.cornell.edu/gettingaround/demand.html.

De Leon-Menjivar, D. (2006, February). Solar project christened Wednesday will provide 40 percent of campus power needs. *Napa Valley Register*. Retrieved from www.napavalleyregister.com/articles/2006/02/23/news/local/iq_3313657.txt.

Eco League. (2006). About the Eco League. Retrieved from www.ecoleague.org/about/index.php.

Energy Action Coalition. (2006). Campus Climate Challenge. Retrieved from http://climatechallenge.org

Harvard Green Campus Initiative. (2006). The Green Campus Loan Fund. Retrieved from www.greencampus.harvard.edu/gclf/index.php.

Los Angeles Community College District. (2006, October). Proposition A/AA. Retrieved from www.propositiona.org.

Middlebury College. (2006, October 30). Middlebury College ski facility takes carbon neutrality to new heights. Retrieved from www.middlebury.edu/about/pubaff/news_releases/2006/news632977987165870677.htm.

Mount Wachusett Community College. (2006). MWCC Biomass Conversion Project. Retrieved from www.mwcc.mass.edu/renewable/conversion.html.

Oregon State University. (n.d.). Reser Stadium expansion. Retrieved from http://oregonstate.edu/sustainability/projects.html.

Orr, D.W. (1994). *Earth in mind: On education, environment and the human prospect*. Washington, DC: Island Press.

Renewable Energy Access. (2005, September). Cal State agrees to landmark clean energy policy. Retrieved from http://renewableenergyaccess.com/rea/news/story?id=36910.

Ruibal, S., & Upton, J. (2006, May 31). Sports facilities can be Earth-friendly. *USA Today*, p. C-2.

Tufts Climate Initiative. (2003). Chicago Climate Exchange. Retrieved from www.tufts.edu/tie/tci/CCX.htm.

United Nations World Commission on Environment and Development. (1987). *Report of the World Commission on Environment and Development: Our Common Future*. Oxford: Oxford University Press.

University of California. (2006, July). University of California sustainability policies and best practices. Retrieved from www.ucop.edu/facil/sustain/welcome.html.

University of Colorado Environmental Center. (2006). Renewable energy at CU. Retrieved from http://ecenter.colorado.edu/energy/cu/renewables.html.

University of Connecticut. (n.d.). Retrieved from http://advance.uconn.edu/2005/050314/05031410.htm.

University of Georgia. (2006). Environmental literacy requirement. Retrieved from http://bulletin.uga.edu/bulletin/prg/uga_req.html.

University of Michigan Plant Operation Division. (n.d.). Stadium recycling program. Retrieved from www.plantops.umich.edu/grounds/recycle/stadium_recycling.html.

University of New York at Buffalo. (2006). You have the power. Retrieved from www.buffalo.edu/youhavethepower/yhtp.html.

U.S. Environmental Protection Agency. (2006a). 2006 college and university green power challenge. Retrieved from www.epa.gov/greenpower/partners/hi_ed_challenge.htm.

U.S. Environmental Protection Agency. (2006b). EPA Green Power Partnership partner list. Retrieved from www.epa.gov/greenpower/partners/gpp_partners2.htm.

U.S. Green Building Council. (2006, October). LEED initiatives in governments and schools. Retrieved from www.usgbc.org/ShowFile.aspx?DocumentID=691.

Glossary

carbon neutrality—Reducing or offsetting an individual or organization's carbon dioxide emissions so that there are no net emissions. This is achieved through reducing energy-consuming activities, using cleaner technologies to reduce carbon emissions, and offsetting emissions indirectly. (See *carbon offsets*.)

carbon offsets—A means by which individuals, companies, and organizations can compensate for the carbon dioxide emissions that are a result of their energy use. Offsets can be purchased from third party companies and organizations, which then invest in projects that will compensate for these emissions such as energy efficiency, emissions reductions, renewable energy, and carbon sequestration projects (usually through reforestation).

carbon trading—A means for reducing net carbon dioxide emissions (and other greenhouse gases) by setting a limit or cap that any institution or entity is allowed to emit. Institutions that emit carbon dioxide beyond the specified limit must purchase credits or allowances from the regulating body. As an incentive to reduce emissions, those that emit less than their allowance may sell their credits.

DDT—Carcinogenic and mutagenic pesticides used for mosquito spraying that were banned for most purposes in the United States in 1972. They persist in the natural environment for decades to centuries, enter the food chain, increase in concentration as one moves up the food chain, and are stored in human fat tissue.

polychlorinated biphenyls—Carcinogenic chemicals used in electrical transformers whose new production was banned in 1977 in the United States. They persist in the natural environment for decades to centuries, enter the food chain, increase in concentration as one moves up the food chain (e.g., tuna and whales), and are stored in human fat tissue.

sustainability—Literally, the ability to maintain a positive status or set of conditions over time. The term is also used interchangeably with *sustainable development,* which is "development that meets the needs of the present without compromising the ability of future generations to meet their own needs" (United Nations WCED, 1987).

CHAPTER 17

Campus Recreation Careers and Professional Standards

NIRSA and Douglas S. Franklin, CRSS, PhD, Assistant Dean for Recreation and Wellness, Ohio University at Athens

> Choose a job you love, and you will never have to work a day in your life.
>
> *Confucius*

The complex nature of campus recreation and the influence of recreation and sport, student development, and business on the operations of programs greatly influence standard knowledge in the field. It is an interdisciplinary field, and career opportunities exist in diverse places. This chapter is divided into two sections. The first covers careers in campus recreation. It explores the progression of campus recreation career options, ranging from a student employee to a full-time professional. Average job salaries and years of experience are also included. The second section of the chapter covers industry and professional standards in campus recreation and provides information regarding professions, the accountability cycle, and the role standards and outcomes play in—as well as the process of knowledge development and dissemination that guides—the practice of recreational sport professionals.

CAMPUS RECREATION CAREERS
NIRSA

Professional Preparation and Progression

As with any career, academic preparation and experience are paramount in the field of recreation. Jobs in this field range from full-time professional to part-time seasonal. Employment opportunities exist with the National Park or Forest Service, state park systems, municipal park and recreation departments, private health clubs, hospitals and health care organizations, camps, hotels and resorts, cruise ships, YMCAs, community service organizations, U.S. military organizations, colleges and universities, the travel and tourism industry, theme parks, commercial recreation, private entrepreneurship, corporate settings, and correctional institutions. The opportunities are endless, and it is often a combination of preparation, skill set, work ethic, personal attributes, and being in the right place at the right time that lands that first job or begins that ideal career.

The range and scope of jobs and careers in campus recreation are also quite broad. Smaller universities may employ one person to teach academic classes, coach a varsity team, and schedule and maintain the intramural program within one facility shared by three departments. In contrast, the largest universities may employ over 30 full-time professionals and paraprofessionals and 500 or more part-time students to support the broad

campus recreation programming that takes place in numerous indoor and outdoor facilities.

Obtaining a professional position in the campus recreation field is not often the goal of incoming freshmen. Most high school students don't even realize that careers exist in higher education that aren't academic or research related. They may not know that the residence hall assignment they receive, the menu planned for their dining hall, the movie scheduled at the student union, or the afternoon kickboxing class were most likely coordinated by a career professional. Students often find out about these careers when they start looking for jobs on campus. A common career path for the campus recreation professional may include a progression from student employee, to student supervisor, to graduate assistant or intern, to professional.

Student Employment Options

As a job-related field, campus recreation enables a large segment of students planning to enter the employment market to receive training and experience in recreation programming and facility management. Student employees are often given a great deal of responsibility and learn how to deal with the challenges of providing recreation services and programs to a large, diverse, and demanding population. Those experiences enable them to pursue a job in the "real world" within the profession of campus recreation and parks and recreation (Lewis, Jones, Lamke, & Dunn, 1998).

Students often seek employment on campus for convenience and familiarity. Student jobs are often very flexible, offering a variety of opportunities to work around academic schedules. Some positions may require specific skills and **certifications.** Many programs require that at a minimum staff be certified in basic first aid and CPR. Some common student positions in a campus recreation program, and a brief description of each, follow:

- *Facility greeter, identification check.* Many campus recreation programs have a controlled entry into their facilities. Students, faculty, and staff generally present their university IDs to gain entry.

- *Equipment checkout.* Equipment that is often checked out to facility users includes balls, racquets, safety equipment, towels, locks, and lockers.

- *Lifeguard.* Aquatics facilities generally have guidelines on the number of lifeguards that must be on duty based on the number of pools and users present. Lifeguards require certification.

- *Intramural official.* Depending on the number of intramural sports offered and the number of participants, officials are hired and trained for a variety of seasonal sport offerings.

- *Fitness instructor.* Fitness instructors are hired to teach a variety of classes such as aerobics, yoga, Pilates, and conditioning. Certifications are often required.

- *Personal trainer.* Personal trainers instruct users on the proper use of weight and fitness equipment and may help develop fitness plans and programs for users. Certifications are often required.

- *Instructional program instructor.* Instructional programs are often based on the desires of the users. Instructors may offer classes in martial arts, swim lessons, bicycle maintenance, or dance. Certifications may be required.

- *Outdoor equipment manager.* Separate from the facility equipment checkout, outdoor programs check out more specialized equipment such as canoes, kayaks, tents, sleeping bags, camping gear, and snow sport equipment. People in this position are often required to maintain, clean, and provide instruction on how to use the equipment.

- *Climbing wall instructor.* People in this position may teach individuals or classes about proper climbing techniques and equipment. Certifications may be required.

- *Outdoor guide.* Outdoor guides plan and lead outdoor trips for a diverse group of participants. They often teach outdoor skills and safety. Certifications may be required.

- *Safety education instructor.* These instructors teach a variety of safety classes to various individuals and groups. Instructor certifications may be required.

- *Sport safety staff.* People on sport safety staffs provide emergency response and care for campus recreation sport events. Certifications may be required.

- *Retail cashier.* Users of a campus recreation program often pay for classes, rentals, and memberships. A program may also have a pro shop where equipment, clothing, food, and beverages are sold.

Those who intend to pursue a career in campus recreation can benefit from the training and experience they will obtain as student employees of their campus recreational facilities.

William A. Cotton, Colorado State University.

- *Clerical workers.* Generally, people with clerical jobs work in offices and may assist with answering phones, scheduling reservations, answering questions, and data entry.

Supervisors

Many of the areas listed in the student employment section also have supervisors. These positions are generally filled by experienced students who have performed responsibly, can anticipate problems and take charge of a situation, relate well to customers and staff, and have acquired a general knowledge of the department's programs and services. They may assist with the staff training, scheduling, and evaluation in their particular area.

Graduate Assistants

Campus recreation graduate assistantships are often the bridge between student employment and a professional career. In the most recent salary census conducted in 2007 by the National Intramural-Recreational Sports Association (NIRSA), 292 colleges and universities reported data on approximately 2,000 professional positions in campus recreation. Over 65 percent of the positions were filled by people who had earned a master's degree or higher. Over 300 colleges and universities listed in the 2006 NIRSA *Recreational Sports Directory* (2006a) offered graduate assistantships in an area of recreational sports.

Many academic fields provide preparation for a career in campus recreation. Following are the most common:

- Recreation administration
- Sports management
- Exercise science
- Student personnel administration

Occasionally, a master's degree, regardless of the discipline, meets the degree requirement of the hiring institution. The work experience, references, and interview get the person hired.

Graduate assistant job responsibilities in campus recreation programs are almost as varied as the people who hold the jobs. At some institutions the recreation program may be administered entirely by graduate students and supervised by one or two professional staff. These types of positions give people a wide range of experiences. At larger schools a graduate assistant may be assigned to one program area for the entirety of a two-year assistantship. If possible, many graduate assistants choose to "specialize" in at least two areas to broaden their experiences and make them more marketable when looking for employment. Areas of specialization include the following:

- Intramural sports
- Facility management or programming
- Informal recreation
- Health and wellness
- Fitness
- Outdoor recreation
- Aquatics
- Sport clubs
- Marketing
- Instructional programs
- Other

A graduate student or assistant is generally given more responsibility than a student employee

or supervisor, often being involved in the broader departmental planning and scheduling. People in these positions gain experience by hiring, training, and evaluating staff; developing, promoting, and administering programs; becoming involved in the campus community by serving on university-wide committees; and joining or continuing their memberships in professional associations.

Colleges and universities that are able to hire graduate assistants gain valuable contributions to their programs. Often, graduate students come from smaller or larger universities, from a different part of the country, from a different academic background, or from a different supervisory style—all contributing factors to growing and evolving a program that is open to new and different ideas.

Some universities choose not to hire graduate assistants, for a variety of reasons. Often, the changeover in staff every one or two years is very stressful. Also, the hiring and retraining process is time-consuming. Others concentrate on providing opportunities to entry-level professionals, knowing that there may be a turnover, but probably not as often as every one or two years.

Professionals

The paths that lead people to the campus recreation profession are as varied as the people themselves. In a brochure developed to recruit student members to the National Intramural-Recreational Sports Association (2006b), there are two noteworthy citations. One statement reads:

> Not studying a recreation-related career? That's okay! Many students and professionals did not begin their careers in recreational sports. It is never too late to begin to gain experience and exposure to the rec sports world, and it can all start with NIRSA!

Anne MacDonald, from Rowan University, stated;

> I got my degrees in communication disorders and child development. When I realized how much I enjoyed my job at my campus recreation center, I knew that getting involved with NIRSA was the next step in pursuing a career in recreational sports.

Both of these situations are more common than most people outside the field would expect. Once a person has chosen a career in campus recreation, finding the first professional job becomes the challenge.

One of the best resources for finding a job is the National Intramural-Recreational Sports Association (NIRSA). NIRSA has an electronic jobs board (www.bluefishjobs.com) that posts professional, graduate assistant, and internship opportunities from around the country in a variety of campus recreation specialty areas. In addition to the online postings, NIRSA offers a Career Opportunities Center, which is held in the spring at its annual national conference.

How specific should a person be when looking for a job? If the main criterion is to gain professional experience while being employed in a recreation-related field, then the organizations to consider are numerous. As mentioned in the introduction to this chapter, employment opportunities exist in many different places.

If a person wants to limit the criteria to colleges and universities only, the opportunities for related experience are still broad. Many "student affairs" opportunities provide related experiences while still offering the opportunity to work with students. Broadening a search to include residence life, campus activities, student unions, or athletics opportunities will provide valuable experience in a collegiate setting.

Almost every college or university employment posting must be listed through the university's human resources or related department. A person looking for a position at a specific college or university should go directly to the institution's human resources department or Web site to view current employment opportunities.

Professional associations may also have job listing services. The National Association of Student Personnel Administrators (NASPA) has an online career center (www.naspa.org) that has employment listings in the areas of health, wellness, and drug and alcohol; student activities and student union; and "other."

The Association of College Unions-International (ACUI) has an online career service (www.acui.org) that lists positions in the areas of campus activities, computers and technology, facilities and operations, indoor recreation, marketing and conference services, outdoor recreation, and "other."

The *Chronicle of Higher Education,* a weekly publication available by subscription, has a career section insert in every publication. Many of the positions are academic or administrative, but related areas may include athletics, recreation, residence life, and student activities and services.

Working with students and learning about the higher education environment can prove to be invaluable when taking the next step to a career in campus recreation.

Titles, Responsibilities, and Salaries

Position titles, responsibilities, and salaries in the campus recreation field can vary greatly, as can reporting structures of campus recreation departments. The most common divisions that campus recreation departments report to include student affairs, athletics, and academic units.

The size of a recreational sport department varies depending on the number of users as well as the variety of programs and services offered. Figure 17.1 shows an example of an organizational chart.

Titles

There is no one consistent, or recommended, title for any professional position in campus recreation. Specific job titles vary from one university to the next, depending on the faculty or staff classification system they use. A staff position on an organizational chart at university A generally may have similar responsibilities to a staff position at the same level at university B; however, their titles could be very different. Even though one may be called a coordinator and the other a director, a closer look at their job responsibilities may reveal commonalities.

- *Directors* are generally responsible for the overall leadership of the department. They report to someone outside of their department, at the next administrative level.
- *Associate directors* are usually senior members of the staff. They report to the director of the department.
- *Program or facility directors* are often responsible for one or more program areas (aquatics, intramural sports, sport clubs) or facilities. This is often a third level of staff, and people in this position generally report to an associate director (for larger programs) or to the department director.

Qualifications and Responsibilities

A combination of academic preparation, skill set, work ethic, and personal attributes will assist people in securing employment and advancing up the campus recreation ladder.

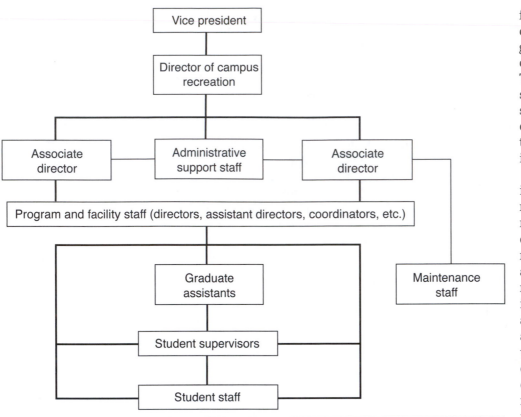

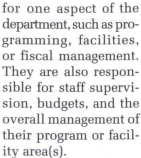

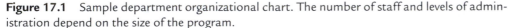

Figure 17.1 Sample department organizational chart. The number of staff and levels of administration depend on the size of the program.

Directors are generally responsible for providing overall leadership to the department staff (full-time staff, graduate assistants, and student employees) in the development and implementation of the recreational sport programs and services for the university. They need to be able to develop effective working relationships with their own staff as well as other university faculty, staff, and administrators. They are responsible for staff supervision, programming, and facility management (indoor and outdoor) and the fiscal management of the department (state or private funds, student fees, fund-raising). The years of experience and degree requirements for a director are often correlated to the size of the university or department.

Associate directors are usually senior members of the staff and report to the director. Associate directors are most often found in larger programs, where the organizational chart will allow for more vertical layers, or in departments in which years of experience may be recognized with a title change, but not necessarily a change in duties or responsibilities. In larger departments, associate directors may be responsible for one aspect of the department, such as programming, facilities, or fiscal management. They are also responsible for staff supervision, budgets, and the overall management of their program or facility area(s).

Program or facility directors are often responsible for one or more program areas or facilities. They are responsible for their area's budget, programming, and staff. Depending on how large these areas are, there may be additional levels of staff within a program. For example, an aquatics or intramural director may supervise one or more coordinators to assist with the implementation of the program. Whether these positions are considered entry level depends on the educational and related-experience requirements of the position.

In addition to related experience and academic preparation, specific program areas may have additional requirements when hiring staff. Many programs require that, at a minimum, staff be certified in basic first aid and CPR. Also, if the job involves driving university vehicles, a driver's safety course may be required. Additional certifications may include the following:

- *Aquatics.* Adult, child, and infant CPR, first aid, and AED certifications; lifeguard, lifeguard instructor, or water safety instructor certifications; certified pool operator (CPO); aquatic facility operator (AFO) certificates.

- *Outdoor recreation.* Adult, child, and infant CPR, first aid, and AED certifications; wilderness first aid or first responder certifications; specific skill trainings or certifications.

- *Fitness and wellness.* Adult, child, and infant CPR, first aid, and AED certifications; group exercise or personal trainer certification from a recognized governing body.

Campus Recreation Salaries

A 2007 salary survey conducted by the National Intramural-Recreational Sports Association yielded responses from 292 colleges and universities, representing over 2,000 positions. These responses provided valuable information on salaries in the field of campus recreation. Following is a brief summary of position titles, responsibilities, and key statistics:

Director (13.1 percent of reported positions). Directors are responsible for the overall administration of the campus recreation program, including intramural sports, sport clubs, informal recreation, and outdoor recreation.

> Average age: 45.9
>
> Average number of years in current position: 9.3
>
> Average number of years in recreational sport profession: 18.7
>
> Percentage of directors who have a master's degree or higher: 95.7 percent

Senior associate director (2.3 percent of reported positions). Senior associate directors share with the recreational sport director the overall administration of the program. They rank above the assistant director(s) and other associate director(s).

> Average age: 42.2
>
> Average number of years in current position: 8
>
> Average number of years in recreational sport profession: 16
>
> Percentage of senior associate directors who have a master's degree or higher: 87.2 percent

Associate director (6.9 percent of reported positions). Associate directors share with the recreational sport director the overall administration of the program. They rank above the assistant director(s).

> Average age: 42
>
> Average number of years in current position: 6.7
>
> Average number of years in recreational sport profession: 15.6
>
> Percentage of associate directors who have a master's degree or higher: 87 percent

Senior program director (3.1 percent of reported positions). Senior program directors share in the administration of programs and rank above other program director(s) (e.g., aquatics, intramurals, marketing).

> Average age: 38.1
>
> Average number of years in current position: 4.5
>
> Average number of years in recreational sport profession: 9.8
>
> Percentage of senior program directors who have a master's degree or higher: 80.6 percent

Aquatics professional (5.7 percent of reported positions). Aquatics professionals are responsible for the administration of recreational programs and activities associated with swimming pools or marinas.

> Average age: 34.5
>
> Average number of years in current position: 4.4
>
> Average number of years in recreational sport profession: 7
>
> Percentage of aquatics professionals who have a master's degree or higher: 57.5 percent

>> *continued*

>> continued

Facilities professional (11.6 percent of reported positions). Facilities professionals are responsible for any number of facilities administered by the department, both indoor and outdoor.

Average age: 35.9

Average number of years in current position: 4.8

Average number of years in recreational sport profession: 7.7

Percentage of facilities professionals who have a master's degree or higher: 58.8 percent

Fitness professional (10.1 percent of reported positions). Fitness professionals are responsible for programming that encourages the development of physical fitness.

Average age: 32.3

Average number of years in current position: 3.6

Average number of years in recreational sport profession: 5.6

Percentage of fitness professionals who have a master's degree or higher: 73.4 percent

Informal recreation professional (1.9 percent of reported positions). Informal recreation professionals are responsible for the administration of leisure programs for the campus community (free-time, family recreation, and cultural activities).

Average age: 31.6

Average number of years in current position: 2.7

Average number of years in recreational sport profession: 5.2

Percentage of informal recreation professionals who have a master's degree or higher: 59 percent

Instructional programs professional (2.1 percent of reported positions). Instructional programs professionals are responsible for the administration of noncredit instructional programs.

Average age: 37.6

Average number of years in current position: 6.5

Average number of years in recreational sport profession: 10.5

Percentage of instructional programs professionals who have a master's degree or higher: 56.7 percent

Intramural sports professional (10.6 percent of reported positions). Intramural sports professionals are responsible for the administration of structured contests, tournaments, and leagues within the institutional setting.

Average age: 31.7

Average number of years in current position: 4.5

Average number of years in recreational sport profession: 6.3

Percentage of intramural sports professionals who have a master's degree or higher: 73.6 percent

Marketing professional (3.0 percent of reported positions). Marketing professionals are responsible for the administration of promotional activities and departmental marketing.

Average age: 34.1

Average number of years in current position: 4.4

Average number of years in recreational sport profession: 5.7

Percentage of marketing professionals who have a master's degree or higher: 46.6 percent

Outdoor recreation professional (6.1 percent of reported positions). Outdoor recreation professionals are responsible for the administration of nonacademic outdoor recreational programming.

Average age: 35

Average number of years in current position: 4.6

Average number of years in recreational sport profession: 7.3

Percentage of outdoor recreation professionals who have a master's degree or higher: 66 percent

Sport club professional (3.9 percent of reported positions). Sport club professionals are responsible for the administration of recognized student organizations that may provide instruction, recreation, or competition in specific sport activities.

Average age: 33.2

Average number of years in current position: 5.2

Average number of years in recreational sport profession: 7.8

Percentage of sport club professionals who have a master's degree or higher: 82.6 percent

Technology professional (1.5 percent of reported positions). Technology professionals are responsible for the administration of technology support, systems, and related activities (computers).

Average age: 34.5

Average number of years in current position: 3.4

Average number of years in recreational sport profession: 5.0

Percentage of technology professionals who have a master's degree or higher: 10.7 percent

Wellness professional (2.1 percent of reported positions). Wellness professionals are responsible for the administration of nonacademic health and wellness programs that are coordinated or sponsored by the campus recreation department.

Average age: 34.3

Average number of years in current position: 3.7

Average number of years in recreational sport profession: 6.5

Percentage of wellness professionals who have a master's degree or higher: 69 percent

Other professional (11.9 percent of reported positions). This category encompasses professionals whose job titles or descriptions do not match any of the preceding.

Average age: 42

Average number of years in current position: 6.6

Average number of years in recreational sport profession: 8

Percentage of other professionals who have a master's degree or higher: 28.2 percent

Salaries

Several factors may affect the salaries of campus recreation professionals, including whether the school is public or private and the regional location of the school. Following are other factors that may affect salaries:

- Educational background
- Institution size (enrollment)
- Level of supervisory responsibility
- Number of years in current position
- Number of years in the recreational sport or a related profession
- Supervisory position (number of employees supervised)
- Amount of time required to fulfill job responsibilities
- Institutional limitations through pay grades and scales
- Salary-to-benefits ratio
- Work performance

Table 17.1 shows a comparison of positioned salaries over a four-year period:

The campus recreation field saw an overall boost in professional salaries from 2003 to 2007 of over 10 percent. Campus recreation facilities are also expanding. According to NIRSA's Collegiate Recreational Sports Facility Construction Report for 2004-2010, 333 colleges and universities reported that during the six-year period from 2004 to 2010, over $3.17 billion would be expended by those schools on new construction, additions, remodels, and expansions of their campus recreation facilities. The expansion of facilities, the growing role of campus recreation departments in the recruitment and retention of students, and the value students place on their participation in these programs all lead to a professional field that is expanding and growing in a positive direction.

Conclusion

Campus recreation is a valued component of the higher education environment. On average, over 75 percent of the student population at any college or university participates in at least one aspect of campus recreation programming. Student employment and leadership opportunities abound in this area as well. Staff are challenged to be on the cutting edge of programs, services, and facilities, with a significant percentage of participants changing from year to year with the influx of new students. The field is an exciting, challenging, and rewarding choice for a career.

Table 17.1 Campus Recreation Professional Salaries

	2003 ($)	2005 ($)	% change (2003-2005)	2007 ($)	% change (2005-2007)
Director	57,012	61,547	+7.95%	64,342	+4.54%
Senior associate	49,990	59,320	+18.66%	58,054	-2.13%
Associate	48,273	51,997	+7.71%	55,931	+7.57%
Aquatics	35,238	37,702	+6.99%	37,786	+0.22%
Facilities	36,598	38,607	+5.49%	40,034	+3.70%
Fitness	34,716	36,239	+4.39%	37,520	+3.33%
Informal recreation	34,649	36,698	+5.91%	35,505	-3.25%
Instructional programs	34,922	39,060	+11.85%	42,920	+9.88%
Intramural sports	34,359	35,356	+2.90%	37,637	+6.45%
Marketing	35,797	38,877	+8.60%	40,827	+5.02%
Outdoor recreation	33,785	36,081	+6.80%	37,268	+3.29%
Sport clubs	38,150	37,454	-1.82%	39,422	+5.25%
Technology	39,802	40,036	+0.59%	48,623	+21.45%
Wellness	36,475	36,686	+0.58%	37,783	+2.99%
Other	34,819	35,377	+1.60%	37,555	+6.16%

INDUSTRY AND PROFESSIONAL STANDARDS IN CAMPUS RECREATION

Douglas S. Franklin

The field of campus recreation has a rich history of practitioner-developed knowledge dispersed through an apprenticeship model that facilitated the growth of the profession from the early 20th century. However, the construction of increasingly complex recreation facilities, the management of multimillion-dollar budgets, and a change in focus toward student learning and development necessitate a new method of knowledge development and diffusion.

A critical construct underscoring a profession is the concept that good theory informs practice and good practice is reflected in theory. The cyclical nature of this principle (from theory to practice and back) is based on discipline-specific knowledge, doctrine, and skill manifested in the use of industry and professional standards and guidelines. This knowledge is established by members of the profession, not ordained or determined by external entities. This does not mean that external controls are nonexistent. The field of campus recreation, like all occupational fields, is subject to industry and regulatory restrictions from various agencies implementing federal, state, and local laws, as well as institutional policies and procedures. Compliance with access requirements dictated by the Americans with Disabilities Act of 1990 (ADA) and the handling of blood-borne pathogens as predicated by the Occupational Safety and Health Administration (OSHA) are examples of legally mandated practices that are outside the control of practicing professionals. However, self-regulation and compliance with standards or principles of best practice established by professionals within the field elevate the stature of a vocation to that of a profession.

Professions

An early 20th-century definition suggests that a **profession** is an occupational field with a unique and distinct body of knowledge gained through an academic discipline, which provides a societal service for the greater good. Abraham Flexner's 1915 address to the National Conference on Charities and Corrections is the first document to discuss the elements of a profession and forms the basis for most future statements, opinions, and research regarding professions (Iwabuchi, 2004). In answering the question, What are the elements of a profession? Flexner suggested that professions are essentially intellectual operations with great responsibility that derive raw material from science and learning; work up to a practical and definite end; possess an educationally communicable technique; self-organize; and are increasingly altruistic in motivation. During this period professions were confined to the fields of law, medicine, religion, and the military (Rudolph, 1962). Flexner's definition was refined throughout the 20th century, and each adjustment accommodated the growth of new and diverse vocations. The modern definition and the one most closely associated with campus recreation suggests that a profession is a social service occupation that possesses a unique and distinct body of knowledge gained through an academic discipline and practically applied using a set of accepted standards.

The basis for any profession is the unique body of knowledge within the specific field and the ability of the practitioners and researchers within that field to develop and disseminate new knowledge. Campus recreation uses knowledge from various disciplines and is therefore considered an interdisciplinary field that requires practitioners and researchers to review and apply the knowledge developed in the fields of recreation and sport, college student personnel, higher education, and business.

Professionalizing the field of campus recreation began in 1950 with the development of the National Intramural Association (NIA), the predecessor to the National Intramural-Recreational Sports Association (NIRSA). The NIA formed a research committee in 1960 and initiated a discussion of professional preparation during its 1969 annual conference. The following year an entire section of the association's annual conference was dedicated to professional preparation (Clarke, 1978). In 1976 a comprehensive plan for professional preparation was presented to the executive committee of NIRSA, which led to formalizing the *Recreational Sports Curriculum: A Resource Guide* (Clarke, 1978). This document, and its subsequent editions, provided academic program faculty with suggested practical knowledge necessary to administer successful campus recreation programs. This publication is periodically reviewed and adjusted based on new knowledge, as defined by professionals in the field, through NIRSA's Curriculum Task Force. A more thorough history of the profession is available in chapter 2.

The strength of the field of campus recreation remains the experience of its practitioners and the ability of industry leaders to share best practices through professional development opportunities in national and regional conferences and specialty institutes. The *Recreational Sports Journal* and other trade journals provide another channel through which to share knowledge of current practices and scholarly work in the field. However, the complexity of campus recreation and the increased pressure to be more productive and accountable require a thoughtful and systematic approach to its practice. The use of an accountability cycle promotes the integration of and interplay between practitioner and researcher to promote knowledge development and dissemination.

Accountability Cycle

Institutions of higher education are under increased pressure to be more accountable and productive. In order to address these demands, higher education professionals, including those in campus recreation, use various tools to enhance their impact on students. One of these tools is the accountability cycle, a formalized version of the concept of "from theory to practice and back." The accountability cycle consists of five areas interconnected by a series of questions (see figure 17.2). The areas of the cycle are practice, standards, outcomes, assessment, and feedback. Ideally, the cycle begins with compliance to industry and professional standards, but practically speaking it can begin at any point within the system.

Throughout this book various authors have provided practical knowledge and techniques necessary to providing a good recreational experience in the form of a modern campus recreation program. In almost all cases this information has focused on practical knowledge and skills. The operationally focused chapters form the basis for the cycle's *practice* area. Chapter 14 specifically provides a discussion of the quantitative and qualitative measures of *assessment* in an effort to evaluate program success, and it also provides methods of *feedback.* Each of these elements is necessary to good practice but is limited in its ability to intentionally develop the profession. To truly conduct good practice and advance the field, the campus recreation

professional must measure his or her practice against industry **standards** by establishing and measuring *outcomes* relative to those standards. The use of standards and outcomes thus completes the accountability cycle and provides an opportunity to move both the practitioner and the field forward through the development and dissemination of knowledge.

Knowledge Development and Diffusion

Chapter 13, Risk Management, provides information regarding liability and the risk facing the campus recreation professional on a daily basis. The basis of a sound risk management plan is qualified professionals who possess the requisite knowledge and skills to perform their duties prudently within the community. The appropriate knowledge and skills are gained from participation in undergraduate or graduate academic programs, professional development, and journals and publications.

Professional standards are established by the professionals within the community of practice as manifested by participation in professional associations. In addition to NIRSA, relevant professional organizations for the campus recreation professionals include the American College Personnel Administrators (ACPA), the National Association of Student Personnel Administrators (NASPA), the National Recreation and Park Association (NRPA), the National Association of College and University Business Officers (NACUBO), and the National Association of Campus Auxiliary Services (NACAS). Other specialty associations exist in aquatics, fitness, and outdoor pursuits.

The development of standards, a code of ethical principles, a certification program, and a national registry standardize the knowledge and skills deemed necessary to work in the field of campus recreation. They also provide an avenue for distributing that knowledge.

Standards and Outcomes

In the best-selling book *The World Is Flat: A Brief History of the Twenty-First Century*, Thomas L. Friedman (2006) indicated that standardized computer software for scripting is the prime factor for the exponential growth of the Internet. Friedman stated, "Once a standard takes hold, people start to focus on the quality of what they are doing as opposed to how they are doing it" (p. 83). The

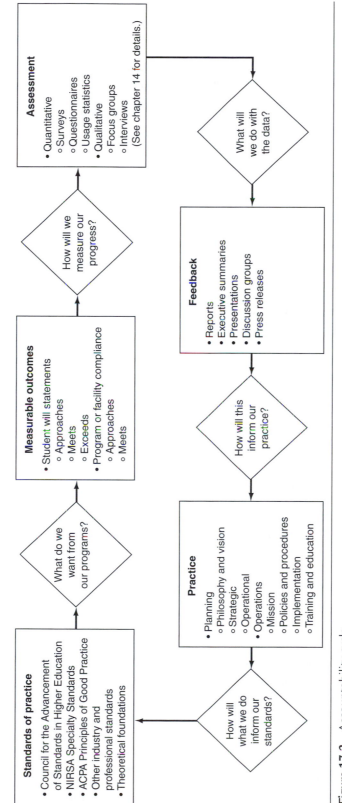

Figure 17.2 Accountability cycle.

concept of quality brought about by the application of standards is desirable for the growth of the field of campus recreation. A standard is a principle established by authority, custom, or general consent as a model or example; it is something set up and established by authority as a rule for the measure of quantity, value, or quality. Standards related to professions are linked to Flexner's 1910 report *Medical Education in the United States and Canada: A Report to the Carnegie Foundation for the Advancement of Teaching,* in which he cited the lack of standards for professional schools as the cause of problems in medical education (Flexner, 1910; Iwabuchi, 2004).

Standards and best practice have become the foundations of many professional fields. The American College of Sports Medicine (ACSM) sets the standards for certifying professionals involved in health and fitness programs in clinical applications as well as for the management of fitness facilities (American College of Sports Medicine, 2007). The Medical Fitness Association develops standards to shape and foster the growth of the medical fitness industry (Medical Fitness Association, 2006). The National Council for the Accreditation of Teacher Education (NCATE) (2007) identifies standards and benchmarks for teacher education programs, including those associated with physical education, the historical foundation for recreational sport programs. The American Academy for Park and Recreation Administration for the National Recreation and Park Association developed standards based on input from practitioners and educators. Until 2007 the two primary sources of standards for campus recreation were the *NIRSA General and Specialty Standards for Collegiate Recreational Sports and Assessment Instruments* (NIRSA, 1996) and the recreational sports chapter in the *Council for the Advancement of Standards (CAS) Book of Professional Standards in Higher Education* (Dean, 2006). In 2007, with the approval of the NIRSA executive committee, the NIRSA standards committee consolidated the general standards with the CAS standards to form a single unified set of general standards for the profession. Specialty standards were not affected.

NIRSA General and Specialty Standards for Collegiate Recreational Sports and Assessment Instruments

The *NIRSA General and Specialty Standards for Collegiate Recreational Sports and Assessment Instruments,* published in 1996, was the culmination of work by dedicated campus recreation professionals through their participation on the aquatics, fitness, standards, and wellness committees of NIRSA. The document is divided into three sections: general standards, specialty standards, and assessment instruments. The general standards portion of the document includes the "minimum criteria for any recreational sports program" (p. 8) and consists of areas necessary for all programs. These sections include mission, human resources, ethics, programs and services, developmental structure, facilities, equipment, funding, publicity and promotion, recognition, safety, planning, relations, legality, and evaluation. Each section has a "must" statement and clarifying information to assist the practitioner in meeting the standard. The specialty standards portion of the document highlights standards relative to aquatics, extramural programming, fitness, information recreation, instructional programs, intramurals, outdoor recreation, special events, sport clubs, and wellness. Each of these sections also has a series of must statements and clarifying information to guide the implementation of the standard. The final portion of the document provides assessment tools for both the general and specialty standards. This document is no longer in print, having been replaced by the CAS Recreational Sports standards in 2007. However, *NIRSA General and Specialty Standards* continues to be used by many recreational sports directors, particularly in dealing with various specialty programs.

CAS Professional Standards for Higher Education

The Council for the Advancement of Standards in Higher Education (CAS) was formed in 1979 as an interassociation consortium of student affairs educators and practitioners. The primary purpose of the CAS is to formalize standards associated with the student service areas within higher education through the publication of *CAS Professional Standards for Higher Education* (Dean, 2006). The "blue book of standards" was first published in 1986 and addressed 19 functional areas of higher education programs related to student services and the academic programs related to student affairs preparation (Nuss, 2003). The publication, now in its sixth edition, represents 37 associations representing a myriad of student service professions, including recreational sport, and provides "a comprehensive and valid set of criteria to judge support program quality and effectiveness" (Nuss, 2003, p. 3) by setting best practice standards.

Each association within the consortium subscribes to the 13 standard areas, including mission; program; leadership; organization and management; human resources; financial resources; facilities, technology, and equipment; legal responsibilities; equity and access; campus and external relationships; diversity; ethics; and assessment and evaluation. Of particular interest to the accountability cycle is the learning outcomes portion of the program standard. CAS identified 16 learning outcome groups to be used in establishing compliance with this standard. This portion of the standard identifies outcome domains for all student service–related programs. These include intellectual growth, effective communication, enhanced self-esteem, realistic self-appraisal, clarified values, career choices, leadership development, healthy behavior, meaningful interpersonal relationships, independence, collaboration, social responsibility, satisfying and productive lifestyles, appreciating diversity, spiritual awareness, and personal and educational goals. Specific learning outcomes will be defined within the program. The use of "student will" statements helps identify the student as the focus of the learning outcome. "The student will demonstrate knowledge of policies and procedures relative to the student recreation center" or "the student will apply conflict resolution skills in dealing with problematic patrons" are student will statements. The CAS publication *Frameworks for Assessing Learning and Development Outcomes* **(FALDO)** (Strayhorn, 2006) provides theoretical constructs that support the learning outcomes and other information to assist in implementing this standard. In addition to standards and guidelines, CAS provides an internal assessment tool to use in program evaluation.

In addition to providing criteria for good practice, the CAS standards and guidelines can be used as a map for self-study, as an aid to the development of new programs and services, to provide criteria for staff development, and as a resource for academic preparation.

NASPA Standards of Professional Practice

Because campus recreation usually exists within an office or department of student affairs, campus recreation programs must comply with standards related to this area. The National Association of Student Personnel Administrators developed and adopted *Standards of Professional Practice* in 1990. This document guides student affairs professional practice in 18 areas: professional services,

agreement with institutional mission and goals, management of institutional resources, employment relationship, conflict of interest, legal authority, equal consideration and treatment of others, student behavior, integrity of information and research, confidentiality, research involving human subjects, representation of professional competence, selection and promotion practices, references, job definitions and performance evaluation, campus community, professional development, and assessment. These standards are not designed to stand alone; rather, they reference compliance and alignment with existing industry and professional standards, including those identified in the *CAS Professional Standards for Higher Education* (Dean, 2006).

ACPA Good Practice in Student Affairs

Good, or best, practice statements are a less stringent but no less important form of guidance. The American College Personnel Association (1996), one of two associations for professionals in the field of student affairs, subscribes to the following statement:

> *Good Practice in Student Affairs.* This document indicates student affairs engages students in active learning, helps students develop coherent values and ethical standards, sets and communicates high expectations for student learning, uses systematic inquiry to improve student and institutional performance, uses resources effectively to achieve institutional missions and goals, forges educational partnerships that advance student learning, and builds supportive and inclusive communities.

Certification

Certification is the term applied to the process whereby an individual voluntarily submits his or her credentials for review based on clearly identified competencies, criteria, or standards. Certifications common to campus recreation professionals are associated with the specialty areas. Certifications related to aquatics operations include the aquatics facility operator (AFO) from the National Recreation and Park Association and the certified pool operator (CPO) certification managed by the National Swimming Pool Foundation (NSPF). Aquatics instructional and lifeguarding certifications, as well as life safety certifications for facility and program employees, are provided by the American Red Cross (ARC). Outdoor programs and challenge courses are subject to specialty standards and certifications through the Association of Challenge Course Technology (ACCT) and the Association of Experiential Education (AEE). Fitness professionals can find certifications from the American College of Sports Medicine and the American Council on Exercise (ACE), among others.

NIRSA developed a certified recreational sports specialist (CRSS) certification in 1981. This certification established criteria to standardize the level of knowledge held by professionals entering the field. The lack of a standard academic curriculum used in the preparation of recreational sport professionals and the low number of professionals holding the certification limited the effectiveness of the CRSS. In 2004 the NIRSA board of directors suspended the CRSS exam and moved forward with the implementation of a professional registry.

National Registries

As this text is being published, NIRSA and NASPA are investigating the development of national registries for professionals working in the fields of recreational sport and student affairs. A national **registry** relies on an identified body of knowledge that supports the practice and guides professional development activities, regardless of one's academic preparation and practical experience. The NASPA national registry (see Resources) uses knowledge found in *CAS Professional Standards for Higher Education* (Dean, 2006) identified in student affairs professional preparation programs. The NIRSA national registry (see Resources) uses the six core knowledge areas of recreational sport management, philosophy and theory, programming, management techniques, business procedures, facility management and planning and design, and research and evaluation (Barcelona, 2001).

Ethical Codes

Ethical codes form the foundation for the way campus recreation professionals conduct themselves and establish levels of acceptable behavior that form the profession's character standard. The guiding ethical principles associated with campus recreation are found in the NIRSA Code of Ethics (see Resources). However, because campus recreation is multidisciplinary, the field is guided by ethical codes from other professional associations. These include ACPA's

Ethical Principles and Standards; the NACUBO Code of Ethics and Core Ideology, Purpose, and Values; and the CAS Statement of Shared Ethical Principles (see Resources). Chapter 15 provides a more in-depth look at the importance of ethics in campus recreation.

Conclusion

The purpose of this chapter is to provide information relevant to the development and dissemination of knowledge in the field of campus recreation and the use of that knowledge in professionalizing the field. The movement from an apprenticeship model of knowledge dissemination to a professional preparation model is being accomplished by professional organizations associated with the field and through the use of standards and other professional development opportunities, as well as certifications provided by these associations. The accountability cycle facilitates the use of this knowledge and enhances the ability of practitioners to justify the role campus recreation plays in the holistic development of students.

Resources

American College Personnel Association (ACPA)
Principles of good practice: www.acpa.nche.edu/pgp/principle.htm

American College Personnel Association (ACPA)
Statement of ethical principles and standards: www.myacpa.org/ethics/statement.cfm

American College of Sports Medicine (ACSM)
www.acsm.org/AM/Template.cfm?Section=ACSM_Certifications&Template=/CM/HTMLDisplay.cfm&ContentID=6162

American Council on Exercise (ACE)
www.acefitness.org

American Red Cross (ARC)
www.redcross.org/services/hss/courses

Association of Challenge Course Technology (ACCT)
www.acctinfo.org

Association of Experiential Education (AEE)
www.aee.org/customer/pages.php?pageid=28

Council for the Advancement of Standards in Higher Education (CAS)
Statement of shared ethical principles: www.cas.edu/ethicsstatement.pdf

National Association of College and University Business Officers (NACUBO)

Code of ethics: www.nacubo.org/Documents/about/NACUBOCodeofEthics.pdf

Core ideology, purpose, and values: www.nacubo.org/Documents/about/NACUBOCoreIdeologyPurposeandValues.pdf

National Association of Student Personnel Administrators (NASPA)

Registry for student affairs professionals: www.naspa.org/programs/registry.cfm

Standards of professional practice: www.naspa.org/programs/standards.cfm

National Intramural-Recreational Sports Association (NIRSA)

CAS standards: www.nirsa.org/about/documents/cas.aspx

Code of ethics: www.nirsa.org/about/documents/code_of_ethics.aspx

Registry: www.nirsa.org/education/files/national_registry_proposal.pdf

National Recreation and Park Association (NRPA)

Academic program standards: www.nrpa.org/content/default.aspx?documentId=1037

Certification: www.nrpa.org/content/default.aspx?documentId=551

National Swimming Pool Foundation (NSPF)

www.nspf.com/cpo.html

References

American College of Sports Medicine. (2007). *ACSM's health/fitness facility standards and guidelines* (3rd ed.). Stephen J. Tharrett, James A. Peterson, editors. Champaign, IL: Human Kinetics.

American College Personnel Association. (1996). Principles of good practice in student affairs. Retrieved from www.myacpa.nche.edu/pgp/princple.htm.

Barcelona, R.J. (2001). An analysis of the perceived competencies of recreational sport managers: Toward a competency-based model for academic and professional development. Doctoral dissertation, University of Indiana. UMI Number: 3024235.

Clarke, J.S. (1978). Challenge and change: A history of the National Intramural-Recreational Sports Association. West Point, NY: Leisure Press.

Dean, L.A. (2006). *CAS professional standards for higher education* (6th ed., pp. 285-291). Washington, DC: Council for the Advancement of Standards in Higher Education.

Flexner, A. (1910). *Medical education in the United States and Canada: A report to the Carnegie Foundation for the Advancement of Teaching* (New York, 1910; reprint edition, 1972). Stanford, CA: The Carnegie Foundation for the Advancement of Teaching.

Flexner, A. (1915). Is social work a profession? In *Proceedings of the National Conference of Charities and Corrections at the Forty-Second Annual Session*, National Conference of Charities and Corrections, Baltimore, MD.

Friedman, T.L. (2006). The world is flat: A brief history of the twenty-first century. New York: Farrar, Straus & Giroux.

Iwabuchi, S. (2004). The pursuit of excellence: Abraham Flexner and his views on learning in higher education. *The Japanese Journal of American Studies, 15*, 139-161.

Lewis, J., Jones, T., Lamke, G., & Dunn, J.M. (1998, December). Recreational sport: Making the grade on college campuses. *Parks and Recreation*. Retrieved from www.findarticles.com/p/articles/mi_m1145/is_12_33/ai_53479082.

Medical Fitness Association. (2006). Medical fitness standards and guidelines released. Retrieved from www.medicalfitness.org/displaycommon.cfm?an=1&subarticlenbr=58.

National Association of Student Personnel Administrators. (1990) Standards of professional practice. Retrieved from www.naspa.org/programs/standards.cfm.

National Council for the Accreditation of Teacher Education. (2007). Revised NCATE unit standards in effect in fall 2008. Retrieved from www.ncate.org/.

National Intramural-Recreational Sports Association (1996). NIRSA general and specialty standards for collegiate recreational sports and assessment instruments. Corvallis, OR: Author.

National Intramural-Recreational Sports Association. (2006a). *2006 NIRSA recreational sports directory*. Champaign, IL: Human Kinetics.

National Intramural-Recreational Sports Association. (2006b). Student membership is your path to success [Brochure]. Corvallis, OR: Author.

National Intramural-Recreational Sports Association. (2007). *2007 NIRSA salary census*. Corvallis, OR: Author.

Nuss, E.M. (2003). The development of student affairs. In S. Komives, D. Woodward, & Associates (Eds.), *Student services: Handbook for the profession* (4th ed., p. 76). San Francisco: Jossey Bass.

Rudolph, F. (1962, 1990). *The American college and university*. Athens, GA: The University of Georgia Press.

Strayhorn, T.L. (2006). *Frameworks for assessing learning and development outcomes*. Don G. Creamer, Ted K. Miller, and Jan Arminio, editors. Washington DC: Council for the Advancement of Standards in Higher Education.

Glossary

certification—The process whereby an individual voluntarily submits his or her credentials for review based on clearly identified competencies, criteria, or standards.

FALDO—*Frameworks for Assessing Learning and Development Outcomes;* a CAS publication providing theoretical constructs that support the development of student learning outcomes within the program standards of CAS.

graduate assistant—A student pursuing a graduate degree who is employed by the university, often in a department related to the student's field of study. Employment could include teaching, research, or other department-related responsibilities.

profession—An occupational field with a unique and distinct body of knowledge gained through an academic discipline, which provides a societal service for the greater good.

professional association—An organization composed of members of a particular profession. The association may set or maintain standards for the profession and it may aid in the professional development of its members.

registry—A list of professionals in a particular field who support the practice and guide professional development activities in the field.

standard—A principle established by authority, custom, or general consent as a model or example; something set up and established by authority as a rule for the measure of quantity, value, or quality.

GLOSSARY

account total (the bottom line)—A one-page summary of the financial forecasts section in a business plan that puts the total picture in perspective by summarizing the key points articulated in the expense and revenue projections sections.

acknowledgments—A statement in a business plan that recognizes and thanks those who contributed to its research and writing.

activity or class fee—The price charged to the participant for an activity, class, or course.

actual harm—What the plaintiff suffered as a result of negligence, such as harm to or loss of property; past, present, or future medical expenses; loss of income; and extended care.

administrative fee—A fee assessed by some programs in addition to the class fee, generally to cover the administrative costs of registration.

air changes—The total volume of air in a room that is turned over in one hour.

amortization detail—A chart or table in a business plan that lists the amortization details on the debt.

ancillary areas—Subordinate areas that help to "round out" recreation centers, insuring a wide range of services and bringing in clients who may not typically use recreational sport venues.

arm's-length approach—Adminstrative model for sport clubs in which students operate teams that are independent from the institution, but a coach or faculty advisor employed by the school provides education and guidance. The students are not agents of the school, but the coaches and faculty advisors are and can create liability for the institution.

attrition—A decline in participation following the formal registration period.

automated external defibrillator (AED)—A device designed to administer a controlled shock to a pulseless victim.

body composition assessment—A procedure used to determine body density in which fat mass and lean body mass are expressed as relative percentages of total body weight. Examples include skinfold assessment and hydrostatic weighing.

bouldering—A type of climbing that is ropeless and generally occurs only a short distance off the ground. It generally requires a pad and partner spotting.

branding—An advertising method that repetitively exposes the brand or logo of an organization in order to establish widespread recognition of the brand or logo and thus recognition of the organization it represents.

business description—A section of a business plan that contains a detailed description of the major areas of a campus recreation department: its participation levels, the philosophy that drives the business functions, its pricing strategies and priorities, and its values.

business plan—A comprehensive document that discloses the recent financial and operational history, the current operational and financial status, and the projected operational and financial outlook of a campus recreation department. It serves as a tool to emphasize campus recreation department accomplishments to the public and the institution, and it provides a blueprint for achieving fiscal self-sufficiency, stability, and success.

campus recreation—A major sector of recreation programming designed to meet the needs of older teenagers and young adults in college settings; often used interchangeably with *recreational sports*.

capital reserve and requirements—A section of a business plan that outlines plans to create and enhance capital reserve funds that are expected to pay for capital repairs and replacement of indoor and outdoor facilities.

capital reserve fund—A budgeted account whose purpose is to provide the necessary funding for immediate and long-term capital expenses on indoor and outdoor recreational facilities.

carbon neutrality—Reducing or offsetting an individual or organization's carbon dioxide emissions so that there are no net emissions. This is achieved through reducing energy-consuming activities, using cleaner technologies to reduce carbon emissions, and offsetting emissions indirectly. (See *carbon offsets*.)

carbon offsets—A means by which individuals, companies, and organizations can compensate for the carbon dioxide emissions that are a result of their energy use. Offsets can be purchased from third party companies and organizations, which then invest in projects that will compensate for these emissions such as energy efficiency, emissions reductions, renewable energy, and carbon sequestration projects (usually through reforestation).

carbon trading—A means for reducing net carbon dioxide emissions (and other greenhouse gases) by setting a limit or cap that any institution or entity is allowed to emit. Institutions that emit carbon dioxide beyond the specified limit must purchase credits or allowances from the regulating body. As an incentive to reduce emissions, those that emit less than their allowance may sell their credits.

cardiorespiratory (CR)—The ability to perform large muscle, dynamic, moderate-to-high intensity exercise for prolonged periods. Related to the capacity of the heart-lung system to deliver oxygen for sustained energy production. Also called cardiorespiratory endurance or aerobic fitness.

certification—The process whereby an individual voluntarily submits his or her credentials for review based on clearly identified competencies, criteria, or standards.

certified pool operator (CPO)—A certification offered by the National Swimming Pool Foundation. May also refer to a person responsible for swimming pool maintenance in a recreation facility.

class meeting—The specific time when members of the class meet for instruction. If the class meets twice a week for six weeks, it has 12 class meetings. A class meeting is not referred to as a session.

codes of ethics—Principles and standards voluntarily developed and agreed to by professionals for the purpose of protecting the public from harm. These codes are intended to secure the public trust and to be useful for the induction of new members of the respective profession.

commutative justice—The moral position that justice is achieved when one gets what one has earned. Students earn grades. Accordingly, it would be morally unjust for a teacher to assign grades without regard to merit.

compliance—The state or act of conforming with or agreeing to do something.

constituent group—Those people residing within an institution's service area who currently participate in intramural sport programs and those who are interested but not currently participating.

contract—An agreement or promise between two or more parties that creates a legal obligation either to do or not to do something. Some examples are client–trainer contract, informed consent, assumption of risk, and employee contract.

contraindication—Any condition that renders a particular activity inappropriate.

contributory negligence—Refers to conduct by an injured person who contributes to his or her injuries or damage by failing to take reasonable care for his or her own safety.

cost recovery—The level to which a program generates revenue to offset its cost. Cost recovery information should always specify whether the calculation includes indirect as well as direct expenses.

course description—Information that explains what activity will be taught, what skills or knowledge will be gained, and the potential benefits that will result from taking the course.

credit and noncredit courses—Participants who complete a course may receive academic credit, or there may be no academic credit offered to participants who complete a course.

current major departmental goals—Goals derived from the sustained operating goals of a campus recreation department. They outline a series of actions to take to accomplish certain ends during the identified year.

current status—The section of a business plan that provides a current snapshot of key areas of the campus recreation department.

data analysis—The process of examining quantitative information to extract meaning.

DDT—Carcinogenic and mutagenic pesticides used for mosquito spraying that were banned for most purposes in the United States in 1972. They persist in the natural environment for decades to centuries, enter the food chain, increase in concentration as one moves up the food chain, and are stored in human fat tissue.

debt service requirements—The annual payments on debt incurred by a campus recreation department.

defendant—In a negligence lawsuit, the person sued for allegedly acting negligently.

deontology—Ethical theories that view moral obligation as duty without regard to its consequences. For example, one can take the moral position that capital punishment is wrong and sustain that position without qualification no matter what the circumstance or consequence.

department history—A brief synopsis in a business plan of the milestone events that have occurred in the campus recreation department during its existence.

direct costs (expenses)—Direct costs are those specific costs associated with a particular program or activity, such as instructor salary, equipment, supplies, and so on.

director (primary author) letter—A one-page letter from the head of the recreational sport program that is generally addressed to his or her supervisor as part of a business plan. It reports that the plan is complete and encourages suggestions, feedback, and input.

discrimination—The unfair treatment of one person or group, usually due to prejudice about race, religion, ethnic group, age, or gender.

distributive justice—The fair distribution of good and evil. According to this normative theory, equals deserve comparable treatment. While we distinguish between the punishment of juveniles and adults found guilty of crimes in our system of justice, we expect all juveniles to be treated the same, and likewise for adults. In the distribution of goods, the same idea applies—equals are entitled to their fair share.

duty of care—An obligation to protect someone from unreasonable risk of injury.

emergency action plan (EAP)—A comprehensive plan for responding to emergencies at a given facility.

emergency medical services (EMS)—The prehospital response, normally an ambulance and crew that are in the community.

emergency procedures—A set of guidelines and protocols for employees and others present in a facility to follow in an emergency situation such as an accident, fire, bomb threat, or tornado.

emergency response plan—A plan for dealing with a wide variety of emergencies.

emotional wellness—The ability to express feelings in an appropriate manner. It encourages participating in activities that focus on emotional self-care, including relaxation, managing stress, building self-confidence, and developing inner resources. It includes an awareness and acceptance of one's own feelings and the feelings of others.

employee evaluations—A necessary and valuable tool to help all instructors adapt and grow in the department. In addition to recognizing past achievements, the goal of an evaluation is to improve the effectiveness of the employee. Evaluation helps identify areas that need refinement or additional training.

enrollment—See registration.

ergometer—An exercise machine equipped with an apparatus to measure the effects of exercise.

ethical dilemma—A moral problem without a satisfactory solution—for example, having to make a decision that will result in harm.

ethical egoist—A person who believes that whatever is in his or her best interest is morally correct. These individuals may not break the law, simply because going to jail or having to pay a fine is not in their interest. At the same time, ethical egoists see no value in helping others unless they believe it is in their interest to do so. The ethical egoist does not believe in or practice altruism or beneficence.

ethics—Ethics is moral philosophy, a branch of philosophy concerned with reasoning, judgments, and thinking about moral problems. The philosophic study of morality.

executive summary—A one- to two-page condensed version of the business plan that serves as an attention-getter and provides a frame of reference. It captures the essence of the plan and includes only the most general and important concepts, such as programs, facilities, participation, budget, and staff.

exercise prescription—The development of an exercise program to elicit a behavioral change that improves the participant's health.

expense projections—The expenses a campus recreation department predicts it will incur during the period of time covered by a business plan.

extramural sport programs—Programs that allow for competitive sport experiences between individuals and teams from different organizational settings.

facilitation skills—The set of interpersonal and group management skills required to manage groups in the field.

FALDO—*Frameworks for Assessing Learning and Development Outcomes;* a CAS publication providing theoretical constructs that support the development of student learning outcomes within the program standards of CAS.

fill rate—The number of people enrolled compared to the number of spaces available.

financial forecast—A forecast of expense and revenue projections for the life of a business plan.

financial threats—Any impact reductions in income or revenue will have on the campus recreation department.

fitness programs—Programs linked to the physical realm of wellness that offer structured and unstructured activities that enhance cardiorespiratory endurance, as well as muscular strength, power, and endurance.

focus group—A group discussion used to generate a large amount of concentrated data in a short amount of time.

friendship—An achievement between people that is freely formed for the sake of the other and without contractual obligations. There are various types of friendships. Aristotle distinguished between friendships that exist between superiors and subordinates, fleeting friendships of utility and pleasure, and the perfect and enduring form, where the moral excellence of the other is admired for its own sake.

functional training—A form of strength training that utilizes multiple muscle groups in a single exercise and trains the body for activities performed in daily life. This is an advanced form of training that includes balance, stability, and core function (abdominal and lower back) in each exercise.

games—Activities that are organized, are structured, have rules and regulations, have specific strategies, occur within a defined time frame, and use specific facilities and equipment.

graduate assistant—A student pursuing a graduate degree who is employed by the university, often in a department related to the student's field of study. Employment could include teaching, research, or other department-related responsibilities.

hands-off approach—Administrative model for sport clubs that are independent from the educational institution. Under this approach, sport clubs are contracted independent organizations. Contracted independent organizations are not agents, servants, or employees of the university, but rather are independent contractors that manage their own affairs. Club activities are run by students who are not working on behalf of the school for liability and insurance coverage purposes. Faculty and staff are removed from sport club activities, even in an advising capacity.

hands-on approach—Administrative model for sport club activities that are part of an educational institution. A coach, recreation director, or student affairs director plans and supervises team activities as an agent of the school. Club staff keep records and documents. The school is responsible for team activities and risks through its employees. The team leadership is covered by the institution's liability insurance policies.

hazing—An intentional action taken toward any student, on or off campus, by a student organization or any of its members to produce humiliation, physical discomfort, bodily injury or ridicule or to create a situation [in which] humiliation, physical discomfort, [or] bodily injury occurs (James Madison University, n.d.).

highlights (of a business plan)—The major points of a business plan, usually presented as a bulleted list in the plan.

image building—A campus recreation department's efforts to enhance the positive image of the institution and increase recruitment and retention of academically prepared and qualified students by providing a comfortable, friendly, enjoyable, clean, and safe environment for all participants.

independent contractor—A legal term referring to a provider of services purchased by contractual agreement. Some programs use independent contract instructors to teach all or some courses; others hire instructors as employees of the institution.

indirect costs (expenses)—Costs that are determined through extensive analysis or a complex formula to account for overhead expenses incurred as part of an activity or course. Such expenses can include facility maintenance, administrative salaries and benefits, utility and custodial costs, insurance, and so forth. Often this analysis results in an overhead percentage that is then applied to the total of direct costs incurred as part of an activity or course.

informal, or open, recreation schedule—A schedule outlining the drop-in use of a wide range of activities offered by recreation departments.

informed consent agreement—A document that includes a written expression of what will occur during a specific activity as well as verbiage stating that a person has voluntarily accepted the known dangers by participating in that activity. This document should be orally explained and should include a statement confirming that the person was offered the opportunity to ask questions about the procedures to be followed during the activity.

inherent risks—Risks that, if removed, would fundamentally change an activity at its core.

in-service training—Regular or topic-specific training given to staff by their employer that is designed to maintain currency of specific job-related skills.

instructional program—A program that offers classes, activities, or courses designed to provide a participatory or learning experience that promotes physical health or develops lifelong recreational skills, or both. An instructional program can be an entire organization unto itself or part of a larger division or department.

intellectual wellness—Stimulating the mind through activities that are mentally challenging; a sense of being internally energized. It encourages continued learning and the ability to grow from experiences, especially through problem solving and decision making.

intramural—Derived from the Latin words *intra,* meaning "within," and *muralis,* meaning "wall." The term is usually paired with other words such as *sports, athletics,* or *activities* and, when so combined, implies that these programs are conducted "within the walls" or imaginary boundaries of some organization or institution.

job description—A written description of a position of employment that addresses the function and primary objectives of the position and accountabilities.

justice—The equal treatment of equals, classically studied as being either commutative or distributive. Plato considered justice the central question for political thought.

law—A rule of conduct or procedure recognized by a community as binding or enforceable by authority; an act passed by a legislature or similar body.

lead—A type of climbing that requires the climber to establish a line from the ground upward, thus generally increasing the fall potential.

leisure—Unencumbered time, free from class, study, or other obligations, in which to participate in structured or unstructured activity.

logistics of the excursion—Making reservations, being familiar with an emergency action plan, going over transportation details, and looking into permitting if necessary.

long-term capital replacement schedule—A schedule that identifies any items that will need replacing, the predicted year for replacement, and the predicted cost of the replacement (usually 3.5 percent per year).

management overview—A section of a business plan that describes the hiring process; lists the highest degrees earned by administrative, professional, and support staff; and lists the cumulative years of professional experience within a campus recreation department.

management section (of a business plan)—A section of a business plan in which positive aspects of the department are highlighted and staff are commended for their work.

market research—To analyze data pertaining to a target audience in order to glean information that may be relevant for program planning, sponsorship sales, or assessment.

marketing management—The analysis, planning, implementation, and control of programs designed to create, build, and maintain beneficial exchanges and relations with target markets for the purpose of achieving organizational objectives.

marketing plan—A detailed road map for the planning and supervision of all marketing activities for the following year. It addresses the four basic questions in planning: (1) Where are we now? (2) Where do we want to go? (3) How do we get there? and (4) Are we there yet?

marketing planning cycle—A continuously reoccurring cycle of planning that involves analysis, research, plan development, implementation, and evaluation.

medical information sheet—A document that includes questions pertaining to the medical and health history of the participant. This document should be completed during the pretest portion of a fitness assessment.

natatorium—An aquatic facility.

needs assessments—Systematic inquiries about the needs, attitudes, behaviors, and patterns of all constituents.

negligence—The unintentional harm to others as a result of an unsatisfactory degree of care. It occurs when a person does something that a reasonably prudent person would not do, or when a person fails to do something that a reasonably prudent person would do.

Occupational Safety and Health Administration (OSHA)—The federal agency responsible for the development, administration, and enforcement of employment-related health and safety regulations.

occupational wellness—Taking pride in one's work as well as maintaining a healthy balance between work and leisure. It encourages participation in activities that build skills for excelling in the workplace, including people skills and planning for the future.

occupiers (premises) liability—The responsibility of the owners to ensure that their premises are free of hazards.

organizational values—What is important to a campus recreation department.

outdoor adventure programs—Programs that provide adventure trips, instructional clinics and classes, climbing equipment rentals, and in some cases challenge courses for team building and leadership development and focus on experiential learning and environmental awareness.

overview—The part of a business plan that provides a perspective and justifies its direction.

PAR-Q—A self-administered questionnaire that serves to alert those with elevated risk to consult their physician (or other appropriate health care provider) prior to participating in an exercise program.

participation categories—Different programming options or divisions that participants can choose from, based on their needs. Some examples are competitive level, sex/gender, and place of residence.

participation levels—A benchmark of the success of, and satisfaction with, campus recreation departments. These provide some evidence of trends, shifts in interests, and participant needs, particularly when individual program and facility use are tracked.

permanent, or standing, blocks of time—Periods of time that are reserved, usually on a semester or quarterly basis, for recurring events.

personal liability—The liability that attaches directly to the individual who has been found negligent.

PEST analysis—An organizational analysis of political, economic, social, and technological factors.

philosophies—Consistent reference points that organizations use to make decisions.

physical wellness—Taking care of the body through education, disease prevention, and management of illness and injury. It encourages participation in regular activities and a lifestyle that promotes optimal health.

physician's statement—A document that is completed by the participant's physician clearing the participant to engage in an initial fitness assessment and a daily exercise program. Also called a physician's clearance.

plaintiff—In a negligence lawsuit, the person who was harmed and who brings about legal suit.

play—A behavior that is self-motivated and carried on for intrinsic purposes; it usually involves sport or recreational activity.

point-of-sale (POS) system—A sophisticated computer system to manage and record sales transactions.

policies—Broad, general statements that flow from an organization's philosophy, goals, and objectives.

policy interpretation—An explanation or establishment of the meaning or significance of something; further explanation on how to comply with a law or regulation.

polychlorinated biphenyls—Carcinogenic chemicals used in electrical transformers whose new production was banned in 1977 in the United States. They persist in the natural environment for decades to centuries, enter the food chain, increase in concentration as one moves up the food chain (e.g., tuna and whales), and are stored in human fat tissue.

pricing strategies—How a campus recreation department charges participants for access, programs, and services.

prime time—The term applied to those hours in which facilities have the heaviest use and demand.

principles of Leave No Trace—A set of guidelines that help outdoor users understand their actions with respect to resources.

priority usage—A statement about the priority for the use of indoor and outdoor campus recreation facilities. The campus recreation department reserves the right to prioritize space usage based on need, usage patterns, and availability.

pro forma budget—A budget that lists projected revenues and expenses for each year of a business plan.

products liability—The responsibility that applies when an injury was caused by some defective or hazardous aspect of a product or piece of equipment.

profession—An occupational field with a unique and distinct body of knowledge gained through an academic discipline, which provides a societal service for the greater good.

professional association—An organization composed of members of a particular profession. The association may set or maintain standards for the profession and it may aid in the professional development of its members.

program administrator—The person with immediate administrative responsibility for the overall operation of the instructional program. Within institutions, titles may be program coordinator, program director, or assistant director.

program and facility guiding principles—Principles on which a campus recreation department proposes to operate in regard to revenue generation, marketing practices, lifestyle enhancement, and priority usage and access.

program-related rules—Rules that guide the behavior of participants and staff. More specific than sport procedures, they stem directly from policies and procedures and provide a clear set of expectations.

promotion—"The persuasive flow of marketing communication," including advertising, sales and sales force, promotions, public relations, publicity, packaging, point-of-sale displays, and brand name or identity (Green et al., 1999).

protocol—A set of guidelines to follow when performing a fitness test to measure a specific component of cardiorespiratory health.

proximate cause of harm—A judgment made when evidence proves that the harm caused was the direct result of the carelessness or negligence of the defendant.

psychographics—Statistics that describe a target audience's lifestyle, education, approximate income, types of careers, leisure activities, reading habits, and so on.

public relations—Management of relationships with media outlets and the general public to strategically communicate information about an organization, program, or event.

purpose of the plan—A succinct statement describing why a business plan was undertaken, who was involved in the writing, why it was written, the direction the department will take as a result, and the overall tone of the plan.

random sample—A sample in which all members of the population have an equal chance of being included.

recommendations—A section of a business plan that lists the plan's recommendations and provides a time line for their completion, the area and people responsible for their completion, and a list of revenues or costs.

recreation—Time or activity used to renew and re-create ourselves.

registration—The act of signing up for, or enrolling, in a class or activity. One person taking one class or activity is considered one enrollment or registration. One person who takes two classes is considered two enrollments or registrations. Any fees due are collected at the time of registration.

registry—A list of professionals in a particular field who support the practice and guide professional development activities in the field.

regulations—Official rules or orders stating what may or may not be done or how something must be done.

relative knowledge—The notion that a product manufacturer is expected to know more about a product than a consumer is expected to know, and an owner or occupier is expected to know more about a facility hazard than a user is expected to know.

retributive justice—Commonly understood as "an eye for an eye, and a tooth for a tooth," retributive justice is based on the moral defense of punishment as a means of balancing the consequences of harm. This position is in contrast to more forward-looking moral principles embodied in forgiveness, where resolution of an unjust act has to do with advancing the possibilities for moral enlightenment. For example, being sorry—having genuine feelings of guilt—can change the way a person reasons and behaves in the future and can justify forgiveness over retribution.

risk stratification—A set of categories that individuals are placed in following the identification in them of coronary artery disease risk factors or signs or symptoms of cardiovascular, pulmonary, metabolic, or other known disease. The categories include low risk, moderate risk, and high risk.

round-robin tournament design—A popular tournament format familiar to most participants. It guarantees the opportunity to continue playing regardless of wins and losses, as long as there are still games on the schedule.

route setting—Designing and implementing specific climbing routes via holds and wall features.

sampling—Taking a portion of the population, collecting data on this group, and then generalizing the findings to the population.

section—A class or course may offer one or more sections. The sections may vary by day, time, instructor, or skill level. Each section is considered a separate class, independent of the others. If one course title has three sections, that would be considered three different classes with three different enrollments. A section is not the same as a single class meeting.

session—A period of time, usually 4 to 12 weeks, during which classes take place. Because recreation programs typically follow the academic schedule, a session can be equal to the length of the quarter or semester. In addition, the quarter or semester may be divided into two or more several-week sessions. A session is not the number of times a class meets during a given quarter or semester, and it is not the number of classes offered.

social wellness—Contributing to the human and physical environment for the betterment of the community. It includes participation in activities that help to develop healthy relationships while enhancing the ability to enjoy social situations.

spiritual wellness—A guided sense of meaning or value in life as well as an understanding of and an ability to express one's purpose in life. It addresses values and ethics and the degree to which one's actions are consistent with one's values.

sponsorship—A relationship between organizations for the purpose of enhancing a sport event through cash donations, in-kind support, media attention, or staff expertise.

sport—A team or individual competitive activity.

sport club—A group of students (and if the institution allows, faculty, staff, and community members) who voluntarily organize to further their common interests in a sport through participation and competition.

sport format—The way an intramural program is designed and delivered. Sport can be offered as competitive leagues, informal opportunities, special events, or instructional opportunities.

sport procedures—Specific actions or steps designed to carry out sport policy. Procedures

provide more information than, are more specific than, and further define the actions associated with policies.

sport program design—The systematic process of planning and providing structure for sport and recreation programs.

sport rules—Rules that govern the play of participants during sport contests. They are specific to each sport activity.

standard—A principle established by authority, custom, or general consent as a model or example; something set up and established by authority as a rule for the measure of quantity, value, or quality.

standard of care—A determination made by the courts based on factors such as the nature of the activity and particular circumstances involved. The courts rely on published standards and current industry practices when deciding what the current standard is.

stratified sampling—A system for choosing subjects based on their representation of specific demographics, such as year in college, gender, ethnicity, or income. Stratified sampling allows for comparison between various subgroups of a population.

student development—The process of growth and maturation of students in a particular environment.

submaximal cardiorespiratory test—Used to measure cardiovascular fitness, submaximal testing relies on the measurement of the participant's heart rate as increased workloads are performed. During this test, a participant is typically taken to 85 percent of his or her age-predicted maximal heart rate.

subsidy—Any monies not coming from direct fees for services. Subsidies include tuition reimbursement from state agencies, monies from a central institutional office, or staff salaries paid by means other than class registration income. To determine the percentage to which the program is subsidized, divide the subsidy income by the total income for a full recovery of all program expenses.

summary—A recap of a business plan.

summary of financials—The heart of a business plan that provides intricate details of the entire financial side of a campus recreation department.

sustainability—Literally, the ability to maintain a positive status or set of conditions over time.

The term is also used interchangeably with *sustainable development,* which is "development that meets the needs of the present without compromising the ability of future generations to meet their own needs" (United Nations WCED, 1987).

sustained operating goals—Unchanging, general, long-lasting goals that are based on the missions of the institution and the campus recreation department.

SWOT analysis—An organizational analysis of strengths, weaknesses, opportunities, and threats.

systematic sampling—A system for choosing subjects from a population that involves drawing names from a list at a specific sampling interval, such as every second, third, or fourth name. The number of subjects needed must first be decided. Then the population of possible subjects is divided by the number of subjects needed. The answer to that equation becomes the sampling interval.

target audience—The market for whose needs and wants the program or service is developed.

teleology—Ethical theories that view moral obligation as aiming for the greatest good. In contrast to deontological theories, consequences matter. The aim is to end up doing the least harm while achieving the greatest happiness.

Title IX of the Education Amendments (P.L. 92-318, 20 U.S.C.S. section 1681 et seq.)—Landmark legislation that bans sex discrimination (against either males or females) in schools in both academics and athletics.

top rope—A type of climbing in which the climber is protected from above; this generally minimizes the fall potential.

tournament design—An essential component of intramural sport programming that refers to the style and format used to organize and schedule competitions. Tournament design has perhaps the largest impact on participants' perceptions of the program

values—Generally considered a common conception of what is good, useful, important, or desirable. A nonmoral value is in the utility of something, such as a "good" car. Moral values are good simply because they are moral.

vision and goals—A section of a business plan in which the campus recreation department lists operating principles, purposes, and program-user priorities.

voluntary assumption of risk—When a person consents to participate in (or watch as a spectator) certain activities such as contact sports (hockey or football), there is no liability if harm is caused by normal hazards inherent to the activity.

waiver—An agreement between an organization (the service provider) and the participant by which the participant agrees to absolve the service provider of any fault or liability for negligence of the service provider or its employees.

wellness center—In recreation facilities, an area devoted to providing individuals the opportunity to learn how to prevent illness and prolong life and to make choices that lead to better physical and mental health.

INDEX

Note: The italicized *f* and *t* following page numbers refer to figures and tables, respectively.

ABOUT THE CONTRIBUTORS

Robert J. Barcelona, PhD, is an associate professor of recreation management and policy at the University of New Hampshire. His professional career has included stints as director of intramural sports and sport clubs at the University of Mississippi, assistant director of sport clubs and intramural sports at the University of California at Berkeley, and lecturer in recreational sport management at Indiana University. He also worked with Cal Athletics, focusing on community outreach and youth summer camps. Barcelona's doctoral dissertation, *An Analysis of the Perceived Competencies of Recreational Sport Managers: Toward a Competency-Based Model for Academic and Professional Development,* was completed in 2001, and set the stage for articles published in the *Journal of Park and Recreation Administration* and the *Recreational Sports Journal (RSJ)*, among others. A NIRSA member since 1992, Barcelona has served as state director, *RSJ* Editorial Board member, chair of the Curriculum Subcommittee, Certification Task-Force member, and member of the Professional Registry Task Force. He also received the NIRSA Foundation Award for Outstanding Writing in the *Recreational Sports Journal* in 2003, 2004, and 2007.

Kathryn G. Bayless, CRSS, MSPE, is the director of campus recreational sports and assistant dean of the School of Health, Physical Education, and Recreation at Indiana University in Bloomington, Indiana. She was hired as the first full-time staff member for women's intramural sports at Indiana University in 1974, and experienced the challenges of building such a program from the ground up during an era characterized by a male-dominated culture. When she obtained her current position in 1992, Bayless became the first female director of recreational sports in the Big Ten. Bayless was also the only female administrator involved in the planning and opening of the Student Recreational Sports Center at Indiana University in 1995. She co-authored *Recreational Sport Management* (Human Kinetics, 2005), the first of its kind as a comprehensive text. A founding member and chair of the NIRSA Affirmative Action Committee, Bayless has also served on NIRSA's Professional Development Committee and as the keynote speaker at NIRSA's 25th anniversary breakfast celebrating re-admittance of women into the membership of NIRSA (NIRSA Annual Conference, 1997). In 1979, she received the National Service Award for outstanding service to NIRSA and leadership with affirmative action.

Diane K. Belz, CRSS, MA, is the building and equipment services manager at the University of Colorado in Boulder, Colorado, where she previously served as the instruction program coordinator. During that time, she developed policy and procedures regarding registration, publicity, cost analysis, and overall program instruction success. Belz is an active member of NIRSA, serving on the instruction program committee and making presentations at the state and national level. She received a National Service Award for her work in co-authoring the NIRSA publication *Instructional Programs: A Resource Manual* (1995). From 1997 to 1999, she served as the NIRSA Region V vice-president. In 2001, she received the NIRSA National Service Award for compiling and orchestrating membership in the International Association for Continuing Education and Training (IACET) and developing CEU guidelines for the association.

Anthony D. Cortese, PhD, is the president of Second Nature, Inc., a nonprofit organization which seeks to help universities create a sustainable future. His work with Second Nature provided a catalyst for the Education for Sustainability movement in higher education, today embraced by 800 college and university presidents worldwide. Cortese has also worked as the Tufts Dean of Environmental Programs and the commissioner of the Massachusetts Department of Environmental Protection. He was the founder of the Higher Education Association's Sustainability Consortium, a group of higher education associations (including NIRSA) that considers sustainability the foundation of their work. For his work, Cortese received the Presidential Environmental Award from President George H.W. Bush in 1991, and he became a fellow of the American Association for the Advancement of Science in 2001.

Julian Dautremont-Smith, BA, is the associate director of the Association for the Advancement of Sustainability in Higher Education (AASHE) in Portland, Oregon. He earned an honors degree in environmental studies from Lewis & Clark College in 2003. While attending college, he spearheaded a successful and nationally recognized effort to bring the college into compliance with the emissions targets of the Kyoto Protocol on climate change. Dautremont-Smith is the author of *Guidelines for College-Level Greenhouse Gas Emissions Inventories*, an instruction manual for performing greenhouse gas emissions inventories for colleges and universities. He also cofounded a business to produce biodiesel while studying sustainable development in Barbados on a J. William Fulbright scholarship.

Elizabeth A. Davis, CRSS, MA, is the associate director of the department of recreational sports at The Ohio

State University. During her 29 years in recreational sports management, Davis has created the assessment area within the department of recreational sports at Ohio State, partnered with the student affairs assessment office to develop a university study reflective of the department's needs, and worked as the department's director of assessments. In addition, she serves on the Big Ten Research Committee and received the Ohio Special Olympics Honorary Coach Award in 2001. Throughout her 27 years in NIRSA, Davis has belonged to and chaired numerous committees. For her service, she received the NIRSA National Service Award in 1989 and the NIRSA Region III Award of Merit in 2002.

Gerald S. Fain, PhD, is a professor at Boston University's School of Education and visiting professor at Springfield College. Fain began his career at the Children's Village in New York City, where he worked as a recreation specialist with emotionally disturbed and adjudicated youths. In 1971, he joined the faculty at the University of Maryland, College Park, as coordinator of the therapeutic recreation curriculum. Since that time he has published more than 40 papers, delivered more than 100 lectures in the United States and abroad, published 3 edited volumes, and served as principle investigator of more than 30 federally funded projects. He has served as coordinator of the Leisure Studies Education Program at Boston University since 1978, where he also served as coordinator of health education, for 22 years, and chairman of the department of special education, for 17 years. Fain is the World Leisure and Recreation Association representative to the United Nations and has served as president of the American Leisure Academy and chairman of the AALR J.B. Nash Scholar Committee.

Douglas S. Franklin, CRSS, PhD, is assistant dean for recreation and wellness at Ohio University in Athens, Ohio. In this position, Franklin has consolidated campus recreation programs into the division of campus recreation, established the undergraduate campus recreation curriculum for the recreation studies program, and developed and implemented the first graduate-level course for concepts and issues in campus recreation. His doctoral dissertation focused on recreational sports directors' awareness, perceived importance, and applications of standards in campus recreation programs across the United States. Additionally, Franklin currently serves as the chair of the NIRSA Standards Committee (2007-2008) and is the NIRSA representative to the Council for the Advancement of Standards (CAS) in Higher Education. He is a frequent presenter at NIRSA national, regional, and special conferences.

Evelyn Kwan Green, MBA, MS, is an instructor of tourism management at the University of Southern Mississippi. Green was one of the first full-time marketing professionals hired by a campus recreation department. For 10 years, she served as the director of marketing, public relations, and sales in the division of recreational sports at the University of Southern Mississippi. A member of NIRSA, Green played an instrumental role in the creation of NIRSA's Marketing Special Interest Committee. As part of that committee, she has served as a consultant (1999-2000) and chair (1998-1999). In 1999, she initiated and presented NIRSA's first pre-conference marketing workshop and developed the inaugural marketing symposium the following year. For her contribution to recreational sports marketing, she received NIRSA's National Service Award in 2000.

Jennifer Gudaz, MS, is the director of the Noyes Community Recreation Center at Cornell University. Gudaz has 10 years of experience in aquatics management and helped to establish the first aquatics programs and facilities at Western Washington University. She is also a water safety instructor trainer; lifeguard instructor; an instructor of CPR, first aid, and water safety; and a certified aquatics facility operator (AFO). As part of her involvement with the American Red Cross, Gudaz served as a member of the American Red Cross Health and Safety Board. A member of NIRSA, Gudaz has served on the Aquatics Institute Work Team (2005 and 2007) and as the Washington State director (2004-2006).

Danell J. Haines, PhD, is the director of the National Research Institute for College Recreational Sports & Wellness (which is in partnership with NIRSA) and administers the assessment program for the department of recreational sports at The Ohio State University. Haines' other professional accomplishments include serving as a research scientist in the department of family medicine and aquatic director in the department of recreational sports. A NIRSA member since 1988, Haines has received two association National Awards for Outstanding Achievement in Research.

Sarah E. Hardin, CRSS, PhD, is an associate director of campus recreation at DePaul University. She has 20 years of experience in the field of recreational sports, including previous positions as a recreational sports director, an assistant professor in recreation administration, and as a Florida board of education articulation specialist. This range of experience has provided Hardin the opportunity to see higher education organizations from several different perspectives. She served as chair (2003-2004) and faculty member (2001-2005) for the NIRSA School of Recreational Sports Management, where she presented on the topic "crossroads of theory" and its implications for the application of the myriad of theories in the work setting. During the 2004 NIRSA annual conference, she initiated the discussion of the impact of various academic and theoretical backgrounds through the presentation "How Can We Play the Game if We're Not on the Same Team? A Look at Organizational Culture."

Cher T. Harris, MS, is the outreach educational programs coordinator at the University of Florida's College of Health and Human Performance. She has over 10 years of experience in the fitness industry. She has held positions as personal trainer and group exercise leader; assistant director of recreational sports, at the University of Florida; assistant director of fitness/wellness, at Indiana University; and senior instructor of fitness and administration, at Florida State University. Harris currently serves as the programming work group chair of the Healthy Gators 2010 coalition at the University of Florida and has also served on the NIRSA Fitness Committee.

Jonathan Hart, CRSS, MS, is the assistant director of campus recreation—facilities at the Georgia Institute of Technology. During his time at Georgia Tech, the Campus Recreation Center underwent a 45 million dollar renovation, which included designing the layout of a fitness center and purchasing exercise equipment. Hart is a certified personal trainer and he served as the cochair of the NIRSA Fitness Committee (2004-2006) and as a consultant to the Fitness Committee (2006-2007).

Vicki D. Highstreet, CRSS, MPE, is a senior assistant director of campus recreation at the University of Nebraska in Lincoln, Nebraska. She began her career at the University of Nebraska in 1982, working for the University Health Center in the development of noncredit fitness classes and wellness programming for students, staff, and faculty. In her current position, Highstreet is responsible for the oversight of instructional programming, fitness and wellness, and outdoor recreation. She programs the academic credit recreational activity courses and noncredit instructional classes, and identifies and facilitates staff development opportunities. An active member of NIRSA since 1988, Highstreet served as the NIRSA Region V vice-president (2005-2007), was elected NIRSA president-elect (2007-2008), and will serve as NIRSA president (2008-2009). She was a co-author of the NIRSA *Instructional Programs* manual, chair of the Instructional Programming Committee, chair of the Fitness Committee, and coordinator of two instructional program preconferences at NIRSA national conferences.

Aaron Hill, BA, is a student and graduate teaching assistant completing a master of science degree in public policy at The New School in New York City. He holds a bachelor of arts in speech communication from the University of Southern Mississippi, where he received mentoring from co-author Evelyn Kwan Green. Hill has worked in campus recreation as a professional marketing manager and was the director of marketing for NIRSA from 2000 to 2003.

Ian McGregor, PhD, is the president of Ian McGregor & Associates Inc., a consulting company in Vancouver, British Columbia, specializing in sport and recreation risk management. He is also a former president of the Canadian Intramural Recreation Association (CIRA). McGregor has taught courses on legal liability and risk management at four universities in Canada and the United States and has developed creative and highly functional tools to assist professionals with risk management planning. Within NIRSA, he is regarded as the expert on risk management. He has served as a

consultant in sport and recreation risk management for over 15 years and has written and published several manuals and articles on risk management. One such manual was the *Risk Management Manual*. Published in 2000, the second edition, for which McGregor served as the primary author, is the only manual on risk management published by NIRSA. For his work with NIRSA, he received the Outstanding Service Award in 1992.

Paul R. Milton, PhD, is an assistant professor of sport management at Ashland University. Previously, Milton was the director of recreational services at Kent State University in Kent, Ohio. An administrator in the field of recreational sports for 28 years, Milton developed the first strategic plan at the department level in Kent State's history. He has written and been published on various topics in recreational sports. His most important publication was an empirical study of gender and the need for a recreational facility. It provided statistical evidence that men and women are equally likely to want a recreational facility on campus. He has been on the editorial board of NIRSA's *Recreational Sports Journal* and currently serves as its editor. He is also the vice-chair of the National Research Institute for College Recreational Sports and Wellness.

Josh Norris, CRSS, MA, is the coordinator for climbing and adventure education at Oregon State University. He has worked for four universities and seven commercial outfitters, and founded his own commercial guide service with operations throughout the United States and Mexico. He was instrumental in the creation and establishment of a multifaceted university outdoor recreation program at the University of Mississippi, which included the inception of an academic minor and extensive course offerings. Norris has served as an instructor/guide for wilderness medicine, white-water kayaking, rafting, challenge courses, and more. As part of his work in outdoor education, Norris was a script writer and technical advisor for a series of instructional rock climbing videos (see www.GuideTricksFor Climbers.com). He is currently a member of the NIRSA Outdoor Committee.

Nicole Olmeda, CRSS, MED, is an assistant director with the division of recreational sports at The University of Texas at Austin. From 1996 to 1998, while pursuing a graduate degree at Oregon State University, she worked with OSU's outdoor program and challenge course. She spent the next eight years administering the outdoor recreation program at The University of Texas at Austin, receiving certifications as a wilderness first responder, a Leave No Trace (LNT) trainer, and a swift-water rescue technician. As a member of the Association of Outdoor Recreation and Education (AORE), Olmeda served on the AORE board of directors from 2000 to 2003. As a member of NIRSA, she served on the Outdoor Recreation Committee from 2004 to 2005 and chaired the committee the following two years.

Mila L. Padgett, MS, is the assistant director of programs in the department of campus recreation at Oakland

University in Rochester, Michigan. She has been involved with the opening of wellness facilities at the University of Southern Mississippi, Ohio University, and Oakland University. In her position as fitness director at Ohio University and Oakland University, she built comprehensive fitness and wellness programs from the ground up—creating recreation facilities, hiring and training staff, developing manuals, and implementing programs. Padgett is certified as a health fitness and CPR/first aid instructor and also holds certifications in personal training, cycling, and primary group exercise. She has taught a variety of group exercise classes for over 10 years. As a member of NIRSA, Padgett served on the Fitness Committee from 2003 to 2005, the Fitness Symposium Work Team from 2004 to 2005, and the Wellness Committee from 2005 to the present.

Gary Pogharian, CRSS, MSSEd, is the aquatics director at the University of South Carolina. In addition to his 13 years in university aquatics, Pogharian has been an aquatics facility operator (AFO) instructor for 10 years and an AFO instructor trainer for 5 years. He is a member of the AFO Council for NRPA. As part of the NIRSA Aquatics Committee, he helped found the NIRSA Aquatics Institute in 2001. Pogharian also co-authored the *NIRSA Aquatics Director Manual*, which has helped further the role and status of aquatics in NIRSA.

Nancy L. Rapp, BA, is director of parks and recreation for the city of Santa Barbara, California. In this position, she provides overall administration of the department, including park planning and development, business services, park operations, recreation, municipal golf course, and creek restoration and water quality improvement program. Previously, she worked as the recreation manager of fitness and instructional programs for UCLA Recreation. Rapp served as chair of the NIRSA Instructional Programs Committee from 1984 to 2000.

Erin Rausch, MS, is the director of the University of the Pacific's Center for Community Involvement. After seven years of outdoor programming, Rausch changed paths to follow her love of helping students build opportunities that impact their local communities.

Thomas M. Roberts, CRSS, MSPE, is the director of recreation and wellness at the University of Richmond in Richmond, Virginia. For more than 20 years, he has been involved in the organization and administration of sport clubs. Before obtaining his current position, Roberts was the instructor for the NIRSA On-line Sport Club Administration course and an instructor of sports administration at San Diego State University. As a speaker, he has been featured in the United Educators Insurance Company Telephone Roundtable program on the topic of sport clubs, and he has also presented at state, regional, and national conferences. A member of NIRSA, Roberts was the chair of the Sport Club Committee in 1991-1992 and the program chair for the Sport Club Symposium in 1993. Roberts was the

co-editor of the second edition of *NIRSA Sport Clubs: A Resource Guide* and has also produced and published a recreational facility risk management employee training CD.

Peter D. Schaack, CRSS, MS, is the associate director of facility operations for the division of recreational sports at The University of Texas at Austin. He has 20 years of experience as a recreation professional. During his time at The University of Texas at Austin, he oversaw the renovation of the Gregory Gymnasium and the construction of its accompanying aquatic complex. Schaack has been a member of pool construction and pool consultant search committees in Lakeview, Texas. As a member of NIRSA, Schaack has served on the Professional Development Certification Subcommittee (1988-1989); the Outdoor Subcommittee (1989-1992); the Research Committee (1993-1996), for which he served as chair in 1995 and 1996; the Professional Ethics Committee (1999-2000); and the Conference Exhibits Committee (2003-2006).

Lisa Stuppy, MS, is the assistant director of fitness programs at Boise State University in Boise, Idaho. During her 10 years in university recreation, Stuppy has worked at Boise State University and Purdue University in fitness and wellness programming. At Boise State, she implemented a comprehensive fitness program, which includes group exercise, fitness testing and training, instructional classes, incentives, employee wellness, and educational outreach. Stuppy served as the NIRSA Fitness Committee chair (2004-2005) and the chair of the 2007 NIRSA Fitness Institute. She also assists in test development for the American Council on Exercise as a subject matter expert for their group fitness and personal training exams.

Carrie Tupper, MS, is the director of aquatics at the University of Maryland in College Park, Maryland. Tupper has 12 years of experience in the aquatics field, serving as assistant director and director of aquatics at the University of Maryland. She has been a member of the American Red Cross National Capital Area Instructor Support Committee and was the American Red Cross National Capital Area Aquatic Volunteer of the Year in 2001. Tupper was also the NIRSA Aquatics Committee chair in 2005 and served as the chair of the 2007 NIRSA Aquatic Institute.

Paul E. Wilson, CRSS, BS, is an adjunct instructor in health and exercise science at the University of Oklahoma in Norman, Oklahoma, where he earned a bachelors degree in law enforcement. At his alma mater, he is currently teaching several courses in the department of health and exercise science. A professional lifetime emeritus member of NIRSA, Wilson served as the University of Oklahoma director of intramural-recreational sports for 31 years. He has since retired from that position and is now the appointed NIRSA national historian. His interest in history has given him the opportunity to be an invited presenter and speaker on local and national levels.

The NIRSA Education & Publication Center

a partnership of NIRSA and Human Kinetics

NIRSA and Human Kinetics have partnered to create the NIRSA Education & Publication Center, available online at **nirsa.HumanKinetics.com**. Working with Human Kinetics, NIRSA will be able to increase the number of publications and resources it can develop—including online courses, CEU opportunities, videos, and software—increasing NIRSA's educational offerings. This book, as well as a host of other new products, is a product of that partnership. For the latest titles, visit the NIRSA Education & Publication Center, or call **800-747-4457** to request a catalog.

**For NIRSA books, videos, and more,
visit the NIRSA Education & Publication Center
nirsa.HumanKinetics.com**

NIRSA

www.nirsa.org • 541-766-8211
4185 SW Research Way
Corvallis, OR 97333

HUMAN KINETICS
www.HumanKinetics.com • 800-747-4457
P.O. Box 5076 • Champaign, IL 61825-5076

Mail Code: 2335

1/06

USER INSTRUCTIONS FOR CD-ROM

System Requirements

You can use this CD-ROM on either a Windows®-based PC or a Macintosh computer.

Windows

- IBM PC compatible with Pentium® processor
- Windows® 98/2000/XP
- Adobe Reader® 8.0
- 4x CD-ROM drive

Macintosh

- Power Mac® recommended
- System 10.4 or higher
- Adobe Reader®
- 4x CD-ROM drive

User Instructions

Windows

1. Insert the *Campus Recreation CD-ROM: Essentials for the Professional.* (Note: The CD-ROM must be present in the drive at all times.)
2. Select the "My Computer" icon from the desktop.
3. Select the CD-ROM drive.
4. Open the "start.pdf" file.

Macintosh

1. Insert the *Campus Recreation CD-ROM: Essentials for the Professional.* (Note: The CD-ROM must be present in the drive at all times.)
2. Double-click the CD icon located on the desktop.
3. Open the "Start.pdf" file.

For customer support, contact Technical Support:

Phone: 217-351-5076 Monday through Friday (excluding holidays) between 7:00 a.m. and 7:00 p.m. (CST).

Fax: 217-351-2674

E-mail: support@hkusa.com